Adaptive Mainstreaming

A PRIMER FOR TEACHERS AND PRINCIPALS

MAYNARD C. REYNOLDS

JACK W. BIRCH

THIRD EDITION

Longman

New York & London

**Adaptive Mainstreaming: A Primer for Teachers
and Principals, Third Edition**

Longman Inc., 95 Church Street, White Plains, N.Y. 10601

Associated companies:
Longman Group Ltd., London
Longman Cheshire Pty., Melbourne
Longman Paul Pty., Auckland
Copp Clark Pitman, Toronto
Pitman Publishing Inc., New York

Executive editor: Ray O'Connell
Production editor: Louise M. Kahan
Text art: J&R Art Services
Production supervisor: Judith Stern

Library of Congress Cataloging-in-Publication Data

Reynolds, Maynard Clinton.
  Adaptive mainstreaming.

  Rev. ed. of: Teaching exceptional children in all
America's schools. Rev. ed. 1982.
  Bibliography: p.
  Includes index.
  1. Special education—United States. 2.Mainstream-
ing in education—United States. I. Birch, Jack W.
II. Reynolds, Maynard. Clinton. Teaching exceptional
children in all America's schools. III. Title.
LC3981.R45 1988   371.9'046   87-17081
ISBN 0-582-28504-6

Compositor: Best-set Typesetter Ltd
Printer: The Alpine Press, Inc.

88 89 90 91 92 93 9 8 7 6 5 4 3 2 1

Contents

Chapter 10   Severe and Profound Handicaps   286

Chapter 11   Facing the Future   311

Preface

In preparation of the first two editions of this book we agonized, waivered, argued, and compromised over issues of structure, specifically about how to deal with the various categories of exceptional children and special education programs. Finally, however, we wrote books with quite a traditional structure, including chapters on each of the common eight or nine categories of handicapping conditions. At the same time, we predicted and advocated changes toward much less narrow categorization.

In this third edition, we've turned a corner and have omitted separate chapters on learning disabilities and the milder forms of mental retardation and emotional disturbance. But some of the same awkwardness and compromise are still with us. Many school programs are still organized quite strictly by categories, and our readers need to know that. On the other hand, textbooks ought to tell about practices that are reasonably well confirmed by research or by tested professional experience. Most of the categorizations of students and programs do not meet that "state of the art" test, so we've decided to speak as forthrightly as we can about the matter.

In this book, there are separate categorical chapters only in domains in which we believe there is quite a clear and distinct knowledge base for teaching. In the vision area, for example, there are distinct approaches to the teaching of reading (braille), mobility, and orientation that require teacher preparation and skill well beyond anything included in the repertoire of "regular" teachers. Similarly, a case can be made for special categories of hearing impairments, severe and profound handicaps, and speech impairments. The categories of physical impairments and the gifted and talented do not cohere in such distinct ways, but they are among topics treated in separate chapters.

In a sense, we've substituted major sections of this third edition on the topics of effective and adaptive teaching for what might have been separate treatments of learning disabilities, educable mental retardation, and behavior problems or mild emotional disturbance. This represents a judgment about the knowledge base in special education and its relation to practices in the schools. We see the regular schools as challenged now to become more effective and adaptive, in the process reducing substantially the rates at which exceptional children in the milder ranges of these handicapping categories are referred to special education. To put it differently, we now envision an ongoing process, which we also advocate and support, of renegotiation between regular and special education by which the regular schools accommodate most exceptional children now served in special education pullout programs. We do not see this as entailing the demise of special education or even a cutback. Rather, we foresee a redeployment of specialists as support personnel operating mainly in mainstream environments.

Our views on the current trends and needs in special education have been influenced by two in-depth experiences. One is a recent review and synthesis of research and practice in most aspects of special education that will be reported in a three-volume publication to be available almost simultaneously with this book (Wang, Reynolds, & Walberg, 1987). The other is involvement with the field of adaptive education as a research and development theme (Glaser, 1977; Wang & Birch, 1984). Through both of these experiences, we've been reinforced in our belief that to serve exceptional students in a quality way, it will be necessary to make major changes in both regular and special education and that the most promising approach to such changes is to implement adaptive education for all students. It is within this framework that successful mainstreaming of handicapped students is likely to take place.

That explains why we've addressed this third edition of the book mainly to regular teachers and school principals. We intend that it should be useful as an introductory volume for special educators as well. It also explains why we have changed the title to *Adaptive Mainstreaming: A Primer for Teachers and Principals.*

The book is somewhat unusual in that it is explicit about its advocacy of the *mainstreaming*, or "least restrictive environment," principle. It is clear, we think, that much of special education has developed on the basis of rejecting from the mainstream children who are different or inconvenient to teach and that similar exclusionary trends have been evident in all too much of community life. That legacy of rejection and segregation remains with us and needs to be turned around if persons with disabilities are to be well served. For us, mainstreaming is no casual matter; rather, we see it as a deeply moral challenge as well as a difficult technical problem. Also, we see mainstreaming as no minor swing of the pendulum, soon to be reversed. Instead, we believe it is part of a major, continuing cultural trend to be recognized and supported.

Finally, we acknowledge the good help and cooperation of the Council for Exceptional Children, the publishers of the first two editions of this book. That was an experimental venture for CEC and for us, one that we enjoyed and appreciate. We welcome now the opportunity to join the other fine publications of the Longman series in special education.

Maynard C. Reynolds
Jack W. Birch

Selected Key Dates and Events

in the Development of U.S. Public Education, 1776–

1776 The 13 states unanimously declared their independence and their joint commitment to "life, liberty and the pursuit of happiness."

1779 Thomas Jefferson's School Bill for Virginia; First state school system proposal.

1791 Passage of Tenth Amendment to the United States Constitution reserves education to the states.

1817 First educational program for exceptional children and youth formally established in the United States—American Asylum for the Education and Instruction of the Deaf (now American School for the Deaf), Hartford, Connecticut.

1818 First grants of money paid by the federal government to states.

1821 English high school for boys organized in Boston.

1823 United States' first normal school for teachers privately established in Vermont. Kentucky established the first state school for persons who were deaf.

1826 First nursery school of the nation opened in New Harmony, Indiana. Bowdoin College first in United States to award a degree to a black person, John Russwurm.

1829   Massachusetts passed first state high school law. First residential school for blind students in the United States incorporated in Watertown, Massachusetts; initially called the New England Asylum for the Blind, now the Perkins School for the Blind. First state schools for students who were blind established in Boston and New York City. Publication of *Essay on the Construction of Schoolhouses* by William A. Alcott.

1837   Horace Mann discusses school hygiene in his first report to the Massachusetts Board of Education.

1839   State supported normal school for teacher training started at Lexington, Massachusetts.

1840   Rhode Island passed first state compulsory education law.

1845   First statewide associations of teachers founded in New York and Rhode Island.

1848   Edouard Seguin came from France to describe his educational procedures with mentally retarded pupils and to urge the establishment of schools for mentally retarded children and youth in the United States.

Dorothea Dix confronted the Congress with the inhumanity of many programs for the "mentally ill."

The Massachusetts legislature enacted a three-year experimental scheme to instruct ten selected children considered mentally retarded, with a total budget of $7,500.00.

1852   Pennsylvania's appropriation to Elwyn Institute in Philadelphia was the first use of public monies to support education for children with handicaps in a private facility.

Massachusetts passed the second compulsory school attendance law.

1854   First U.S. federal direct participation in education of handicapped children and youth through founding by act of Congress of Columbia Institution for the Instruction of the Deaf and Dumb, and the Blind. Extended to college level in act signed by Abraham Lincoln in 1864 and designated in 1865 specifically for persons who are deaf. In 1954 became officially known as Gallaudet College.

1855   The United States' first kindergarten established in Watertown, Wisconsin.

1857   National Education Association formed, initially called the National Teachers' Association.

1859   Nation's first residential school for persons with mental retardation started in South Boston under the name Massachusetts School for Idiotic and Feeble-Minded Youth. Samuel Gridley Howe, than head of the Perkins School for the Blind, was most influential in enlisting legislative and public support for this new facility.

U.S. Congress initiated a perpetual fund to help educate blind persons through the American Printing House for the Blind, located in Lexington, Kentucky.

1867   Congress created a National Department of Education, later to become the United States Office of Education, under the Secretary of Health, Education and Welfare.

1869   First day classes for any exceptional children were begun for deaf pupils in Boston, Massachusetts.

1873   Nation's first permanent public kindergarten initiated by the St. Louis, Missouri, Public Schools.

1878   Day classes for mentally retarded pupils proposed by August Schenck of Detroit in a speech before the American Teachers Association.

1880   Los Angeles Board of Education requested school personnel to be aware of classroom ventilation and temperatures.

1890   Dr. Samuel Durgin, Health Commissioner, Boston, Massachusetts, established a system of medical inspection following a series of school epidemics. Fifty "medical visitors" (physicians) appointed to visit schools daily to examine children suspected of having communicable diseases. Suspected cases were quarantined at home.

1891   Teacher training launched at Gallaudet College in education of deaf pupils.

1892 First public school medical officer in the United States appointed in New York City.

1893 Committee of Ten report promulgated the initial report of a series on curriculum from the National Education Association.

1895 United States educators with management responsibilities formed the American Association of School Administrators.

1896 First public school day classes for mentally retarded pupils initiated in Providence, Rhode Island.

1898 National Congress of Mothers organized; now called National Congress of Parents and Teachers.

1899 First public school day classes for crippled children and youth started in Chicago, Illinois.

  First state law relating to medical inspection of school children passed in Connecticut, also required teachers to test pupils' eyes once every three years.

1900 First public school day classes for blind students begun in Chicago, Illinois.

  Two states, Wisconsin and Michigan, authorized subsidies to expand classes for deaf pupils in local public schools, the first such state financial support for excess educational cost for any exceptional children and youth.

1904 Vineland Training School started summer training sessions for teachers of the retarded.

1905 E. L. Thorndike conceptualized and planned a scale to measure educational achievement.

1906 Approximate date medical inspections were introduced in the schools for the detection and prevention of contagious and infectious diseases.

1908 Establishment of first public school day classes for children with lowered vitality.

  Speech correction initiated in New York public school.

1909   First White House Conference on Children and Youth.

National Education Association cities the Goddard translation and revision of the Binet-Simon Scale of Intelligence as a useful test with exceptional children and specifically with mentally retarded children.

1910   Nation's first public junior high schools opened in Berkeley, California, and Columbus, Ohio.

First formal lunch program installed in public schools.

1911   Countrywide survey by United States Bureau of Education found 6% of cities reporting special classes for gifted pupils.

Establishment of Joint Committee on Health Problems in Education of the NEA and the AMA.

1913   Roxbury, Massachusetts, and Cleveland, Ohio, started first classes for partially seeing pupils.

1915   *Laggards in Our Schools* by Leonard P. Ayres was published; it became one of the first special education texts.

Minnesota initiated state aid of $100 for each child attending a special class and required certification of teachers to instruct such classes.

1916   Organization of American Federation of Teachers as an affiliate of the American Federation of Labor.

Lewis Terman produced the Stanford–Binet Scale of Intelligence Tests with an elaborate standardization and the inclusion of the intelligence quotient concept proposed by Stern in 1912.

1917   Federal support for vocational education furnished through Smith–Hughes Act.

New York City started special school programs for children with cardiac and other health problems.

1919   All states had legally effective compulsory education.

The Seven Cardinal Principles of Secondary Education was published.

The foundation was laid for special education cooperatives and intermediate units by Pennsylvania laws allowing school districts to join together to provide special education.

White House Conference on Child Health and Protection stressed that healthful school living was the most important phase of education and made recommendations for environmental factors and the school day. Planning the school day, arrangement of the curriculum and discipline were some of their concerns.

1920   First presidential proclamation of American Education Week. School census taking initiated in Massachusetts to determine the number of handicapped children in each school district; required of local boards of education and financed by the state. Special classes mandated where ten or more mentally retarded children found.

Federal Civilian Rehabilitation Act signed by President Woodrow Wilson.

1921   Malden Study showed that health education was practical, could change children's health habits and could influence the child's growth.

1922   Founding year of The Council for Exceptional Children.

1923   World Confederation of Organizations of the Teaching Profession organized in San Francisco; original name was World Federation of Education Associations.

Oregon laws enacted to include gifted children as educationally exceptional children needing special education.

1925   The National Congress of Parents and Teachers promoted the Summer Round-Up Campaign to promote among parents a realization of their responsibility for sending children to school prepared through adequate medical attention.

1926   First prototype of teaching machine and programmed instruction invented by Sidney Pressey at Ohio State University.

Health of teachers was emphasized in a report by James Frederick Rogers. First attempt to stress importance of teacher's health as part of school health program.

1930   In a national conference on child health protection called by President Hoover, one committee was assigned to study the needs of exceptional children.

1931   A section on exceptional children was formed in the United States Office of Education and a professional educator was named a Senior Specialist to head the unit.

1940   White House Conference on Children in a Democracy stressed mental health and need for health education in elementary and secondary schools.

1941   The National Society for the Study of Education devoted a yearbook to the education of exceptional children.

1944   Initial GI Bill for veterans' education passed by Congress.

1946   The National School Lunch Act (Public Law 396) passed by Congress, served as impetus for development of kitchens and cafeteria facilities and services in public schools throughout the country. Act made federal funds available, and with the installation of kitchens and cafeterias increased emphasis on maintenance of sanitary and safe cooking and eating facilities and equipment. Importance of hiring healthy food handlers stressed.

1950   National Association for Retarded Citizens formed; other parent groups with focus on specific exceptional conditions also began to press for special education and other necessary services. Thirty-four states had laws subsidizing public school classes for all recognized groups of exceptional children.

Mid-Century White House Conference on Children and Youth focuses attention on handicapped child.

The Mid-Century White House Conference provided optimum standards for lighting, heating, ventilation, cooling, and other environmental factors; school nutrition, and factors related to the school day.

1952   Federal Communications Commission reserved more than 200 channels for noncommerical television, providing functional base for educational television.

1957   Cooperative Educational Research Program launched by the U.S. Office of Education, with problems of mentally retarded children a priority concern.

1958   National Defense Education Act approved by Congress to improve instruction in sciences, mathematics, and languages. Congress passed Public Law 85-926 to provide $1 million to be allocated to colleges and to universities to train professional ˙ educators for special education of mentally retarded pupils.

1960   First book published on programmed instruction.

         White House Conference on Children and Youth considered hearing and vision screening, dental and medical examinations, tuberculin testing, prevention and control of diseases, health records, immunization, the handicapped child, and health service facilities.

1961   Congress added funds to support preparation of teachers of deaf children and youth.

1963   Congress legislated funds to support training of educators for all recognized groups of handicapped children and youth and to subsidize research regarding their education.

1965   Elementary and Secondary Education Act provided major breakthrough in federal support of the schools, particularly for programs serving disadvantaged children and youth.

         National Commission on Architectural Barriers established to study access and mobility problems facing persons with physical disabilities.

         National Teacher Corps approved by Congress. Head Start was made a year-round program. Elementary and Secondary Education Act authorized educational benefits directed mostly toward low income families.

1966   Regional educational research and development centers and laboratories established through the United States Office of Education.

1967   Education Professions Development Act adopted by Congress.

1968   Federal Handicapped Children's Early Education Assistance Act approved to establish demonstrations of early education and to furnish models for state and local educators.

1969   Federal Elementary and Secondary Education Act amended to provide technical assistance to states for special education of gifted and talented pupils and to support teaching and research on children considered learning disabled.

1971   Special study of educational needs of gifted and talented pupils initiated by United States Commissioner of Education.

1972   Conclusions from legal actions in Pennsylvania and in the District of Columbia initiated a national move to open and improve education for all exceptional pupils within the context of regular education to the fullest extent possible and with guarantees of due process.

1973   Rehabilitation Act amendments guarantee rights of handicapped persons in employment and in educational institutions that receive federal monies.

Section of 504 of the Rehabilitation Act of 1973 dealt with the physical accessibility of buildings and public programs to the handicapped.

1974   U.S. Supreme Court upheld right of non-English speaking students to bilingual compensatory education in English (*Lau v. Nichols*).

1975   Education of All Handicapped Children Act (Public Law 94-142) passed by the Congress and signed by President Gerald Ford.

Passage of Public Law 94-142 also known as The Education of All Handicapped Children Act. Designed to assist the states to assure that all handicapped children have available to them free, appropriate public education. Together with Section 504 or Rehabilitation Act of 1973 emphasized "mainstreaming."

1976   All states have laws subsidizing public school programs for exceptional children and youth.

The National Education Association and the American Federation of teachers pass resolutions in support of teaching exceptional children in regular classes (mainstreaming) with appropriate support personnel and facilities.

Four states require by law all regular class teachers to have preparation to include exceptional pupils in their classes.

1978   Public Law 94-142 (The Education of All Handicapped Children Act) became effective, assuring all handicapped children a full public education and a variety of accompanying rights.

1979   The Office of Comprehensive School Health was established to coordinate many federal efforts in school health services, instruction and environmental programs.

1980   Cabinet level U.S. Department of Education officially instituted on April 1.

Year-round schooling for children with certain handicaps made law in Delaware and ordered by court in Pennsylvania. Public Law 95-626, the Congress appropriated an additional $10 million specifically designated for grant programs to deter smoking and use of alcoholic beverages among children and adolescents.

1981   This year proclaimed by United Nations as International Year of Disabled Persons. Main purpose to encourage rehabilitation of the approximately 450 million handicapped persons in the world and to help them achieve full participation in the social and economic life of their communities.

Department of Education and Department of Health publish a document entitled "Health Promotion Through the School." The document is an assessment guide to provide a process for reviewing specific areas of school health policy, curriculum and services.

1986   Public Law 99-457 passed by Congress and signed by President Ronald Reagan; it amends Public Law 94-142 with the special feature of mandating education for handicapped preschoolers (ages 3 to 5) and encouraging programs at even earlier ages.

1987   U.S. Department of Education launches priority attention to transition programs (bridging from school to community employment) "regular education initiative" to strengthen general education resources for handicapped students.

CHAPTER 1

Mainstreaming: Concept and Practice

In this chapter, we introduce some of the various forms of special education, stressing its most recent development, called mainstreaming. *Mainstreaming* means providing special education and related services to exceptional children while they attend regular classes and schools. It is a simple idea in some respects, as most big ideas are. Yet it is far from easy to put into action, because it requires professionals to acquire new ideas and skills and it calls for changes in school organizations, educational policies, and funding systems. Such changes are hard to bring about. In this chapter, we show how mainstreaming came into prominence as an educational concept. We also explain adaptive education, the practical basis for mainstreaming.

Mainstreaming seems here to stay, a desirable full partner with more conventional ways of educating exceptional children. Thus the content of this chapter is fundamentally important to the remainder of the book, if readers are to learn about effective pupil management and teaching today.

In 1941, Dr. Samuel Kirk, a leader in special education, wrote:

There appears to be some confusion in the minds of certain educators on who should care for or educate exceptional children. One group alleges that exceptional children should be educated in special classes, while the other group maintains that exceptional children should be educated by the regular teacher in the regular grades....Actually the education of exceptional children is not wholly the responsibility of any one group of

Every teacher is a teacher of exceptional students.

1

teachers. Each teacher, therefore, is to some extent a teacher of exceptional children, and should utilize with some modifications the techniques employed to teach...handicapped or gifted children. (p. 35)

In the 1940s, Kirk's was only one of a number of voices calling for more joint responsibility for exceptional children between regular and special educators. For example, Haitema (1947) pressed for the study of segregation versus nonsegregation of exceptional children.

Special education and regular teachers have much to learn from each other.

Kirk urged special educators to contribute their knowledge and special skill to all other teachers to help improve education. We add a similar challenge for regular class teachers to reciprocate. They and the supervisors and principals with whom they work have abilities and skills that, if shared, can be of great help to special educators. The education of *all* children can be improved through the collaboration of *all* educators, but that process will take time and commitment in every school and community. The challenge is still broader, it must be added, since no change in public schools of the magnitude we discuss here can succeed without understanding and support from the public at large.

CHANGE UNDER WAY IN EDUCATION

Today's schools are involved in urgent, far-reaching change toward improvement and coordination of teaching for all children. The report of the National Commission on Excellence in Education (1983) under the title *A Nation at Risk* caused an unusually deep, broad, and sustained effort for the improvement of the schools. Dozens of state and local initiatives have added their energies to school improvement efforts. Advocates for children who have special needs have stressed the need for maintaining concern for *equity* (equal opportunities for all children) while also seeking *excellence* (NCAS, 1985).

Mainstreaming is occurring in a context of deep concern about schools in general.

Regarding special education, the trend today is toward a partnership of special and regular teachers to work more and more together with exceptional children who are attending school in the same classes as all other children. Coordination is needed because disjointedness has developed in school programs for exceptional pupils and others who need adapted education. The system had become too complex and scattered through the development of many separate, narrowly framed programs conducted mostly outside mainstream classes. The objective today is to bring about more coordinated programs for all students and to help all teachers increase the flexibility and the adaptability of programs so that exceptional students can get the attention and help they need in regular classes.

This movement toward integrated cooperation has both advocates and critics. Both are needed if the change is to be accomplished in the best interests of children now and in the future. All educators must be ready to respond professionally to questions such as "Why change?" "Will students be better served?" "Is it practical?" "Won't teachers resist?" "Can we afford to put present funding practices at risk?" and "Won't the new schemes be misused just to save money or to serve the convenience of administrators?" Parents and the public look to educators for answers to such questions. Good answers, we think, will involve professional integrity and much creative work to improve the schools in general as well as the special programs.

Strong forces press for cooperative integration.

Several forces have moved regular and special education toward closer cooperation. External pressures come from outside the teacher-pupil relationship, even from outside the school itself. Internal forces arise within education.

External Forces

One external pressure for change arises from the equal protection clause of the Fourteenth Amendment to the U.S. Constitution, which assures the individual's rights to personal liberty and equality of opportunity.

A second pressure is philosophical. It is represented by a principle called *valorization* (a concept known earlier and perhaps still more widely known in a slightly different version as *normalization*), which argues that any education, care, guidance, recreation, housing, employment, or other human service for exceptional persons should affirm the value of the social role of such persons and be supplied in normal or everyday environments (Flynn & Nitsch, 1980; Nirje, 1969; Wolfensberger, 1972, 1983).

Special education programs are costly and receive close political scrutiny.

A third force is economic and political. Special education programs have grown rapidly and are expensive; but in the long run, it is also expensive to neglect such programs. The growth of special education has had its troublesome aspects, in that the definitions of the various categories of exceptionality have not been carefully drawn or observed. Political leaders are concerned to contain the further growth of special education, and many educators are intellectually and morally frustrated by a widely used, unreliable, and sometimes hurtful system of categories and labels that is used to structure special programs for children. The widely heralded deinstitutionalization of handicapped persons and their return to community settings has resulted in dollar savings, but these have not often been transferred to schools and other local agencies. This causes many economic and political difficulties.

A fourth influence, one likely to be basic to the future of programs for all children, is the development—essentially for the first time in the history of education—of a substantial knowledge base founded on research for the improvement of education. Known by such names as the "effective schools" and "effective instruction" literature, this compilation of well-confirmed knowledge about teaching and learning provides a new basis on which the renegotiation of relations between regular and special education can be conducted. (We will return to this topic later.)

Handicapped persons are increasingly acting as advocates for themselves.

Fifth, but not least among external forces for change, has been the advocacy of both articulate handicapped persons and parents of exceptional children. Young adult handicapped persons, now found increasingly on university campuses and in other parts of the community, have fashioned a new identity for themselves. They aggressively reject what they sometimes call the vulgarities of labeling and segregation. They work for a respected image of handicapped persons and insist on their right to full opportunity to enter and participate in mainstream institutions of all kinds. Parents of exceptional children have been no less insistent, usually stressing both access and quality in school programs.

Nirje used the term *mainstream* in 1969 in a community-wide sense to help define the principle of normalization. The normalization principle means making available to handicapped persons patterns and conditions of everyday life that are as close as possible to the norms and patterns of the mainstream of society.

Five specific changes have resulted from the five external forces just discussed.

All children have a right to education.

1. *A wave of judicial pronouncements emphasizing children's right to an "appropriate" education in the least restrictive environment.* Following a 1971 federal court case (*Pennsylvania Association for Retarded Children v. Pennsylvania*), the state of Pennsylvania was obligated to search for all retarded children of school age and to initiate programs to provide each such individual with an appropriate education. The settlement agreement specified that the children should be educated in regular classes whenever possible and that, in other cases, there should be the least possible separation from normal school and home environment—that, in brief, is the principle of least restrictive environment.

What Does the Principle of LRE (Least Restrictive Environment) Mean?

Q: Does LRE mean that all students with disabilities will be placed in the regular classroom?

A: No, although this idea is not as farfetched as it might seem initially. Children labeled trainable mentally retarded and autistic already attend regular classes at several schools across the country. The principle of LRE does not necessarily mean mainstreaming in regular classes. However, it does mean that children with disabilities can and should be integrated into regular school buildings, activities, and programs to the maximum extent appropriate.

Q: Does LRE mean trading quality for integration?

A: No. Just as living in society does not guarantee the "good life" to anyone, integration in public schools does not guarantee a good education for students with disabilities. LRE simply affords students with disabilities access to the same opportunities as those enjoyed by their nondisabled peers.

Q: How does the principle of LRE apply to students with severe hearing impairments, multiple handicaps, and severe and profound mental retardation?

A: Even students with the most severe physical and mental disabilities are attending special classes in regular public school settings at an increasing number of locations throughout the country. Many school districts—including Madison, Wisconsin; Tacoma, Washington; Albuquerque, New Mexico; Birmingham, Alabama; and Philadelphia, Pennsylvania—have closed their segregated schools for students with severe and profound handicaps.

Q: I want my child to be as independent as possible as an adult. With this goal in mind, is it preferable to have my child in an integrated setting?

A: If the goal of education is to prepare children for the future—and we want handicapped children to have a future that includes freedom of choice and maximum independence—we have no choice but to educate them in environments where they will develop the skills necessary to be independent, just as we do with all children.

Adapted from *OERS News in Print, 1(2),* Summer 1986.

2. *Passage of extremely important federal legislation relating to special education*—the cornerstone being Public Law (PL) 94–142, the Education for All Handicapped Children Act. Since its passage in 1975, this law has dominated much of the planning and development of special education in the United States. Major principles of the act will be detailed throughout this book, but in brief they are as follows:

    a. *Zero reject.* Schools must provide appropriate education for *all* handicapped children.

    b. *Nondiscriminatory evaluation.* Classification and educational planning must live by procedures that assure fairness to all.

    c. *Individualized educational programs (IEP).* Educational plans must be explicit and specific, based on the individual needs of the handicapped student.

    d. *Least restrictive environment.* To the maximum extent appropriate, handicapped children must be educated with children who are not handicapped.

    e. *Parent participation.* Parental participation in decision making about their handicapped children is assured. This includes, among other things, the right of parents to be notified before any special assessments are made of their children for purposes of identifying handicaps and related educational planning.

In 1986, an important amendment to PL 94–142 was passed (as PL 99–457) that affects early education programs. The law requires that by the 1990–1991 school year, appropriate public education be provided for children aged 3 through 5. That extends earlier provisions of PL 94–142 so that the total range of rights under these laws extends from age 3 to 21. PL 99–457 also created an incentive program for states to provide special programs for handicapped children from birth through age 2.

3. *A virtual shutdown on exclusions, excuses, expulsions, and suspensions from school.* In 1975 (in *Goss v. Lopez*), the Supreme Court moved to further student rights to education by making it clear that school principals and teachers invite legal action if students are suspended or expelled from school for any but the most compelling reasons and even then only by following procedures that recognize pupil and parent rights.

Deinstitutionalization has produced marked dislocations and new community awareness.

4. *The return of many persons from residential institutions to their communities and the local schools.* Many state-operated and private residential school and hospital populations have been reduced by more than half. Others have closed. This shift affects most aspects of local schools: busing, class size, and school board agendas.

Long-accepted classifications are changing because of new knowledge and attitudes.

5. *Serious objections to prevailing classification systems of children for special education.* For example, California educators had to limit the use of individual intelligence tests because of court decisions that such tests had been used unfairly to classify and stigmatize some minority children (*Larry P. v. Riles*, 1972). In New York City, a two-year after-school training program was required for all teachers (numbering about 70,000) as a result of a court decision on the classification of so-called emotionally disturbed students (*Lora v. Board of Education*, 1979).

Internal Forces

Increased flexibility of the elementary and secondary curricula and grade structures permits more interaction of special and regular education programs. This flexibility allows the individual child and the school to accommodate to each other. It is now accepted that all children in the class do not have to work on the same topic or the same level at the same time. A steadily growing mass of both anecdotal and research evidence shows that segregated or separated programs frequently do not work well and that it is feasible and desirable for most exceptional pupils to be educated with other children, with benefits to both (Wang & Birch, 1984). Here are some illustrations of specific internal forces.

1. *Developments in educational technology and methodology make special education much more portable.* Recorders, programmed and adaptive instruction, calculators, team teaching, use of aides and volunteers, computers, magnifiers, amplifiers, self-instructional and self-pacing material, curriculum- and criterion-referenced assessment, cooperative goal structuring, teacher-to-teacher consultation, peer tutoring—these are but a few of the recent innovations now employed by educators. Their use in all classes would mean that special-needs pupils would no longer have to be pulled out to go to separate places in the school building for special education. Rather, special and regular teachers team up to bring such procedures to pupils who need them in the regular class. Under such conditions, much of the distinction between regular and special pupils becomes instructionally irrelevant.

Technological advances can be used to increase the adaptive power of schools.

2. *Programs conducted in local schools are now found effective for pupils formerly believed to be uneducable.* The press is on to extend schooling to children and youth whom the schools previously excluded as unteachable. In 1971, on recommendations of a special policies commission, the Council for Exceptional Children, the major professional organization of special educators, adopted a policy whose first sentence was "Education is the right of every child" (Reynolds, 1971). That collective voice said that the time had arrived for the formal enrollment in school and the teaching of literally all children. No longer was lack of toilet training or any other reason to be considered sufficient to exclude any child from education. The right-to-education principle was established firmly by PL 94–142. Use of new measurement and instructional tools, such as behavior analysis procedures, have been employed in remarkable demonstration efforts that now show how even severely handicapped pupils can learn self-help and socialization skills that make their lives richer and less dependent on others. These successful projects conducted in regular schools have helped persuade school and community leaders of the feasibility of policies for the total function of handicapped students in the schools.

The "right to education" principle has support of the professional community.

3. *Boundaries between regular and special education are already breached, and mainstreaming policies and practices are growing.* The refer-test-classify-place procedures of the past, by which children were pulled out of regular classes and schools and sent to special places, are coming into disfavor. The pullout approach is seen as less effective and more troublesome than many educators had realized (Sansone, 1984; Wang, Anderson, & Bram, 1985). Many exceptional students now receive the education they need in regular classes through special education instruction and ancillary supports provided there.

"Special" doesn't mean separate.

4. *Indirect support roles are increasing for special education teachers, including team teaching and consultative relationships with parents and other educators.* As fewer exceptional children need to be referred out of regular programs, specialists have been enabled to work in the regular class. Teaming with regular teachers, they join in activities to assess, plan for, and teach exceptional children. More teachers now individualize instruction for all their pupils and use assistance from special educators, school psychologists, and others to prevent problems from arising and to teach students who need intensive, highly structured help.

Teachers are doing more consulting about problems and less referring of pupils as problems.

5. *Recognition is growing that special education and adaptive regular*

Special education is adaptive education.

education have a great deal in common. Exceptional child education has passed through a great change, from the earliest definition of *special education* as "instruction that cannot be carried on in the regular class" (NSSE, 1949) to the modern one of "individualized adaptations that make regular education more inclusive" (U.S. Congress, 1983). That great change highlights a major shift in expectations on the part of professionals and parents. Adaptive education means that instruction is geared to the individual needs of students and that students also learn to be adaptive to meet their own needs in increasingly complex environments.

Special and regular school programs are moving closer together.

The external and internal forces noted have a common effect—*the inclusion of more children who have special needs into the mainstream of school, family, and community life.* They reverse the rejection-oriented philosophy that permitted schools to pick and choose among the children to be educated. They also signify the demise of the "two-box" theory of education, that is, the view that there are two kinds of children (exceptional and normal) and two kinds of school systems (one "special" for the exceptional children and one "regular" for normal children).

The new kinship between regular and special teachers is a major national and international theme. The why, the how, and the practical consequences of that closer relationship make up much of today's professional teacher preparation. Making it work in the improvement of education for all pupils is an important part of the challenge to educators. By adapting the examples and by applying the guiding principles and preferred practices provided in this and later chapters, growing numbers of teachers should find increased satisfaction in working with the broad range of students they now find in their classes.

Good Schools

The characteristics of any good school are the same characteristics required to provide quality education for exceptional children. The differences, if any, are a matter of adaptation.

Requirements of All Children	*Requirements of Exceptional Children*
Instruction suited to their various learning abilities and limitations	Same
Safe, comfortable, healthful, orderly surroundings	Same
Curriculum content in academic, vocational, and other subjects that is appropriate for their level of development	Same
Opportunities that constantly challenge them to	Same

grow intellectually, physically, emotionally, and aesthetically	
Chances to excel and win praise for doing well at what is within their power to do	Same
Teaching and guidance in acquiring personal, social, and self-management skills and respect for others	Same

In summary, our main theme is that it is feasible, desirable, and economical now for most exceptional children to attend neighborhood schools and take part in regular classes and activities. The feasibility for educating exceptional and other children together concerns parents and teachers most, so information and guidance about that has high priority in this book. The desirability of providing special education to regular schools and classes is explained also. The economic consideration—the effort to offer quality education and services within an affordable range—is important to everyone too. For that reason, cost-quality data are highlighted where the facts are known. The challenge is to carry out practices that will model the best instruction possible considering the present state of the art of education. As we succeed in serving exceptional persons in the ordinary institutions of the community rather than excluding them—sometimes in ways that have personally catastrophic results—there is a gain in *moral* maturity for us all. At least, so we believe.

Education should meet state of the art standards.

THE MAINSTREAM OF SCHOOL AND SOCIETY

The mainstream of education includes all the classes that students attend, from nursery and kindergarten through postsecondary training. Also included are all the social, competitive, and other activities that engage student time outside classes but under faculty supervision. The mainstream is the strong, central current of the physical, social, and instructional life of the school, plus the offshoots and eddies that are open to students who wish to explore them.

The mainstream of the school is more than a classroom.

Mainstream is used outside education, too, in a similar though much wider and more inclusive sense. The mainstream of society includes families and all the other structured systems of human organization that furnish protection, continuity, security, and community identity for its members. The technology of society includes escalators, vending machines, satellites, dishwashers, lasers, buses, telephones, traffic lights, frozen foods, automated banking, ambulances, supermarket checkouts, and countless other contrivances that humans interface with often and that we are expected to be able to use advantageously. Sometimes the systems and the technology lack flexibility to accommodate persons who are handi-

Mainstreaming occurs outside of schools as well.

capped, but the challenge to extend that flexibility in all aspects of community life is clearly there. Life in the mainstream of society is the general goal for which life in the mainstream of school should supply appropriate preparation.

Origin of Separate Special Education

It has not always been possible to teach exceptional students effectively in the school's mainstream. That was strikingly evident in the early 1900s when large group, mass instruction predominated in urban environments. All students were expected to learn at the same pace and in the same ways. The mainstream was narrow and tightly circumscribed. Individual differences in background, motivation, and capabilities were neither well understood nor tolerated. Under those conditions, many children and young people found no benefit in school and left, uneducated or undereducated.

The first forms of special education involved separation of handicapped students from regular classes and schools.

In the early 1900s, few special programs for handicapped students were started in the public schools. Some of the new technologies, such as the individual intelligence test, created by Alfred Binet in France around the turn of the century and adapted quickly for use in the United States and other parts of the world, were used to predict which pupils would succeed in the regular schools. Pupils predicted not to do well were set aside in special classes, not because they were expected to do better in special places, but simply because they were expected (predicted) to do poorly in regular school places.

In most instances, the early special classes were copied after residential schools that had been started about a half century earlier. The teachers and the curriculum came from places like the Vineland Training School, a private center for retarded persons in New Jersey, and from residential schools for children who were blind and deaf. By the early 1920s, there had been enough growth in concern for the education of handicapped children to stimulate a group of teachers and allied human services personnel (social workers, psychologists, and physicians) to establish the Council for Exceptional Children. The CEC members spoke out for what they called special education for the young people who were denied regular education because they did not fit into the fixed or rigid programs of the early 1900s. That group began the movement toward a special education, administratively and instructionally separated from what came to be called regular education.

Teachers of the handicapped have joined together in the CEC.

Early efforts to individualize instruction did not extend to exceptional pupils.

In the 1920s and 1930s, a variety of experiments in individualizing instruction were conducted in schools of the nation, but most lasted for only a brief time. Rarely did these efforts include individualization for exceptional pupils. The main thrust of early special educators was to obtain education for the "outcasts." Separation from regular education made their special students highly visible, encouraged philanthropy in their direction, and avoided confrontation with regular education. Indeed, the separation drew plaudits from many regular educators. The result was a growth in special classes and special schools, a growth that would later accelerate beyond all expectations.

A related trend that started in the early 1900s and continued for many decades was for definitions of exceptional children to expand. For example, in 1910 the American Association on Mental Deficiency extended the definition of mental retardation to include morons; the category is now considered offensive, but in the early part of the century, it was applied to a great many persons with lesser degrees of cognitive limitations, who consequently qualified for special education. Programs for blind pupils were extended to include pupils with partial sight. A day class for partially seeing children opened in Roxbury, Massachusetts, in 1913 (Wallin, 1955), followed nationwide by others. The residential education programs for deaf children were extended to include day classes for hard-of-hearing children; such a class was opened in Lynn, Massachusetts, in 1920 (Wallin, 1955), and similar ones appeared soon in other cities. In later years, the concept of educational difficulties associated with mental illness among children was extended to those with "behavior problems." Still later, in the 1960s, a very large residual category (children who were not profiting from instruction in basic curriculum areas but did not fit any of the other categories) was added; this was the learning disability category. Most such expansions of categories were accompanied by development of part- or full-time special classes in regular schools. In these ways, the concept of exceptionality was extended, and the separation between regular and special education became larger, if less sharply defined.

During the first half of the twentieth century, students assigned to special education programs for blind, partially seeing, deaf, hard-of-hearing, crippled and health-impaired, speech-defective, socially maladjusted, emotionally disturbed, brain-injured, mentally retarded, slow-learning, and mentally gifted pupils had growing numbers of special, categorically trained and certified teachers to instruct them. Special classes and schools were designed and constructed to house them. States provided designated funds for particular types of special education, over and above support for the schools in general, if certain standards were met. Usually these standards included the categorization and some public labeling of the children. More labeled children meant more money. The new state special education standards also encouraged full or partial separation of the exceptional children from the mainstream of education because schools were eligible to receive extra funds only when special placements were made. Up to about 1970, special education based on that separation model grew in professionalism, gained public acceptance and respect, and increased enormously in size and influence. In the 25-year period between 1945 and 1970, the number of children identified as handicapped and placed in special programs increased by about 700 per cent.

Thus from about 1920 to the early 1970s, a "two-box" pattern of edu-

A separate special education system grew as categories expanded.

Categorizing children and placing them in separate places brought money to local schools.

cation, regular and special, took root. Several generations of Americans were acculturated to it. For years, the two developed in a relatively steady state of symbiosis. The two "boxes" maintained and developed unique structures and styles of education.

Emergence of the Mainstream Movement

Separation was not totally accepted even among special educators.

Even in the 1930s and 1940s, however, some educators and parents did not agree that the delivery of quality special education was incompatible with student life in the mainstream. John Tenney, a major early figure in special education, is quoted as saying, "Mainstreaming has been in existence in some form since 1930." There were early efforts to integrate children into regular programs at the Kellogg School in Michigan (Aiello, 1976a, p. 251). Educators in both public and private schools experimented with various ways of affording exceptional children the instruction and services they needed while going to their neighborhood schools with their brothers, sisters, and friends.

Beginning with the Supreme Court racial integration decision (*Brown v. Board of Education of Topeka*) in 1954, a wave of personal and civil rights sentiment and actions developed a powerful political and philosophical counterforce to separation that continues to this day. The chief advocate for the defense in the *Brown* decision, John W. Davis (who had been Democratic party candidate for the presidency of the United States in 1924) argued that if separate schools for black children were unconstitutional, surely it would be found that separation of handicapped students would also be unacceptable (Gilhool, 1976). He was right. Literally hundreds of laws and regulations that embodied or implied discrimination because of race, sex, age, handicap, religion, or national origin have been rewritten or dropped altogether. National public policy changes tipped the scale toward the view that separation was no longer defensible except in extreme cases and then only for short, intense instruction or treatment that required a specialized setting.

Both philosophy and technology began to encourage integration.

By the 1970s, the more flexible mainstream was not just for the regular students anymore but could accommodate a very wide range of exceptional children (Reynolds & Birch, 1977, 1982). The heightened interest in closing the special-regular education gap was in part a response to Lloyd Dunn, who said in 1976, "We need to take the whole concept of least restrictive alternative and put meat on it. . . . How is the process accomplished in terms of the regular class?" (Aiello, 1976a, p. 251).

Mainstreaming Enters the Everyday Vocabulary

The term *mainstream* became current in the early 1970s to describe the education of exceptional children in regular classes and schools by providing adaptive, specialized instruction and services there. Instances of the successful practice of mainstreaming, though, were reported many years earlier—so much earlier that we have not been able to identify the first. Here are some early examples:

1951   Blind children were given special education while integrated with sighted children, beginning in nursery classes and continuing through the school yeaars, in Temple City Unified School District in California. Program elements included starting children to school together, use of special-regular educator teams for planning and instruction, relating to community resources, and linking with specialized vocational guidance. Georgie Lee Abel and Florence Henderson of the American Foundation for the Blind were leading a national movement toward mainstreaming of children who were blind in the same period of the early 1950s. The famous Pinebrook Report articulated this philosophy and trend (American Foundation for the Blind, 1954).

Education for the blind with the sighted was an early mainstreaming move.

1956   *Autistic* children of preschool age were enrolled and provided specialized instruction in regular nursery classes in Toronto, Canada, in 1956. The children were described as unresponsive at the time of initial enrollment, lacking speech, unable to play, and quite retarded intellectually. Yet they made rapid and substantial progress in the nursery classes, some attaining normal school progress as early as second or third grade. The program elements included beginning school together with other children, a teacher-therapist available at the outset for one-to-one intensive work part of the day for each child (becoming less necessary over time), and special-regular educator teamwork (Lovatt, 1962).

1956   In the District of Columbia, a group of boys, aged 8 to 10, described as having severe learning disabilities and behavior disorders moved from full-time separate education as inpatients on a closed ward to attending and receiving special education in regular school classes every day. The step-by-step transition took three years. At the end, the boys received only occasional tutoring from special teachers when the regular teachers requested. Salient program elements were a combination of individual psychotherapy and planned school activities by special educators, intensive tutoring during transition; pupil self-management skill training, teamwork among psychotherapists and special and regular educators, and periodic joint evaluation of progress (Newman, 1959).

Other mainstreaming situations were reported, too, before the term itself was widely used. They included children with cerebral palsy, spina bifida, thalidomide-caused deformities, hemophilia, and other crippling and chronic illness conditions (Anderson, 1973); gifted secondary and elementary school children (Dunlap, 1955; Mallis, 1955); severely mentally retarded children (Ziegler & Hambleton, 1976); mildly mentally retarded children (Haring & Krug, 1974); and deaf children (Connor, 1976). These are only a few examples of the many that could be listed. The program elements that helped to make those early efforts effective have since been identified, analyzed, sharpened, and expanded.

Mainstreaming in the 1970s and 1980s called for two forms of action. One was "bringing the children back," a sequence of step-by-step plans for the reentry of pupils who had been enrolled in separate, segregated special education programs. A second action called for was "never moving them away," a new emphasis on enrolling, maintaining, accommodating, and supporting exceptional pupils full time in regular education curricula and settings to the greatest extent possible (Birch & Reynolds, 1981).

"Never moving them away" clearly called for an extension of the special education and service continuum to recognize and support the teaching of children with special needs in regular classes. The "new service continuum" at the start concentrates on the waves of children who reach school entry age each year, keeps them in the mainstream, and develops ways to meet their needs in regular classes through all the grades. In the past, the states provided standards and financial support formulas for the teaching of children with special needs, so long as they were separated from regular classes for some or all of the time. Now both the legislative history and the language of PL 94–142 press the States to provide financial support for exceptional children's special-education and related needs while the children are in regular classes. The legal and philosophical intent is plain, but long-entrenched practices are difficult and time consuming to change (Wang & Reynolds, 1985).

Halfway moves do not satisfy the mainstream principle.

The forceful mandate of PL 94–142 was not meant to be easily satisfied, we believe, by such limited measures as resource rooms, where exceptional children would spend part of their time with a special educator away from regular classes. A 1983 congressional commission made that explicit by expressing dissatisfaction about compliance with PL 94–142's intent and by calling on state and local education agencies to

> establish more flexible and individualized options in the regular education program. . . . First, very substantial economies of time, effort and money can be achieved simply by expanding the instructional options that are included in the "regular" education program. Second, [schools] can develop time-limited, intensive special education strategies for those students who do require services not available in the regular program. (U.S. Congress, 1983, p. 10)

The commission emphasized that exceptional children should *not* be

Special placement of children shoud not reinforce programmatic separations.

regarded as "assigned" to special education in a way that reinforces programmatic separation and eliminates demands on general education programs for increased flexibility and inclusiveness. . . . Special Education means "specially designed instruction" to meet the "unique needs" of a handicapped child. For many handicapped children, specially designed instruction may not be needed or may be needed only temporarily as the child develops and the regular education environment becomes flexible and responsive. (pp. 11–12)

A pointed recommendation of this same commission is that state and local school systems

> *should adopt rigorous requirements that the needs of students be met in regular programs before any formal special education identification or evaluation occurs. These should include formal meetings among district administrators, teachers and parents to design and test individualized education programs within the regular education context.* (p. 12)

Equally important with the congressional commission report is the report of a special task force created by the National Academy of Sciences (Heller, Holtzman, & Messick, 1982). The NAS membership is comprised of the most distinguished scientists of the nation, the agency to which the president and other high civic leaders turn for advice on top-priority subjects of scientific character. In this case, the U.S. Office of Civil Rights had approached the NAS for advice on issues concerning the placement of students in special education, noting especially the disproportionately high rates of classification and placement of minority and male students in the "educable mentally retarded" category. The final report of the task force indicated that a child's placement in a special program should be based on evidence that the child will be better served there than in the mainstream. Furthermore, they suggested that categorical delineations should be used in placements only when there is evidence of educational advantage for a specific group or category of children. Their studies suggested that for most mildly handicapped children, there is little if any evidence to justify special placements (Heller et al., 1982).

Special placements should always require positive evidence that the child is likely to be better served in the special arrangement.

The commission's recommendations and the NAS report are consistent with the view taken by many modern educators, namely, that the *mainstream* and *special education* can best serve exceptional students when the two truly join resources, that is, when quality special education is provided for exceptional children *while they are in regular classes*, not separately in resource centers or special classes.

Limitations on mainstreaming are sometimes necessary, of course. However, as the commission indicated, the child deserves first a serious attempt on everyone's part to provide the needed accommodations without removal from the regular class.

THREE FORMS OF MAINSTREAMING

Mainstreaming takes three general forms: physical, social, and instructional.

Mainstreaming comes in more than one form.

Physical space mainstreaming means that exceptional children are physically and visibly present in the same school facilities as other children including those who are nonexceptional. In its plainest form, all the children attend the same school and use many of its facilities at the same time. Severely handicapped pupils may be segregated for instruction in special rooms, and that time is not counted as physical space mainstreaming, but there is at least some interaction in the building as a whole. Also, some pupils may not yet be able to socialize or to communicate readily, but all children, their teachers, and their parents have daily opportunities to recognize that they are citizens of the same world and that their life spaces often overlap. *A very small number* of exceptional children, mainly youngsters who have not yet learned to communicate with others, are able to participate in school at *only* this level of mainstreaming. It is not always a gain for students to be mainstreamed physically unless efforts are made to provide social and instructional mainstreaming as well.

Simple physical mainstreaming can be wrong and cruel because it's incomplete.

Social interaction mainstreaming is a step beyond simply being together in the same facilities. It calls for social interactions, both incidental and deliberately arranged by the school staff. It means that teachers, principals, aides, and parents plan and monitor the mingling of exceptional and other children in ways that encourage mutual understanding, support, and learning. The students get to know one another as persons and to engage in personality-building social relationships. It can be seen that physical space mainstreaming is a necessary precondition for social mainstreaming. *All* exceptional children can *profit* from the assistance of teachers and fellow students in the social aspect of mainstreaming.

The most complex form is *instructional mainstreaming*. It builds on physical mainstreaming and is enhanced by social mainstreaming. Exceptional and other pupils receive instruction in the same subject (although they are not necessarily being taught the same things in the same ways). Mainstreaming in its fullest sense is achieved when all three aspects of mainstreaming are at their maximum. This depends heavily on teachers skilled in adaptive instruction (described in Chapter 3).

Complete instructional mainstreaming is the goal.

Duration of mainstreaming refers to the portion of time during the school day a pupil spends in an effective mainstreaming program. A student might, for instance, be scheduled for full-time (six-hours-per-day) physical space mainstreaming, one hour of which is also at the social level of mainstreaming, but with no time in instructional-level mainstreaming. Another pupil could receive all needed special education and related services under a schedule of full (six-hours-a-day) instructional mainstreaming. Consideration of the temporal element allows several dimensions of mainstreaming to be quantified in days and hours (or percentage of the school day).

The Mainstreaming Profile

The aspects of mainstreaming can be represented in the "mainstreaming profile." The hypothetical case of Fred, shown in Figure 1.1, depicts a

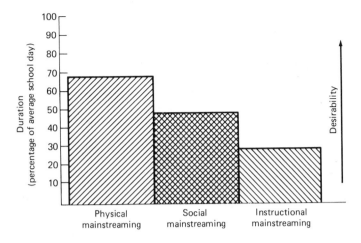

Figure 1.1. Mainstreaming Profile—"Fred: A Sample Case"

student who spends about 70 percent of his time in mainstream settings. This calculation includes time when the student is physically present with general groupings of students, including both exceptional and nonexceptional members. This estimate includes the formal clock hours of classes, plus ordinary extracurricular activities and busing time. Fred spends about 30 percent of his school time in a resource room for handicapped students, and that is not counted as time of physical mainstreaming. In only about half of his school experience is Fred fully integrated in a social sense; that is, he has opportunities to learn to interact readily and successfully with both exceptional and nonexceptional classmates, is accepted by other students, participates in voluntary group activities available to all students, and so on. For instructional purposes, Fred is mainstreamed for only about 30 percent of the time, as noted in Figure 1.1.

Clearly there is a hierarchical relationship between physical mainstreaming and the other two forms of mainstreaming. Social and instructional mainstreaming may not surpass the level of physical mainstreaming. In Figure 1.1, the arrow pointing upward suggests that the desired direction for development is toward fullest possible mainstreaming in all three aspects. Fred's profile shows room for improvement in all three dimensions.

Instructional mainstreaming assumes physical mainstreaming.

It is possible for a profile to show special patterns of discrepancy. Consider the case of Amelia, for example, as shown in Figure 1.2. She is blind and has mastered braille and all other necessary technical skills for academic tasks, mobility, and orientation. The matter of concern is that she is not interacting with other students, nor are they taking initiatives to interact with her. The teacher and the vision consultant have noted the problem and have discussed it with Amelia and her parents, but so far efforts for improvement in social mainstreaming have not succeeded. She is physi-

Instructional mainstreaming does not assure social mainstreaming.

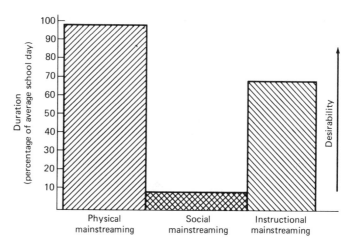

Figure 1.2. Mainstreaming Profile—"Amelia: Social Isolation"

cally mainstreamed and participates successfully in her mainstreamed instructional program but is isolated, unhappy, and dangerously asocial. The solution to her problem will involve significant changes in the behavior of her classmates as well as in her own. Perhaps her teachers will need to learn about new approaches to teaching social skills and grouping practices. If an extended study shows that other students who are blind in the same school system have similar mainstreaming profiles, a schoolwide approach will be required to solve the problem of limited social mainstreaming.

Time in the mainstream can be either good or bad for the pupil.

It needs to be understood, of course, that *time in the mainstream by itself* is not always a good indicator of the suitability of an exceptional child's educational program. As in any program for any child, the program must be appropriate for the individual student. One or more of the mainstream classes may be a poor choice on someone's part, perhaps because of too marked age differences, perhaps because the exceptional child is scheduled to only one or two meetings a week for a class that meets four or five times a week, or perhaps because the scheduled mainstream classes are not ones that the child really needs or can succeed in. Sometimes, too, an exceptional child may be scheduled to an age-appropriate grade for the full number of periods every week, but part of the time is spent with one section and part with another, where differences in pace of instruction, assignments, and social groups are added obstacles.

Interruptions and inconsistencies in placements can interfere with instruction and learning.

Such poor professional decisions, harmful rather than helpful, are sometimes made about pupils. In studies that encompassed 39 schools, for example, only 2 schools were found to be free of all the kinds of scheduling problems just enumerated. For example, considering all 39 schools, only about 40 percent of the exceptional children ($N = 844$) who were going to regular classes were actually scheduled to the full instructional sequence for all the regular education subjects they were taking (Sansone, 1984, pp. 51–56). In only 5 of the 39 schools were exceptional pupils assigned to grade-appropriate groups when attending regular classes. In only 7 of the 39 schools did the exceptional pupils attending regular classes continue with the same group of regular students each period during the same week; in fact, in 46 percent (18 out of 39) of the schools, more than half the exceptional children *were not* scheduled consistently with a fixed group of regular students in mainstream classes (pp. 42–48). Quite clearly, such practices are not favorable for learning and put the exceptional child at a broad and serious relative disadvantage with respect to regular class pupils with full, consistent schedules.

Inconsistent scheduling is wrong. It should be called *dumping*, not mainstreaming. Figure 1.3 shows what might be considered a "dumping" profile. The student is mainstreamed physically, but virtually no success has been shown in social or instructional mainstreaming. Indeed, no decent effort had been made in those dimensions. Because such conditions do exist, it is essential for pupil welfare that whoever controls scheduling assess carefully that time is used well. Zigmond, Vallecorsa, and Silverman (1983) employ the following three criteria as a starting point in looking at how time is used:

Time must be used well.

> The exceptional child in a mainstream class should be with a grade-appropriate group of students; that is, the children should all be in an age range that allows reasonable social compatibility.

> The exceptional child should stay with the same group of students for all regular class experiences.

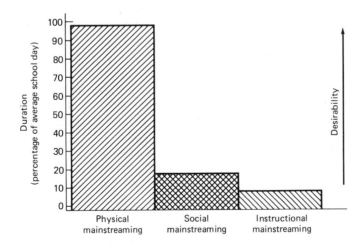

Figure 1.3. Mainstreaming Profile—"A Case of Dumping"

The exceptional child should attend the full sequence of instruction in each regular class subject.

We agree that these three considerations are fundamental to appropriate programming. They should be given detailed attention in every individualized educational program (IEP).

The models presented in the mainstreaming profiles and related discussions outline several salient aspects of mainstream education for exceptional students. Attention is given to the three dimensions of mainstreaming and the duration of each. An extremely important cautionary note about avoiding discontinuities in social grouping and instructional sequence is added. Obviously, quality of instruction and effectiveness of learning are of ultimate importance; we believe that with effort, it is now possible to implement mainstreaming at the highest level for most of the school program for most exceptional students.

Effectiveness of learning is the ultimate criterion for judging all school placements and experiences.

Illustrations of the Model

For some youngsters, only an elemental form of physical space mainstreaming may be possible at a given time. An example might be a group of autistic children, aged 12 to 14, who attend a middle school. The children, with a teacher, an aide, and consultant services as needed, might occupy an area near the school's center. It could be, at this time, that the students require instruction full time by special educators and are not yet able to participate at all in regular classes or other school activities. In fact, their characteristics, such as the steady concentration on themselves and their constant daydreaming or fantasy, may render them virtually inattentive to one another, much less to the busy swirl of young humanity populating the rest of the school. But they are in the school, known to other children and teachers, *and are not kept from their opportunity* to engage in social or instructional mainstreaming if they might profit from it.

Not all students can be successfully mainstreamed.

An example of limited social mainstreaming might be a small group of children who show markedly slow cognitive development (perhaps called severely or profoundly handicapped) and who have their own assigned space in a regular elementary school. Their teacher and aides stimulate and assist them in language development, feeding, learning to play, toilet training, and other skills that will be essential as they mature. These youngsters may not yet have reached the developmental levels of typical kindergartners. They are, however, responsive to attention, music, affection, and simple recreation like rocking and clapping, and they recognize and greet children and adults in their surroundings. Thus there can be meaningful social interplay with others in the school if the interactions are deliberately engineered to occur in ways that are mutually pleasing and helpful to both the exceptional children and the other children. Student volunteers from regular classes, under teacher or aide direction, can help the exceptional children learn to feed themselves, talk about their surroundings, recognize objects and colors, and otherwise achieve a moderate level of social mainstreaming.

Illuminating examples of mainstreaming at the instructional level are found among children who are deaf or blind. Modern preschool preparation, technology, and support systems are so well developed today that many children who cannot hear at all, even with hearing aids, and children who cannot see at all, even with glasses, can enter kindergarten at the usual age and continue through school without ever leaving their regular classmates. Not all do, but that is mainly because the needed and available know-how, technical facilities, and special education support services are not yet being brought to them while they attend regular classes. The same is true for large numbers of learning disabled, disturbed, gifted, and otherwise exceptional students, if appropriate adaptive educational procedures are applied by the regular and special teacher team.

Mainstreaming at the instructional level is the most complex form.

To sum up, mainstreaming means that children who need special supports are receiving good special education while they enjoy the personal and social advantages of life in regular school classes with all the other neighborhood youngsters of their age. It also means that good regular and special education go on at the same time, complementing each other. Further, it means that the regular teacher coordinates pupil activities with colleagues made up of special educators, aides, the school principal, and other specialists. With parents, these professionals make up a team whose central concern is to provide top-flight instruction for all children.

RESEARCH ON THE EFFECTS OF MAINSTREAMING

A natural question is "Does mainstreaming work? What is the evidence, one way or another?" A key point to keep in mind in this context is that it is the *alternative* to mainstreaming that needs to be justified. Unless and until there is research or other credible evidence to suggest that pullout or other special placements will offer advantages to the child, the preferred placement is in the mainstream. That is the meaning of the principle of the least restrictive alternative.

It is too early to answer questions about the relative outcomes of mainstreaming and other forms of special education with absolute certainty. There are two chief reasons: the limited amount of research involving control or comparison groups and the relative newness of mainstreaming. However, even with those limitations, some useful conclusions can be drawn.

Lack of Comparative Information. Dozens of articles and books report successful mainstream programs. They range from preschool to college

Research on mainstreaming is only beginning to be instructive.

and include exceptional students of all varieties. The elements of success given in most such reports are that (1) teachers, parents, and pupils express positive reactions, from satisfaction to enthusiasm, with the mainstream program and procedures; (2) the few problems at the outset are usually resolved after the process is under way for a time; and (3) over time, the number of pupils referred for possible special placements decreases, and regular-class consultation on pupils increases. Few of these reports, however, involve controlled investigations. Encouraging as they are, they nevertheless lack the rigor associated with reports from comparative studies. That has led to a number of efforts to examine the effects of mainstreaming through more tightly designed comparisons and contrasts with conventional special education arrangements like special schools, special classes, and resource rooms.

Early estimates of the effectiveness of mainstreaming tend to be positive.

Relative Newness of Mainstreaming. The usual way to obtain comparative information is to try out two or more approaches under controlled conditions, that is, keeping all conditions essentially the same except for the specific matters being compared. Then, given an equal start, equal time, equal resources, equivalent pupils, equivalent teachers, and faithful implementation of the several approaches, the outcomes are measured and conclusions are drawn. Actually, it is extremely difficult to put together such tightly controlled field investigations in education, even under the best of circumstances. The fact that widespread mainstreaming is a relatively recent development makes it doubly difficult to conduct well-controlled comparative studies. Even so, a significant amount of research has been done, and its results are available (Madden & Slavin, 1983).

A spate of studies was conducted quite early, mainly in the 1950s and 1960s, comparing special class and regular class placements for mentally retarded children at the educable level. The findings of these so-called *efficacy studies* were equivocal. "They did not support regular or special classes as the most appropriate placement for retarded children" (Kaufman, Agard, & Semmel, 1985, p. 9). The lack of evidence in support of special arrangements for this large group of exceptional pupils undoubtedly served as part of the rationale for mainstreaming.

A large descriptive study, called Project PRIME (Programmed Reentry into Mainstreamed Education), was conducted in the early 1970s on educable mentally retarded (EMR) children in the public elementary schools of Texas, where a variety of efforts pointing toward mainstreaming were under way. Both children and their instructional environments were studied intensively in regular classes, resource rooms, and special classes. One important conclusion was that "if mainstreaming EMR learners is to enhance their education, administrators and teachers must effectively integrate regular and special education services" (Kaufman et al., 1985, p. 410).

The most instructive investigation of the usefulness of mainstreaming was a rigorous synthesis (technically known as metanalysis; Glass, McGaw, & Smith, 1981) of studies published from 1975 to 1984. All the

studies reported in that period were conducted in a time when the least restrictive environment principle was quite explicit as public policy (*PARC*,
1971; PL 94–142, 1975). It was also a period in which vigorous efforts were
beginning to be made in many places to provide for the integration of
special and regular education programs. It was possible to find 264 studies
of mainstreaming done during that nine-year period. Of the 264, only 85
studies reported empirical data on the effects associated with mainstreaming. Of those 85 studies, 50 presented adequate data to allow comparisons
with control groups of some kind, and it was that set of 50 studies on
which the detailed analysis was performed. The analyzed studies included
3,413 students, representing all grade levels from preschool through high
school. The pupils fell into the following classifications: mentally retarded,
learning disabled, hearing impaired, academically handicapped, low achieving, and gifted (Wang et al., 1985).

Wang and colleagues (1985) raised four key questions, stated here
with short summaries of the answers the investigators found. The results
appear to apply across all the categories of exceptionality included in the
studies.

1. "Are there significant differences in the social and academic outcomes for handicapped students in a mainstream program and for those
students placed in special education classes?"

Yes, the handicapped students in mainstream programs tended to be
significantly superior in social and academic outcomes. The social and
academic outcomes included performance effects, attitudinal effects, and
process effects. "Performance" referred to achievement measures in subjects such as mathematics, reading, language arts, social studies, and
quality of play. "Attitudinal" effects encompassed self-concept measures,
attitudes toward school and learning, attitudes toward nonhandicapped
classmates and the reverse, and teacher and parent attitudes toward mainstreaming. "Process" effects covered types of interaction between students
and teachers and among students.

2. "Are there significant differences in student outcomes for part-time
mainstream programs (e.g., pull-out resource rooms) and programs that
mainstream handicapped pupils in regular classes on a full-time basis?"

All three outcome measure types (performance, attitudinal, and process) were noticeably higher for handicapped students in full-time mainstream programs than for those in part-time programs, although the effects
did not reach statistical significance. Similarly, outcome measures were
uniformly higher, though not statistically significant, for full-time and part-
time mainstreamed pupils than for handicapped pupils in self-contained
special classes. Thus the conservative answer to the question is that outcomes do not seem to be *significantly* influenced by the *degree* of mainstreaming, when comparing among full-time, part-time, and self-contained
settings, although any *observed* differences appear to lean in favor of higher
levels of mainstreaming.

Metanalytic procedures in research are impressive but controversial.

3. "Are there significant differences in the social and academic outcomes for mainstreamed handicapped students and those for their nonhandicapped classmates?"

Of the 50 studies analyzed, 24 included comparisons of student outcomes for mainstreamed handicapped students and their nonhandicapped classmates. The comparisons showed that the nonhandicapped students did consistently and significantly better on measures of performance, attitude, and process than the handicapped students. Thus mainstreaming did not prove to be a cure-all. However, again, the mainstreamed handicapped students fared better in comparison with their nonhandicapped classmates than handicapped students who were not mainstreamed.

Success in mainstreaming depends on application of principles of good instruction.

4. "What are the programming characteristics associated with demonstrably effective mainstreaming approaches?"

The mainstream programs that showed greater effects in student and teacher performance, attitude, and process outcomes did tend to employ certain instructional procedures more often. There were observed effect advantages tied to the following strategies:

a. Continuous assessment of student achievement
b. Alternative routes or methods of instruction
c. Variety of materials available for use in teaching
d. Explicit individualized instructional plans
e. Student self-management in parts of the school program
f. Peer assistance among students
g. Instructional teaming of teachers and other staff
h. Use of consulting teachers

Overall, mainstreaming programs that employed these strategies had more positive effect. Differences across the various instructional strategies were not statistically significant, however.

So far as relative cost is concerned, there is still too little information to reach firm conclusions. From the few studies that have been done, though, it appears that mainstreaming may be no more costly per pupil or per unit of growth in achievement than other approaches and may even be less costly (Wang & Birch, 1985).

On balance, research shows mainstreaming to be holding up well.

On balance, mainstreaming seems to be holding up well as an approach to providing good special education. That is particularly impressive in view of its position as the "new kid on the block," not yet having had time to work out all its problems, in contrast to longer-established approaches, such as special classes and special schools.

CONTEMPORARY MAINSTREAMING AS AN INTERNATIONAL MOVEMENT

The trend toward joining regular and special educational strengths to improve schooling in general is not confined to the United States. In fact, many of the techniques and procedures that make effective mainstreaming feasible were pioneered and developed elsewhere. Witness this statement about special education in Sweden:

> Stress has been laid during the last decade on efforts to integrate handi-capped pupils as far as possible into ordinary education.
>
> At one time the characteristics of special education could be summed up as individualized teaching methods, specially constructed programs, step-by-step learning, a psychological approach to the child's problems and dif-ficulties, mental hygiene as an aspect of the methods and treatment adop-ted by teachers, and so on. On the whole, the emphasis was not only on the pedagogic aims of education, as evaluated in terms of knowledge, skill [and] achievement, but also on the social and emotional development of the child. All these criteria, however, have now been incorporated in modern education and it is therefore no longer reasonable to regard special education as fundamentally different from general education. Throughout the world the general school systems seem to have changed their characteristics. In Sweden, the modern school aims at a method of work whereby each student can obtain exactly what he requires in respect [to] teaching, upbringing and care. The aim is to offer each individual student a course of study that suits his particular aptitudes and needs and gives him an opportunity to perform according to his ability.
>
> The aim...is also valid for special teaching. It implies the creation of better opportunities in the school system as a whole for children and young people with some sort of special difficulty or handicap. Special edu-cation in Sweden nowadays can thus be described as an essential part of general education, as one of the elements designed to make it possible for all pupils, including the handicapped, to benefit by access to learning or training. At the same time, special education requires a greater degree of specialist contributions, coordinated with the pedagogic work in "or-dinary" education. Medical, technical, social and psychological experts are needed, as are specially trained teachers and specially devised teaching aids combined with ordinary materials. Hence, it is still correct to talk of special education as a reality in the sense that it involves concentrated edu-cational efforts for the individual handicapped pupil. (Lundstrom, 1974, pp. 119–120)

Mainstreaming is a worldwide movement.

In London, the Fish (1985) report to the Inner London Education Authority called for the mainstreaming of handicapped students, includ-ing even the most severely handicapped, to the maximum extent pos-sible. The report called for the appointment of a "befriender," a person to help parents in advocating for their handicapped children.

Vaughan and Shearer (1986), two Britons writing from their respective associations with the Centre for Studies on Integration in Education and the Campaign for People with Mental Handicaps in London, have sum-marized American experience in mainstreaming—especially in Massachu-setts —for an international readership. They concluded that to serve young people in England and Wales there is need for "far stronger public pro-

U.S. mainstreaming is being monitored on a worldwide basis.

motion of the philosophical ideals...to reduce segregation of people with handicap" and "for more flexibility in the regular schools' structure and curriculum" (p. 35).

In Indonesia, recent approaches to rehabilitation have stressed the goal of integration. The quality of mainstreaming is measured not merely in terms of frequency of the disabled person's contacts "outside the primary group" but also in terms of "actively creating such contacts... rather than passively accepting them" (Semiawan, 1980, p. 1). And in mainland China, attitudes and approaches are moving in a similar direction:

"Other pupils have to shoulder the job of settling them in."

> China's programme for the care of the disabled stresses one basic point: integration....Those disabled people who can work are encouraged to take jobs in a normal environment. It is the same for the children: schooling where possible with physically sound children, and if the other pupils have to shoulder the job of settling them in, so much the better. (Yi Shui, 1981)

Such reports from other nations, plus many reports of direct observations of practice here and elsewhere, lead to the conclusion that mainstreaming in education is an international movement. Also, the salient characteristics of the movement are very much the same from place to place.

CHARACTERISTICS OF MAINSTREAMING TO LOOK FOR IN SCHOOLS

Program characteristics formerly reserved for special settings are being moved to the mainstream.

The chief observable characteristics of mainstreaming in the United States and elsewhere are well illustrated in Figure 1.4. The characteristics represented are a small sample of the kinds of organizational elements that are required to make mainstreaming work. Under this scheme, regular classes are made educationally more powerful, in that they have more human and material resources. They are made more diverse, in that the regular class personnel and materials have, among them, a greater variety of knowledge and skills. Modern adaptive education *systems* (see Chapter 3) are employed to manage individualization for all students. Self-management skills ("school survival" or "coping" plus achievement-oriented and social interaction skills) are deliberately taught. Students are trained to be self-responsible and mutually helpful.

Regular school spaces are treated acoustically. Amplification and illumination are provided as needed to accommodate sensory deficits. Carrels and "time-out" areas are included if teachers wish to employ them. Equipment needed by individual pupils for mobility and participation (found only in special schools in the past) is made available. Priority is given to

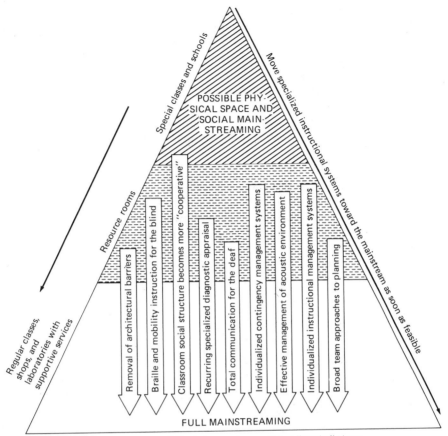

Figure 1.4. Changes Occurring in the Cascade. The term *cascade* is used because of the figurative resemblance to a waterfall (Deno, 1973). Note the trend toward fewer specialized places and more diverse regular places.

moving the various forms of specialized instruction into the regular schools (see the arrows in Figure 1.4).

Practically all children start school under full mainstreaming conditions, in regular classes. But some separate, specialized placements remain, for after a thorough trial, it is found that regular class cannot be made flexible and accommodative enough for every child. Conditions such as the following require special placements outside the mainstream.

1. Intensive, short-term educational facilities and programs for children who need concentrated instruction to learn not to be destructive to themselves or others.
2. Situations in which children with severe and profound *multiple* ex-

ceptionalities require a totally specialized curriculum all day, every day, for extended periods.

3. Children suffering from traumatic injuries or who are undergoing surgery or other treatment that alters their mental or physical state so that they need specific reeducation in various developmental, cognitive, or social skills.

4. Children who are in stable physical and mental condition but must have maintenance environments (e.g., mechanical respirator, dust-free living space) that cannot be readily made available in regular class groups.

Children are moved to specialized environments for only a limited number of clearly specifiable educational purposes that are demonstrably impossible to achieve in regular schools.[1] Such special settings are ordinarily staffed by special education personnel who have targeted their advance training on work with highly specific educational procedures and who are also available as consultants to their special and regular education colleagues who work in the mainstream.

CLUSTERS OF PROFESSIONAL CAPABILITY: PREPARATION TO IMPLEMENT MAINSTREAMING

Changes affect preparation programs.

The mainstreaming trend is causing many changes in the functions and roles of teachers and other school personnel in dealing with exceptional students and special education. In a national survey of teacher training institutions (Sattler & Graham, 1984), just over half (52 percent) required at least one course in special education for preservice elementary teachers, and nearly 4 out of 10 (38 percent) had such a requirement for secondary teachers. Universities can expect to increase such programs, not only by requiring a course or two in special education for all teachers but in much more basic ways as well. Changes are likely to affect *all* teachers.

A view covering a common body of practice for all teachers is emerging.

To help guide those changes, significant national groups and states have recognized 10 clusters of capabilities that should make up the common body of knowledge and practice for all educators (Reynolds, 1980a). They are summarized briefly here. They constitute a checklist of professional competencies that are needed if mainstreaming is to be effective.

---

[1] There are noneducational reasons for removing children from school, of course, like delinquency or communicable disease. Appropriate education should be supplied to such children, wherever they are. If they are to be away from their home schools for more than a few days, remedial catch-up programs should be given on their return to close any educational gaps that have developed.

Use this checklist for personal status assessment and as a planning tool to write a teacher education plan for acquiring the requisite competencies.

CHECKLIST OF PROFESSIONAL COMPETENCIES NEEDED IN TODAY'S
SCHOOLS BY ALL PROFESSIONAL PERSONNEL

Do I have the competencies in this cluster?

Yes   *Maybe*   *No*

_____   _____   _____   1. *Curriculum.* All teachers and other school personnel should have a broad understanding of curricula for grades kindergarten through 12 and should be prepared to analyze and modify them to meet individual student needs.

_____   _____   _____   2. *Individualization of instruction.* All educators should be prepared to study individual pupils, devise explicit plans for their instruction, and function in organizational systems that feature teamwork in providing educational diagnosis and individualized instruction.

_____   _____   _____   3. *Basic skills.* All educators should be prepared to teach the basic literacy, life maintenance, and personal development skills.

Every teacher should be able to teach the basics.

_____   _____   _____   4. *Class management.* All educators should be skilled in managing students in complex activities, maintaining on-task behavior, setting necessary rules and teaching students to follow them, creating a positive climate, managing crises, and teaching students to participate in management functions.

_____   _____   _____   5. *Student observation and referral.* All educators should be skilled in making systematic observations of individual students in a social setting and in other forms of data gathering. They should also be skilled in making referrals to other professionals and agencies for help when needed.

6. *Student-student relationships.* Teachers and other school personnel should be prepared to create social structures in classrooms and other school settings where students learn to understand and appreciate diversity in human characteristics, are helpful to one another, and are able to work effectively in cooperative and orderly ways.

Consultation skills are increasingly important.

7. *Consultation.* Teachers and other school personnel should be skilled in consultative relationships, that is, in helping one another to serve student needs. This is based on the position that under new policies, the first duty of a teacher, upon observing that a student may need help beyond the teacher's ability, is to call in a consultant rather than to make a referral or remove the student from the mainstream.

8. *Parents and family.* Educators should understand family life and know how to work with the parents of their pupils. Particular emphasis is needed on developing an understanding of minority groups and other "disenfranchised" families and on work with parents of handicapped and gifted students.

9. *Exceptional conditions.* All school personnel need to understand the exceptional conditions that influence the lives of some students (such as slow or unusually rapid intellectual growth, sensory deficiencies, physical limitations, emotional

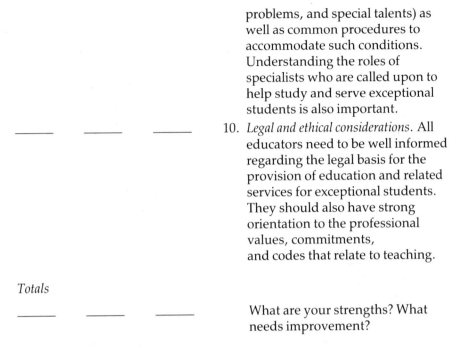

problems, and special talents) as well as common procedures to accommodate such conditions. Understanding the roles of specialists who are called upon to help study and serve exceptional students is also important.

10. *Legal and ethical considerations.* All educators need to be well informed regarding the legal basis for the provision of education and related services for exceptional students. They should also have strong orientation to the professional values, commitments, and codes that relate to teaching.

Totals

What are your strengths? What needs improvement?

All regular educators, special educators, school psychologists, speech and language therapists, and other specialists need the listed competencies and more as they work together as a support system for students. The "clusters of competency" listed are clearly derived from an analysis of the least restrictive environment, or mainstreaming, principle. The list could well be extended to include areas of principled teaching derived from the "effectiveness" literature—a matter, treated later in this book that is receiving increased attention in organizations of teachers and teacher educators.

All teachers need these capabilities to assure proper instruction for all children.

PREVAILING AND PREFERRED PRACTICES

To aid in understanding the rapidly shifting dimensions of special education, this chapter and most others of this book include a list of *current* or *prevailing* practices in the education of exceptional pupils. Each list is related to the content of the chapter in which it appears. Contrasted with that is a list of *preferred* practices, also related to that chapter's content.

Prevailing practices are those that are still in widespread use. Preferred practices are actually found in everyday use, increasingly but still not necessarily in the majority of U.S. schools. Both philosophy and research show the preferred practices to be advances that are appropriate, effective, and feasible.

Practices are continually evolving.

Here are the lists for this chapter. It is best to read and discuss them in same-numbered pairs.

Prevailing Practices	*Preferred Practices*
1. Special education is conducted mainly in separate, specialized settings, such as special classes, resource rooms, or special schools.	1. Special education is conducted as an integral part of the unified school system; as much of it as possible is made portable and provided in regular classes and schools. Specialized settings are used only for essential purposes and for limited periods of time.
2. Special education is managed mainly by highly centralized and specialized officers of the school system, all distinctly set apart from the leadership of the general educational system.	2. The administrative management of special education is highly decentralized and in the hands of regular school principals, other line officers, and the teachers in the schools.
3. Educational programs for most exceptional children tend to start at 5 to 6 years of age, with some special programs, such as those for blind or deaf children, starting earlier.	3. Special education begins at birth or as soon thereafter as a special need is identified.
4. Exceptional children are placed in special settings often before a real effort has been made to help the regular class teacher to make realistic accommodations for them.	4. Exceptional children are separated from regular classes only when necessary for specific forms of instruction and after methods of mainstreaming instruction have been tried but failed; consequently, even children with severe handicaps remain in regular school settings all or most of the time. Categorizing and labeling of students are minimized.
5. Special educators, school psychologists, speech and language clinicians, school social workers, and other specialized staff members provide services to exceptional	5. Special educators, school psychologists, speech and language clinicians, school social workers, and other specialized staff members emphasize training as a

children and their families only outside regular classes.

professional function and work to "give away" as many of their competencies as possible to teachers and other staff members; in addition, they work collaboratively with regular teachers and directly with exceptional students in regular classes.

6. As spaces for instruction, schools consist mainly of series of "boxes" that have little provision for variety, easy assess, or flexibility.

6. Schools, as physical settings for education, provide barrier-free, safe, interesting, flexible spaces for all children, including those who are exceptional.

7. Instructional materials for exceptional pupils are limited and available only to special education instructors.

7. Adequate instructional supplies and materials are provided for all teachers, thus improving their accommodative power in dealing with individual differences among learners.

8. Teachers refer special problem children to specialists.

8. Teachers call in teams of assisting regular teachers or consult with specialists to help with problem children right in the classroom as the preferred first step.

9. Parents are usually informed about the specialized programs that are provided for their children.

9. Parents participate fully with teachers and other staff members in all decisions on programs for their children.

10. Reading instruction is conducted at multiple levels in most elementary school classrooms, but other aspects of the curriculum are standardized for all children.

10. Modern management systems for instruction and curriculum differentiation permit considerable variety in programming to accommodate individual readiness and needs in all subjects.

11. Some children start every year in the regular classes of their schools, whereas others always start and are officially enrolled only in special education programs.

11. All children, handicapped and nonhandicapped, begin their first year of schooling and every successive year in a regular school program.

It is an instructive class project for students to look into their home school districts or others in the region to determine the present status of these practices.

CONCLUSIONS

The recent history of education for exceptional children shows one steady trend: progressive inclusion.[2] In less than two centuries, exceptional children have progressed from almost total neglect, first into isolated residential schools (for just a few) and then into isolated community settings (mostly in the form of special classes and schools), to today's more integrated arrangements. In the 1970s and 1980s, there began what undoubtedly will be recorded by future historians as a remarkable reversal of the negative attitudes that relegated handicapped children to isolated classes, hospitals, and residential centers. Virtually all children are now in school, increasingly in regular schools. The agendas of school boards in communities all across the country now reflect the influx of children with complex and sometimes severe educational problems, and almost every principal and teacher in every school district now faces difficult challenges concerning the accommodation of more exceptional children in regular classes and other school activities.

Heinz (1971) summarized the trend as follows:

> From a historical perspective, special education may be viewed as developing through three successive stages: (1) treatment through the segregation and restriction of resources for survival appropriate for people called different; (2) caring for people regarded as different by providing resources required for their physical existence; and (3) instructing such people so that they may be incorporated into existing, dominant social systems. (p. 9)

Neighborhood elementary and secondary schools are being transformed to make them more inclusive of exceptional students. Some special settings remain and will continue to operate for some time. Although almost all pupils could be well served in the mainstream, there is always a "social progress lag" between what we can do and what we do in fact. But the trend is a definite one, and the processes that result in the assignment of students to special settings will be more and more closely monitored and increasingly difficult to justify.

---

[2] *Progressive inclusion* was the term applied by the late Dr. Henry Bertness who, in the early 1950s, spearheaded the integration of special and regular education in school districts including the city of Tacoma and surrounding Pierce County, Washington, perhaps the first districtwide and all-category application of *mainstreaming* in the sense in which the term is used in this book.

Historical and international perspectives suggest that the current mainstreaming trend is not a minor pendulum swing or a temporary enthusiasm, but it would be naive to assume a straight-line, uncomplicated progression. There are and will be ups and downs. Nevertheless, fundamental forces appear to be at work supporting the general move to join special and regular education on behalf of all or nearly all children in the mainstream. Administrative arrangements are increasingly regarded as dependent variables that can be modified to meet individual needs rather than as certitudes for the disposition of children "carved by nature" to fit isolated "special" places.

The changes toward mainstreaming appear to be permanent.

The changes now occurring in special education need to be broadly understood, not only by educators but also by parents and citizens. Mainstreaming can expand only if people are persuaded that it can work in their localities and that it provides advantages for all. Until people are convinced about this matter and celebrate it as a moral and technical achievement, all the legal decisions, the legislation, and the efforts of advocates may come to naught. Educators ought not underestimate the difficulties of making the fundamental changes discussed here. They present enormous challenges in every sense—professional, technical, political, and moral.

TOPICAL BIBLIOGRAPHY

History and General

Bodgan (1983)
Dunn (1968)
Hallahan & Kauffman (1980)
Kirk & Gallagher (1986)
Sarason & Davis (1979)
Ysseldyke & Algozzine (1984)

Administrative Arrangements

Deno (1973)
Goldstein, Moss, & Jordan (1964)
Kaufman, Agard, & Semmel (1985)
Reynolds (1962)

International Developments

Loring & Burn (1975)
Warnock (1978)

Legal Considerations

Abeson (1976)
Ballard, Ramirez, & Weintraub (1982)
Gilhool & Stedman (1978)
Jones (1981)
Weintraub, Abeson, Ballard, & Lavor (1976)

Adaptive Education

Glaser (1972, 1977)
Strother (1985)
Wang (1980)
Wang & Birch (1984)

CHAPTER 2

The Classification of Students

One can think of a day as a continuum of light shading into darkness and back again or, in a simpler way, as made up of just two parts, night and day. Americans, perhaps more than some other groups, tend to interpret observations in broad categories rather than as continuous spectra. Because it is difficult to think in many dimensions at once, many of us tend to classify, type, or categorize experiences and even human beings in simple ways.

Sometimes there is a choice to think in terms of either categories or continuous variables.

The classification of human beings, however, involves more than simple perception, and it is far more serious. Classification is a social act that is used at times to cast deviants from the community. Hodges (n.d.) tells of a time when the municipal code of the city of Chicago banned people classified as ugly from the city's streets. In some ancient societies, infants classed as handicapped were left unattended in remote places to die. Yet some individuals, by their classification, became entitled to extraordinary interventions on their behalf. So it is with many exceptional children today.

Classifying human beings is, in part, a social act.

Currently, the classification systems applied to exceptional students are anomalous. In the past, the categories were used to keep children with special needs out of the mainstream of education and society, but now, under Public Law 94–142, children assigned to the same categories are required to be included in the mainstream, and educators are expected to make that feasible.

Some degree of public labeling often follows classification of children.

Classification is often conducted in a public way; for example, a child almost inevitably becomes known as mentally retarded when added to a group already classed as retarded. Thus a potentially beneficial educational opportunity conducted by a teacher specially licensed to teach, say, retarded students or emotionally disturbed students carries with it a potentially damaging stigma.

Some labels are highly stigmatic.

Very strong feelings are associated with the classification and labeling of students. Some labels, such as "mentally retarded," are frequently regarded as especially stigmatic and are deeply resented and resisted; they have led to court cases in which parents pleaded for the removal of the label from their child. By contrast, classification may be regarded as reassuring when it is considered to be a sign that the child has been authoritatively diagnosed and that appropriate treatment will ensue. The treatment following the diagnosis or classification makes much of the difference; if the diagnosis leads to highly valued services that clearly and quickly improve the child's educational standing, the stigma is minimized.

Attitudes about classification are more positive if classification leads to successful or valued programs.

The importance of classification in the lives of children can hardly be overemphasized. In the summary report of an important study of classification conducted in the early 1970s, Hobbs (1975) warned that "nothing less than the futures of children is at stake" (p. 1) in the way they are categorized. Hobbs viewed practices of child classification as anomalous; he saw the current system for classifying handicapped children as "a major barrier to the efficient and effective delivery of services to them and their families and thereby [impeding] efforts to help them" (Hobbs, 1980, p. 274) but essential nevertheless because it serves to "open up opportunities for exceptional children, facilitate the passage of legislation in their interest, supply rallying points for volunteer organizations, and provide a rational structure for the administration of governmental programs" (Hobbs, 1975, p. 13).

Diagnosis and classification of handicapped pupils are inexact and controversial.

Scriven (1983) was more definite in his criticism of classification processes in special education, describing them as "scandalous." Glass (1983), a noted educational researcher, seemed to concur when he commented that "most pupils who are labeled 'handicapped' in our schools are diagnosed so arbitrarily because of nonspecific symptoms that most questions of treatment efficacy are, perforce, irrelevant" (p. 65).

Special education does what is left undone by regular education.

In this chapter, we consider issues and practices in child classification. This topic is one of considerable turbulence, even controversy, in special education—indeed, in education in general—because the functions of special education are not well defined or are defined in a residual way by what is left undone or incomplete by regular education.

The categories commonly used in schools in the United States are shown in Table 2.1, along with the current numbers and percentages of students for each category (based on a count of children served on December 1, 1983, reported to the U.S. Department of Education). The categories are used by the states to report the children enrolled in special education programs, as required under Public Law 94–142. Thus for the nation as a whole, 4,341,399 handicapped children were served in the 1983–1984

TABLE 2.1. U.S. CHILDREN AGED 3–21 YEARS WITH A HANDICAPPING
CONDITION SERVED UNDER PL 94–142 DURING THE 1983–1984
SCHOOL YEAR

Category	Number Enrolled in Special Programs	Percentage of Handicapped-Child Population
Learning disabled	1,811,489	41.7
Speech impaired	1,130,569	26.0
Mentally retarded	750,534	17.3
Emotionally disturbed	362,073	8.3
Deaf and hard of hearing	74,279	1.7
Multihandicapped	67,537	1.6
Orthopedically impaired	56,209	1.3
Other health impaired	54,621	1.3
Visually handicapped	31,576	0.7
Deaf and blind	2,512	0.1
Total	4,341,399	100.0

More than 80 percent of handicapped children are reported in just four categories.

SOURCE: U.S. Dept of Education (1985).

school year. That represents 10.89 percent of the estimated total child population (ages 3 through 21) in the United States.

The categories for children, as listed in Table 2.1, tend to be used to classify professionals also; that is, states typically issue teaching licenses in the same categories used for children. For example, it is common for a teacher to be prepared and certified as a teacher of learning-disabled children or emotionally disturbed children. Currently, most states issue eight or nine different kinds of special education certificates, some covering two or more child categories. Teachers may be further limited to practice at the elementary or secondary level (and sometimes preschool), depending on their basic preparatory studies in education.

The same categories and labels tend to be used for both handicapped pupils and their teachers.

The foregoing data and discussion do not include gifted and talented students. No regular reports on gifted students are required by the U.S. Department of Education. Most states make limited special provisions for gifted students, though usually the funding is not so generous as for students who are handicapped. National data on programmatic operations are not available. It seems safe to assume, however, that at least an additional 2 to 3 percent of children could be added to the totals provided in Table 2.1 to estimate the totals of exceptional (handicapped and gifted) students who need special education and related services.

Gifted students are less well reported than handicapped students.

SOME BASICS

The Purposes of Classification

As a starting point in examining practices and issues in classification, it is important to consider the purposes of classification. As Robbins (1966) put

Classification processes should be judged by how well they serve specific purposes and goals.

it, a system of classification "implies that the category chosen is good for something" (p. 5). We propose that classification in the schools ought to serve the purpose of getting each child the kind and level of instruction that is appropriate. That is not an easy thing to accomplish. The knowledge base for classification of children in the schools is quite limited. Sharma (1970) reminded us that mental hospitals existed before the emergence of the scientific disciplines that created the classification of psychiatric patients. With improvement in classification of mental patients, services improved, but even now diagnosis is a major problem in the mental hospitals. Indeed, people with all kinds of problems are taken to general hospitals by amateurs. Even in general hospitals, the sorting and diagnostic processes are not always useful or precise, but they serve as starting points for the beginning of treatment. So it is in the schools.

Causes of handicaps often have little to do with planning instruction.

Zubin (1967), a clinical psychologist, cited three purposes for the diagnosis and classification of people with problems: (1) to search for etiology or cause, (2) to make a prognosis, and (3) to select a therapy. It is clear that classification merely according to *etiology*, Zubin's first purpose, is not broadly useful in education. Knowing the cause of poor sight is of little help in deciding how the child with poor sight should be taught. Knowing the causes of disorders is, of course, very important in preventive work of some kinds. For example, adding iodine to salt to prevent goiter and the giving of smallpox vaccinations could not even be considered until the etiology of the disorders they prevent was understood. For educators, etiologic variables are only occasionally useful, and then only in the context of the educational decisions to be made.

Similarly, general *prognosis*, Zubin's second classification purpose, has limited usefulness for instruction. Knowing the course and outcomes of disease processes is undoubtedly important in the field of health, but in education a different kind of prognosis has held a prominent position. Often developed on the basis of intelligence test results, educational prognosis leads to general predictions of or "expectations" for educational progress and may lead to the "tracking" of students on the basis of "special needs" or the adult roles they are expected to play. Educators, however, are employed to *influence* children's learning, not simply to predict it. Educational decisions require attention to variables or characteristics that interact with instruction, that is, that help educators make a difference in the lives of children rather than make simple predictions about learning and development. Thus general prognostic formulations are seldom useful in planning instruction. In any case, predictions of educational progress from tests of any kind are quite limited in accuracy, especially for individual pupils.

When the aim is to provide appropriate education for each student, the problem of prediction becomes one of choosing or designing an appropriate individual program. The prediction of different outcomes for different individuals within a single, fixed instructional program is not the problem. Rather, the challenge is to predict and plan across alternative instructional approaches to enhance outcomes for each individual. This requires that we consider simultaneously the variety of instructional approaches that may be offered in the school and the differences among individuals and thus foster optimal programmatic choices for each individual. This is the ATI (aptitude-treatment-interaction) idea.

Simple prediction of educational outcomes is not very useful in improving instruction.

In technical terms, an ATI requires demonstration that a student's aptitude or attribute is acted upon positively by a treatment. For example, if there are two possible instructional procedures, the variable that produces an interaction with the treatment provides the basis for decision making. Teachers are constantly making informal ATI decisions. For example, a teacher may decide that Fred learns best when he is given short, closely monitored assignments, while Jenny is able to organize her own work over long time segments. By acting on this knowledge, the teacher matches instruction to the particular needs or most promising approach for each student. This is far different from using procedures, such as general scholastic aptitude tests, just to make academic predictions.

As a further example of the ATI model, suppose that there are two ways of teaching a unit in social studies on the Bill of Rights. Method **I** (see Figure 2.1) is the read-lecture-memorize approach. Note that the correlation between IQ and achievement under Method I is relatively high, as shown by the steep slant of the regression line. Method II involves use of sociodrama, in which students create courtroom scenes that illustrate basic rights. Notice that the slant of the regression line showing the relation between IQ and achievement is lower in Method II. If one were to predict achievement under Method II from IQ scores, the accuracy would be very low. Because the two regression lines intersect, they show what is called

ATIs have their informal analog in daily decisions by teachers on individualizing instruction.

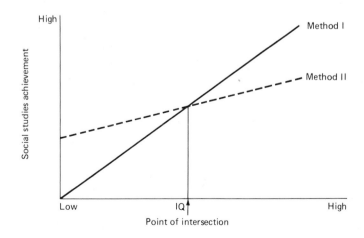

Figure 2.1. Relationship Between IQ and Achievement in Social Studies

disordinal interaction. This aptitude-treatment-interaction suggests that pupils with slowed cognitive development may achieve better under Method II, while pupils with accelerated cognitive development may achieve better, as measured in this case, under Method I.

Thus the ATI analysis shows clearly that the teacher will maximize the achievement for all children by using *both* approaches to teaching the material on the Bill of Rights. That calls for a step toward individualization, with some students being better accommodated by one method and some by the other. The ATI decision was possible, of course, only because alternative programs and appropriate data on individuals were available.

Aptitude information usually is not helpful in adapting instruction unless the aptitude and treatment interact—more specifically, unless the regression line relating aptitude to achievement under one treatment crosses the regression line for the alternative approach, as illustrated in Figure 2.1 (Cronbach & Gleser, 1965). An aptitude measure that validly predicts success within both treatments may have no value in deciding which treatment to use. This implies that general ability is likely to be a poor basis for differentiating instruction, because it correlates with success in most instruction (Cronbach, 1967, p. 30). Unfortunately, school records tend to be "loaded" with general aptitude data (such as IQs) that tend to predict school progress in many dimensions but have limited value in making instructional decisions.

Zubin's third purpose for classification, the *selection of treatment*, is relevant in the educational context (if we substitute *instruction* for *treatment*) because in schools the important purpose of classification is to design or select the most appropriate plan for *what* and *how* we teach. Two general classes of treatment should be distinguished, however. The first is oriented to negative criteria, in which case we use terms like *prevention*, *cure*, or *amelioration*. The second is oriented to positive criteria, in which case we use terms like *development*, *competency*, or *achievement*. In the second case, the concept of prevention does not have its ordinary meaning or relevance.

Educational treatments are almost always positive, that is, oriented to competency or achievement. Their purpose is the promotion of learning, not the recovery from defects or the simple prevention of problems. The educator "prevents" reading failure, for example, not by creating antibodies but by teaching reading or its prerequisites with greater resourcefulness and better effects to more children. Thus to be educationally relevant and to engage the teacher, "treatment" must usually focus on positive learning and development.

There are occasions, of course, when teachers work for what might be called "negative" learning, in the sense that they wish to eliminate or minimize some already learned but undesired behavior. For example, the child who is assaultive toward others or self needs to be taught to reduce that tendency. But even in such cases, where the teacher wishes to reduce the rate at which the child engages in unacceptable behavior, it is often

Variables that predict achievement are not always useful in making decisions about how to provide instruction in the same domain.

Education is oriented to positive goals: competencies.

Reductions in undesirable behaviors can often be achieved by teaching more desirable alternative behaviors.

possible and more desirable to proceed positively by teaching alternative behaviors. The child who spills or throws food can be taught to eat properly. On occasions, it may be necessary to use so-called aversive (punishing) procedures to reduce undesirable behavior directly. This leads readily to controversial topics, which we leave for later discussion.

The view on classification presented here is consonant with Zubin's third purpose, but only in a context of a developmental rather than a deficit-oriented concept of treatment. Unfortunately, there is still much talk among educators about deficits and disabilities, as if they were the starting points of education and as if recovery from or remediation of deficits were the goal. That is the so-called medical model. Obviously, one prevents problems and creates a kind of invulnerability to life's problems whenever important competencies are developed, but remember that learning and competent performance are the goals of education.

Systems of classification and labeling used in special education are under modification in many places to make them more useful. For example, in the California Master Plan for special education, launched in 1974 but fully carried out only in the early 1980s, exceptional children are referred to as "individuals with exceptional needs." The children participate in programs that bear labels of a kind, but the use of traditional categories is diminished, and the students are not labeled except as having "exceptional needs."

In the states of Massachusetts and South Dakota, the practice of labelling children according to the traditional categories of exceptionality is extremely limited. In those two states as well as in New York, New Jersey, and some others, it is becoming common to categorize children for reporting purposes only. Clearly, the trend is growing toward the use of traditional classification systems in special education only for the statistical reports that are required by state and federal government, thus avoiding the attachment of labels to individual children. This trend portends major changes in the diagnostic processes used in the schools, as well as in the roles of many specialists, particularly school psychologists and special teachers. Increasingly, instructional planning is coming to the fore.

Categories and labels for children are sometimes used just for reporting purposes.

> The system should deemphasize the familiar but gross categories of exceptionality. It should specify instead the services required to assist the child or his [or her] family and school in the interest of the child's fullest development. (Hobbs, 1975, p. 234)

In each state, province, or other political unit, it is necessary, of course, to understand the required eligibility and classification systems used in special education and to operate within their regulations. If such systems seem inappropriate, one can work through professional and political processes to modify them, but in the meantime, to the extent that they have the force of law, they require observance. We must try to manage all

If one disagrees with a mandated classification system, solutions require political action.

aspects of the assessment processes such that they produce no gross over-simplification in categorization and placement decisions and no stigma for the children involved.

A special purpose of classification is to facilitate communication among researchers. In this case, a rather open definition of a category suffices. The aim is to achieve better understanding in a field, and the boundaries of concepts cannot always be predicted. Definitions used for purposes of scientific exchange often have no particular relevance to applied fields.

Classification for purposes of scientific communication often do not have relevance in schools or other applied settings.

An example of a definition used for scientific purposes is that of mental deficiency as advanced by the American Association for Mental Deficiency (Grossman, 1983). Recent editions of the classification manual of the AAMD define mental retardation in terms of low rate of cognitive development (at least 2 standard deviations below the mean for the general population) concurrent with deficits in adaptive behavior, manifested during the developmental period (Grossman, 1983). Leaders associated with the development of that definition would undoubtedly urge that it not be applied routinely in the placement of children in special education programs or for any other kind of treatment.

The definition is not used consistently even as a basis for communication among researchers, however, and that is a problem. Taylor (1980) examined all articles published in the two journals of the AAMD (*American Journal of Mental Deficiency* and *Mental Retardation*) for a six-year period after the AAMD issued the 1973 *Manual on Terminology and Classification in Mental Retardation* (Grossman, 1973). The definitions announced in 1973 were a distinct change from earlier definitions. Only 28.1 percent of the articles examined over the six-year period had used the terminology and classes proposed by the AAMD's definition.

Researchers must carefully describe the subjects used in their research.

The problem of inconsistent uses of classes is not restricted to the field of mental retardation. It has also been very difficult to obtain agreement on what is meant by the classification "emotionally disturbed." Wood and Lakin (1979), after a review of research reports on "emotionally disturbed" children, concluded that procedures for classification were described so inadequately by the researchers that it would be impossible to replicate the studies, and "we are deceived if we think we know about whom it is that most authors of research reports are writing" (p. 44).

To help solve the problem of communication among researchers, Keogh has proposed a system of "marker variables" (Keogh et al., 1980). According to this plan, a set of descriptors agreed on by special education researchers would be used in all research so that each study might be compared meaningfully with others. For example, reports could be compared with greater ease if researchers routinely provided data on the subjects of their research on variables such as age, grade, ethnicity, language background, general ability, reading achievement, and exclusionary criteria and on details of the context and program used in the research. With such information, researchers would have a fair chance for accurate replication and for valid synthesis of results over several studies.

The key point on the purpose of classification in the schools is that it should serve to improve instruction and learning. If the classification process does not lead to valuable differentiation in teaching and learning, according to needs of individuals, it is not worth doing. As put by the NAS panel (Heller, Holtzman, & Messick, 1982), "it is the responsibility of the placement team that labels and places a child in a special program to demonstrate that any differential label used is related to a distinctive prescription for educational practices...*that lead to improved outcomes*" (pp. 101–102, emphasis added). This view requires that specialists, such as psychologists, social workers, and physicians, learn to scan what they know for what may be relevant to instructional decisions whenever they are called on by educators to assist in the diagnosis of and planning for students, and it proposes that educators should insist on the primacy of decisions about instruction whenever teams are assembled in the schools to diagnose individual pupils.

Classification in the schools should lead to improvement of instruction.

Screening Efficiency

Screening systems are used to make preliminary decisions about students who may have special needs and in whose cases special diagnoses should be undertaken. They tend to be subjective in that they use "broadband techniques," rather superficial scanning across broad domains. Two kinds of errors can occur in screening: *false positives* and *false negatives*. A false positive is the incorrect identification of a person as having a problem; a false negative is the failure to detect a real problem. In general, there is more concern during screenings for avoiding false negatives than false positives; you do not want to miss the child who has a significant problem or need. However, screening procedures can be highly inefficient when they simply refer too many children as having problems.

Standards of *efficiency* and *effectiveness* are sometimes used in connection with screening. A procedure is said to be effective if it actually identifies all or most of the positives. It would be very easy to be effective, of course, simply by calling every child a positive. The concept of efficiency takes account of this problem. Efficiency is defined as the percentage of positives or referrals for educational diagnosis that are correct (Pegnato & Birch, 1959).

With handicapped students, it is usually more important to avoid false negatives than false positives when screening for problems.

Classes Versus Taxons

Another of the basic considerations in classification is to distinguish between a class or category (used interchangeably) and a taxon. All taxons are classes, but not all classes are taxons (Meehl & Goldberg, 1983). Most

All taxons are classes, but not all classes are taxons.

classes or categories as they are used in education are determined by setting a cutoff point on certain variables used to describe children. For example, children are usually classified for entrance to kindergarten by date of birth; in many places, children are admitted to kindergarten for the year in which they reach age 5 by September 1 (or some other near date). Similarly, students are often defined as learning disabled when the degree of discrepancy between measured achievements and estimated "expectations" for achievement exceed some specified magnitude. The classes or categories so created are not defined causally or with any theoretical significance; they are not "types" or categories in any fundamental sense. They are invented more or less as administrative conveniences rather than true types. Such classes are not totally arbitrary; they are more like standards for admission to college. These classes or categories are much influenced by the adaptive capacity of the regular schools, the local and state definitions, the amount of money provided by legislators or school boards for special programs, how bothersome pupils are to their teachers, and the persistence of advocacy groups on behalf of the students with certain characteristics, among other factors.

A taxon is not necessarily a useful classification for differentiating instruction.

A taxon, by contrast, is "nature carved at its joints." There are fundamental, causal, theoretically interesting, and significant groupings that would exist whether special education had been invented or not. Down syndrome, a genetic disorder usually associated with mental retardation, is taxonic, whereas mental retardation in general is not. Whether a class is taxonic is not the same as whether it is useful for any given purpose. It is entirely possible that a given student who has Down's syndrome might be taught in the same fashion as students in other categories. Many discussions on the categories of special education proceed on the assumption that they are true types or taxons. Occasionally it is made to seem almost sinful that a child is misclassified as retarded or emotionally disturbed, the assumption being that there really is a "taxon out there"—in some Platonic sense—and that the child is the victim of a poor diagnosis. Textbooks, too, frequently discuss "causes" of learning disabilities or behavior problems as if they were dealing with taxons, failing to recognize that to a very considerable extent, they are dealing with terms designed for mere administrative convenience or to accommodate economic constraints.

To say with credibility that someone is misclassified requires that one be clear about correct classifications as well.

Contextual Variations in the Uses of Categories

Categories used in schools are often different from those used in other agencies.

Another basic element in understanding classification is to recognize that categories used for educational purpose may be distinctly different from those used for other purposes. A person who is "blind" for educational purposes is one who needs to be taught to read by braille methods or by other nonvisual means. Whether the person would be classified as blind by the Internal Revenue Service (IRS) for income tax purposes is another matter. The IRS standard for blindness is set at 20/200 in the corrected better eye; most individuals with that degree of vision can be accommodated easily in school and get along quite well in daily life.

Home as Part of the Context

I went to visit a home of a very disturbed child. The mother was anxious to show me that he could do something really well. I was standing on the porch talking with the father and she pushed the kid out the screen door saying, "Go on, go on, show the teacher." And she stood behind the door with this big ruler in her hand. The poor little kid just stood there with tears rolling down his face. I said, "What is it, Kenny?" He said, "She wants me to say the time tables, and I can't." So I tried to explain to the mother that we don't teach the time tables in the first grade. (Bower, 1973, p. 22)

Diagnosis should look beyond the child to the child's school and general life situation as well.

In 1969, the President's Committee on Mental Retardation issued a major report titled *The Six-Hour Retarded Child*, the implication being that some children are considered retarded only during school hours. That idea may seem illogical, even repugnant, to some observers. However, it is entirely possible that a classification or category is useful in school, however dysfunctional it may be in other settings.

During World War II it was noted that the traditional psychiatric classifications were useful in no more than about 10 percent of the psychiatric casualties (APA, 1965). Presumably, there was something unique about the stresses of war that made the traditional diagnostic categories less than useful. Similarly, the demands made on children in school are different from those of other settings, and it should be no surprise to find that the categories used are different.

Categories vary with context.

U.S. Court Tells New York to Aid More with Learning Disabilities

A Federal judge has ruled that New York State's method of identifying children who have learning difficulties violates Federal law and has ordered the state to tell tens of thousands of parents their children may now be eligible for help....

New York City screens an average of 5,000 pupils a month for learning disabilities. So far, 23,413 have been identified as having the handicap throughout the state. Citing the testimony of experts across the country, the plaintiffs in the current case argued that if screening procedures were less arbitrary, the figure would be nearly four times as great....

Where an eighth-grade pupil with a reading score of 4.6 would have been

Boundaries of the categories are set in many ways.

> denied special help in the past, because his reading level was above the 50 percent mark (fourth grade), he now most likely would be entitled to special tutoring....
>
> In the city alone this year the parents of more than 50,000 children asked for special placement. Of these only 10,000 were selected. (*New York Times*, July 2, 1980, pp. Al, B3)

Public Law 94–142 requires that children first be identified as handicapped and, second, that a determination be made about their needs for "special education and related services." This two-stage identification policy proposes that at the first stage the identification be context-free, that the child simply be found to be "handicapped." That first step in child study presents enormous difficulties, especially in cases of what have been called judgment categories or mild handicaps, and leads to the suggestion that a one-step process be designed and used specifically for education. This topic will have recurring attention in later sections of this book.

David's Story

David's story illustrates progress and how classifications may change over time.

David was the second of six children born to his parents. A 3 lb., 8 oz. baby, he was born prematurely after a pregnancy of only six and one-half months. His early development, both intellectually and physically, was slow. He sat up at one year, walked at three, and began to speak at five. After unsuccessful attempts at school in Germany and in Denver, Colorado, David was admitted to the State Home and Training School at Grand Junction, Colorado, on November 30, 1964, at the age of eight.

Certainly, in 1964, mental retardation would have appeared to many to be an accurate assessment of David's status. Yet if other psychologists, educators, and physicians in other locations had studied David at that time, he might well have been considered either learning disabled or brain injured rather than mentally retarded, based on the same evidence. The important thing was David's educational program, not his label.

Much learning occurs in places other than schools and homes.

Almost 11 years later, a confident young man, David was released from the Training School to seek his place in the world, not as he entered, but as an ambitious youth ready to face success or failure on his own.

During the course of his 11 years at the School, David progressed through numerous training and therapeutic programs, both within the institutional school and in the nearby public school system. David, who attended Grand Junction High School, is one of a small number of institutionalized persons who have scored a touchdown for a state championship caliber football squad.

One of David's earlier adventures was as a Scout, when he was selected to attend the National Jamboree, traveling to Idaho in the process. David later became a member of the State Home and Training School's Jaycee chapter, the first organization of its kind to be based on the campus of a residential school for the developmentally disabled.

David's family has maintained a close interest in his progress through the Training School, often contacting David by telephone and arranging for visits to various family members from as distant a place as Georgia and California.

At the time of graduation in the Spring of 1975, David had participated in the school district's "Work Experience—Study Program" and had improved both his work and academic skills. His teachers estimated his reading level at between the 3rd and 4th grades and his arithmetic skills at the 5th and 6th grade levels. He had completed Driver's Education, earned letters in football and track, and been selected as the "Spirit King Award" recipient and reigned over one of the school dances. He had also been recognized as an outstanding local student by one of the local banks. His formal educational program, which began in the institution, progressed far beyond what was thought possible when he was admitted in the mid 1960's.

David's participation in the Work Study program included work activities as a grocery carry-out clerk, a dishwasher at the fraternal lodge, and as a clean-up man for a local drug store. With the money earned in these various endeavors, he has opened a private checking account and is making his own purchases in the community.

Total independence is the long-range goal.

A few weeks prior to his release from the Training School, David expressed his great desire to become totally independent and a realization that he has much to learn in order to become so. He stated a reluctance to brag about his achievements but also pointed out that many students in "Special Education" can surprise others if given the chance to show their abilities. He spoke of his long range goals of working in construction or as a grocery stocker or cashier.

David has not yet achieved his goal of total independence and is still living in a somewhat restricted environment, that of a group home. He has, however, been able to move himself out of the institutional setting, both by his own efforts and that of the Training School staff and community programmers. He will have his successes and he will have his failures in the months and years ahead, but David Jones' story is one worthy of notice. (Smith, 1976, pp. 7–8)

David's early childhood status might have been classed as "severely retarded"; with the improvement brought about by education, training, and strong motivation, however, his performance could no longer be described in that way, and his development can continue. As Grossman (1977) suggested:

Education may result in the changing of classifications for a child.

> An individual may meet the criteria of mental retardation at one time in life and not at some other time. A person may change status as a result of changes or alterations in his intellectual functioning, changes in his adaptive behaviors, changes in the expectations of society, or for other known or unknown reasons. (p. 14)

Orders of Disposition

A further basic point is to distinguish between definitions that are curriculum based and those that involve dispositional elements (Meehl, 1972). If a child is diagnosed strictly at the "level of the lesson," that is curriculum

Diagnosis and classification can be provided at different levels for different purposes.

based. However, definitions of categories or classes often go well beyond the curriculum level.

Consider the case of a child who has phenylketonuria (PKU), a genetically determined disorder that under certain dietary conditions can result in severe intellectual limitations. Note the ordering of various elements of disposition. The child shows very poor academic achievement in school (1st order), arising presumably from limited general intelligence (2d order), stemming from an inappropriate diet (3d order) for a child who is PKU genotype (4th order), which, in turn, is based on the genetic carrier status of the parents (5th order). In this case, it is possible to order a series of dispositions or conditionals that eventuate in a particular problem. If we defined the problem simply at the first-order level of the poor academic achievement, going into detail about the child's educational status, we would be making a curriculum-based classification. Usually, however, the diagnosis involves studies by psychologists and others, giving attention to conditionals or predispositions that may help to explain the problem.

Diagnoses at the level of the lesson are most meaningful to teachers.

The field of learning disabilities provides another example of thinking through levels of disposition as an approach to classification. A widely used definition of learning disabilities proposed by the U.S. Department of Education requires the finding of a significant discrepancy between ability (or "capacity") and achievement in a basic area (for example, reading) *plus* evidence of "disorder in one or more of the basic psychological processes involved in understanding or in using language" (U.S. Office of Education, 1977, p. 42478). The reference to "basic psychological processes" (meaning attention, perception, memory, etc.) moves the definition beyond the curriculum level to the presumed predisposition.

Classifications that involve remote dispositional elements tend not to be well confirmed as a basis for educational planning.

In schools, it is very common to move from a curriculum level to a psychological level of disposition. The most common predispositional attribute studied by psychologists is intelligence. On the basis of results on intelligence tests, psychologists often make predictions about progress in the school curriculum or reasonable achievement expectations. From there, the psychologist's analysis can spread to aspects of personality, motivation, specific cognitive abilities, and other characteristics. Then the analysis may make a further shift to an organic level, representing a new order of disposition; at this level, physicians may well be called on to assist. Cruickshank (1972) illustrates this process when he says all learning disabilities [first-order] are "essentially and almost always the result of perceptual problems [second-order and psychological] based on the neurological system" [third-order and organic] (p. 383).

Including in the definitions of classes unproved assumptions about the causes of disorders tends to lead to controversy.

Definitions that cut across several orders of disposition are enormously complex and usually difficult to justify on the basis of clear research evidence in the field of special education. That is one of the reasons there has been such great difficulty in defining what is meant by learning disabilities. The definition used by the federal government, which has important implications nationwide because of the legal entitlements and funding for the supplemental services involved, includes an assumption about dispositional aspects of the problem. It is made all the more difficult because there are no clear measuring techniques for all the variables included in the definition, and the relevance of the "psychological processes" as conditionals for learning disabilities is much in dispute.

> As generally practiced, the division of students into groups and tracks assumed to ensure considerable likeness in attainment is a meat-ax approach to problems requiring much more sensitive curricular and pedagogical approaches. (Goodlad, 1985, p. xii)

The learning disabilities dilemma is similar to the problem encountered by the American Psychiatric Association, which, in its second version of the *Diagnostic and Statistical Manual* for mental disorders (DSM II; 1968), defined the psychoneuroses in a way that presumed the validity of the psychoanalytic view of causation. Getting out of that complex trap in the preparation of DSM III (APA, 1980) was a major professional and political challenge. A similar challenge now faces special education.

An Approach That Makes Few Assumptions About Predispositions: Applied Behavioral Analysis

Applied behavioral analysis is the name given to methods of behavior modification based on the work of B. F. Skinner; it depends on controlling the consequences of the person's present behavior. In simplified form, it operates from the principle that behavior that is reinforced systematically will continue and can be brought to substitute for behavior that is not reinforced. A substantial literature testifies to the efficacy of that principle as applied to academic learning (Homme, 1970; Lindsley, 1972). The measurement technology developed by behavior analysts serves as a useful approach to learning problems whether or not one uses behavioral principles as a main orientation to teaching (Deno & Mirkin, 1977).

This approach aims to reshape or reduce the rate of existing behaviors that are inappropriate, incorrect, or otherwise unproductive and to increase behaviors that are more consonant with desired educational outcomes. Methods involve the precise specification of learning objectives and the management of instruction focused on those objectives in accordance with principles of operant behavior. Measurement activities are a frequent and direct aspect of the instruction. Proponents of applied behavior analysis include the leaders cited so far, Haring and Schiefelbusch (1976), Lovitt (1978), and many others. Haring (1975) offers an excellent and relatively brief exposition of this design for teaching. Deno and Mirkin (1977) have provided a total system for measurement and decision making in special education within this framework.

Behavior modification by methods of the behavior analysts has not yet

Measurement is a frequent, integral part of instruction by behavioral methods.

Behavior analysts tend to teach directly toward specific goals.

demonstrated applicability over the full spectrum of educational functions. Its advocates are very optimistic, but skeptics believe it has a very restricted range of effectiveness. Proponents of behavior modification arouse defensive reactions and provoke counterattacks on two highly sensitive points. The behavior analyst expresses no need for the notion that deeper roots of human behavior must be uncovered, understood, and rearranged to bring about lasting and balanced changes in humans. Instead, the behavior and its cause are all one; there is no gain either in insight or in technique of management by noting the behavior on the one hand and probing for separate causative factors on the other. Also, the direct approach of behavior modification (and perhaps the expression itself) smacks to some observers of the denial of human freedoms, particularly free will and freedom from domination and direction by others. There is a substantial and growing literature on these and related issues; see Skinner (1971) or Carpenter (1974).

The prevailing classification system for special education is in trouble partly because educators tend to turn to psychologists, physicians, and other specialists whose orientation and experience are outside the classroom and who tend to make classifications on the basis of dispositional states that may be unrelated to teaching and learning. Teachers often find the diagnoses and classifications to be useless. Classifying and labeling may be necessary to secure special funding, but often they serve little or no purpose in instructional planning, the matter of prime importance in the schools.

Consider the case of Chris Nassar. Chris had always been a "good boy," outgoing and quick. His father, a successful pharmacist, enjoyed Chris, and so did his mother. Two years ago, however, clouds began to mar the school scene.

The second-grade teacher had been uncertain about whether Chris should go on or stay another year. He was promoted, but slow school progress persisted. The family's concern mounted along with that of the third-grade teacher. Chris struggled with language arts skills. His arithmetic computation progress was satisfactory, and so was his writing. But he came home with mostly Ds and Fs in reading and spelling (of course, he could not be expected to spell and write words he could not read). Mischief and class disruption were on the rise, too.

Behavior problems often appear collaterally with learning problems.

At home, he was not the same easygoing funster. He did not want to talk about school and was irritable in response to his family's often repeated "What's wrong, Chris?" The notes about misconduct in school grew more urgent. His early promise of achievement and good adjustment had evaporated, replaced by discouragement and evasion. His mother's words about that time were, "I'd say we were worried about him, and upset, too. We were afraid to talk or think about the future."

Chris's personal dissatisfaction with marginal, increasingly weak, and unrewarding school performance was growing. The directions appeared to be set toward heightened hostility, truancy, frustration-induced aggression, and finally, dropout.

As one important developmental phenomenon, the ability to communicate, articulate, and organize through spoken and written language one's internal and external experiences has a profound impact on behavior. Thus, learning disorders theoretically can lay foundations of vulnerability for delinquent and criminal behavior, for severe mental illness, for emotional problems, and for social dysfunction. (Hersh, 1976, p. 27)

Yet within a year, these conditions were completely reversed. Chris's school attainments satisfied him and his parents. Both could see ahead to using education to help toward competent citizenship and productive adulthood, including pleasure in employment and worthy use of leisure.

How was this magic worked? What happened to shore up Chris's faltering educational development and to establish a firm foundation where there had been serious gaps, slippage, and danger of collapse?

It was not a miracle, though Mr. and Mrs. Nassar might not agree. It was the result of the solid, systematic, professional work of Chris's homeroom teacher and a special education teacher who joined forces on his behalf. Outlined in brief, as they are here, their services seem too simple. Quality professional teaching has an appearance of elegant simplicity that belies the energy, concentration, and control it demands of the teachers conducting it. *Planning is critical to good teaching.*

First, the teachers studied Chris's records and interviewed his parents and his previous teachers. They obtained the parents' approval to have various tests administered if the test information might help the teachers discover how to assist Chris. They *listened* to what the parents and other teachers had to say. They probed to get information about what had and had not been done when Chris first appeared not to be responding satisfactorily to the instruction offered in his classes. *Parents can provide valuable information about their children.*

Second, they asked Chris to talk with them about his school experiences. They were careful to keep this on a positve and nonthreatening plane. They let Chris take the lead and question them, as he wished, regarding the purpose of the discussions and where they might lead. Chris's record had some good spots in it. The teachers showed Chris that they were favorably impressed with that part of his record.

Third, they spent considerable time analyzing what the records and interviews had produced. They started with the question "What is the simplest possible formulation of Chris's education situation?" It turned out to be inadequate learning of the most rudimentary word analysis skills. If *The teachers tried procedures at the level of the lesson first.*

that was what had happened (or failed to happen), and if it had not been subsequently corrected, it would explain Chris's erratic and far-below-par performance in reading and spelling.

Fourth, they talked with Chris again. They asked him, in private, to read aloud from some samples of second-, third-, and fourth-grade texts. When he stumbled on words, they watched and listened to see how he proceeded in trying to determine what they were. Then they asked him to tell how he went about trying to unlock the pronunciation of an unfamiliar word. It was true; they saw that he lacked an orderly way of attacking new words. Their empathic attitude encouraged Chris to talk more about himself and his schoolwork than he had for a long time.

Failure to master early rudimentary skills can lead to mounting difficulties in learning complex skills.

They tried Chris on some nonsense words they had made up, like *stelp, trug, enol, whelgat,* and *wistob.* They taped his efforts, studied them later, and confirmed their earlier impression that he was applying a haphazard, self-designed set of procedures that were of limited effectiveness in determining how to pronounce a word unfamiliar in print.

The fifth step taken by the teachers was to consider *why* Chris had not mastered word analysis skills. It was tempting to think of some nonschool factor—undetected minimal brain damage, an emotional block, a perceptual disability. Did not his recent record of irritability, poor attainment, and disruptive behavior suggest something like that? Perhaps they should turn to physicians for the answers. If there was any indication that Chris had a medically significant problem, he should be referred to a physician, whether or not it might relate to instructional procedures to be used.

Perhaps the source of the problem was in the school.

The teachers knew, of course, that there were dozens of transitory conditions that were more likely culprits: fatigue, wandering attention, an illness that kept him out of school at the time of key lessons, temporary hearing impairment, concerns about social relations, and many others. They also knew that teachers cannot always monitor their pupils' mastery of skill and content as thoroughly as they would wish. So the working strategy they elected to follow, at least for a start, was to reteach the basic skills that had been missed in initial teaching.

A different approach in early instruction might have helped.

It is important to notice where the responsibility rested. There had probably been something wrong with the way in which Chris was taught and with the follow-through of that first teaching. At the same time, allocating responsibility was not considered the same as allocating blame or impugning the competence of prior teachers. Most of Chris's classmates had prospered under the same teachers. It was a recognition that teachers, like all professionals, operate with an acknowledged margin of error.

The sixth step was to plan, put in writing, and carry out a personalized instructional program to teach Chris the word analysis skills whose absence appeared to be playing havoc with his school life. The teachers conferred with Mr. and Mrs. Nassar, explained the special education program they wished to try, and obtained approval to do so. Most of the work was done in the regular class. Chris was helped to work on his own much of the time. An aide and an older pupil volunteer took part, too, under teacher supervision. The Nassars helped at home. Chris kept track of his own improvement on frequent teacher-made, criterion-referenced tests. At first, rewards in the form of special privileges were often necessary to keep him at the tasks. Success bred increased satisfaction, and keeping a chart of improvement became reward enough in itself.

Being clear about goals and objectives makes a positive difference.

After a few months, the teachers were able to take the seventh and final step. At a conference with Chris, his parents, and the school principal, they proposed that the special education program be discontinued. A special program as such was no longer necessary. Individualized instruction would continue, but as a normal part of the ordinary course of school events. The special education teacher left the door open to consultative aid, however, if desired in the future. The special educator had been a partner in the whole operation concerning Chris.

The story of Chris illustrates the many facets of learning problems and their *educational* management. Certainly not all work out as smoothly as this one (which had many rocky stretches along the way). But the principle is there: Many learning problems can be diagnosed quite well at a curriculum-based level. Often the problems are traceable to initial instruction that did not correspond to pupil needs. Knowing what to do about such a circumstance, as these teachers did, can turn the problems around.

Meeting pupil needs by adapting instruction is every teacher's responsibility.

Reliability and Validity

A system of diagnosis and categorization ought to meet ordinary scientific standards of reliability and validity. This says that classifications of children ought not vary widely from one examiner or place to another. The procedures used in classification ought to meet the criterion of public testability, or replication, rather than depend on private skills and insights available only to a limited few.

A very troublesome part of special education classification with regard to reliability has been at the level of the mild or so-called judgmental handicaps such as learning disabilities, educable mental retardation, and behavioral disorders. Other conditions, like vision or hearing handicaps, may appear nonjudgmental, that is, they may appear to be taxonic and to have universally accepted criteria or boundaries. But for educational purposes, vision, hearing, and other physical handicaps are quite judgmental, too. Ysseldyke and his colleagues at the Institute for Research on Learning Disabilities at the University of Minnesota, one of five such federally funded institutes in the early 1980s, studied problems of reliability of the learning disability classification exhaustively. Among their findings were the following:

Nonreliability of classification is a problem with mildly handicapped students.

> It is the interpretation of the test scores made by a test user that needs to be validated, not the test itself. (Ebel, 1983, p. 10)

Learning disabled students do not show distinct and reliable differences from other low achievers. (Ysseldyke et al., 1982)

Using seventeen of the common procedures for identifying students as learning disabled, as many as 80 percent of nonhandicapped students could be defined as learning disabled. (Ysseldyke, Algozzine, & Epps, 1983)

In classification, LD rates are up and EMR rates are down.

Tucker (1980) has produced data showing a sharp shift in classifications of children from the educable mentally retarded (EMR) category to learning disabled (LD) in a political context showing resistance to the EMR label, particularly as applied to black students. This kind of shift appears to be occurring nationally. Between 1976 and 1984, the number of pupils reported nationally as "mentally retarded" dropped from 969,547 to 750,534 while the figures for "learning disability" were up from 757,213 to 1,811,489 (see U.S. Department of Education, 1985).

Clearly, there are many difficult problems in the conceptualization of the categories as used in special education, especially "learning disability." There is a kind of hydraulic or seesaw interaction among the several categories, such that an increase in one (such as LD) is often associated with a decrease in another (such as EMR). Even in the low-prevalence areas such as sensory and physical handicaps, there are difficulties about classification procedures, though that may not be so widely acknowledged because they are not so much in the limelight as other categories and less money is at stake.

It is difficult to justify continued classification of mildly handicapped students into EMR, LD, and ED categories.

In view of the major problems of reliability in the classification of children, it can be fairly concluded that for the present, instruction for exceptional children ought to proceed mainly on the basis of highly individualized evaluations of both children and their situations, disregarding such classification criteria as EMR, LD, and ED (emotionally disturbed), except for required noninstructional purposes such as pupil accounting. In time, developments in conceptualization, measurement techniques, and research may provide the field with useful categories and education-relevant terminology. The next section offers suggestions in that direction through the dimensional concept.

> The legendary spectator from Mars would certainly remark on how easy it has been to get children removed from regular school and classes and how difficult it has been to get them back in. If all the children now getting along in regular grades were moved out to special education programs and were

required to pass through the the complex processes set up in many places for readmission, it is doubtful if more than half would make it.

Categorical Versus Dimensional Approaches

A final basic consideration here is the distinction between categorical and dimensional approaches to human differences. At the simplest level, one could say, for example, that persons with IQs below 70 are mentally retarded while those at 70 and above are "normal." Alternatively, one can treat IQ as a continuous variable and leave it at that, in which case intelligence test results would be used in planning educational programs but without resorting to typologies such as "retarded" and "normal."

Dimensional approaches should replace categorical classifications for mildly handicapped students.

Eysenck, Wakefield, and Friedman (1980), in their review of the third edition of the *Diagnostic and Statistical Manual* of the American Psychiatric Association, urged that the next version be more strictly dimensional rather than categorical. They went on to say that categorical diagnoses may be appropriate when there is a "specific causal species of pathogen." But most problems encountered in the schools are not of such kinds, and "the alternative to categorical diagnosis is dimensional assessment" (p. 185).

Reynolds and Balow (1972), some years ago, suggested an analogy to weather in making assessments. Just as we find it possible to describe a unique place and time in terms of variables such as temperature, humidity, cloud cover, barometric pressure, wind velocity, and wind direction, so, perhaps, we can understand unique individuals using variables such as age, intelligence, specific abilities, temperament, cognitive style, motor abilities, and the like. One can envision a complex hyperspace within which an individual is located; going further, if a significant number of people tend to cluster, creating densities in certain regions of the hyperspace, we may have what could be termed a class. Thus an approach through dimensions may yield concepts of classes, but diagnosis and planning would rest mainly on dimensional assessments.

Towering above all other dimensions of relevance for the educator is that of achievement in the domain of instruction. To teach reading, one should know how well the child reads *now*; likewise, to teach social behavior, one needs to know what the child's repertoire and habits of social behavior are *now*. Beyond those essentials, the teacher welcomes whatever assistance can be provided through detailed studies of the child and the environment, remembering that the test of relevance in education is always the question "Does it help in instruction?"

Curriculum-based dimensions are most important.

CLASSIFICATION AS PROBLEMATIC

The classification of a child is not always benign. It can create troubles. In this section, we include a brief discussion of five kinds of difficulties associated with the categorizing and labeling of children: stigma, resistance by minority families, "capping," disjointed incrementalism, and funding disincentives.

Stigma

Labels seem often to be hurtful.

Almost inevitably, when children are given negative classifications ("retarded," "disturbed," "disabled"), a degree of public labeling tends to occur. Wood (1981) suggested that labels should be used only in ways "that stimulate a therapeutic, healing response from the student's eco-system" (p. 59). Unfortunately, the labeling process appears often to fall far short of the high standard Wood proposed and to provoke, instead, a negative value judgment of the labeled children, especially when they are separated from the mainstream institutions of the community on the basis of the labeled condition.

Research results on effects of labeling are equivocal.

The specific evidence on the effects of labels on children's self-concepts and social positions is equivocal (Guskin, Bartel, & MacMillan, 1975; MacMillan, Jones, & Aloia, 1974). Researchers have noted the difficulty of separating the effects of prelabeling behavior that may have been viewed negatively and caused stigmatizing effects even before the labeling took place. MacMillan and Meyers (1979) expressed doubts, "given the complexity of dynamics involved,...that the kind of research controls necessary...to clarify the relationships" (p. 180) can be achieved.

Sometimes parents are relieved by labels.

The rash of court cases in which objections have been raised to the application of negative labels to children reflects resistance to labels. But there is clinical evidence that parents are sometimes comforted when a label is given to a child's condition. For example, when parents have struggled for years to get help for their son's reading difficulties, they may feel relieved when the clinic staff finally tells them that the boy has dyslexia, whether for ill or good, for treatment or neglect.

Minority Group Resistance to Labels

In minority communities, the labeling of children by categories has provoked considerable resistance. Following the case of *Larry P. v. Riles* (1979) in California, IQ testing leading to the classification of children as mentally retarded was totally abandoned in some places and seriously curtailed in many other parts of the nation. A key part of the evidence in *Larry P. v. Riles* was the data showing the high rate of EMR labeling of black children.

In a similar case, however, exactly the opposite conclusion was reached in an Illinois court in 1980. Again, the plaintiffs claimed that the IQ testing used for categorization and placement of children in EMH (educable mentally handicapped) classes unfairly discriminated against members of minorities. The judged reviewed the tests, including the Wechsler Intelligence Scale for Children, in detail and even printed test items along with his analysis of them in his findings and decision. He concluded that the tests, when used by professionals, were not unfairly discriminatory (*PASE v. Hannon*, 1980).

Using data collected by the office of Civil Rights for 1978, the report by the NAS panel (Heller et al., 1982, p. 12) summarized enrollments in EMR classes by racial and ethnic status as follows:

Rates for negative labeling are higher for minority children.

Nationwide Percentages in EMR Classes

American Indian or Alaskan native	1.73
Asian or Pacific islander	.37
Hispanic	.98
Black	3.46
White	1.07
All students	1.43

The rate for black children was more than three times as high as for white children. The panel concluded that problems of validity in assessment and quality of instruction were the prime issues, however, more so than the disproportionate numbers of minority children placed in EMR classes.

Major revisions in classification procedures have been ordered by courts.

In New York, the case of *Lora v. Board of Education* (1979) centered on the classification of minority students as emotionally disturbed. It resulted in a court order for the retraining of all 70,000 teachers and of other professionals in the New York City school system on procedures for the referral and placement of exceptional students and on problems of racial and ethnic bias in assessment processes.

Most efforts to provide appropriate special education in public schools for emotionally disturbed students—the anxious, phobic, violent, and chronically disruptive....—have focused on younger, elementary level students. Older disturbed students have been permitted or encouraged to be absent from class frequently or to leave school early without graduating....

If one acknowledges the stress and avoidance behavior stimulated in us by bigger, older, stronger, sexually more mature, seriously emotionally disturbed students, it is easier to understand the tendency of teachers and administrators to exclude them rather than plan for their education. No other group arouses so strongly the contradictory impulse to punish as well as to heal. (Wood, 1980, p. 1).

Figures published by Design for Change (1983) show that "Chicago's black students are assigned to EMH (educable mentally handicapped) classes at twice the rate for white students" and that "Chicago has more than three times as many black students in these classes as any other school system in the United States" (p. 1). The argument was made that these results follow "a web of misguided policies and practices" (p. 2). Chicago advocates argued also that because "there is no evidence of the long-term benefit of being in an EMH class,...the programs themselves must be changed radically" (p. 3).

A possibility exists that the classification of children as handicapped will be regarded as so stigmatic and become so resented and resisted that errors will be made on the side of underreferral. Early in the history of implementing P.L. 94–142, many large cities in the nation tended to have low rates of participation in the program, possibly because of this reluctance to offend minority families by referring their children for special education.

Underreferral could become a problem.

Many people believe that the classification of children by school authorities is cultural and is used to preserve a social and economic system that reserves privileges for some and disadvantages for others (Oakes, 1985). Commenting on the possibly favorable developments heralded by the passage of P.L. 94–142, Levin (1978), for example, argued that in the past, individualization and differentiation were practiced in the schools to prepare children for unequal social roles, depending on their social origins. This line of thinking is consistent with a concept of deviance advanced by Becker (1963), which suggested that "deviance" is defined by the social groups that make the rules, any infractions of which constitute deviance. By extension, then, people who lack power are particularly likely to be labeled negatively and to be excluded from the best opportunities in school and elsewhere.

Some theories suggest that school classification is part of a broad pattern of social injustice.

In sum, racial and ethnic minorities often deeply resent the high rates of classification by psychologists and special educators of their children as "retarded," "disturbed," or "maladjusted." In fact, however, the problems of disproportionality begin at least as early as the referral. The rates at which teachers refer children for special study are about as uneven among the various racial and ethnic groups as the classification decisions by psychologists and other specialists (Foster et al., 1984).

Racial disproportionality appears at the point of referral as well as after classification.

Disjointed Incrementalism

The rapid expansion in the development and support of special education programs during the 1960s and 1970s was mainly in the form of narrow categorical programs. For example, federal programs in support of special education began in the area of mental retardation, then spread to the deaf and later to a variety of other areas. Other categorical programs were created for students classified as migrant, economically disadvantaged, bilingual, Indian, and so on. Each program had its own bureaucracy, time line, and evaluation monitoring system. The assumption appears to have been that no program interacts with others, but the facts contradict this assumption. Programs for economically disadvantaged students (Title I programs under the Elementary and Secondary Education Act) have been administered apart from special education programs despite the evidence that the children covered have much in common with those assigned to special education. In some communities, even simple audiovisual equipment, such as overhead projectors, purchased out of one program's budget could not be used in another program and had to be maintained on separate inventories. Thus, beginning with doubtful classification practices, the schools have created increasingly disjointed special programs. Almost inevitably the result is waste and inefficiency because of duplication and lack of coordination of valuable professional services. In such cases, it is the students who are the losers.

Bureaucratic management has tended to encourage separateness, not interaction among programs.

In virtually all categorical programs, there has been a turn to mainstream or regular classroom teachers for help and cooperation. The result is that students classified in the various categories often spend some time with regular teachers in regular classrooms and some with specialists, usually in resource rooms or special classes. When properly designed, scheduled, and monitored, these so-called pullout programs can be helpful. But in actual practice, negative results such as the following have been found with alarming frequency.

Everybody wants time to communicate with mainstream teachers!

1. The pullout system results in many discontinuities or interruptions in curricula and daily routines for almost all teachers and students. These discontinuities occur when labeled students travel to and from their regular classrooms and Title I classrooms, speech therapy laboratories, learning disability resource rooms, and so on, in scattered ways throughout the school day.

2. Special and compensatory education programs cause a narrowing of leadership and a loss of control by local school personnel (e.g., the school principal) as growing numbers of programs come under the "ownership" of Title I supervisors, members of bilingual communities, special education advocacy groups, and administrative specialists in categorical areas.

3. School staff time is used more and more simply to make eligibility or entitlement decisions. For example, many school psychologists have been withdrawn from practicing the broader aspects of their profession and required to concentrate on simple psychometric gatekeeping, that is, on making decisions about which children are eligible for the various categorical programs; the result is a severe loss of morale and program development potential among psychologists.

4. Categorical political constituencies have tended to protect their narrow but hard-won territories and to neglect, even oppose, systemic approaches to school improvement.

The disjointedness among school programs that has grown with the proliferation of categorical programs has become a major problem to be confronted by educators, but the problem extends beyond the schools. Rogers and Farrow (1983), in a study of state strategies to promote interagency collaboration, found that "initial classification directly and substantially affects how handicapped children and their families are treated by

Disjointedness of categorical programs has become a major problem.

multiple systems—and the differences in classification can be a significant barrier to interagency programming" (p. 11). The same researchers noted especially that various agencies have organized and limited their services according to categorical funding systems, "each of which has its own eligibility requirements, provider networks, and perception of the primary needs of its clients" (p. 9).

Funding

Funding practices and programmatic policies are sometimes at cross-purposes.

A feature of the categorizing problem that causes much difficulty is that classification has been linked to special funding. Most states and the federal Department of Education deliver special education funds based simply on a count of children who have been categorized and placed in special programs. Lynn (1983) noted that these procedures put all special education funding on the "input" side. It matters not whether the categorizing and programs do anyone any good; the pay comes anyway. Thus a kind of "bounty hunt" mentality arises—the greater the number of children identified as handicapped and given special education, the more money is received.

Excesses in categorizing can be costly.

Maintaining the children in narrowly separate categorical programs can be very costly and lead to complaints by legislators, school board members, and taxpayers. For example, in small schools and rural areas, categorical special education teachers may have very small case loads and occupy regular classroom spaces. The alternative of busing children to schools in neighboring districts to achieve full case loads and more efficient use of space is expensive and wasteful of the children's time. If noncategorical or cross-categorical groupings can be formed without disadvantage for pupils or if pupils can be mainstreamed with adequate supports, the cost savings may be significant (Sage & Fensom, 1985).

Wang and Reynolds (1985) have described a kind of catch-22 situation in which students were moved from special education classes to regular classes for a systematic adaptive education program. Evidence showed the program to be successful in terms of achievement gains and social acceptance. Some 30 percent of the handicapped students were decertified as handicapped at the end of the first year of the program. The dilemma came when state officials declared that the state's categorical special education funds could not be applied to the mainstream program. The local board of education then ordered that the handicapped students be returned to their special programs! This situation demonstrates graphically how programmatic and funding policies can conflict. The programmatic policy is that students should be mainstreamed whenever feasible, but in this case, adherence to the policy is at the expense of losing all special education funding. Obviously, this policy problem must be solved.

Since about 1950, there has been much success in building categorical funding systems for special education in which the basic triggering event or unit is the individual handicapped child in a categorical program. It has worked marvelously well in producing dollars (Bernstein et al., 1976). Consequently, the resistance to change is high. Even educators who agree that change is needed cling to what someone has called the "Tarzan" theory: When you swing through the jungle on vines, don't let go of one vine until the next is securely in hand.

The public wants funding systems that emphasize educational outcomes.

Alternative procedures are available. As noted earlier, Hobbs (1980) has proposed that funding be related to service or program elements; for example, categorical funds might be disbursed for specialized tutoring or specialized diagnostics on an hourly basis. The purpose would be to get away from "child in category" as the funding unit and to move to a service unit. Another possibility is simply to reimburse local school districts a percentage of the salaries for specialized personnel. In such a case, each community would present a plan and be reimbursed for the major cost elements, the personnel. The functions of people in the reimbursed positions would be publicly identified in the plans, and the persons in the positions would be held accountable for acceptable performance. Thus there would no longer be a need to label individual children and to reward schools financially for doing so (Magnetti, 1982). The funding would be based on a new kind of unit.

Perhaps it is inevitable, even under such a plan as Hobbs's or the personnel reimbursement system, that special programs and services will become labeled, sometimes negatively, and that the labels will become associated with children assigned to them (Leinhardt, Bickel, & Palloy, 1982; Reynolds & Balow, 1972), but some social gains seem likely for all concerned if we make funding changes of the kinds Hobbs suggested. It may be possible to limit negative effects if the labels for special programs are positive and developmentally oriented, for example, the "braille laboractory," "total communication program," "mobility instructor," "intensive academic instruction lab," or "basic skills support system."

Classification can provide labels for programs, not children.

An idea often advanced in connection with special education funding is the so-called excess cost principle. The basic idea is that the state and federal governments ought to provide local education agencies with an amount of funding that covers all "excess costs" of educating exceptional students. That is, it should cost the local schools no more or less to educate exceptional children than it costs to educate others. Such a plan presumably neutralizes decisions about special placements and services, at least on the financial side. Estimates of excess can be used, but with funds transfers triggered on the basis of Hobbs's type of units or the personnel unit rather than on detailed accounts and calculations of excess cost for every pupil or school.

Capping the Categories

A policy problem of importance has arisen over the limits or caps assigned to special education categories. The federal government has placed a general cap of 12 percent on the total number of handicapped children for whom reimbursements may be claimed under P.L. 94–142. Hocutt, Cox, and Pelosi (1984), in a policy-oriented exploration of identification and placement practices, observed, "If a State Education Agency feels significant pressure from any source regarding over-identification or over-representation, that SEA is likely to change its definitions and eligibility criteria" (pp. 8–9), which is another way to cap a category. The particular category that has grown most rapidly and presents the most capping difficulties is learning disabilities.

The LD classification may be "out of control" in some places.

Special educators tend to make contradictory assumptions in this context. On the one hand, they sometimes assume that the categories are taxonic and that handicapped children are "really out there" in fixed numbers. On the other hand, considering the review of reliability problems in classification and, further, assuming a broad, ecological framework for defining the categories, there are no clear boundaries; the numbers of children currently classified as learning disabled or deficient in some other way are indefinite. It is not at all clear, from this viewpoint, that some definite set of specific clinical types really exists. The numbers of children in a category could expand quite freely, as indeed some have. It is this openness of definition and the costs associated with the proliferation of child counts that has caused legislators and others to think about capping the categories.

Such a move, of course, could lead to embarrassments about entitlements. What happens to the first child identified as handicapped in some category after the school district has passed the magic limit? Do that child's parents have a right to participate in planning an individualized education program and in other activities guaranteed by P.L. 94–142? What about the frustration that teachers feel in denying services to a child who is just over the new borderline established to define the category in more restricted ways?

It is in this complex context that a necessary renegotiation of the relation between special and regular education has been launched. For example, the U.S. Department of Education supported some 260 Dean's Grant Projects in the late 1970s and early 1980s in which deans of education were assisted in leading programs for revising regular teacher preparation programs to take into account the needs of exceptional students when they are placed in regular schools and classes (Reynolds, 1980a; Sharp, 1982). This is also the context in which proposals for waivers for performance strategies have been advanced (Reynolds & Lakin, 1988; Reynolds & Wang, 1983). Under such waivers, selected school districts would be authorized to use innovative noncategorical approaches to instruction that would direct the efforts of special educators to problems of prevention and the full range of children's learning problems without the use of the traditional categorical system. With waivers of some of the rules and regulations, local education agencies would be permitted to offer experimental programs without losing categorical funds.

All teachers need preparation for work under emerging new policies.

> To the extent that we remain trapped in programming definitions and funding models dominated by traditional labeling and categorization, to that same extent we will fall short. The basic educational issue. . .is not finding something to call them [the children] so we can put money in a pot with a label on it. The basic issue is providing an educational program that will allow them to learn better.
>
> _____
>
> Madeleine C. Will (1986), Assistant Secretary, Office of Special Education and Rehabilitation Services, U.S. Department of Education

Proceduralism

The use of detailed categorical approaches to special education also leads to a great deal of regulation of the categorical boundaries. The expanded federal role in education, especially since passage of P.L. 94–142 in 1975, has led to increases in the procedural requirements placed on teachers and school administrators. Individualized educational programs have had to be prepared, formal notices for and meetings with parents have been required, and so on. In a study of the kinds of program evaluations conducted at state and local levels, Cox (1984) observed that the major effort "was designed to determine the extent to which administrative procedures are being followed" (p. 2), thus showing the highly procedural orientation in monitoring activities by governmental agents. When mere procedures consume too much time or prove to be without value, attention and resources are subtracted from the education of children, which the services were intended to improve. Several other problems ensue.

First, procedural rather than than substantive norms are used to monitor an increasingly disjointed school system. In some systems, monitoring has been conducted not only by state and federal education authorities to check on adherence to regulations but also by court-appointed "masters" who are assigned to shore up compliance with court decisions. Second, a litigious attitude in procedures sometimes heightens distrust among teachers, parents, and administrators when in fact more trust is needed.

In periods of rapid change, monitoring sometimes attends just to procedures, neglecting substance.

Finally, by being caught in a complex web of procedures designed to protect the rights of individual children, teachers have sometimes been denied participation in the "moral victory" represented by Public Law 94–142. Daniel Lortie (1978), at a conference on the future of education, put it something like this: "Teachers feel that they are left at the tail end of a long chain of moral insight." Teachers, among other educational personnel, tend to resent the implication that a sense of moral justice is found mainly in Washington, D.C. (or in their state capital) and the fact that the

Procedural preoccupations distract and divide.

impact of the legislation on them is mainly procedural. The problem is to keep procedural demands at tolerable levels while encouraging progress on the substantive front, which is in the arena of effective instruction.

CONCLUSIONS

Considering the many difficulties in the classification of students, the use of pullout programs, and the coordinating of specialized programs, what can be suggested to correct or improve the situation? These critical matters affect the entire structure of special education, indeed, all education. We offer five major conclusions, all to be discussed.

Some special education categories are well justified.

1. There is good reason to treat certain topics categorically (which we do in separate chapters of the book): hearing impairments, visual impairments, severe and profound disabilities, advanced cognitive development (giftedness), and speech and language impairments. Each of these fields has a substantial and growing knowledge base. Treating them categorically *does not* exempt them, of course, from moving their practices into the mainstream of local elementary school and secondary school classes. In fact, in some instances, such as integrating and teaching visually impaired students, these "legitimate" categories have led the way for others. In each of these categorical areas, there is a reasonable and predictable opportunity for challenging and rewarding professional careers. Children characterized by these categorical terms do, indeed, have specialized needs, which can be summarized quite distinctly by category. Obviously, each child in each category must be understood as a unique individual in a unique environment, but the categories are useful as first approximations in understanding and planning for them.

The delineation of these categories is consistent with a predictive study (using Delphi procedures) conducted in 1973 by Reynolds for the Council for Exceptional Children as part of a professional standards project. A questionnaire was sent twice to a broad sample of educators; the results of the first round of questioning were summarized and then returned to the respondents. Then they were asked to respond to the questions a second time. The responses were interpreted to suggest that by about 1983 only five special education categories and licenses would be offered by state departments of education, in the following fields: hearing impairments, visual impairments, speech and language therapy, severe and profound handicaps, and mild-to-moderate (or noncategorical) handicaps. It appears that trends are moving in the predicted directions, but only a bit behind the predicted pace.

Other categories should simply be removed as organizing rubrics for special education.

2. With respect to children in the judgmental or mild categories, we prefer to proceed on a noncategorical basis, urging, above all, that special education and regular teachers work together to create a more powerful regular school environment that will prevent the necessity for the categorical portrayal of children's needs and will serve them well in the mainstream. This approach is detailed in the next chapter and is followed generally in the organization of this book.

3. In a separate chapter of this book, we treat processes of communication among members of the school staff and between staff members and parents. Many children's problems can be treated through teaming practices and consultation, thus reducing or limiting the number of referrals for classification and enrollment in special education programs. We regard the improvement of communication in the school as an essential part of serving exceptional students.

4. We feel that the screening and assessment of students in the schools should be dimensional rather than categorical, and first attention should be given to curriculum-based screening and assessment tools and procedures. When measurements are continuous, they should not be segmented by category that diagnosis should be expressed mainly in curriculum-based terms. Analysts who wish to push diagnosis to levels or orders of disposition beyond the curriculum level should be held to a very high standard of evidence that their procedures are useful before they are admitted to practice in the schools.

Effective communication is essential in effective schools.

5. Assessment processes undertaken in cases of students who show special needs should be applied not only to the student but also to the class and school and to each student's broader life situation.

PREVAILING AND PREFERRED PRACTICES

Prevailing Practices

1. Financial and other incentives encourage the identification of students as handicapped.

2. Diagnosis and classification of students is strongly oriented to etiology and simple prognosis.

3. Categories of exceptionality are highly "medicalized" and assumed to be taxonic.

4. Diagnosis is mainly categorical or typological

Preferred Practices

1. Through strengthened mainstream programs and changed funding systems, efforts are made to limit the number of students classified as handicapped.

2. Diagnosis and classification of students is oriented strictly to the improvement of instruction; they are mainly curriculum based.

3. Most categories of exceptionality are recognized as administrative conveniences and as education specific.

4. Diagnosis is mainly dimensional, preserving in detail all relevant assessment data.

5. Assessment in special education is a two-stage operation, first determining that a child is handicapped by category, then considering educational needs.

5. Assessment is based directly on educational needs and does not assume a context-free classification of the child as handicapped.

6. Mildly handicapped students are classified as EMR, LD, ED, and so on.

6. Mildly handicapped students are taught on the basis of noncategorical assessment and planning.

7. Categorical teachers negotiate with mainstream teachers for accommodations in the regular classroom.

7. Noncategorical special education teachers work in regular classrooms to enhance service to a broad range of students who have special needs.

8. Special funding is linked to classification of pupils in a handicapping category.

8. Special funding is linked to services or to personnel (at a level approximating "excess cost") rather than to children per category.

9. Special education categories are capped by legislators to limit expenditures.

9. Special education renegotiates its relations with regular education, to serve preventive purposes as well as to serve children counted into special education.

TOPICAL BIBLIOGRAPHY

Classification of Human Beings

Becker (1963)
Elstein, Shulman, & Sprafka (1978)
Grossman (1983)
Heller, Holtzman, & Messick (1982)
Hobbs (1975)
Reynolds (1984)
Tucker (1985)

Funding Systems

Bernstein, Kirst, Hartman, & Marshall (1976)
Hobbs (1975, 1980)
Magnetti (1982)

CHAPTER 3

Instruction
in the Mainstream

It is a classroom in an ordinary school. The special education teacher and the regular teacher work together in that setting. The special education teacher spends only about an hour each school day in any one classroom, usually when basic-skills instruction is offered, but an aide may stay on for an additional two hours to extend the work of the special educator.

Together the teachers have defined the goals and objectives of the school's basic curricula in reading, language, and mathematics and written all of this down in a kind of shorthand on "prescription sheets," which they use to record progress and make plans for each pupil. Units of the program relating to each objective in each skill area have been defined and sequenced, and together the teachers have agreed on mastery examinations to use for each segment. The prescription sheets list the instructional materials, such as the basal series and workbooks, plus a variety of additional books, games, and computer exercises that can be used with each unit. Because the teachers are working together, they have quite an extensive list of approaches they can use to work toward each objective. Some of the materials and methods require one-on-one teaching or small group instruction that only the special education teacher is prepared to offer.

Special education teachers and regular teachers can and do work together in the same classroom.

Not all pupils will do all the work with all materials; that will depend on individual diagnosis of needs and progress. Pupils will advance individually through the basic skills progress as they show mastery of units or segments.

The school psychologist does more than test children.

The regular teacher meets with small groups for direct instruction on curricular topics for which pupils show readiness. Grouping varies considerably from time to time, depending on pupils' specific progress and needs. The special education teacher joins the elementary teacher and attends carefully to pupils who show poor progress or present special problems, such as lack of attention or disorderly behavior. The special education teacher also instructs small groups of selected students or individual students directly on carefully chosen elements of the curriculum. The special education teacher concentrates on students who show slow progress and need detailed diagnosis or on exceptionally rapid learners.

Sometimes the school psychologist is called in for consultation when additional ideas and skills are needed to map out a program to meet especially challenging pupils or instructional situations. The school psychologist also participates in twice-annual formal assessments of the entire class operation, for example, checking on the ALT (academic learning time) rate for each pupil and for the class as a whole and on the rate of each pupil's academic progress. Rate of progress is checked simply by having the school's computer print out the relative amounts of time taken by all pupils to move through the various elements of the curriculum. Informal and formal testing are used occasionally.

Children learn to use data on themselves and to help plan the school program.

Self-management skills are taught as children learn gradually to collect and use data on their own performances as the basis for planning. Pupils make choices about how their schoolwork should be ordered for the school day or week, always accommodating the teacher's general plans for direct instruction. For example, pupils may schedule themselves at various times in one or more of the five systematically organized learning centers in the classroom on topics such as math maintenance, computer literacy, "winter poetry," watercolor painting, and map reading. The centers contain materials adapted to various levels of prerequisite skills, and they are changed quite often with help from all staff members associated with the class.

In this classroom, all regular testing of students is curriculum based. It corresponds exactly to the domains of the curriculum for this school and is used integrally with instruction. Children proceed to more advanced topics or units only when they have demonstrated mastery of earlier units. The interpretation of test results involves no comparisons with classmates; it is criterion referenced. A child passes a test when a preset criterion level of performance is reached. A kind of norm-referenced assessment is achieved indirectly simply by noting how much time the pupil has needed to reach a given point in the curriculum.

Pullouts can be reduced, with advantages for both pupils and teachers.

This classroom differs from those in many schools in the nation where as many as 10 children in one class may be removed for part of each day for pullout programs. The children may be labeled learning disabled (LD), educable mentally retarded (EMR), behavior disordered (BD), or disadvantaged, and they are sent out of the regular classroom to special resource rooms, where they are taught by teachers bearing the same labels, LD pupils going to LD teachers, EMR pupils going to EMR teachers, and so forth. In the classroom we have described, nearly all the "special" children are retained all day in the regular classroom. They are fully mainstreamed. They receive special help as needed, but it is part of the systematic operation of a teaching and learning situation that is adaptive for all pupils.

School officials may be required to report to the state and federal government on certain pupils by categories (LD, EMR, etc.), but these reports are regarded as only rough accountability checks; they are not the basis for instructional classification or grouping. Legal requirements for individualized educational plans (IEPs) are met chiefly by doing IEPs for all pupils, albeit more formally and completely in cases of children who show the least progress, behavior problems, or other special needs. Due process guidelines are followed for all pupils and their parents. This means that parents are fully and respectfully involved in all major aspects of child study and school planning for their children and that they are aware of their rights to appeal decisions with which they disagree.

Ultimately, IEPs can and should be provided for all students.

The educational scene and operation we have described are not typical at this time in the United States, but there are hundreds of such classrooms around the country, and the procedures for creating and maintaining them are well developed. In such classrooms, research, development, and professional insights have been implemented from several fields: adaptive instruction, effective instruction, and modern special education. Bringing together these several aspects of knowledge and skill to create educational environments that are more effective, especially in accommodating individual differences, is truly a major challenge to educators today, and it is the challenge addressed in this chapter. By acting on the full range of insights and procedures outlined in this chapter, powerful forms of instruction and services are made available to exceptional students, permitting them to remain in the mainstream.

Special education is the extreme part of adaptive education.

The focus in this chapter is mainly on students who are referred to as mildly handicapped, commonly to students labeled EMR, LD or ED. We also include students who have speech, sensory, or physical impairments but no additional complicating disabilities. The only clear exclusions are students with severe or profound disabilities (chronic or temporary) that make special placements outside the mainstream a necessity.

LINKING IDEAS AND PRACTICES

Just as the principle of the least restrictive environment requires special educators to renegotiate their relations with regular teachers and work toward integration in the regular school, so too is it important that integration occur among ideas and practices derived from various elements of the research community and the professions in education. In this chapter,

Renegotiation means that all parties have something to contribute.

therefore, we discuss ideas from several fields that have developed separately but now require linkage.

Adaptive instruction has been the subject of much educational research in regular education. Now, as greater numbers of exceptional students appear in the mainstream, the time has come to suggest a negotiated arrangement between adaptive and special education and even to suggest that special education can be defined as an aspect of adaptive education.

Glaser (1977) described adaptive instruction in terms of modifying school environments to correspond to student differences and teaching students to be adaptive to variations in school environments. This two-sided approach, emphasizing adaptations both in the environment and by the learner, is followed here. Consider, for example, the obvious environmental manipulation made when a classroom is treated acoustically to make it easier for students to hear. Correspondingly, the learner with a significant hearing loss makes an adaptation in such an environment by using an electronic hearing aid. Adaptive instruction is not isolated individualized instruction (a child sitting alone completing a worksheet); it may involve ordinary or even greater amounts of direct group instruction. It requires individualized planning that takes into account the developmental level of the student and other characteristics that lead to good decisions about instruction. The same is involved in preparing IEPs, which is a good reason for seeking bridges across the fields of adaptive and special education.

Both environments and students can be adaptive.

Individualizing does not mean solitary education.

A notable feature of research and development in adaptive education is the increasing emphasis on variables that can be manipulated by educators to change the environment, the student, or both. For example, instead of characterizing differences among students in terms of relatively static abilities, such as IQ, more attention is now given to such items as student achievement in specific skills, the processes by which students manage information, and the application of modern management systems in schools. These are matters that make a difference and that teachers can control.

A major assumption undergirding this chapter—indeed, this entire book—is that the best condition for mainstreaming exceptional students exists when adaptive instruction is provided for *all* students. In such a case, special education is only the more intensive or extended form of adaptive education. In this view, there is no sharp dividing line between special and regular education, and few special referrals or displacements of pupils to special classes or centers are necessary. If a true bridging is achieved between adaptive and special education, communication is improved, and the successful mainstreaming of exceptional pupils is an expected outcome.

Handicapped students are best served when programs are adaptive for all students.

Also to be considered is the impressive recent research on effective schools and effective instruction. For example, it may sound somewhat like rediscovering Niagara Falls, but educational researchers have made it clear that to learn efficiently, students must spend time in active learning. When more time is spent attending to school tasks and completing them successfully, learning tends to improve. If teachers teach directly to students, in situations in which good order is maintained and expectations for performance are high and clear to the students, learning tends to improve. When student work is monitored regularly and feedback on successes and mistakes is given promptly, learning also tends to improve. Much has been learned about how schools and classes can be made effective by using the various effectiveness principles. Classes and schools in which these principles are not applied will be ineffective, especially in the case of students whose situation is marginal, thus increasing the likelihood that they will be referred out of the mainstream to special education resource rooms, classes, or schools. In contrast, when the mainstream class is especially effective, it becomes a useful resource for more of the students who have special needs, and rates of referral to special education can be expected to drop.

Creating effective schools and effective instruction should be an objective for all educators.

   A summary of recent research on effective instruction and schools is provided in Table 3.1. In the leftmost column, a number of the effectiveness principles are listed. To the right are listed four general kinds of educational outcomes and 13 subsidiary outcomes. Shaded areas indicate the particular outcomes that are influenced by specific effectiveness features. For example, "Management of instruction that permits each student to master many lessons through independent study" has been shown to be related to one or more specific kinds of outcomes in each of the four general categories.

JOINING ADAPTIVE EDUCATION, EFFECTIVENESS PRINCIPLES, AND SPECIAL EDUCATION

In the next part of this chapter, we provide detailed statements to show how ideas from adaptive education, effective instruction, and special education can be brought together. Each topic is treated in three phases. First, we introduce the topic, give definitions as necessary, and identify the knowledge base that confirms the idea as educationally sound. Second, we show how the principles involved can be implemented in the school environment. Third, we discuss adaptations that can be made to serve the particular needs of exceptional pupils. It is sometimes argued that schools give too much attention to negative characteristics and needs of exceptional pupils—a kind of "child-blaming" approach—rather than to diagnosing the instructional situation and outlining a positive plan for children with special needs. Here we suggest that one always needs to attend to both the environment and the child. This is sometimes called an ecological approach, one that attends to environment but recognizes the child as a central, active figure in that environment.

Common variables of effectiveness can be used to describe both programs and students.

TABLE 3.1. EXAMPLES OF FEATURES OF EFFECTIVE CLASSROOM LEARNING ENVIRONMENTS AND EXPECTED RELATED STUDENT OUTCOMES

Expected Student Outcomes

Features of Effective Classroom Learning Environments	Mastery of Subject-Matter Content		Acquisition of a Variety of Learning Skills			Development of Positive Attitudes toward Learning				Development of Positive Self-Perceptions			
	Mastery of content and skills for effective functioning	Mastery of content and skills for further learning	Ability to study and learn independently	Ability to plan and monitor learning activities	Ability to obtain assistance from others	Enjoyment in taking part in learning activities	Viewing help-giving and help-receiving as positive experiences	Special interest in certain learning areas	Motivation for continuing learning	Confidence in one's ability as a learner	Confidence in oneself as a contributing member of the school/community	Confidence in one's ability to take self-responsibility for learning and behavior	Perceptions of internal locus of control
Instructional content that is essential to further learning		■											
useful for effective functioning in school and in society at large	■	■											
clearly specified	■												
organized to facilitate efficient learning	■	■		■						■		■	
Assessment and diagnosis that provide appropriate placement in the curriculums				■									
provide frequent and systematic assessment of progress and feedback			■		■			■	■			■	
Learning experiences in which ample time and instructional support are provided for each student to acquire essential content	■	■				■			■	■			■

disruptiveness is minimized

students use effective learning strategies/study skills

each student is expected to and actually experiences success in achieving mastery of curriculum content, and accomplishments are reinforced

alternative instructional strategies, student assignments, and activities are used

Management of instruction that permits each student to master many lessons through dependent study

permits each student to plan his or her own learning activities

provides for students' self-monitoring of this progress with most lessons

permits students to play a part in selecting some learning goals and activities

Collaboration among students that enables students to obtain necessary help from peers

encourages students to provide help

provides for collaboration in group activities

* The shaded sections indicate that extant findings from studies on effective teaching and learning suggest relationships between the implementation of specific features and the achievement of particular student outcomes.

SOURCE: M. C. Wang, M. C. Reynolds, & H. J. Walberg (1986, September). "Rethinking Special Education." *Educational Leadership, 44*(1), 26–31.

Excellence and Equality

In our search for the solution`to the problems of educational equality, our focus was almost exclusively on the characteristics of the children themselves. We looked for sources of educational failure in their homes, their neighborhoods, their language, their cultures, even their genes. In all our searching we almost entirely overlooked the possibility that what happens *within* schools might contribute to unequal educational opportunities`and outcomes. (Oakes, 1985, p. xiv)

Equity and excellence in schools need not be incompatible.

Special education referral comes only after attempts to modify the mainstreams.

Recent major reviews of special education practices have stressed the importance of creating healthy, effective environments for children as a first concern when planning for them. For example, the report of a special panel created by the National Academy of Science (Heller, Holtzman, & Messick, 1982) proposed that before any student is referred to special education, the child's regular school situation should be examined, and adaptations that seem promising should be made there. Only in cases where such efforts have been made and found unsuccessful, the panel suggests, should a child be referred officially to special education. In the discussion that follows, we make suggestions that facilitate this important policy advanced by the NAS panel. First we treat obvious problems of physical and social access, then move on to topics more centered on instruction.

PRINCIPLES AND PRACTICES IN THE MAINSTREAM

Physical Access

Physical access to programs is the essential first step.

A first requirement of schools and classrooms is that they be accessible to all students, including those with disabilities. They have the right of access to public buildings and other public facilities. Section 504 of the Rehabilitation Act enacted by Congress in 1973 makes *access* a matter of right; it reads, in part:

> No otherwise qualified handicapped individual in the United States... shall solely by reason of his [or her] handicap be excluded from participation in, be denied the benefits of, or be subjected to discrimination under any program or activity receiving Federal financial assistance. (29 U.S.C. 794)

The Environment. In school, providing access means such things as providing ramps and elevators so that pupils, teachers, and parents with disabilities that prevent their using stairs can enter and move about the school. It may mean putting the piano and the choral group rehearsal room on the first floor of the school so that students who use wheelchairs can reach them. It means that careful attention is given to the acoustical treatment of all instructional spaces so that persons with hearing problems have improved opportunities to hear. Space and facilities are arranged flexibly and with variety so that a wide range of instructional activities can be supported.

The Individual. In addition to environmental adaptations, handicapped pupils also need good supporting help. For example, elevators may not operate during fire drills. At such times, prearranged teams of fellow students should be ready to assist a disabled student to leave the building.

Individuals can develop abilities to manage access.

Every child using a hearing aid needs training in its use and maintenance.

Special arrangements for transportation to and from school are necessary for some pupils, especially those who are physically disabled or, for example, those who come to the school from the juvenile detention center. To the maximum extent possible, however, students should be taught to manage their own transportation and to use special arrangements only as a last resort. Every individual's school situation needs review to ensure that there is full physical access.

Social Integration

One clear effect of the mainstreaming movement has been to increase the diversity of characteristics of children in regular classes and schools. Gifted and handicapped students are brought together with others in very heterogeneous groups. Teachers, by contrast, have been oriented mainly to teaching children in homogeneous groups. This divergence creates an obvious problem. When exceptional children remain in or are returned to regular classrooms, the result can be very negative for everyone if too little is done to make the social environment of the classroom more accommodative. It is not only the teachers who must be accepting and helpful; all the students must share the responsibility for creating acceptable social environments. Thus the policy of mainstreaming requires major efforts to establish social structures and processes that encourage positive interactions among the students.

Students must help set reasonable policies for dealing with differences among their classmates.

The Environment. In many classrooms, desks are still lined up in rows so that students look at the backs of other students' heads. When students try to talk to each other, they may be accused of cheating. The atmosphere in such rooms is often competitive, and cooperative group activities get little or no encouragement, instruction, or recognition. It is cruel for administrators and teachers to place exceptional students in such an environment.

Student interaction in class can be positive in effects.

Developing Acceptance and Positive Integration

Even if researchers were to document that nonhandicapped children exhibit an intolerance for their handicapped peers that includes a willingness to engage in overtly cruel behavior, this should pose a challenge to educators rather than a limitation. Surely such behavior of presumably "normal" children is as susceptible to change as the behavior of severely handicapped children, now apparently acquiring skills once thought unattainable. What is needed is a determination on the part of those in the educational system to give children—handicapped and nonhandicapped—the opportunity and the necessary assistance to develop positive interaction patterns in integrated community and school settings. (Voeltz, 1980, p. 463)

Students should have every reason to be helpful to one another.

Now imagine a situation where some class time is given to small group work, and the groups are formed deliberately to be heterogeneous. Goals set for each group require helpful interactions among the students. Each student contributes an essential part of the group process, as if each were a piece in a jigsaw puzzle. The teacher explains the group structure, pointing out that individuals will be evaluated and rewarded according to the group processes and outcomes. The teacher serves as consultant to the groups to help further interpersonal and group skills. Suppose that a group of students is given the task of presenting a skit on jury selection in the American court system. The pupils learn to work together to do the necessary research, create the skit, rehearse it, and present it. Some students are best at background work; others can contribute in writing the dramatic dialogue; still others will create the physical set. Projects are designed to require frequent, helpful, and supportive interactions among pupils. Only under such conditions can one expect the development of mutual understanding, positive feelings, and a sense of safety and trust.

Cooperative Learning

Competition has its place; but so does cooperation.

Cooperative learning occurs when teachers have students work together in small groups on a task toward a *group goal*—a single product (a set of answers, a project, a report, a piece or collection of creative writing, etc.) or achieving as high a *group average* as possible on a test—and then reward the entire group on the basis of the quality or quantity of its product according to a set standard of success. (Oakes, 1985, p. 210)

Teachers can learn to create social environments that encourage cooperation and reduce the likelihood of attaching stigmas to differences. Johnson and Johnson (1975), for example, described in detail methods by which teachers can teach for cooperation as well as for competition or strictly individualistic (solitary) behaviors. Skillful teachers will choose to structure their classes differently at different times for various purposes, and one important purpose is to increase positive interactions between handicapped and nonhandicapped students. A variety of helpful materials for teachers is now available for use in teaching nonhandicapped children about handicapping conditions and about how exceptional children prefer to be treated. These include children's books about handicapped persons and guides for teachers on managing the introduction and instruction of exceptional students in regular classes (Benham, 1978; Bookbinder, 1978; Cohen, 1977; Madsen, 1980; Sapon-Shevin, 1982; Shaver & Curtis, 1981).

Students should learn to be cooperative in heterogeneous groups.

The Individual. Some individuals who have particular difficulty in social or behavioral problems may require special help beyond the kinds of general environmental arrangements just considered. Thus in addition to the effective general practices the teacher uses to create a desirable social environment, a special education teacher and the school psychologist may need to work intensively with certain pupils to improve their social behavior. Quay (1972) has described a number of ways in which students may exhibit inadequate or unacceptable social behavior; let us look briefly at four such patterns.

1. *Conduct disorder (aggression).* Conduct disorder is recognized by "the presence of a pattern involving aggressive behavior, both verbal and physical, associated with poor interpersonal relationships with both adults and peers" (p. 9). Overt behavior includes combinations of disobedience, disruptiveness, destructiveness, fighting, profanity, defiance, impulsiveness, irritability, lawlessness, and distrust of others.

Some patterns of student behavior are observed frequently and have implications for treatment.

2. *Personality disorder (withdrawal).* Personality disorder encompasses "such traits as feelings of distress, fear, anxiety, physical complaints, and open and expressed unhappiness. It is within this pattern that the child who is clinically labeled as an anxiety neurotic or as phobic will be found" (p. 11). Other observed behavior includes seclusiveness, timidity, shyness, and hyperactivity.

3. *Immaturity.* This cluster is less distinct. It is characterized by habitual actions that are significantly below those expected for the child's age. "Such behaviors are at variance with either the expectations of self, parents, or educational and other social institutions" (pp. 13–14). Behaviors often cited as characteristic of immaturity are preference for younger playmates, passivity, poor coping skills, short attention span, and clumsiness; they are much like those associated with mental retardation.

4. *Socialized delinquency.* Quay calls special attention to this cluster by saying that it "represents behavior which is neither generally a source of personal distress nor clearly maladaptive when one considers social conditions under which it seems to arise" (p. 14). For example, in communities where gang activities constitute a way of life for adolescents, the socialized

What is maladaptive in general may be adaptive in specific situations.

delinquent teenager is a "good citizen" of the gang subculture, cooperating with peers in planned robberies, in habitual truancy, and in showing close allegiance to a coterie of peers. All the while, though, the behaviors are at sharp variance with the mainstream's social and personal norms.

An example of an educational design that took off directly from the base built by Quay is the structured learning approach of Goldstein, Sprafkin, Gershaw, and Klein (1980). Noting that the Quay descriptions focus on the inappropriate behaviors of youngsters, they proposed a modified approach:

The goal is to augment prosocial behavior.

> From a skill-deficiency viewpoint it is...profitable to examine what each youngster does not do. Thus the aggressive adolescent...may also be deficient in such prosocial skills as self-control, negotiation, asking permission, avoiding trouble with others, understanding the feelings of others, and dealing with someone else's anger. The withdrawn youngster...may lack proficiency in...having a conversation, joining in, dealing with fear, decision-making, dealing with being left out, responding to persuasion, and dealing with contradictory messages. (pp. 4–5)

Social skills are not always learned incidentally; they may need to be taught.

A skill checklist of prosocial developmental tasks serves as an objective basis for evaluating pupil behaviors. Pretest and posttest scoring is used to measure performance change. The Skill Checklist Summary includes 50 elements, divided into six major skill areas (Goldstein et al., 1980): beginning social skills, advanced social skills, dealing with feelings, alternatives to aggression, dealing with stress, and planning skills. The first area is divided into seven specific developmental tasks: listening, starting a conversation, having a conversation, asking a question, saying thank you, introducing yourself, and introducing other people.

Other major areas break into specific tasks in a similar way. Having established the list of 50 prosocial developmental tasks, specific lessons are constructed for each. Then a training program aimed at direct teaching of the prosocial skills is initiated. Such training may be appropriate at any level in elementary or secondary education. Regular teachers may find it useful to call on special education teachers, a school psychologist, or a school social worker to help plan and conduct a teaching program in this area.

Things to Think About While Watching TV or Reading a Story That Involves a Disabled Person

Is the disabled person a main character?
Is the disabled person the villain, with the disability used to suggest evilness?
Is the disabled person present as "interesting scenery"?
Is the disabled person the hero or heroine?
Is the presentation of the disability accurate and free of stereotyping?

Is the disabled person portrayed as a person to be pitied?

Does the disabled person have as much control over important events in his or her life as nondisabled characters do?

Does the disabled person appear to lead a normal, satisfying life?

Does the disabled person appear to "feel good" about himself or herself?

Is the disabled person generally respected by other characters in the story?

Is the disabled person a victim of a physical assault or otherwise victimized, suggesting greater helplessness than likely?

Do advertisements contain disabled persons? (Shaver & Curtis, 1981, p. 51)

The regular teacher should call for consultation and assistance in cases of extreme problems of social behavior. Special education teachers and school psychologists, among others, are increasingly able to offer help in both diagnosis and instruction of students who show problems in social behavior. Also, varieties of procedures for general improvement in the social structuring of classes and in the teaching of social skills have become available, and specialists can be expected to help deliver them to regular school operations. Note that the approaches suggested are quite strictly educational rather than psychiatric or medical. There are occasions, of course, when the social behavior of an individual is so extreme that it cannot be tolerated or treated in the mainstream environment; in such cases, referrals will of necessity be made to special schools, psychiatric facilities, or, perhaps, if appropriate, the police.

The approach is educational, oriented to developing competencies.

Good Order and Management

Poor learning or problem behavior in school is by no means entirely a function of the characteristics of children. Poor class management by a teacher who provides inadequate or inconsistent cues or who fails to bring the group to attention when necessary leaves children confused and disoriented. If a teacher fails to clarify expectations before activities are completed, permits materials to be left in poor order, or handles the consequences of misbehavior inconsistently, the result is usually disorder and what may be labeled misbehavior by students. When behavior disturbances occur in a classroom with some frequency, the problem should not be sought in the students alone. Diagnostic studies should be made of both the teaching and the classroom environment. Treatment may be required for the total classroom situation. The diagnosis in that case would point to an absence of good management and would require improved teacher preparation and consultation as well as special education for the child. Teachers need not feel inadequate or guilty in these matters. The challenge of management and order in today's schools is very great, and it is a sign of professional strength for a teacher to acknowledge difficulties and to be open to help when it is needed.

The teacher is not the only manager in the class.

It is a sign of good teaching to ask for consultation on management problems when needed.

The Environment. Fortunately, class management has had significant recent attention in educational research and in the professional literature. For example, the Research and Development Center on Teacher Education at the University of Texas at Austin focused in the early 1980s on class management problems and developed materials for use by teachers who wish to become better managers. One of the strategies used at the center was to visit classes that were orderly and productive and to contrast them with classes known to be disorderly and to have frequent referrals of students for being troublesome and nonresponsive in learning situations. An outcome of such studies is a focus on the first few weeks of each school year as a situation in which teachers have the opportunity to teach students how to go to school and to establish good management procedures that will last the entire school year. Teachers who clarify expectations for student behavior, class rules, and sanctions for rule breaking at the start of the school year tend to have well-functioning classes, according to mid-year and later observations. In effect, the researchers propose teaching children how to go to school, followed up with regular monitoring to support appropriate behavior. The manuals for teachers provided by the Texas R&D center are not especially remarkable in the particulars covered. Indeed, good teachers will recognize most of the ideas. But what the center literature conveys quite forcefully is the importance of early, continuing, and consistent adherence to good management practices (Evertson et al., n.d.; Emmer et al., 1981).

Teaching children how to go to school is especially important at the beginning of every school year.

Another approach to good management is contained in the Borg training materials (Borg, n.d.), which were developed to translate the observational work of Kounin (1970) into a teacher training system on classroom management. Use of the system is intended to reduce the incidence of disturbing behavior in regular classrooms. Kounin observed, for example, that disorder often occurs when teachers lack skills to achieve the attention of an entire group when that is what they want. Borg has transformed that observation into several ideas and practices designed to solve the problem. For example, if a teacher wants to maintain group attention during recitation activities, it is important to ask the question first and *then* call on a particular student for a response. The teacher should say, for example, "In what directions would you expect most rivers to flow in Missouri? John," not, "John, in what directions would you expect most rivers to flow in Missouri?" Similarly, in oral reading, the order in which children will be called on should not be predictable; if it is, the *group* alert is lost. Individual students tend to be "on task" (academically engaged) only when they expect to be called on soon. If academic engagement is lost, learning suffers and problems mount.

The results of some research have been transformed first to teacher training, then to classroom applications.

The highly skilled teacher may consider many other approaches to classroom management. Using contingency contracts with a group is often effective. For example, an ingenious male teacher used his beard as a point of focus for his class. He wrote a contract in which he gave points to the class for positive behaviors resulting in good "climate" and learning and promised that when and if a sufficient number of points was earned, he would shave off his large and growing beard—at school, in front of the class. When the point total was achieved and the shaving episode was scheduled, an ingenious student arranged for a local TV station to send a crew and camera to record the event. Behavior in the class improved remarkably during the contract and for a surprisingly long period afterward.

Contingency management techniques can be used with groups as well as with individuals.

The Individual. Even when classes are generally well managed, some individuals will present extreme problems, possibly because they are uninvolved or do not understand the situation. It is important in such cases to be as precise as possible about the diagnosis. Deno and Mirkin (1977) described a simple measurement procedure that special and regular teachers can use collaboratively to specify the problem. While the class goes on as usual under the leadership of the regular teacher, the special teacher observes the child with problems for perhaps 30 seconds, recording whether the child is on task as expected by the teacher, distracted, or disturbing others. Then the special teacher observes a randomly chosen classmate, using the same recording period and behavioral categories. This is followed by a second observation of the problem child and then of another (different) randomly chosen classmate. After 6 to 10 pairs of observations, it becomes possible to make statements of the following type:

Direct observation of the classroom is often the most useful form of observation.

1. The child's rate of distraction during directed class activities is twice as high as that for his classmates.
2. The child's rate of disturbing behavior is four times the average rate of students in his class.

With such data as a beginning point, the teachers can work together to devise a plan for dealing with the child's problem and use the measuring technique to check on progress. The plan may include alterations in his assignments, closer monitoring of his work, use of contingency management systems, changing his seating, more time in direct instruction in small groups, more one-on-one tutoring by the special education teacher and classroom aide, consulting and planning with parents, or other procedures. It may also require giving the child a detailed review of class operations and expectations and then reteaching him the skills necessary for self-management and appropriate class behavior. In later checks on the student's behavior, it may be possible to say that the student's rate of distraction has been reduced by one-half or some other precise amount.

Teaming by teachers solves many difficult problems.

Contingency Management

1. A pupil's specific behavior is chosen for attention. It can be any behavior from learning an addition combination, carrying a tune, maintaining

fingernail hygiene, using polite language, or reducing disruptive behavior.

2. Systematic attention is given to reinforcing the pupil's desired behavior
when it occurs. The teacher who is not familiar with the basic principles
of reinforcement should carefully study materials on the optimal conditions for achieving and maintaining rate changes (Haring & Phillips,
1972; Haring & Schiefelbusch, 1976; Lovitt, 1978).

3. Systematic records are kept on the pupil's progress toward mastery of the
desired behavior, and reinforcements are changed as necessary to maintain progress and attainment.

*Systematic
reinforcement is
the key.*

The Premack principle (Higbee, 1981; Premack, 1959) is a special case
of operant conditioning in which learning activities themselves are used as
positive reinforcement. Desirable learning activities are the immediate
positive consequence of desired behavior on a less appealing learning task.
For example, if a child who loves music is allowed to go to music activities
right after she has performed well in the mathematics lessons, which the
child values less highly, the result should be a better rate of performance in
mathematics. The principle can be made operative in various school settings and with all kinds of pupils at all levels.

*Changes in rates
of specific
behaviors are the
objectives.*

Teachers may wish to involve special education teachers or school
psychologists as advisers and consultants in the application of contingency
management or behavioral principles. The consultant can make in-class
observations to pinpoint behaviors that need to be influenced, establish the
rates at which they appear, and design systems of reinforcing change. The
most frequent failures in the use of contingency management procedures
result from inconsistency and from not keeping systematic records. The
use of a consultant is recommended to help install a workable system for
dealing with behaviors that need to be either accelerated or decelerated.

Increasing Academic Learning Time

Just attending school regularly or just allocating an hour of class time each
day to a basic subject, such as reading, is not sufficient for adequate learning. Pupils' active engagement with the materials, problems, and processes that are the objects of teaching and learning is required. This positive
kind of engagement is referred to as academic learning time (ALT). It is
especially important to watch for ALT problems in students who show
poor progress in learning. If they become inattentive, perhaps because
assignments given to them are too difficult or not monitored thoroughly,
a snowball effect can result in their spending very little productive time on
learning tasks and falling ever farther behind in achievements.

The Environment. Industrial engineers emphasize the importance of keeping workplaces safe and efficient by preventing the intrusion of unneces-

sary and distracting objects or materials. The same general principle holds for the teaching space of teachers and aides and the learning space of pupils. Noises, objects strewn about, garish and clashing colors, and strong light contrasts produce testiness and irritation when anyone, especially an exceptional child, is trying to concentrate on a meaningful activity. By eliminating clutter, the effective use of space can be increased, attention can be focused on the specific task of learning, and distractions can be reduced.

If it's distracting, get rid of it.

An uncluttered environment does not imply a Spartan one. Nor does the reduction of distractions demand the closeting of pupils away from each other to a noticeable degree. Rather, it is a call for the simple, uncomplicated, and orderly organization of an instructional space (by both pupils and teacher) to permit the conduct of group or individual activities under conditions of mutual respect and consideration.

A device called a teacher call is used to help organize teacher-student interactions as part of one instructional system, the Adaptive Learning Environment Model (ALEM; Wang, 1980b). Many varieties of teacher calls are used, but they are simple devices featuring one color on top and a different color on the bottom. For example, a simple block of wood might be painted half orange and half black. Each student has one on his desk, to be turned orange side up whenever the attention of a teacher or an aide is desired—to answer a question, clarify procedures, or check work. Instead of raising hands and waiting for help, pupils are expected to turn up the teacher call when they need help. While waiting for the teacher to respond, students are expected to go ahead with whatever work they have at hand or to turn to a special set of activities that all students have for gaps between assignments. By using teacher calls and preparing students to avoid empty waiting time, the amount of ALT is increased in ALEM classes.

Learning requires much time on task, with success.

Other procedures to extend ALT include peer teaching, carefully checked homework, and direct teaching strategies. When procedures for enhancing ALT are not used, the situation of the marginal child is likely to be grossly affected, possibly to the point where referral to special education is necessary.

The Individual: The Case of Erick. Erick, age 5, is observed by his kindergarten teacher to be immature in language and social abilities, somewhat awkward physically, and quite often distracted or inattentive when other children are on task. The observations were made in November of the school year. The first parent-teacher conference had been held in September, but Erick's parents had not indicated any special concern; the teacher, however, had expressed the intention to observe Erick closely. Now another parent conference is in the offing, and Erick's progress calls for a report of "unsatisfactory." The teacher has told the school principal of a growing belief that Erick may have a significant problem. He may need special education and related services, especially because it is so difficult to

Teacher observations are often the starting point in assessment.

get his sustained attention for school tasks. The following are some of the questions considered by the teacher and the principal:

It pays to be very clear about the questions one is trying to answer when considering a problem.

1. What sequence of steps should be taken to pursue this situation, and by whom? Should a special educator or school psychologist be consulted?
2. Does the school have a legal responsibility to identify Erick as a handicapped child and to write an IEP for him?
3. Assuming that Erick has not had a recent medical checkup, how should a thorough examination be secured for him? Who should pay for it? Should the physician be told of the teacher's concerns about attention problems? Might this be a case of petit mal seizures or some other neurological problem?
4. Who should be responsible for integrating all the information gathered on Erick and for consulting and planning with his parents?

Literally thousands of children like Erick who show poor attention on school tasks are identified each year. Each child requires individualized assessment. In the schools, "assessment" refers to the systematic process of assembling and using information to make decisions on the instruction of students.

Special Education Assessment

Assessment is important only in relation to decisions to be made.

A variety of decisions must be made in the typical special education assessment process which can be framed in terms of the following questions:

1. Should the student be studied in detail? (This is the screening problem.)
2. Does the suspected problem actually exist? Are there data to support the need for special concern? Is it accepted by the child's caregivers and others?
3. Precisely what is the nature of the problem, and how serious is it?
4. Is the student eligible for special education or related services?
5. What educational program is suggested? (What goals and objectives should be pursued, and by what means?)
6. Is the student's mainstream educational resource capable of offering the suggested program? If not, how can it be augmented so that it can?
7. Are the results of the assessment and the educational plan in accord with parental perceptions and preferences?
8. Has the plan been put into practice? How effective is it?
9. When should the special plan be terminated?
10. Has anything been learned from this student that has general implications for the teacher, other school personnel, other students, or the school?

Let us return to Erick's case. Suppose that his teacher and other team members decided to do a thorough study, including a medical examination (with the parents' permission). The physician's report on Erick was essentially negative. He is in good health. The tests of vision and hearing were normal. No detailed neurological testing was considered necessary. The physician was interested in knowing the school staff's concerns about Erick's lack of attention in school, his delay in language development, and his awkwardness and distractibility; the physician asked to be kept informed. Nothing in the physician's report or in other available data on Erick's early development was of a nature to predict or explain his school problems.

The psychologist reported a low average level of cognitive ability (WISC-R Full Scale IQ of 92) with somewhat lower verbal than performance abilities (Verbal IQ, 86; Performance IQ, 95). The psychologist also reported on classroom observational studies that had been conducted for several minutes on each of five days, following the procedures described by Deno and Mirkin (1977). Observations focused on *noisemaking, being out of place, unacceptable interpersonal contacts or destructiveness*, and *off-task behavior*. Compared with other children in the classroom who were randomly selected for comparative observations, Erick showed an average amount of noisemaking, twice the average rate of being out of place, an only slightly above average rate of unacceptable contacts and disturbances, but eight times the average rates for off-task behaviors. This finding fully confirmed the teacher's informal observations.

Erick's plan is a BCD type. No etiological data were found to be relevant.

The special education teacher reported general slowness in Erick's language development and specific needs for help in sensitivity to sound similarities (rhyming) and in auditory discrimination of word elements.

The physical education teacher observed Erick and confirmed the informal observation of awkwardness. The problem was considered minor but worth attention by the physical education teacher for some individualized help in gross motor skills.

Needs were pinpointed in several areas.

The classroom was observed to be in good order at most times. Erick seems not to have suffered any stigma in relationships with classmates, but he has no frequent, cordial interactions with them. The regular teacher would need assistance from the special education teacher to offer highly structured help to Erick on an individualized basis; hence, consideration should be given to having the special education teacher spend time in Erick's room to help extend direct teaching for Erick, perhaps by means of a small group in which he is included. Teacher-parent contacts have been minimal so far and would need to be developed, assuming that the parents can be engaged in a collaborative program.

Responsibilities for carrying out the IEP must be clear.

It was agreed by all the professionals that Erick qualified as a handicapped child under the standards of the state, one in need of special education or related services.

Note again the emphasis on approaches that have practical significance in the school situation. In cases of extreme problems, medical

Some "diagnoses" are merely descriptive.

approaches may be needed. For example, a relatively new classification called attention deficit disorder (ADD) has been included in the third edition of the *Diagnostic and Statistical Manual* (DSM III) of the American Psychiatric Association (1980). Such a diagnosis is often heavily dependent on evidence concerning the child's behavioral history, which is presented to physicians by schoolteachers and parents, and thus the ADD diagnosis may not always provide many insights. Drug treatments may be recommended, in which case teachers can be very helpful by observing and reporting changes in classroom behavior associated with the treatments.

Drug Administration in the Schools

Drugs have a definite but limited role in the treatment of students' learning and behavior problems. Drugs can be useful with *some* under *certain* circumstances. . . .

Clear policy promotes effective practices.

The procedure under which medication may be administered varies by school district. It is essential that school personnel check to see if there are established policies for medication administration within the district. Adhere to these policies, if for no other reason than legal protection. The following guidelines will aid school systems in dealing with this situation:

1. Written orders are to be provided to the school from a physician, detailing the name of the drug, dosage, and the time interval in which the medication is to be taken. These orders are to be reviewed periodically.
2. A written request is to be received by the school district from the parent or guardian of the pupil, together with a letter from the physician indicating the necessity for the administering of the medication during the day, the type of disease or illness involved, the benefits of the medication, the side effects, and an emergency number where the parents or guardians can be reached. Both letters should be placed in the pupil's file.
3. Medication must be brought to the school in a container appropriately labeled by the pharmacy or physician.
4. The initial dose at school must be administered by the school nurse. If a teacher is to give subsequent medication, the nurse should discuss the medication, including its side effects, with the teacher.

Drugs should be administered in school only on competent, written others.

5. The school nurse shall prepare a written statement to the building administrator as to the side effects of the drug, if any, and a copy should be placed in the pupil's file.
6. A locked cabinet must be provided for the storage of the medication. Opportunities should be provided for communication with the pupil, parent, and physician regarding the efficacy of the medication administered during school hours.
7. With the parent's and physician's consent, medication of a short-term duration may be administered by a teacher.

8. The school district retains the discretion to reject requests for administration of medicine.

Information will be needed in order to understand and teach a child who is on medication. With written parental permission and through the school nurse, the following information should be obtained from the child's physician:

1. How does the medication work?

2. What change in the student's behavior can be expected?

3. What effect will the medication have on the child's attention span, memory, motor dexterity, personality, sleeping and eating habits?

4. Does the medication have undesirable side effects?

5. What behavioral and/or motoric reactions indicate that the dosage may be toxic or inadequate for the child's needs?

6. How long will the child have to take the medication?

7. Could the child become physically and/or psychologically addicted to the medication?

Teachers can help monitor the effects of drug treatments in collaboration with the school nurse, parents, and physicians.

The most important aspect of chemotherapy is to understand that the use of drugs does not relieve the physician, parent, and teacher of the responsibility for seeking to identify and eliminate the factor(s) causing or aggravating the problem. (Grotsky, Sabatino, & Ohrtman, 1976, pp. 8–10)

Developmentally Appropriate Instruction

Children can hardly be expected to perform long division of whole numbers as part of the mathematics curriculum until they have mastered addition, subtraction, and multiplication of whole numbers. That assertion seems clear and valid, but there is much more to adapting the curriculum so that it is developmentally appropriate. Children develop in many ways, and it is necessary to specify the dimensions of development of most concern. In considering educational plans, parents and teachers tend to agree on subject matter and skills that are required of all students (the cultural imperatives) and those that are deemed less uniformly essential (the cultural electives). Today certain areas of learning are as essential to human beings as adequate calcium for bones. These *cultural imperatives* are the basics of education, the tools of the culture, without which a person is confined to fundamental ignorance and limited choice. For the United States and Canada in the late twentieth century, any list of cultural imperatives by consensus for attention in the schools would, we think include the following five:

Some curriculum domains require careful sequencing of learning or teaching segments.

1. *Language*: Speaking, listening, comprehending, reading, and writing for everyday personal, social, and vocational purposes

There is broad consensus about the importance of certain curricular areas.

2. *Mathematics*: At least the basic skills required in the marketplace and in daily life
3. *Health, safety, and mobility*: The knowledge of self-care, health, protection, and travel
4. *Social skills*: For acceptable behavior in citizenship and in group life (nondestructive, cooperative, etc.)
5. *Career education*: Preparation for an economically useful life, including employment in competitive situations, if possible, and for other life roles

The cultural imperatives are for every student.

A good start on these imperatives is provided in most homes during early childhood. As children enter the schools, a coalition of home and school forms to develop these essential areas further. Some children have difficulty with them, in which case there is great concern and an extraordinary persistence in trying to help the children achieve. Failures to learn in these areas are the causes of most referrals to special education. They are the domains in which most progress is required in mainstream classes if referrals to special education centers are to be limited or reduced. Progress of students in the areas of the cultural imperatives are among the most important dimensions on which assessments must be made in order to plan developmentally appropriate education.

The cultural electives are not uniformly included in every student's curriculum.

The *electives* are different. Our society does not require all students to take up the flute, study the higher branches of mathematics, write poetry, or learn to use the crosscut saw. We are remarkably tolerant of people's lifelong ineptitude in many such areas.

The individual. Tobias (1976), in an analysis of achievement variables as aptitudes in ATI (aptitude-treatment-interaction) studies, concluded that achievement is perhaps the most important variable to consider in individualizing instruction. This is to say, for example, that the present reading levels of a child are extremely important to consider in arranging instruction that is intended to advance the child's reading abilities. Similarly, if one wishes to advance the social skills of a child, the essential beginning point is to know where the child is now in social skills. When teachers work with psychologists, physicians, and other specialists, frequently there is a tendency to be drawn to variables that are considered to be predispositional or to undergird the learning process. The psychologist may stress capacity for learning (often represented by IQ), perceptual abilities, or personality traits. The physician may focus on neurological integrity. All these factors can be important, but the educator is well advised to give primary attention to the child's present levels of achievement and performance and focus on the specific area of learning being considered.

The most important variable in educational planning is what the student already knows in the area of instruction.

Teaching should be started well within the range of a pupil's present skills and understandings, rather than at the limit (Betts, 1946; Birch,

1955). For example, if a child's reading comprehension is at grade 3.5, the day's reading should start with material at a bit lower level (perhaps at grade 3.0) and move on to more challenging material after success experiences; if the difficulty level begins to upset the youngster, drop back a little until the reader regains confidence. The same procedure can be followed in other curriculum areas.

The lesson should yield success from the first lesson.

Many exceptional children and young adults experience more than a fair share of failures in the ordinary course of life. The cumulative effect is expectation of failure. Undercutting, that is, beginning a little below the child's level of development, is a sound tactic to combat such negative expectations in learning. If the instructional sequence is matched to the pupil's present development and deliberately seeded with easy spots, a positive level of self-expectation will be confirmed (reinforced) often enough to keep learning on an upward course.

Children sometimes have a surprising degree of awareness of their own best level and pace for absorbing new experiences. That self-knowledge grows in usefulness as the children have more opportunities to set their own expectations and rates on learning tasks and to participate in broader aspects of managing their own learning. Teachers are well advised to encourage pupils to become aware of their own performance characteristics and to help in the management of the instructional process. "How long shall we plan for this activity to take?" is preferable to "This assignment is due by noon tomorrow." Taking time to set clear purposes for reading or other activities and to design the optimal conditions for study is significant. Helping students become strategic about such matters in their own lives should be an important goal of the teacher.

Students can help set the pace for instruction and can improve it, too.

Special pupil characteristics sometimes influence learning pace significantly and need to be considered in educational planning. Physical limitations of mobility, slowness in writing, or speech impairments are examples. Factors extrinsic to the pupil, such as the relative difficulty of the learning task, other assignments and time commitments, and the adequacy and availability of teacher or tutorial assistance, may also affect a pupil's performance.

Three Outcomes to Be Looked For When Helping Children Set Their Own Pace in Learning Activities

1. The pupil learns to estimate accurately how long it will take to accomplish any new learning task.
2. The pupil learns to set a personal learning pace that will accomplish a task within a reasonable margin of error.
3. The pupil learns to identify and practice techniques for advancing the pace of learning while maintaining standards of comprehension and retention.

The Environment. One of the most important factors in the individualization of instruction to meet developmental needs is the management of structure. Children who show relatively poor progress in the initial phases of acquiring basic skills, for example, seem to profit most from intensive, direct, carefully structured lessons. In such programs, one proceeds methodically from concept to concept and skill to skill, always linking and sequencing activities in smooth steps. This is "high-density" teaching. The teacher does not wait for discovery learning or for the pupil to create structure after trial-and-error but rather proceeds in a direct teacher-centered style.

Highly structured teaching is usually indicated for pupils whose pace of learning the rudiments of a subject is slow.

When children who do not catch on readily to the rudimentary steps of basic subjects are pressed along too rapidly, their initial confusion may turn into serious and long-standing failure to achieve. This is the kind of situation in which the special education teacher is called into the breach to try to solve the student's "learning disability" problem by providing highly structured teaching.

Many special education teachers can be described as experts in highly structured teaching; they know about and are more experienced than most teachers in making micro-level analyses of children's understandings and skills and in offering systematic, carefully sequenced instruction. The challenge now is to provide such highly structured teaching in the regular classroom when it is appropriate, long before problems become serious. This goal may require cooperative work by the regular and special education teachers, perhaps assisted by paraprofessional aides.

Some students do better when they create their own structures for learning.

In some instances, structure is overly tight and some students feel confined and bored. They may prefer to create structures of their own; to discover, on their own, the conceptual linkages of a subject; to learn some details incidentally rather than always by teacher design. There is some evidence that bright and high-achieving students tend to learn better in low-structure situations, just as children who are low in general cognitive ability tend to profit most from high structure (Cronbach & Snow, 1977; Hunt, 1975).

A class in which there is good accommodation to individual differences is one in which the teacher individualizes structure and uses it creatively. Unfortunately, some teachers operate inflexibly in one style or another. Obviously, a teacher's style is something to be considered in the placement of children with exceptional needs.

> The young child's knowledge of himself, his confidence in himself, his willingness to risk himself in new situations, grows out of significant pleasurable experiences.
>
> The young child learns and grows by experiences. (Wood, 1975, pp. 3–4)

Frequent Monitoring, Feedback, Reinforcement, and Review

Among principles emerging from research concerning effective instruction are those stressing the value of frequent monitoring, feedback, reinforcement, and review of student work. According to Glaser (1972), "A student's progress through the curriculum must be adequately monitored by assessment measures and observational judgment by the teacher so that the student's performance dictates the design of a teaching program adaptive to individual requirements" (p. 111). He added the admonition that the adaptation must be made for all students and not just those who are not "making it."

Close and continuous monitoring is also the basis for the ongoing diagnosis of learning difficulties; they should be identified before they become major problems. The best approach, of course, is one in which the data yielded through monitoring is used immediately to provide on-the-spot feedback and instruction for the child. Reinforcement is then provided selectively as the student demonstrates progress.

Close monitoring of classroom performance is required for instruction in an adaptive mode.

It cannot be assumed that all that is learned will be retained. Successful teachers use frequent reviews to remind pupils of what they have already learned. Opportunities to repeat, and thus to see and feel one's own achievements, build and strengthen self-esteem.

Review should be regular, meaningful, and focused. When it includes fundamentals that were learned earlier, the association between those fundamentals and recently learned material should be made explicit. A good way to make review meaningful is to encourage pupils to teach what they have learned to others. Allowing committees of pupils to invent new ways of review or incorporating reviews into such activities as dramatic play, games, or publications is also effective. Almost any approach works, provided it is meaningful, regular, and clearly described to pupils as a review activity.

Memories aren't perfect, so review is necessary.

The Environment. The application of principles relating to monitoring, feedback, reinforcement, and review is a major problem in most classes and schools. A result is that students at the margins, both those who are falling behind and those showing rapid progress, often encounter nonadaptation in their school programs and experience failure for that fact. This result need not occur if regular and special education staff members work together to create adaptive teaching situations.

For example, in contemporary instructional systems, information on performance is turned over to pupils rapidly. There is substantial evidence that the shorter the time lapse between action and reaction, the more learning is facilitated.

It is helpful for pupils to see their progress charted, whether in learning foreign-language vocabulary, reading novels, staying in one's seat,

Pupils are motivated by feelings and by clear evidence of their own progress.

making a set of bookends, or mastering spelling words. Charting often serves as a reinforcement. Although charts can be maintained by the teacher, aide, or a pupil who is "chart coordinator," the technique seems to work more effectively if the learner makes periodic and cumulative entries. They can be very simple graphs or more complicated logarithmic charts as used by some behavior analysts. The important thing is that they reflect learning in a meaningful way. The charts should provide a kind of "external clock" for both pupils and teachers. In addition to feeling progress, the pupils can see it!

Whether charts or other visual displays play a part in pupil feedback, it is crucial that the day-by-day response system be domain-oriented rather than norm-oriented. Pupils gain the most if they can measure their progress against their earlier achievements in a clearly delineated field or domain rather than against a norm (an external criterion made up by averaging the achievements of other pupils).

As a part of systems approaches to instruction in the regular classroom, teachers can create special centers on math maintenance or other topics where students are scheduled in regular ways to review work of past years, semesters, or weeks. Suppose that a given fifth-grade boy knows the basic number combinations (addition, subtraction, and multiplication) up to 12 quite well—at least as shown on tests in fourth grade. Nevertheless, an arrangement is made in his fifth-grade class for the student to complete timed review sessions on the number combinations just to maintain high automaticity (the ability to provide answers very rapidly and accurately). No school that fails to deal methodically with review problems can be considered a fully professional operation.

The Individual. Some children require extraordinarily close monitoring, feedback at the microlevel, reinforcements in rigorous accordance with the principles of behavioral analysis, and daily reviews of work covered only the day before. This is where the special education teacher joins in the classroom to apply principles of effective instruction detail by detail. Indeed, more specialists, such as the remedial physical education teacher and the speech and language therapist, may be involved. Let us return to the case of Erick. The IEP written for him will show details of a collaborative approach.

Erick's Individualized Educational Plan (IEP)

Present Developmental Level. Erick was 5 years and 10 months of age on the day of the planning conference (December 15). His intellectual development is slightly lower than average for his age. It is not clear if that is a permanent condition or if it can be altered favorably. His language development is a bit lower, estimated to be about the level of children just reaching age 5.

Erick is somewhat awkward in motor behavior. For example, he runs slowly and is not able to skip. He grasps and uses pencils and crayons in immature ways. He lacks skills that are necessary for learning to read, specifically in sound discrimination. He will need help in learning to discriminate sound similarities and differences before he can be taught letters and their corresponding sounds. Erick is often inattentive in class. Because regular instruction has not been sufficiently effective, Erick now shows exceptional needs that qualify him for special education and related services.

The first part of the plan summarizes educational problems, thus comprising the educational diagnosis.

Plans for Special Education and Related Services

Beginning immediately after the year-end holidays, the following steps will be taken:

The second part specifies what will be done.

1. Erick will receive tutoring for one hour daily by the special education teacher or an aide, under the joint supervision of the regular and special education teachers. Emphasis will be on pre-reading skills, particularly sound discrimination. This instruction will be provided in Erick's regular class.
2. Erick's teachers will be assisted by the school psychologist in designing and conducting a behavioral management plan to increase Erick's persistence on tasks assigned by the teacher and to reduce off-task behavior. The psychologist will help the teachers establish a daily system for recording results.
3. Over a period of about two weeks, the physical education teacher will introduce instruction in motor activities (running, skipping, hopping) that can later be used by Erick's regular teacher and continued by his parents in occasional formal and informal sessions. The physical education teacher will monitor progress through twice-weekly observation sessions.
4. Erick's regular teacher and the school principal will coordinate these activities and will call conferences from time to time to review progress and plans.
5. Erick's entire program will be conducted in the mainstream, with coordinated activities carried out by parents at home.

Goals Specified in the IEP

1. Erick will show progress in staying on task in the academic assignments given by his teacher.
2. Erick will progress in specific prereading academic skills.
3. In motor skills, as reflected in well-coordinated walking, running,

Long-range goals are agreed on and written out as the third part of the plan.

and other ordinary movements, Erick will show significant improvement.

Objectives

The fourth part contains specific objectives.

1. By February 1, Erick's off-task behavior, as observed by the school psychologist in the regular kindergarten class, should be reduced to a ratio of 2 to 1 (frequency of Erick's off-task behavior compared to the average of his classmates').
2. By April 1, Erick will consistently discriminate the sounds of the letter consonants in beginning and ending positions of words and will be able to match letter sounds with printed letters at the level of at least 75 percent accuracy. He will consistently match short vowel sounds as presented in one-syllable words.
3. By April 1, there will be noticeable improvement in Erick's co-ordination, as judged by his parents and teachers.

Monitoring and Next Conference

The responsible professionals indicate how progress will be evaluated and recorded.

1. In late February and again in late April, (a) the psychologist will repeat classroom observational studies of Erick's off-task behavior compared to that of his classmates, and (b) the special education teacher will repeat informal studies of prereading skills.
2. The special education and regular teachers will prepare weekly charts summarizing results of the behavior management program.
3. The physical education teacher will make progress reports on Erick after each observation.

The staff and parents agree on how they will work together and meet for further planning.

4. The conferees will reconvene in early May (or earlier, if the teacher thinks it is necessary) to review Erick's total program and progress and to consider plans for the next school year. A summer program will be considered.

Other Considerations

1. The parents agreed that a full report of the school's findings and plans for Erick should be sent to the examining physician and that such reports should be made routinely in the future.
2. The legal rights of parents to due process, additional studies, and appeal were explained at the IEP conference.

Interaction of Diagnosis and Instruction

In the past, assessments and diagnosis were used mostly to make pre-dictions about students' learning and to place the students in different programs according to the expectations held for their success. They were not considered integral parts of instruction. Thus children scoring low on

IQ tests would be expected to achieve in academic subjects at only a very low level and would be placed in a special class. According to Glaser (1972), in this "selective educational mode" the

The schools are shifting from a selective to an adaptive mode of education.

> effectiveness of the system is enhanced by admitting only those students who score high on measures of the abilities to succeed. . . . Little change in the educational environment is necessary, and the differences among individuals that become important to measure are those that predict success in this special setting. (p. 122)

Glaser proposed that in contrast to the prevailing selective mode, an "adaptive mode" of education be adopted, one in which many instructional methods and levels are offered in accordance with the needs of individuals. In the adaptive mode, assessment and diagnosis are concurrent with instruction.

On Binet's Test

Accepting the goal of maximizing the effectiveness of education for all children and youth, we must face up to the problem that we have long acknowledged but seldom dealt with effectively—the problem of providing for each individual the educational treatment that will be most effective in developing that person's potential. A good measure of scholastic aptitude is not automatically a good guide to the optimal educational treatment. Binet's test, like others used in education, must be judged in terms of its ability to facilitate constructive adaptations of educational programs for individuals. This is the challenge for the next 70 years. (Thorndike, 1975, p. 7)

Norm-referenced tests tend to be validated on the basis of predictive power.

The shift to the adaptive mode of education entails a general, but less than total, shift from traditional norm-referenced testing to criterion-referenced assessment. Norm-referenced testing in the schools is used to evaluate individual performance against the results or norms for some group. For example, Harold is said to be performing at the 50th percentile as compared with his fourth-grade classmates, Mary is said to score at the level of average third-graders at midyear (grade score 3.5), or Fred is said to score one standard deviation above the mean for his age group on national norms. Such information tells whether a child is above or below average for the age or grade group, but it does not say with precision whether a student has mastered specific content or skills or is ready to proceed to the next stages of instruction. Norm-referenced testing is usually oriented to judging the general progress of students and making predictions about future achievements. It has limited use in planning instruction for individuals.

A contrasting technique is that of criterion-referenced or domain-

Criterion-referenced tests are probably best thought of as domain-referenced.

referenced testing (sometimes known also as objectives-referenced). It focuses on testing a student's performance in relation to a fixed standard in a well-defined domain of content or skill. For example, the question may be "Does the child know the whole number combinations (addition, subtraction, and multiplication) through the tens?" Using a domain-referenced test, the answer to that question can be provided with precision and without reference to how any norm group performs. No reference is made to grade levels, percentiles, or standard scores; instead, the testing specifies precisely how the student performs in a specific content or skill area. It permits interpretation of a student's position in relation to the local curriculum and thus is useful in planning individualized instruction.

Although teachers often find it necessary to develop their own criterion-referenced tests, help is provided increasingly by commercial producers in classroom materials that are organized by specific objectives and include objectives-oriented or criterion-referenced tests.

Norm-referenced Versus Criterion-referenced Tests

If we interpret a score of an individual by comparing his score to those of other individuals (called a norm group) this would be norm-referencing. If we interpret a person's performance by comparing it to some specified behavioral criterion of proficiency, this would be criterion-referencing. To polarize the distinction, we could say that the focus of a normative score is on how many of Johnny's peers do not perform (score) as well as he does; the focus of a criterion-referenced score is on what it is that Johnny can do. Of course we can, and often do, interpret a single test score both ways. In norm-referencing we might make a statement that "Johnny did better than 80 percent of the students on addition of whole numbers." In criterion-referencing we might say that "Johnny got 70 percent of the items correct in a test on addition of whole numbers." Usually we would add further "meaning" to this statement by stating whether or not we thought 70 percent was inadequate, minimally adequate, excellent, or whatever. (Mehrens & Ebel, 1979, pp. 2–3)

Increasingly, norm-referenced tests are needed to make long-range predictions and plans.

Occasionally, it is useful to administer norm-referenced tests so that individuals can compare their rates of development with those of their peers. The information provided in such social contexts helps to judge overall development, relative strengths and weaknesses, and likely future development in special fields. It is useful in making long-range educational and career plans.

Policies set in P.L. 94–142 require education in an adaptive mode.

The Environment. One of the fundamental changes now occurring in schools relates to assessment processes. Public Law 94–142 declared the policy that schools should no longer be selective; all children are to be served—appropriately and in the mainstream whenever feasible. This policy makes irrelevant many of the measurement processes in most schools and makes assessment an integral part of instruction.

Transactional Assessment

Dr. Lauer made the point that any definition of handicap which placed the sole responsibility in the child's deficiencies furthers the very system of evaluation and placement which so many deplore. It encourages removing children from the contexts of their schools and families and allows diagnoses based on their traits and characteristics in isolation of crucial interactive processes. It encourages the separation of diagnosis and remedial planning, the separation of regular and special education. It encourages the selection of a category for every child, a special class for every category, and a bureaucracy for every class. . . .

She [advocated] a process in which an expert aids people—teachers, children, family members, or neighbors—in systematically observing and evaluating what goes on, assessing the outcome of the variations, and enjoying productive interactions.

From *New York State Psychologist* (1979), p. 5, reporting the views of Dr. Rachel M. Lauer.

Peterson, Peterson, Heistad, and Reynolds (1985) have described a set of schools in which diagnostic functions are fully integral with instruction. Every unit in the basic skills curriculum has a mastery examination associated with it, and pupils progress from one unit to the next only when they have passed the mastery exam at the preset criterion level. The number of days required to complete each unit is recorded. In this situation, all the assessment activities are conducted immediately in the context of instruction and used to make decisions about how the child's program should be organized and implemented. The vast majority of assessment activities are conducted in a criterion- or domain-referenced rather than norm-referenced mode.

Sometimes the same test data can be used for both domain-referenced and norm-referenced purposes.

Interestingly, however, merely by keeping track of the numbers of days required by each student to complete each unit, relative rates of progress through the curriculum can be obtained as a simple computer printout. For example, Alfred may have completed the unit on multiplication of two-place numbers after a total of 416 days of instruction in mathematics. It can be determined that the average student reaches this point in the curriculum in 390 days. Alfred's rate of progress was determined to be at the 30th percentile (somewhat below average) for pupils his age. All such norm-referenced data were obtainable totally without special testing; it was a nonobtrusive outcome of systematic use of criterion-referenced testing and keeping track of time as an integral part of instruction. Incidentally, use of time (number of days of instruction) as the variable in producing norm-referenced data on the progress of students provides an interval scale of measurement. Ten days are twice as many as 5, and it costs twice as much to employ a teacher for 10 days as for 5. The quality of information provided by measurements of this kind is far beyond the usual fare provided by norm-referenced tests.

In the future, testing will probably be oriented more to domain-referenced types.

It is not common for schools to operate general assessment and diagnostic systems of the kind just described. Indeed, most college classes for prospective teachers probably still teach measurement procedures useful only in Glaser's selective mode of education. But changes in the direction of the adaptive mode, in which assessment becomes an integral and internalized aspect of instruction, are on the way.

The Individual. A truly remarkable aspect of recent changes in education, especially in aspects relating to handicapped pupils, is the shift of accountability standards to the individual pupil. IEPs are written for individual students, which is to say that goals and objectives are individualized. Measurement systems must also be applied to individuals. Are the objectives stated in the IEP achieved? That is a key question in modern special education.

The accountability of teachers and administration now focuses on individual pupils as well as on general progress of students.

Protections Against Discriminatory Assessment

1. Always use more than one method of measuring important aspects of a child's development and performance (e.g., classroom observations, both informal and formal testing, and case history information).
2. Use two or more persons of different backgrounds (multidisciplinary teams) for critical assessments.
3. In the case of non-English-speaking and culturally different children, include in the decision-making process someone who can provide a special perspective on the child's background and current life situation.

An important way to gain insight into a child's learning behavior is to try to teach the child and make observations while doing so. If the teacher attends to the child's feedback—how the child responds—helpful information usually surfaces to indicate how instruction should be modified or revised to improve the child's learning. Thus all teaching can be used for diagnostic assessment.

We do not know how to teach all exceptional children as well as we would like, but all children can learn!

The special education teacher, the school psychologist, and parents are frequently called on to assist in studies of students with difficulties. By using such teaming, the intensity and range of study are extended beyond what the regular teacher might ordinarily achieve.

It is helpful to systematize thinking about educational diagnosis. The ABCD approach, suggested by Cromwell (1976), is useful not only in thinking about assessment but also in thinking about how a knowledge base relating to diagnosis is structured. The ABCDs involve consideration of the following four general classes of information about individual students:

A: *Historical information*, such as genetic history, family history, medical history, early developmental history of the child, early school performance, including specific successful and unsuccessful curricular experiences, etc. These data are found mainly in records or gathered through interviews.

B: *Current status*, including present levels of development in areas such as intelligence, social maturity (self-dependence), academic skills, motor behavior, speech, personality, interests, and health. These data are gathered by testing, observation, interviews, performance or product evaluations, etc.

C: *Instructional alternatives*, including programmatic options available in the regular and special education programs provided in the child's local school and the larger school system, plus the potential for changing and intermingling parts of all such programs. For example, decisions might be made on types and levels of reading materials to be used in instruction, on methods of instruction to be tried, on level of structure to be used in daily lessons, and on the need to add special tutoring to the daily teaching program. Characteristics of the child's teachers and the school facilities are also considered.

D: *Program outcomes*, including a delineation of the goals and objectives to be pursued.

The problem of diagnosis in this framework is to study the As and Bs (background and present status) in relation to the Cs (program possibilities) and to achieve a match, the best possible combination of pupil and program to optimize D (desired educational results or outcomes).

In educational diagnosis, the challenge is to match the individual with the most promising instructional program.

It is the teacher's responsibility to design and conduct C individually in order to maximize D. The teacher asks for help from parents, special educators, the school psychologist, and other personnel in order to decide on the Cs that are appropriate for a particular child. Much of the attention of those who consult with the teacher may focus on As and Bs, but it is the Cs—the instructional interventions—that are pivotal in educational diagnosis. Teachers are right to insist that discussions about As and Bs be kept strictly relevant to instructional planning.

One can think of the knowledge base for assessment and diagnosis using the structure provided by the ABCD terms. Some knowledge may be of the ACD type; that is, the history (A) of a child may tell us something about how to teach the child (C) to achieve certain objectives (D). Teachers often feel that if a child has failed badly (A) in one system of instruction or series of readers, for example, it is better to use different materials and systems of teaching (C) in later remedial efforts. Knowledge claims of this

Multidisciplinary diagnostic teams focus on instruction as the key problem in educational diagnosis.

ACD type often have a degree of clinical validity and may be worthy of attention in planning.

Sometimes teachers encounter more complicated knowledge claims about diagnosis, such as the following ABCD formulation. "The reading problem stems from perceptual problems resulting from neurodevelopmental problems." In this case, the history (A) of a neurological problem is said to predispose both the perception and reading problems (Bs shown by current observations and testing). In effect it is claimed that there has been an ordering of events or dispositions from neurological to perceptual to reading problems. In such a case, it is not uncommon to suggest that the teacher teach directly to the child's "perceptual" deficits (C) on the assumption that positive results will transfer to reading. Knowledge claims and prescriptions of such complexity are often poorly supported by evidence, and teachers do well to be very cautious about focusing their instruction on goals and objectives far removed from the ordinary school curriculum.

Teachers might well be cautious about diagnostic formulations that seem remote and unconnected to instruction.

It is very common for assessments to fall into a BCD framework. In this case, one is concerned with the careful delineation of a child's present level of development and functioning (B) as a basis for planning instruction (C). In the absence of strong evidence in support of complex diagnostic formulations, it is advisable for teachers to insist that BCD types of diagnosis focus mainly on practical, curriculum-based characteristics of the child rather than on presumed capacities or other attributes not directly linked to instructional planning and management.

Adequate diagnosis depends on an adequate knowledge base.

It is possible, of course, to limit diagnosis to just a CD framework. Behavioral psychologists sometimes assert that history (A) and most pretesting (B) are irrelevant to instruction. Given an objective (D), they are prepared to proceed directly to instruction (C). They proceed in the instructional situation through the immediate management of stimulus materials and contingencies or consequences of the child's responses.

Continuity in Content, Sequencing, and Staff

A major difficulty in programs involving pullouts of selected students from regular classes to go to resource rooms or remedial classes of various kinds is the discontinuity introduced in the school life of the child and the regular teacher. Just the breaking up of the school day to travel to the resource room at a particular hour often interrupts instruction. Also, regular and special teachers may use different materials, sequences, and methods of instruction, which confuse the child. When several teachers work in separate settings with the same students, they often are left struggling for time to talk with each other about individual students and programs.

Effective instruction requires that it not be interrupted by pullouts or anything else.

The Environment. The cleanest and clearest way of achieving continuity in context, sequencing, and staff for exceptional students is for the program to be delivered as fully as possible in the mainstream environment. Consider the following example of coteaching in regular secondary school classes.

In the first year of the program, the special education teacher teamed with a teacher of sophomore English and a teacher of modern American history. Clusters of about 8 to 10 exceptional students were placed in each of these classes. The special education teacher spent three periods a day as a coteacher, working cooperatively with the regular teacher on general improvement of instruction so that all students were able to profit from the class. The possibilities for exciting ventures into new and varied methods of instruction increased dramatically with two teachers in the classroom. Sometimes tape-recorded reports or dramatic presentations were substituted for written reports. Interesting adaptations were made in reading materials, and the number of field experiences and experts visiting the classes was increased. Systems for measurement were adapted.

Intensive teaming expands the adaptivity of instruction.

In a sense, the special education teacher provided the extra "developmental capital" needed for a period of time to enrich instruction in two of the most important courses offered in the high school. Not only were the clusters of exceptional students served well, but the nonhandicapped students (about 20 in each class) were stimulated as well. By the end of the first year, there were long waiting lists for the following year's enrollment in these two classes.

In the second year, the special education teacher worked with a science teacher and reduced the amount of time spent in classes she had targeted the year before, sophomore English and modern American history. An increasing number of other teachers volunteered to coteach in future years and to expand their roles in serving exceptional students. Everyone agreed on the importance of making special arrangements for students who are gifted as well as for those who have disabilities (Smith & Smith, 1985).

Success is contagious.

The Individual. Clearly it is important to examine the situation of the individual pupil in this context, to make certain that there is good continuity in curriculum and sequencing of topics. Also, it is essential to have consistent experience for each child across the various teachers who are providing instruction. Inconsistencies in programs for individuals can be a cause for major difficulties and need to be corrected when not in good order.

Learning How to Learn

Insights about learning need not be the exclusive domain of teachers. It can be extremely helpful for students to learn about their own learning and take responsibility for managing their learning activities in strategic ways.

The coach explained to Bruce that every time he was guarded very closely in basketball, he tended to turn to his dominant hand for dribbling and turn to the right. Knowing this, Bruce was willing to practice very hard at dribbling with his left hand and becoming more adept at left turns when under pressure. Gradually it became automatic for him to use either hand in an unpredictable fashion and to go either way even when the opposing guard was "in his face." Bruce gained awareness about his own performance and used that to design a program for learning. As new and better performance was made automatic, Bruce was free to give his attention to still more complex aspects of his development as a basketball player. By becoming a more thoughtful observer of his own performance and a better planner for his own development, his own ingenuity was added to that of his coach.

Students can learn about learning, just as teachers do.

All children can benefit from acquiring insights into how and under what conditions learning—especially their own learning—takes place. Learning about learning (1) gives pupils a realistic perspective on their own cognitive, affective, moral, and motor development; (2) explains interpersonal differences in style or approach to learning; (3) makes pupils more knowledgable participants in arranging their own learning experiences; and (4) helps pupils understand the concept of development as it relates to different ages and stages of growth (Palincsar, 1986).

An important general goal is to help students become metacognitive *about their own learning and to* take charge *of it.*

Encouraging elementary and secondary pupils to learn how they learn does more than provide theoretical knowledge, important as that can be. It helps pupils to make the theory operational, in parallel to the professional work of the teacher, and it helps increase their skills in managing their own learning.

The Environment. Ideally, every teacher takes time to foster in students valuable kinds of awareness about learning. For example, the teacher who expects students to read some materials for detailed mastery and to approach other reading assignments for sheer enjoyment will introduce the tasks differently and encourage the students to maintain awareness of their own awareness. The student may reflect on how she reads everything the same way, taking notes to prompt detailed recall of the story. If such a student can be made aware of her inflexibility in the approach to reading, perhaps changes can be made, just as Bruce learned to dribble with both hands.

Important recent research on metacognitive processes, a kind of second-order awareness of awareness by students, deserves the attention of all teachers. Not all the ideas about metacognition are new. The reader who "wakes up" to realize that he has been reading for two pages without comprehending a thing shows a kind of metacognition. If he then proceeds to analyze the situation to discover, for example, that he reads best when not too tired, at an uncluttered desk, and with occasional stops to reflect on what he is reading, real progress may have started. Teachers who talk through plans for learning activities can serve as guides for students who wish to become strategic about their own learning.

The Individual. Some students have extraordinary difficulties in matters such as comprehension, systematic study, or test taking. They may not be capable of self-analysis to understand their problems and devise plans for improvement. Such students may well need the attention of special education teachers or psychologists to diagnose their situation. The goal then should be to make plans for improvement and to enable the individual gradually to take charge of his or her own diagnosis and planning. This will often involve a series of steps that together provide a scaffolding process by which the student becomes progressively more effective in self-management. In an important sense, individuals become independent and self-responsible when they have established good metacognitive skills for managing their own behavior and further development. They have learned to learn.

Students need good models and the help of teachers and parents to become metacognitive about their own learning and lives.

Reflecting on One's Own Performance

A high school student made a brief presentation to the class on abortion laws and then led a spirited half-hour discussion. Afterward, the student asked, "How did it go? How did I do?"

"Don't you know?" asked the teacher. "Can't you tell from what you saw and heard?"

"No. That's the first time in my whole school career that I ever did anything like that!"

Encouraging Constructive Divergent Thinking

Many children appear to lose their imaginative abilities during the school years. Constructive imagination is a wholesome quality. It may well be the precursor of adult artistic, literary, or scientific creativity. The conscious ability to think in divergent ways is also important in its own right for problem solving in childhood and youth.

Thinking should be more than simple recall and finding right answers.

The Environment. Teachers can take deliberate steps to foster positive forms of creative thinking in all aspects of the school curriculum. There is no child, high achiever or low achiever, who cannot profit from procedures such as the following as a part of the teacher's daily instructional behaviors.

1. Planning a "what if" element in every lesson. What if suddenly no one in the world could see colors? How would that change our lives? What if the average temperature of the world rose 2 degrees for a year? What if the South had won the Civil War? What if no one in the world could hear? What if there were no insects? What if Columbus had not received backing for his explorations?
2. Checking to see that lesson plans, homework, and tests strike a

Education should be productive, not just reproductive.

balance between questions with only one satisfactory answer and questions that allow pupils to reason through to alternative appropriate responses.

3. Encouraging each child, at least once a day, to introduce a divergent thought into whatever is being studied.

These three procedures should not preclude situations in which only one answer is correct. The world is full of such one-answer situations. It would be a disservice to pupils not to teach the kind of convergent thinking that is needed in those instances. What is wanted is a reasonable amount of time for acquiring skill in and learning to value the constructive divergent thinking on which so much of each pupil's future and that of society might depend.

The Individual. Some students have great difficulty in accepting assignments or structuring from anyone in a position of authority. They have an extraordinary need to design their own approaches to schooling. Perhaps they are eager to read widely on broadly framed topics and to engage in creative discussions about them but resist and resent directions by teachers to focus on particular knowledge and skills. Adolescents who drop out of regular schools to enroll in street academies or school-within-a-school arrangements may be seeking more opportunities for divergent and creative thinking. They may be best served when encouraged to explore and create on their own if, for a given period of time, they are unable to tolerate a given educational diet. Such students need to be identified and served in flexible ways. Equally, some students show extreme inability to move beyond learning simply what somebody else structures for them. In such cases, giving the children reinforced experiences in creative thinking may be of extreme importance to their development.

Giving the Child Choices

Children must learn to make choices responsibly. This takes carefully graded experience.

The variety of stimuli in today's world makes it imperative that children learn during their school years to make intelligent choices. Happily, to give pupils opportunities for choices is often a helpful way to motivate them toward improved achievement.

The Environment. One way to encourage good choices is to arrange the day's activities so that each pupil can select a personal daily schedule, as long as all parts of the day's work are accomplished (Wang, 1981). Such self-scheduling gives needed practice to pupils who tend to be disorganized. If options are presented carefully, a few at first and more as the child learns to handle them, the teacher will be able to observe the pupil's progress in self-management. Areas of pupil choice can include *what* is to be done, *when, where, with whom,* and, sometimes, *whether* to take on the task at all. It is fundamental, of course, that the teacher monitor the pupil's decisions and performances very closely to be sure that the youngster is neither overwhelmed, on the one hand, nor unchallenged, on the other.

The Individual. Contingency contracting is one of many ways to construct a learning environment for individual pupils, giving practice in how to make wise choices. The pupil and teacher agree that once a certain task is accomplished, the pupil will be free to do one of several other appealing activities. Contingency contracting can be used with more than one pupil at a time.

Sometimes children may need time out from their lessons.

Occasionally, a student may need to be given freedom just to take time out, to plan disengagement-from-school tasks for a while. Special physical spaces for time out are sometimes necessary also for children who experience episodes of extreme incapacity to engage in learning activities. Special education teachers or school psychologists can help plan the use of time out as a student choice.

Giving Children Chances for Leadership

Recent studies have revealed (1) that most talking in elementary and secondary schools is done by teachers and (2) that the overwhelming majority of all questions in those classes are asked by teachers. The consequent advice for teachers is to set up more situations in which the teacher listens and responds rather than talks and questions, giving students a chance to develop and practice leadership skills.

Leadership is a subtle matter, often no more than a feeling in the person who is before the group. Pupils who are comfortable in leadership roles have had practice in leading under teacher guidance, have good ideas, are willing to make them public, and are acknowledged to be ready for the role by the rest of the group.

The Environment. Leadership skills range from the knowledge of parliamentary procedures, which are essential to the conduct of formal organization meetings, to personal control, to the mastery of such techniques as brainstorming. The elements of these skills are important to all pupils. They originate and develop best in classes where teachers do not monopolize informal leadership opportunities. Every class and every school can present opportunities for the development of leadership skills.

The Individual. It is especially unfortunate when particular students who are capable intellectually of strong leadership fail to develop skills and comfort in functioning as leaders. There is very little market for highly capable persons whose judgment in complex affairs is needed and respected but who fall apart when required to lead other persons. By contrast, the abilities of exceptionally able persons can be magnified many times when they have learned to work with skill and personal satisfaction in leadership roles. Some schools provide consultants on gifted students who can assist

The market for leaders is very good.

regular teachers and other staff members in planning experiences for the students who need special help in leadership development.

Modeling Behavior

Models reveal all. Children tend to imitate adults and other children whom they admire. They model their own behavior to conform to the examples of people whom they observe to be interesting and successful. This phenomenon can be turned into a strong and versatile instuctional tool, especially when it is combined with an understanding of the power of positive reinforcement.

The Environment. The teacher, of course, is a model of major dimensions. A teacher who habitually shouts at children reinforces loud talking and shouting by pupils. Students will also tend to imitate the teacher who is calm and thoughtful and who speaks directly in a well-modulated tone. In short, the actions of teachers tend to be mimicked by their pupils.

The Individual. Consider the following situation. A teacher felt that Martha, Jane, and Andy were fine examples of proper pupil behavior, as scholars and as school citizens. The teacher often praised their behavior in view of other pupils, suggesting that it would be well if all of them behaved similarly. When that did not seem to affect students who misbehaved, the teacher asked for consultation.

The teacher pointed out to the consultant specific misbehaviors that the teacher wanted changed. Sylvia interrupted others instead of raising her hand. Billy kept tapping with a pencil or poking the child in front rather than keeping his hands at rest on his desk.

First, the consultant positioned Martha, Jane, and Andy where Sylvia and Billy could see that their correct behavior was often rewarded. When-

Positive behaviors receive teacher attention. ever Sylvia or Billy achieved an objective set for them, even for a short time, the teacher smiled or quietly made a favorable comment to them. From time to time, but not always, when either Sylvia or Billy performed as desired, the teacher told them they could choose a favorite activity. When they had mastered the behaviors set as initial objectives, the teacher then moved on to set new goals that focused on other behaviors.

The teacher had learned how to go about accomplishing two broad goals: (1) to guide Sylvia and Billy toward using certain other pupils as models and (2) to embark on a series of systematic moves to help them find increased satisfaction in more acceptable academic behavior.

PREVAILING AND PREFERRED PRACTICES

The preferred practices described in this chapter represent important convergences in ideas from the fields of adaptive education, effective instruction, and special education. The enriched ideas that emerge from this convergence promise to make the mainstream of education a more powerful resource for dealing with individual differences among pupils. A new context for special education is being fashioned, one requiring a basic renegotiation of the relations of regular and special education. Here is a recapitulation of some features of the renegotiation between regular and special education.

Prevailing Practices	*Preferred Practices*
1. Researchers on topics of adaptive education and special education work in separate environments and with minimal interaction.	1. Researchers on adaptive education regularly consider atypical pupils in both their research and in developmental work.
2. Research and school practices operate on a selective mode, assuming minimal adaptability in classes and schools.	2. Research and school practices operate in an adaptive mode, assuming that both teachers and pupils can make adaptive changes.
3. Accommodating individual differences is assumed to involve homogeneous grouping of pupils.	3. Deliberately created heterogeneous groups in which pupils become aware of differences are one means of accommodating to individual differences.
4. The teacher is considered to be the sole manager of the class.	4. Teachers and students all participate in class management; teaching students to self-manage is a regular part of the curriculum.
5. Referral of pupils to special education centers is based on the aberrational characteristics of the pupils. The problem is seen as residing in the child.	5. Referrals of pupils to special education centers is limited severely and, when necessary, is considered to reflect the characteristics of the child's regular class as well as his or her personal characteristics.
6. Attendance in class is checked, but time in concentrated study is unmeasured.	6. Academic learning time is considered an essential matter for assessment and influence if instruction is to be effective.
7. All students in the regular class are on the same page of	7. Systems procedures make it possible for all pupils to be

the same book in most subjects at any given time.

engaged in developmentally appropriate work and at a proper pace in all basic subjects.

8. Monitoring, feedback, and reinforcement of student performance is infrequent and mostly test-oriented.

8. Monitoring, feedback, and reinforcement are daily activities as regular teachers, special education teachers, aides, and volunteers "travel" regularly in the classroom.

9. Assessment and diagnosis are mostly oriented to prediction and selection.

9. Assessment and diagnosis are integral parts of instruction.

10. Special education teachers work mainly in separate resource rooms and special classes.

10. Special education teachers work mainly as coprofessionals with regular teachers in regular classrooms and other instructional settings.

11. Teachers direct learning activities.

11. Teachers direct learning activities but also assist students in learning how to monitor and manage their own learning.

12. Children listen to teachers.

12. Children have opportunities to lead classroom activities.

TOPICAL BIBLIOGRAPHY

Effective Instruction and Effective Schools

Berbow (1980)
Block (1984)
Wang & Walberg (1985)

Individualized Educational Programs

Dardig & Heward (1981)
Federal Register (Jan. 19, 1981)
Morgan (1981)

Norm-referenced, Criterion-referenced, Domain-referenced, and Curriculum-based Assessment

Exceptional Children (Nov. 1985, entire issue)
Hively & Reynolds (1975)
Mehrens & Ebel (1979)

Materials for Children Telling about Exceptional Persons

Benham (1978)
Bookbinder (1978)
Bower (1980)
Mullins & Wolfe (1975)
Sapon-Shevin (1982, 1983)

CHAPTER 4

Teaching and Teamwork

Teaching has become less of a "lonely profession."

Teaching, said an early morning talk show host, is like "trying to hold 30 corks under water at the same time using only two hands." Indeed, teaching can be such a difficult task, depending on how it is conducted. It has also been characterized as the "lonely profession," consisting of one adult closeted in a boxlike room with 30 students. Fortunately, this instructional design is no longer taken for granted. Now several teachers may work together in a classroom or other instructional environment, with aides and consultants, and in teams that include parents. The effectiveness of this teaching situation depends heavily on the ability and skill of teachers in communicating professionally with one another, with parents, and with educational and health-related specialists. Mutual help is the key to effective teamwork.

Good communication within the school is essential for mainstreaming to work.

With mainstreaming comes increasing diversity in the characteristics of students in regular classes and schools. In turn, teachers need a wider range of knowledge and skills to be effective. Few unassisted teachers are likely to possess all the needed insights or talents. Thus today's elementary and secondary classrooms have been opened to new forms of collaboration among teachers, other specialists, and parents. Staff members who formerly worked only in their own specialized environments are now moving in increasing numbers into regular classes and schools and sometimes into students' homes and neighborhoods to help provide educational and related services. They have come to realize that the "special" places where they worked in the past were also very limited places and that their skills are needed to help open the larger and richer resources of the schools and community to children who are exceptional. Such adaptive education works best when there is mutual trust and the expectation of mutual understanding and growth among teachers, parents, and other collaborators.

Not all the changes are voluntary. By law, parents of certain handicapped and gifted students have been guaranteed a voice in the educational planning for their children. The parents must be notified and assent before their child is subjected to specialized examinations; they have the right to participate in the preparation of the IEP for their child and the right to *due process*. Later in this chapter, we list ways in which teachers can help ensure that exceptional children and their parents receive the assistance they deserve.

"Special" education does not always need to be conducted in special places.

Parents have a right to participate in the planning for their exceptional child.

Due Process Safeguards

According to legal and judicial decisions, safeguards are made available to parents and children in any matter relating to a handicapped child's identification, evaluation, or enrollment in an educational program.

1. Prior notice must be given to parents before any special educational diagnosis of a child is performed.
2. Prior notice must be given to parents before any major change in the child's program is made, such as enrollment in a special program or the participation of a resource teacher in the child's instruction.
3. Parents have access to school records relating to their child's school situation.
4. A surrogate parent may be designated to serve on behalf of a child who is a ward of the state or whose parents are unknown or unavailable.

If disagreements develop about any matter connected with a child's evaluation or program, school districts are obligated to provide impartial due process hearings to resolve the issue. Disagreements are the exception, not the rule. Also, most disagreements are resolved without formal hearings or court cases. It is essential, though, that teachers know what can happen if disagreements persist. When a formal hearing is required, a parent has the right to be accompanied by a lawyer or other counselor, to present evidence; to confront, compel, and cross-examine witnesses; and to obtain a transcript of the hearing or a written decision by the hearing officer. A parent who is dissatisfied with the decision of the hearing officer has the right to appeal to the state educational agency and, if still dissatisfied, to the courts.

Procedures in educational planning must be fair.

The new policies and practices increase the demand for time and conditions conducive for teachers and their collaborators to confer and work together. New functions have been added that together make the roles of regular teachers, special education teachers, school psychologists, speech and language therapists, parents, and consultants more complex but also more promising and interesting. Teaching is assuredly becoming less of a lonely profession. It is essential that teacher contracts, agreements, and assignments be adjusted so that these time requirements can be met by the teacher without hardship.

In this chapter, we consider the communication aspects of the changing forms of education, including a brief examination of the new roles of special educators. But first, we note the larger comparable changes in and challenge to the community at large.

A BROADER SET OF CHANGES

Mainstreaming is occurring in all aspects of the community.

The changes occurring in the schools reflect broad social changes that are reverberating throughout the community. For example, some mental health professionals (psychiatrists, clinical psychologists, and social workers) have left their clinics and now function in various other places in the community. Instead of working directly and solely to "fix" or "cure" the clients who come to them with problems, they turn their energies increasingly to providing environmental supports for the clients. Employers, family members, neighbors, and clergy are enlisted to build support systems to maintain individuals in their familiar surroundings. The diagnostic studies required in such a broad context extend to each individual's total life situation. Similarly, treatment may be directed to the environment as well as the individual. Demands for effective communication have escalated enormously as these changes have occurred.

Employers, neighbors, and others provide support.

In many communities, handicapped persons have banded together to press for better services from public transit systems. Persons with motor handicaps are often unable to board buses in the quick manner required, and those in wheelchairs may find the entire public transportation system inaccessible. Handicapped persons need lifting devices that will help take wheelchairs on board buses or trains. Transit agencies typically offer to send special "handicabs" for them, but handicapped persons have insisted on being mainstreamed, that is, on being able to use the mainstream bus or train system.

Conventions and conferences are being mainstreamed.

At the 1976 convention of the American Association for the Advancement of Science (AAAS), another example of broad changes was evident. Even before the decision was made to hold the convention in the city of Boston, clearances were obtained to ensure that all handicapped scientists attending the convention would have access to all sessions and that hotels and other meeting places would have external and internal ramps to permit scientists in wheelchairs to move readily to meeting rooms, restaurants, restrooms, and hotel rooms. It also meant that the special symphony concert for convention registrants was held in a hall with appropriate ramps. Deaf scientists attending convention sessions were provided with interpreter services in the preferred communication mode. Blind scientists received advance transcripts of presentations that featured visual aids.

During the convention, 400 handicapped scientists met to help map strategies to permit *all* scientific meetings to be mainstreamed. They helped determine how special services could be provided, not just at set-aside stations but also in general admission areas. The AAAS has since published a guide for use by other associations in arranging barrier-free meetings (Redden, Fortunato-Schwandt, & Brown, 1976). Handicapped persons want full entry, opportunities, and participation in all mainstream activities.

Other examples of what is happening in communities include mutual-help groups. For example, many widows are turning to networks of widows for help in dealing with the problems of grief. Similarly, parents of handicapped children are helping one another in broad supportive networks. In such relationships, they find immediate understanding and support far different from what is available from a clinical psychologist or psychiatrist. Indeed, professionals such as these increasingly find themselves involved in creating and supporting the mutual-help networks. Thus many specialists are active participants in changing and developing community structures to serve persons with special needs. They engage in the indirect processes of "helping groups of helpers to help" rather than in direct service to a limited number of clients at very high cost. By taking on an indirect support role rather than a direct service role, the professionals "give away" some of their special insights and skills. So, too, do increasing numbers of specialists in the schools.

Clinical professionals are moving toward more indirect services.

One reason for innovations like walk-in clinics and mutual-help networks is the sheer impossibility of supplying specialized help to everyone who needs it on a one-to-one basis. There are simply too many people who need help and too few specialists. Nor are there enough adequately staffed special environments where people who need help can be served productively. It is doubtful that the nation could afford such individual services, even if the specialist situation could be resolved. But beyond these difficulties, it is clearly preferable that immediate and natural associates make accommodations to handicapped persons' special needs. That is vastly to be preferred, on qualitative grounds, to referral to segregated settings.

DIRECT VERSUS INDIRECT SERVICES

In considering changes, a useful distinction can be made between *direct* and *indirect* services and between *dyadic* and *triadic* processes. A teacher who works immediately with a child is providing *direct* service. It is also *dyadic* in that it involves only two parties—the teacher and the child (or children). If direct service were to be evaluated, it would focus on the child to determine whether the desired communication was effective. Most teaching is direct and dyadic.

"Helping the helpers to help"— indirect service— is an expanding new mode for many professions.

If a special education teacher works with and through a regular teacher to serve a child, three parties are involved; the enterprise is *triadic*, and the service of the special educator is *indirect*. Evaluation in this case would focus on both the regular teacher—did the teacher receive the message effectively?—and the child (or children). Today, many special education teachers spend all or part of their time in *indirect* service, that is, consulting with regular teachers to help solve instructional problems. Equally important, regular teachers often consult with one another, and often regular teachers provide consultation to special teachers and other specialists.

The Consultation Triad

Consultant[1] → Client → Target

Psychiatrists and psychologists who work with members of the clergy to improve the latter's ability to meet the mental health needs of parishioners provide an illustration of consultation in the community. That work is triadic and indirect. Educators who support the development of groups of parents of exceptional students, which then offer assistance to new parents of similar children, are contributing to the work of the groups in a triadic and indirect way. All teachers and related professionals require a great deal of indirect or supportive work from one another to make mainstreaming effective.

EFFECTIVE COMMUNICATION

Suppose that a very strong effort was being made in a school to provide adaptive programs for all students and to include as many handicapped students as possible in the mainstream. Assume that the school principal had anticipated that communication would need to be improved as part of that broad effort. A number of observations could be made in such a school.

---

[1] The consultant may be a special or regular educator, school psychologist, or other specialist. The target is usually one or more pupils, but sometimes it is a parent or another professional. Even then, though, the ultimate beneficiary of work undertaken by school personnel will almost always be a pupil.

1. Every teacher is expected to have problems as well as success; equally, every teacher is expected to seek early help when problems occur. It is regarded as a sign of strength for any teacher to call other teachers, counselors, psychologists, supervisors, and principals for help in solving instructional and management problems.

Principals can and should make it clear that teaching problems are expected to occur.

2. Arrangements have been made whereby every teacher can get help when needed. The principal has been careful to organize programs, staff functions, and procedures so that colleagues and specialists respond immediately to teachers' needs and requests for help.

3. Special arrangements are made to link teachers who are going through similar kinds of programmatic changes. Perhaps the sophomore-level social studies curriculum and texts have just been changed or a new system for reporting to parents of kindergarten pupils has been started. In such cases, teachers making the changes may be linked in ad hoc fashion for the first semester or year, to help each other over the rough spots. Every teacher has at least one nearby colleague working at the same grade level or with the same subject matter who provides consultation or just plain unhurried reflection on problems and plans when needed. These linkages can be prearranged or created and expanded spontaneously by teachers.

Teachers facing similar problems often can be mutually helpful.

4. Regular meetings of teachers (in small groups) are held to discuss instructional and management problems. The principal attends but avoids letting administrative concerns dominate the meetings; the agenda is limited to the teachers' concerns and issues.

5. The full staff of the school works together to plan the curriculum and assessment systems and to purchase and manage instructional materials. All staff members, consequently, know what the curriculum is, how pupil progress is assessed, and what resources are available. By handling these basic matters routinely, time is saved in communicating about particular problems and students.

It pays to be professionally deliberate about building trust with colleagues.

6. The school has an excellent system of records so that, for example, when a student moves from one level to the next, the new teachers are able to get a quick and accurate summary of each student and any special provisions that may be necessary.

7. The school philosophy and operating procedures are well understood by all staff members, students, and parents. This is achieved by hard, recurring work to create common understandings and expectations through meetings, publications, staff development work, and community contacts.

8. In general, there are mutual respect and trust among all parties in and associated with the school. They have developed out of honest, candid, and competent performance in instruction, management, and communication. In-service training sessions on communication have been held and were helpful.

Mutual respect and trust are required for effective communication.

A school that could be described in all these ways has a good chance of meeting its policy goals of adapting programs for all students. It is likely also to be a place where all staff members work hard and experience personal and professional satisfaction.

Most people need special help and stimulus to become adept in dealing with emotions and ideas simultaneously.

If we were to observe the same school from a more detailed perspective and look again at communication, but at the microlevel, we might note certain features among the teachers and others who are attempting to share ideas about a problem.

1. The teachers, staff members, and administrators trust one another, knowing that people can accept help only from those they trust. At times, they express their trust explicitly and thus reinforce their mutual expectations for good motives and shared commitments.

2. They acknowledge the effective or emotional aspects of the problems they discuss; they recognize the need to understand and deal with emotions as well as the content or substance of problems. They are professionally deliberate about helping to build and maintain good staff morale.

3. They listen actively to one another, showing a deep commitment to

TABLE 4.1 AN ACTIVE LISTENING SCALE: RATING YOUR RESPONSES WHILE LISTENING TO OTHERS

Level of Helpfulness	Response to Feelings (Emotions)	Response to Content (Ideas)
Additive (Responses at levels 4 and 5 are helpful.)	5. Goes well beyond the person's expressed feelings. Provides the person with a major new view of the emotions being experienced.	5. Goes well beyond the stated meaning. Provides new insight.
	4. Goes to slightly deeper feeling than that expressed. Helps person to understand his or her own feelings in more depth.	4. Goes slightly beyond meaning stated. Provides some new insight. Is more concise.
Interchangeable (Responses at level 3 are just acceptable.)	3. Results in an accurate understanding of feelings and/or emotions, expressed in your own words.	3. Results in an accurate understanding of the content —a restatement in your own words of what the person said.
Subtractive (Responses at levels 1 and 2 may be worse than none at all.)	2. Results in a slight distortion of the feelings expressed—a near miss.	2. Results in a slight distortion of meaning—just misses.
	1. Evidences no awareness of feelings, the wrong feelings, or a genuine putdown.	1. Is dead wrong—the listener hears the opposite of what was said; a complete miss or an active disinterest.

SOURCE: Adapted from N. A. Sprinthall (1982), *Counseling Skills for Classroom Teachers* (Minneapolis: University of Minnesota, National Support Systems Project).

gaining an understanding of each person's perspective. Active listening goes beyond passivity; it demands checking one's understanding of the other person's ideas and feelings by rephrasing them and asking for confirmation or clarification. It recognizes how limited each of us is by our own experience, life-style, and values. Every effort is made to avoid projecting one's own beliefs, attitudes, and stereotypes onto other persons. (See Table 4.1.)

4. They proceed as coequals, avoiding the intrusion of status differences and paternalism (substituting oneself for the other in decision making).

Status differences often subtract from effective consultation.

5. They try to be nonevaluative toward one another and to seek for understanding instead.

6. They maintain focus on the problem, the child, or whatever brings them together rather than let their personal needs intrude on the situation; thus the communication is strictly professional in character.

A barrier to effective teaching can be raised if any feature of good communication is missing or limited. The failure to listen carefully, the absence of trust, the ignoring of differences in perspective, the failure to recognize one's own emotional elements in the situation, and the like, individually or collectively, can cause difficulties that end up hurting pupils, teachers, and others concerned. The features of good communication should be studied, practiced, and improved in workshops and other forms of in-service education provided in school systems.

CONSULTING

As instructional situations become more complex, there is more need for sharing and mutual helpfulness among professionals and between parents and professionals. In special education, the increasing use of consultation is one means of such mutual helpfulness.

Historically, consultation was seen first as a function of the most senior professionals in a field. Those who knew the most and had the most experience offered advice to colleagues with less knowledge and experience. This is no longer a useful model for educators. It is recognized now that a given educator may have *different* knowledge and experience than another educator but not "more" or "less." As a result, almost any educator may serve as a consultant for another depending on the kind of assistance needed. The first formal uses of consultation were in the fields of mental health and management. By the 1950s, formal training was offered at Harvard University in the field of mental health, largely through the efforts of Gerald Caplan, a psychiatrist. Since then, it has spread rapidly and is now regarded as a distinct function for which specialized training can be helpful. In special education, consultation has received

Consultation was once thought of as a function of just the most senior professionals.

One can get training for consultation now.

growing attention because of its contributions to the mainstreaming movement. Some of the consultation principles developed for "mental health workers" can be adapted for use by educators, but they need to be interpreted with care when applied to the instructional situation.

Consulting relationships may at first seem somewhat unnatural in the sense that the emphasis is on creating a capacity within the consultee (or client) to solve his or her own problems rather than for the consultant to "take them away." The natural response when interacting with a person who has a problem is simply to say, "I will take care of it," and adopt the problem. In consulting, however, the opposite is the case; the consultant does not adopt the problem but works instead to enhance the client's capacity to solve it. In so doing, the consultant may teach, do research, interpret, advise, model, coax, add ideas, engage in therapy, "just listen," slow the pace, examine the organization, or do many other things to help—but always systematically.

Consultants avoid adopting the problems they address.

The use of consultants in most situations other than education is usually voluntary. Also, the consultants generally come from outside the system. However, the use of consultants in schools is often expected if not mandatory, and very often the consultants are insiders, peers within the school system. These conditions create the need for very clear understandings about the control of the circumstances under which consultation occurs. For example, teachers may face a school district requirement that consultation and regular class interventions be tried and systematically evaluated before a troublesome student is accepted for referral to special education. If that is so, the policy needs to be made very clear to all parties. Further, because of the conditions of employment by the school district, a consultant may not be free to break a consulting relationship when the implied contract with a client is abridged in some way. That special condition needs to be understood. Principles of effective consultation should be practiced as faithfully and fully as possible in the school situation, even when the relationship is less than completely voluntary and when both professional parties are insiders.

The same person may be consultant at some times and client at other times.

Some specialists are more likely than others to have training as consultants; this is often true for school social workers, school psychologists, and school counselors. Yet their training may have been aimed at resolving personal problems rather than at the pupil management and instructional procedures for which teachers more often seek help. Teachers and others are given very little preparation to function as clients or consultants, though that lack seems likely to be corrected in the near future. Consultation is a complex relationship between a consultant and a client, and both need to be prepared for this common endeavor.

The client has more power than the consultant in deciding the level at which consulting will be conducted.

Often a problem that becomes the subject for consultation can be dealt with at several levels. Consider the following case:

James, an assertive third-grade boy, seeks every opportunity to leave the classroom, and when he does, there is no telling where he will go. He usually goes on the run, upstairs or down, possibly to the janitor's room, sometimes bothering other pupils and classrooms on the way. Even in his classroom, James is a challenge to Ms. Larson, his teacher. Ms. Larson feels strained whenever she tries to get James to concentrate on his studies or to stop disturbing the several good friends he has among his classmates.

It happens that the class, in general, is quite disorderly. It's noisy. There's a great deal of nonproductive moving about. Only a few students work hard and regularly; others seem almost to be trying to escape from the class—not so obviously as James, but in a similar pattern. This classroom is not a happy place, and it's not productive.

The principal is aware that something is wrong but has chosen to look the other way. There are plenty of problems coming to her office, not only from Ms. Larson's class but from others as well, and she is feeling quite resigned and a bit depressed about the entire situation in her building.

The consultant must start at a level agreed to by the client.

A consultant called to Ms. Larson's room to help with James's problems could start at any one or more levels: Jimmy's immediate behavior, Ms. Larson's general management problems, or the lack of clear leadership by the principal and the resulting schoolwide problem of disorderly behavior. In general, it seems wise for a consultant to start at the broadest or most general level at which success may be expected. Sometimes it is necessary to start at a particular level to achieve credibility with the staff and to gain their permission to go on to other levels. Perhaps the critical guideline in decisions on level of approach, however, is finding out whom the problem really belongs to. If the teacher, Ms. Larson, is the person who has asked for help, she is the one who controls the level at which consulting will start—unless the contract or agreement governing employment gives more freedom to the consultant, the school principal, or someone else. As a rule, the consultant starts at the level the client is willing to have addressed.

Guidelines for Teachers When Using Consultants

1. The teacher is in charge of the problem and the pupil's education or the class procedures that are under consideration.
2. The teacher should be sure to reach early agreement with the consultant on the nature of the problem and on how plans for solution will be made. An oral or written contract on goals, methods, and responsibilities should be agreed on early in the relationship.
3. It should be made clear that the teacher is the client and that all communication flows to the teacher. The consultant is there to help structure the teacher's work, not somebody else's. This relationship does not preclude some direct assessment of children and observations by the consultant, if they are agreed on as part of the contract.
4. Status problems should be avoided. Consultants and clients are coequals.

The regular teacher is in charge.

Consulting relationship must be professional.

5. The teacher should avoid interjecting personal problems. The content of the relationship should center on the student and/or the instructional situation.
6. The teacher usually should seek alternative suggestions from the consultant rather than a single or set plan that might not work.
7. Teachers should try to use each consultation as a learning experience to increase effective communication and listening, build trust, and maximize instructional effectiveness.
8. Each consultation experience should be evaluated objectively, and the teacher should share her or his conclusions with the consultant.

Stages of Consultation

Above all else, teachers who call for consultation should understand that they are entering a process, one that usually follows a reasonably predictable course. Persons who work as consultants are likely to have been prepared in some detail on how to proceed through the various stages of consultation. It seems reasonable that clients—teachers, usually, in the present context—should also understand the process and be prepared to function productively in their role in this complex relationship.

Some questions about values and assumptions should be made clear even before consulting begins.

The number of stages in consultation and their designation vary among scholars in the field, but many similarities are found across most descriptions of the process. Here we outline briefly a five-stage delineation of the process adapted from a schema presented by Brokes (1975). The stages are preentry, entry and contract, problem definition, intervention, and evaluation-termination.

Preentry. Before agreements are made formally to enter a consulting relationship, it is important that all participants be clear about assumptions and values, which are part of the background for the anticipated process. Most important, all parties must agree that the primary objective to be attained is the *best possible instruction for the pupil*, but there can be problems about differences in perspectives and values. For example, the consultant (assume that it is a supervisor, a special education teacher, or a school psychologist) may be strongly oriented toward maintaining exceptional children in mainstream classes and may hold other values (e.g., total objection to school exclusions) that should be understood at the outset by each potential participant in consultation. The orientation may have been required when the role of consultant was first established by the school principal, and the requirement must be articulated. Perhaps the principal feels she or he is a full party in any consulting done in the building, meaning that no material may be withheld on the basis of the confidentiality of the information or privileged relationships among other parties. The school principal will often be in good position to help establish the preentry framework so that consulting relationships are not started and discontinued because of misunderstandings about problem ownership, mainstreaming policies, confidentiality of information, student suspension procedures, or like matters. The consultant is advised to make sure that preentry understandings are well in place before beginning to work with a colleague in a school.

Entry and Contract. Scholars who study consulting practices have come to use the term *contract* to signify the professional understandings rendered between the giver and the receiver of consultation. Really effective consultation almost always starts with explicit agreements that spell out the focus, the procedures, the time schedule projected, and the expected results of the consultation. If written, as we consider desirable, the contract need not be more than a page in length, but frequent reference to it by both parties helps to keep the consultation on track, thus avoiding disappointments and wasted time. A "contract" can be any jointly prepared consultation plan. At the entry stage, the initial contacts are made between consultant and client to get a general description of the problem and its history, a sense of the client's motivation and goals, and awareness of the available resources to solve the problem. The "client" is anyone receiving consultation, such as a teacher receiving consultation from a psychologist. Use of the term does not imply legalistic or income-related relationships like those of the lawyer or broker in the business world. As entry proceeds, the parties try to agree on how the problem will be defined, what goals will be pursued, the level at which the problem will be addressed, who will carry out necessary actions, and the schedule. Details of responsibilities for next steps should be made especially clear at each meeting.

A contract of some kind between consultant and client should be agreed on early in the consulting process.

The contract has critical importance —it is not to be violated.

Problem Definition. The "problem," for educators, is most often a situation or a set of conditions that interrupts or reduces the effectiveness of instruction. It is most productive to state the problem as something the teacher wants to alter or improve. At this stage, data are gathered to specify the problem. A problem concerning how the teacher might improve a given child's behavior, for example, might require the consultant to make informal classroom observations, arrange an interview with parents, give psychological examinations, review school records, and carry on detailed conversations with the client. After the consultant and client agree on the nature of a problem, they must agree on the specific goals they will pursue and the communication pattern they will use in their collaboration. If it is determined that the child whose education is the target of their efforts is or may be legally "exceptional" as defined in that state, the process of problem definition must meet the legal requirements, including the involvement of parents with regard to special assessments and planning. The problem definition then eventually becomes a part of the IEP.

Problems are often unclear at first. Development of a common, mutually clear understanding of the problem is essential.

Intervention. Here the consultant and client work together on the intervention—the enactment of their agreed-on plan for problem solution. The "solution" of a problem in education (as in medicine, family life, business, or the church) does not necessarily mean that the problem is eliminated. Many times we may have to settle for improving the situation somewhat or keeping it from growing worse. The consultant may have helped outline several alternative approaches to intervention, but now a particular plan must be selected and tried. It might involve advising, teaching (of the teacher), or modeling activities (of new procedures for teaching a child or managing a class) by the consultant or other staff members. Always the emphasis is on the client's maintaining responsibility for the problem. The plan is then put into operation, and the consulting relationship continues.

Monitoring attempted solutions to the problem is a part of consultation.

Evaluation and Termination. As intervention proceeds, the consultant and client monitor and evaluate each aspect of the agreed-on procedures. Modifications are made when they are necessary. Attention is always on the goals that were set and on how well they are achieved.

Assuming that progress is made, a time arrives to terminate the consulting relationship. At this stage, all parties should review and evaluate what has been accomplished and learned. If the relationships and conversations have been trusting and candid, termination can promote professional growth for all parties. A teacher, for example, may be able to tell the consultant what was helpful and what was not helpful. Equally, the consultant may be able to discuss concerns about the teacher's limitations, special skills, and resourcefulness. Thus both parties may use the experience to increase personal awareness, professional skills, and future ability to use a consulting relationship productively. Though not essential, a brief written report of the consultation processes and outcomes is often useful. It may be valuable to have the report entered into a child's school records for later use, if all parties agree.

Consulting relationships can be growth experiences if the parties are candid and professional.

Obviously, not all professionals have equal competency in consulting, and that includes teachers. Whatever one's work, one must select appropriate consultants carefully and analytically.

Characteristics of an Effective Consultant

Choosing a competent consultant is a key consideration. Not all consultants cover the same problem "territories."

1. Has state-of-the-art knowledge in the problem areas in which consultation is needed, has a reputation for ability to diagnose and outline alternatives for treatment (instruction), and has built up experience and uses it well.

2. Makes sure all potential clients know in general how the process of consultation works. Offers services in a way that minimizes anxiety and does not stigmatize the recipient.

3. Is honest, spontaneous, courageous, and open to all facts, and makes no exclusions.
4. Is genuinely positive and authentic in expectations of constructive motives about people's competencies and is able to build mutually trusting relationships.
5. Is sensitive and responsive to others and has good knowledge of social dynamics.
6. Is interested in learning with others and communicating about processes of learning through consultation experiences.
7. Has a knack for being concrete and specific about approaches to problems yet is also able to structure problems in broader, theoretical terms.
8. Lacks the need for "professional distance"; prefers coequal relationships even though he or she is much more experienced than most others in the area of consultation. Finds rewards in successful performances by other persons, particularly by consultees or clients. Is noncompetitive and mature. Other people notice the maturity and feel comfortable with the consultant.
9. Has good research abilities; is able to access resources efficiently.

To find a topflight consultant, look for as many of these traits as possible. *To become* a top-flight consultant, practice as many of these qualities as possible.

TEAMING

Educators and parents very often work as teams to plan and carry out programs for exceptional children. In assessment, it is common to have three or four professional staff members—perhaps a special education teacher, psychologist, speech and language therapist, and social worker— working together and with parents to make sure that both the learning situation and the child's developmental levels in various dimensions have been specified. A group of similar size and composition, possibly including even a few additions (e.g., a parent advocate and the school principal), may meet to plan and record an individualized educational plan (IEP). Teamwork of a high order is required in performing these functions and in carrying through the programs that have been designed.

Teaming must be efficient, not only to save on costs but also to keep staff morale high and to make teamwork a genuine service for children. Most important, the content of the meetings must be relevant to the problem being considered. Unfortunately, teaming is frequently not the efficient process it ought to be. The person chairing the meeting and everyone taking part should be careful to stick to the task, not waste time, and try to assure that practical guidance results.

Teacher Assistance Teams

Often the best helpers are nearby colleagues.

Sometimes the problems of elementary and secondary teachers in serving exceptional children can be solved by creating a support system consisting entirely of the other teachers already in the school. Chalfant, Pysh, and Moultrie (1979) have described a system for such supports, which they call the teacher assistance team (TAT). The purposes of the TAT are as follows:

1. To help teachers conceptualize and understand the nature of individual children's learning and behavior problems
2. To provide immediate and relevant support to teachers who are trying to individualize instruction
3. To improve follow-up and evaluation of mainstream efforts
4. To increase attention to referrals at the building level, reduce the number of inappropriate referrals, and use special education personnel more effectively.

The pressure is on to limit referrals to special education; prereferral solutions can often be found.

Teacher assistance teams are formed from the local school faculty. They may be elected by peers, selected by the school principal, or both. TATs use processes that specialized consultants also use: classroom observation, defining problems, advising on curriculum and teaching adaptations, and, perhaps, modeling effective teaching procedures. TAT operations illustrate what sometimes has been called "coordinate-status" helping systems; that is, the persons offering help come from situations much like those in which they offer assistance. Thus no problems of difference in status need be negotiated, and the helpers usually have immediate credibility. In one report of the use of TAT, only 37 percent of the students displaying difficulties were subsequently referred for special education (Chalfant et al., 1979).

RESOURCE ROOMS AND TEACHERS

Resource rooms or centers for exceptional pupils were in some use as early as the 1920s. They proliferated rapidly in the 1950–1975 period. Here is a description of one early resource unit:

Resource teachers may work alone or in teams.

The Resource Center consists of one double-sized classroom that contains private instruction booths, a variety of equipment, and an array of educational materials....Two certified special education teachers...comprise the staff....The Resource Center [serves] 30 to 40 children. The staff has the basic responsibility of maintaining each child as a participating member of his regular class. Thus, a wide range of services and a great deal of communication with regular education personnel are required. (Johnson & Grismer, 1972, p. 96)

Such centers may serve children from one or several of the traditional categories. The two teachers who staffed the resource center described possessed a wide range of competencies and served children across several categories. They worked directly with some children but served more of them indirectly through consultation with regular teachers. These resource teachers were leading figures in the school's diagnostic functions, parent conferences and education, and development of instructional materials and teaching methods. (Resource rooms conducted by a single special education teacher may be more common, but forming teams that work out of a single center is not uncommon in larger schools.)

Typically, part of resource teachers' time is spent on direct services to selected children, either by pulling them out of regular classrooms or by going into the classrooms to serve them there; the remainder of their time is spent in indirect work. There is some evidence suggesting that resource teachers may do less indirect (consulting) work than some observers have assumed. In a study reported in 1980, Evans examined the functions of 48 resource teachers and found that they spent 5 percent or less of their time in consultation, that is, in triadic or indirect work. Pressures to increase prereferral activities, initiate more adaptations in regular classrooms, and limit special education placements are likely to increase the use of consultation in the near future.

Some resource teachers use only indirect methods.

In Vermont, a system in which special education teachers offer *only* indirect services has operated successfully for nearly two decades. The system was developed jointly by the Vermont State Department of Education, the University of Vermont, and the 26 school districts in the state. Special education teachers are prepared professionally to work as "consulting teachers." They are employed in the local districts, but the teachers make use also of the state department of education and the university. When difficult individual school situations are referred to the consulting teachers, the consultants and the local school personnel study the situations collaboratively. The consulting teachers assist in designing and later evaluating improved approaches to instruction for the students. This model gives extraordinary emphasis to triadic or indirect service (Fox et al., 1975).

School psychologists, special vision teachers, audiologists, and many other specialists also work, at least part of the time, indirectly in the schools (Draden, Cosey, & Bonstram, 1985). School psychology has an especially rich professional literature on consultation service, which is useful to persons in other professions as well (Bergan, 1977; Meyers, Martin, & Hyman, 1977).

PARENTS AND TEACHERS WORKING TOGETHER

Most parents of exceptional students are eager to work with teachers.

Parents want their children to be well educated. In the past, parents of exceptional children often had to put first priority on simply getting their children into school and into the hands of teachers. Now more attention goes to the provision of quality instruction. Most parents have enormous faith that teachers can be relied on to bring out the best in their children. And most parents are eager to work cooperatively with teachers, although they usually do not know how. They look to teachers and to other parents to tell them.

Even today, few teachers receive preparation in relating to parents. Also, until recently, most parents knew little more about elementary and secondary schools than what they remembered from the years when they were pupils themselves. However, parents have become informed about schools, and their role has become more active. Mothers and fathers often participate directly in the daily activities of the schools in the following ways:

More parents are in the schools these days and for a wider variety of purposes.

First, parents of exceptional children participate in the screening, assessment, and design of individualized education programs for their children. Second, schools employ more parents, particularly as paraprofessional aides and assistants. Thus many parents are brought into daily contact with teachers and pupils. Third, schools are the focus of the volunteer activities of many community organizations. Parents are often members of groups such as the National Association for Retarded Citizens and the United Cerebral Palsy Association. Finally, parents can help guide school programs conducted for their children. For example, parents of children in Chapter I programs (federally supported programs for low-achieving, economically disadvantaged children) and in early education programs frequently serve on local advisory committees.

Nowadays, teachers, too, take several different professional roles in relation to parents.

1. Teachers supervise parents who are employed or volunteer to assist teachers.
2. Teachers evaluate the educational progress of pupils and report and interpret the evaluations to parents.
3. Teachers work with parents in planning and making decisions on school policies and practices.
4. Teachers consult with parents about school and home situations that seem to affect their children, both positively and negatively.
5. Teachers sometimes act for the child's parent when it is necessary and proper. The teacher role under the doctrine of *in loco parentis* has been eroding in recent years in a legal sense but remains strong in less formal ways.

6. Teachers explain the work of the schools to parents and other citizens in the school district.
7. Teachers take part with parents in organizing and conducting general community improvement and maintenance activities.

Each role carries strains for teachers, even after the best of professional preparation. Many functions are relatively new. Moreover, not all teachers believe that all the functions are appropriate, and they may feel that teachers should not accept responsibility for them. While most parents have strong faith in teachers, some parents are deeply distrustful of teachers, schools, and school policies because their children have not been accepted or have not learned effectively. In such cases, interactions with parents can be difficult.

Teacher-parent communication is often difficult for both.

Some parents seek out and receive the help of psychologists, physicians, social workers, and other parents in working out difficulties with children, especially in the early years. For example, severely and profoundly impaired (SPI) children and those with clearly defined conditions such as blindness or deafness are usually identified while infants. The parents of these children often face critical problems in securing adequate social, medical, and educational information about the children's conditions and ways to help them. It is common to need help in securing developmental assistance for the children; managing health and home crises; helping siblings accommodate the handicapped children; interpreting the children's problems to relatives, friends, and neighbors; and arranging respite care so that the family can have occasional periods of time off.

Parents of obviously exceptional children usually receive assistance at preschool levels.

Most exceptional children—those with mild adjustment, language, learning, and behavior problems—are identified only after they start school. Teachers then become very significant figures in working out interpretations and plans with parents. Because the unusual needs of the children were unnoticed or only suspected prior to school entry, it is often a shock to parents to face the reality that special adaptations are needed to deal with a learning problem, a school adjustment problem, or giftedness.

Some theorists argue that bringing parents and teachers together to focus on a child's development may not always be wise (Litwak & Meyer, 1967). In some cases, they consider it wise to seek closer ties but, in others, to "let well enough alone." Litwak and Meyer warn that because schools are bureaucratic in structure and function (they are meritocratic, rule-governed, relatively impersonal, managed by specialists, etc.), they may cause problems if they intrude too far into the privacy of family life. School staff members who intrude on a family situation out of concern for a child may not be all that different from an employer who enters the family because of concern for the father or mother. Perhaps it would be better to seek "balance" in teacher-parent relations, increasing interactions only in

Close relationships between teachers and parents may not always be desirable.

circumstances that call specifically for collaboration and for limited periods of time. Generally, special educators tend to prefer strong interactions with parents, and perhaps they are frequently justified, but some caution is in order.

What Parents Hope For from Teachers

When parents want help, they make their aspirations for parent-teacher collaboration known in a variety of ways, including group policy expressions and individual statements of concern. The advice from one parent of a handicapped daughter provides important leads (Gorham, 1975). Although she focused on handicapped children, many of her comments and accompanying suggestions apply equally to gifted children; indeed, they apply to all children and parents when attempting to solve challenging developmental problems.

Interspersed with Gorham's comments, quoted throughout this discussion, are suggestions for good practices with parents. The suggestions are particularly applicable to teachers who have the central responsibility for planning instruction for exceptional pupils (Kappelman & Ackerman, 1977; Kroth & Scholl, 1978; Seligman, 1979; Stewart, 1978; Turnbull & Turnbull, 1978).

Assessment of Needs. Gorham's first suggestion relates to assessing a child's educational and related needs:

Parents should not be routinely excluded, even from testing situations.

> Let the parent be involved every step of the way. The dialogue established [between teacher and parent] may be the most important thing you accomplish. If the parent's presence is an obstacle to testing because the child will not "cooperate" in his presence, the setup should include a complete review of the testing procedure with the parent. (p. 523)

The teacher is usually in the best position to communicate credibly with parents.

Note the assumption that the teacher has something to say about whether the parent is involved and about the testing procedure and where and how testing is done. The teacher is often the best person to mediate and arrange assessment for three reasons. First, parents want to have direct and final recourse to the teacher, and they see the teacher as having central control over what happens to their child in school. Second, the teacher usually knows the child, parents, and other professionals in the situation best and is thus in the logical position to assert generalship. Third, the teacher is the person who lives with and uses the results of consultations and assessments and who is ultimately accountable for the child's educational program. For all these reasons, it is correct for parents to see the teacher as playing a key role in all matters relating to a child's schooling.

A Realistic Management Plan

> Make a realistic management plan part of the assessment outcome. Give the parents suggestions for how to cope with [and correct or minimize] the problem on a day to day basis, considering the needs of the child, the capacities of the family, and the resources of the community. Let the parents know that you will suggest modifications in any aspect of the management plan that does not work. (p. 523)

Three things are basic to an effective management plan. First, it must be workable in the real world of home and school. It must deal with the conditions uncovered in the assessment, and it must be feasible—not an unattainable ideal. Second, parents must be involved in making the plan, executing it, determining whether it is working, and helping with needed modifications. Third, communication about the plan must be two-way, and the communication must be of top quality.

Communication is a two-way street.

Knowledge of Community Resources

> Inform yourself about community resources. Give the parents advice on how to go about getting what they need. Steer them to the local parents' organization. (p. 523)

Today almost every exceptional condition is represented by an association in which parents, professional persons, and other public-spirited citizens participate. Some organizations include several exceptionalities (e.g., speech, hearing, and physically disabling conditions). Coalitions among parent organizations are developing in many states, and interstate coalitions are coordinating efforts at the national level. The Federation for Children with Special Needs and the National Coalition of Advocates for Students (NCAS), both with headquarters in Boston, for example, are two organizations that have been especially effective in bringing advocacy groups together on a broad basis.

Sometimes more than one organization deals with the same condition. It is not a simple matter for parents or teachers to determine which group may be most useful for them. Guidance is usually available from supervisors of special education programs or other staff members, such as school social workers or phychologists.

Direct familiarity with local groups is best for both teachers and parents. For example, a teacher looking for resources for a gifted child called an organization that conducted Saturday morning painting lessons to which elementary school pupils showing exceptional talent were recommended. The contact led to a similar program for budding writers. By such actions, teachers can multiply their own resources.

Teachers with direct knowledge of community resources are particularly helpful to parents.

The Parent as a Member of the Team

> Make the parent a team member in the actual diagnosis, treatment, or educational procedures. It will give you a chance to observe how the parent and child interact. (p. 523)

Watching others work with a child can yield important insights.

The more the parents are made partners with the teacher and other professionals, the smoother and more consistent the delivery of instruction to the child can be. Parent participation supplies feedback and new ideas for the teacher. In turn, the parents, who have opportunities to learn how the teacher works, may adapt what they observe to their interactions with their children at home.

Veteran teachers sometimes say they were taught to discourage parents from helping their children with schoolwork at home for fear that mothers and fathers might push too hard, become impatient, or use teaching methods that conflicted with the school approach. Today, however, there is good reason to believe that most parents, with hints from teachers, can be effective in the encouragement and guidance of their children. Careful checking of homework by teachers adds much to its value.

Parents who ask how they can help prepare a young child for school can be told by teachers about positive steps to take. The following principles should guide parental efforts:

Talk to the child. Give direct attention through eye-to-eye contact and actual touch so that the child is fully aware of being the target of the conversation.

Encourage responses from the child, especially those that indicate growth in understanding new words and ideas. Help to expand the child's vocabulary.

Allow the child as much freedom of movement inside and outside the house as safety and maturity will allow. Encourage exploration.

Respond when the child seeks attention or help, even if it is sometimes inconvenient. Encourage the child to initiate interaction, and allow the child to take the lead from time to time.

Add meaning to the child's talk and experiences by elaborating, explaining, and connecting ideas.

Homework is a good idea—when carefully planned and checked.

Parents ought also to be encouraged to try teaching their school-age children at home. There is increasing evidence that a child's educational progress is accelerated when teachers and parents work in close partnership. Homework in its early form consisted of practice, study, and writing assignments. Parental supervision was limited to making sure that the child spent time on the assignment. Now it is more than that. It is individualized, and it calls for active parental involvement as well as supervision. It calls for increased parental monitoring of their own behavior, too, to increase their contribution to the child's educational stability, improved concentration, or acceptable social behavior.

If mothers and fathers can relax and work with their children on interesting tasks for sensible periods of time, they can be very effective in complementing the teachers's efforts. When parents show they would like to try, it is good to set up some homework with which they can help. Keep in mind that short time periods, specific directions, simple and readily available materials, and interesting tasks are conducive to success.

Clear, Understandable Reports

> Write your reports in clear and undestandable language. Professional terminology is a useful shortcut for your own notes, and you can always use it in communication with others of your discipline. But in situations involving the parents it becomes an obstacle to understanding. (p. 523)

Avoid professional jargon in all reports and conferences.

Parental Access to Reports. Gorham recommended that teachers let parents know that they are welcome to see and have copies of the work their child does, the teacher's written comments on the work, and any reports prepared or received about the child. The teacher should tell the diagnostician, counselor, school psychologist, and anyone else who makes reports on the child that he or she expects to receive and use them in a spirit of helpful openness. There are occasions, perhaps, when this point of view presents difficulties. These have to be worked out with the other professionals involved. Contemporary codes of confidentiality, laws, and court decisions, however, are on the side of the open position.

Take the initiative in giving school reports to parents.

Select reports that should be part of a family's records, in your judgment.

> Give copies of the reports to parents. They will need them to digest and understand the information in them, to share the information with other people close to the child, and to avoid the weeks or months of record gathering which every application to a new program in the future will otherwise entail. (p. 523)

With families becoming more and more mobile, school records are very important, especially for exceptional children who may move from one to another area of the country's "nonsystem" of special education (Birch & Johnstone, 1975).

Careful Explanations of a "Diagnosis" or "Assessment"

> Be sure the parent understands that there is no such thing as a one shot, final, and unchanging diagnosis. Make sure he understands that whatever label you give this child (if a label must be given) is merely a device for

The "diagnosis" is never final.

communicating and...may have all kinds of repercussions, many of them undesirable. Make sure he understands that it says very little about the child at present and even less about the child of the future. Caution him about using that label to "explain" his child's condition to other people. (pp. 523–524)

Parents are quick to understand the reasons for repeated careful re-assessments if procedures and purposes are carefully explained. In the same way, if a handicap label must be applied to a child, its use is more readily accepted by parents if the accompanying reasons are expressed in plain and educationally meaningful language.

Child Rearing: A Problem-solving Process

Not everything about exceptional children is atypical.

Help the parent to think of life with this child in the same terms as life with his other children. It is an on-going, problem-solving process. Assure him that he is capable of that problem solving and that you will be there to help him with it. (p. 524)

I am thoroughly convinced, on the basis of the many surveys we have conducted on the subject, that the very best way to increase the productivity of the schools is to establish a close working relationship with parents of schoolchildren....

Parents tell us that they would like to attend seminars, to be held at regular intervals during the school year, which would give them the opportunity to discuss with other parents such matters as discipline, how to motivate students, how to establish good work and study habits, how to deal with alcohol and drugs, and many other matters....

To hold these sessions in school buildings and during evening hours would add little to school costs while adding greatly to student achievement.

George Gallup, in a speech delivered at the University of Akron, October 1980

Child rearing is a joyous process for most parents. Yet it also contains problems—even burdens—whether the children are exceptional or not. Parents range widely in their ability and resources to cope with these problems. Teachers, of course, cannot usurp parental functions. They can, however, provide judicious words of encouragement or warning, depending on the situation, if they do not intrude. Teachers can also bring different parents together to learn and acquire strength from each other. Moreover, they can call attention to parent education programs or other community resources that may address specific concerns that parents have expressed. Sometimes school psychologists or other staff members conduct parent-training programs directly in the schools, but often such activities are held in health centers or community agencies of other kinds. It is advisable for teachers to assist in guiding such parent training to ensure that the training content is realistic and up to date.

Understanding the Child's Assets

> Be sure that the parent understands his child's abilities and assets as well as his disabilities and deficiencies. (p. 524)

Attend to the child's strengths as well as problems.

The way the teacher behaves with the child is perhaps the most important and effective way to "tell" parents about their child. This is also true of the way other significant adults and schoolmates act. When teachers openly recognize and encourage the use of exceptional children's assets, pupils follow their lead.

In one school, for example, a boy with complex multiple disabilities had very good manners that earned praise from the teacher. He was nominated by the pupils in his mainstream homeroom to serve on a school-wide committee on student behavior standards. In another case in a junior high school, teachers encouraged a trio of deaf girls to enter a talent show. They won first prize for the beauty and grace of their signs and gestures in "singing" a popular song. These are examples of how teachers can help to create opportunities. Children and their parents can then seize and capitalize on them.

Dealing with Service Insufficiencies

> Warn the parent about service insufficiencies. Equip him with advice on how to make his way through the system of "helping" services. Warn him that they are not always helpful. Tell him his child has a *right* to services. Tell him to insist on being a part of all decisions about his child. (p. 524)

Be candid with parents about limitations in services.

Few complete and comprehensive "systems" of special education and related services can be found anywhere. Nor are there comprehensive "systems" of social welfare, health care, recreation, public transportation, or other essential community operations that accommodate readily to exceptional persons and their families. In one city, a young man in a wheelchair could not enter the public library building because of steep steps and doors that were too narrow. In the same library, a 10-year-old mentally gifted girl was emphatically denied admission to or borrowing privileges from any but the children's collection, so she, too, was barred from any real use of the library just as effectively. In many places, three great enemies, ignorance, tradition, and prejudice, stand in the way of education for exceptional pupils.

A common lack in many communities is service for parents themselves.

Parents are often quite willing to serve as the shock troops in assaults on community and regional service failings, whether in the schools or in other parts of the public sector. Linked together in organizations or on their own, parents are listened to by legislators, board members, and administrators. Teachers can often help by alerting parents and organizations to educational and related needs.

One frequent gap in community services is in programs for parents themselves. Some parents need opportunities for training or counseling for themselves or for their entire families. Specialized parent and family counseling services are an urgent need and should be considered in broad community planning.

Positive Thinking

Overemphasis on negatives helps no one.

> Some people with whom [the parent] talks (teachers, doctors, professionals of any kind, or other parents) may emphasize the negative. Help train the parent not only to think positively but to teach the other people in his child's life to do so. (p. 524)

Reality ought not to be hidden. However, negative facts can be confronted realistically by parents while they build toward a constructive, positive outcome.

Parents: An Integral Part of the Process

The foregoing suggestions do not apply to all parents or all situations. However, each can be adapted to particular situations. There may be some instances in which it is not wise or possible to establish meaningful interactions with parents. Nonetheless, communicating with and guiding parents is now an integral part of the teacher's responsibility. Other school staff members (counselors, social workers, principals, psychologists, and supervisors) certainly share some of the responsibility, but in the final analysis it is the teacher-parent interaction that is critical.

Conferences with parents about problems tend to be deeply emotional experiences.

Informal Parent-Teacher Conferences. The meeting of parents with their child's teacher often has profound significance for each, especially when the child's educational progress is problematic. The parents are likely to be deeply emotional about any problem they perceive; they may feel guilt, hostility, and inadequacy, and it may take time for them to reach a good working relationship with the teacher. Equally, the teacher may be apprehensive about a meeting with parents. Consider the following principles for teachers and other key school figures when planning conferences with parents of exceptional children. (They can be used as an outline for professional faculty meetings or in-service training meetings as well.)

1. In a two-parent family, *meet with both for all conferences* if possible. Teachers and other professionals who are experienced in conferring with parents almost uniformly warn against the assumption that talking with one parent results in good communication with the second parent.

Don't assume that an absent parent will get a good secondhand report.

Conferring with but one parent when there are two fails to consider the information that the absent parent could provide. It fails to include one of the significant parties in the planning and commitments. Finally, it risks creating or enlarging differences between parents in perceptions of the child and of their particular roles in helping processes. When both parents are involved, they can be assisted in understanding how important their mutual support to each other and to the child may be in creating a healthy environment for growth.

2. *Assume good intentions by the parents.* Even when it appears to teachers that the care and attention to a child at home are minimal or that there have been specific neglects, it is *always* appropriate to assume, when conferring with parents about school problems and plans, that they intend to be helpful and want good things for their children. Similarly, teachers deserve to be regarded as advocates for all children. There is no chance for such positive regard and trust unless it is mutual.

Parents do intend good things for their children.

3. *Take time to listen to the parents.* In conferences, professionals too often assume that they should have the most to say and should set the agenda. Too little time, usually, is left for listening to the parents. It is amazing what teachers *do not* know about children they see only in school. It is genuinely important to listen, and then listen some more, to parents. They know a great deal about their children. Their information grows out of the special sensitivities of home and family and out of the unpredictable aspects of the child's life instead of the regularities of school; it is extremely important information.

4. *Consider all reasonable program alternatives with the parents.* In the process of assessing children and school situations, professionals some-times make tentative plans and decisions and then, essentially, ask only for confirmation by the parents. For example, it may be decided that a child should go to a resource room for a period each day for help in reading, that a child will receive extra help in speech, or that a child is not succeeding in the local school and should be transferred to the behavioral learning center downtown. Professionals then expect the parent conference to come to early focus on the preferred new arrangement.

It is no mere courtesy to back up a bit and include the parents in the discussion of all options for their child. Indeed, the observations of the parents and their views of the options are essential elements in planning. They should be given opportunities to learn about the options through visits, readings, and further conversations with professionals and/or other parents). The parents' preference in school planning should be the one chosen if it is within reason. Even if that preference is not optimal in the

Try to arrive at a plan that is acceptable to parents.

eyes of the professionals, it is often a good place to begin a period of continuing study and planning.

5. *Expect criticism.* When children are not learning and developing well in programs, and when those programs are not well understood, parents can be expected to be apprehensive about their children or feel frustrated by the schools the children attend. Sometimes parents are more aware of the child's special needs and in more detail than current teachers of the child, and they may be tired of and disappointed by the school's short-term outlook. Because teachers represent schools, they sometimes become targets for the aggressions of frustrated parents who sense that teachers are uninformed about their children, even though the school's policies, not the teacher, may be at fault.

Teachers may expect to be criticized at times.

Sometimes this works in reverse. Teachers may allow their own general disappointments in parents in the community to be expressed in aggression toward particular parents. It helps to anticipate the likelihood that as a teacher, one will become the object of hostility and criticism. Usually, it need not be interpreted as a direct, personal attack. The negatives will often erode and a good relationship will grow if a broad perspective is maintained and responses are made only to the realities and constructive aspects of the situation.

6. *Do not expect too much from a single conference.* Because parent-teacher discussions are often deeply emotional experiences, it is unrealistic to expect a great deal of progress in any one session. Facing up to the school's failure to adapt to a child's special needs or talking through the parents' anxieties and concerns about their child's abilities and potentials can be a disabling experience for teachers and parents alike, one that is not always conducive to good listening or rational decision making on anyone's part. When situations become tense or difficult, it is often wise to take a break and resume the discussions after a few minutes or even to schedule a future conference. At the outset of any succeeding conference, it is good to ask the parents and other participants to summarize what was discussed and agreed on at earlier sessions. Memories of complicated or tension-filled conferences are often cloudy; thus careful note taking, summaries, and reviews are important.

7. Understand that *parents will not always be interested in working closely with you* when you are their child's teacher or school principal. Sometimes they need a break and will want you to take over as a professional and do your best, giving them a bit of respite. Sometimes they must give priority to other problems or needs. It may even be a good sign of the confidence parents have in their teachers if the parents feel they can take a bit of time off!

Sometimes parents want teachers to go ahead without them.

The IEP Conference. In addition to informal meetings between teachers and parents, formal conferences may be required to summarize the results of special assessments and to prepare individualized education programs

(IEPs). In each case, the situation calls for a meeting of (1) the teacher or teachers (regular and special) who have responsibility for instructing the child, (2) one or preferably both of the child's parents, and (3) a professional representative of the school other than one of the child's teachers. Usually this is the school principal, another administrator, or a supervisor. The child, too, should be encouraged to take part in the meeting if it appears that he or she can participate meaningfully. The school psychologist or social worker is frequently an additional member of the IEP conference.

Several guidelines are important in planning and conducting the IEP conference. Some are quite similar to guidelines already mentioned, but these are particularly significant in the IEP conference because attention to them will help ensure that everyone's rights and privileges are acknowledged.

1. Keep the proceedings simple. Avoid jargon. Emphasize curricular decisions.

2. Clarify and record the purposes of the conference. Set an agenda and hold strictly to it. Build the agenda around a short series of questions, such as these:

    a. Does the student qualify legally for special education or related services?

    b. What special instruction and related services should be provided, for what purposes (goals and objectives), by whom, where, when, and for how long?

    c. How will progress be monitored, and when will the conferees meet again to review progress and make new plans?

IEP conferences need the discipline provided by a clear agenda.

3. Make the arrangements as comfortable as possible for all participants. Find a convenient meeting place and time; be prompt; proceed informally; keep the number of professionals to a minimum.

4. Encourage the parents and the child's teacher, the persons closest to the child, to be the most active participants.

5. Try very hard to agree on plans for special education and related services that the parents can accept, at least for a trial period.

6. Give first consideration to accommodating the child in the regular class. Consider pullout programs (assignment to special settings outside the regular classroom, part-time or full-time) only for compelling reasons.

Try to provide special instruction in the regular class.

7. Specify how parents can be helpful immediately and over the long term.

8. Clarify the parents' rights to appeal decisions about the plan, to secure additional studies of the child, and to see school records.

Parents of Nonexceptional Children. Changes occurring in education for exceptional students call for broad understanding by *all* parents. Perhaps the least involved and most underinformed parents are those whose

All parents need to be informed about modern special education programs.

children have no "recognized" exceptionalities. Increasingly, such parents hear reports of special programs for gifted and talented students and of handicapped students taking up time in regular classrooms. If they attend PTA meetings, they hear the parents of exceptional children express concerns.

Teachers and other school staff members must interpret the changes occurring in special education to parents of nonexceptional children. Most important of all, perhaps, is the need to supply factual information on what is happening and why. All parents need help in understanding human differences. They need to know how school programs can be developed that are helpful to *all* children—with no exceptions.

Grading for Exceptional Students

Every student's grades should reflect current progress.

One of the challenging problems associated with parent-teacher contacts is grading. If grading is based solely on comparisons of achievement among all students in a class, it is all too easy and common for gifted students to receive high grades for minimal efforts. At the same time, students who have difficulties in academics may be making progress that is very good for them but still receive consistently poor grades when they are compared on the basis of general classroom achievements. The solution to such problems is to grade mainly on the basis of current progress in meeting individual goals and objectives. Only when every student is made sensitive to individual progress do grades serve to motivate everyone to make strong, consistent efforts for improvement.

In grade reports, refer to the IEP if there is one.

Occasionally, however, students and their parents need information on their rates of progress in comparison with age and class groups. For example, students need honest and clear information on how their educational progress compares with that of applicants admitted to professional schools. In general, exceptional students should be expected to take the same standardized tests as other students, with necessary adaptations for sensory limitations or other handicapping conditions.

Another feature of a good grading system is that it reflects, in part, how productive each student is in achieving group goals. Our society stresses individual achievements, but in reality, individuals usually achieve very little unless they are also able to cooperate with others.

Deutsch (1979) described the functions of an ideal grading system as follows:

> An ideal grading system would foster the view among students that they have a positive interest in the educational attainments of one another. Second, instead of emphasizing comparative evaluations, such a system would provide individualized, particularistic feedback aimed at helping individual students and groups of students to function effectively both as individuals and as groups in achieving educational objectives.... Third,

when prerequisites of specific skills and knowledge were necessary for students to engage in a course of study, criterion-referenced rather than norm-referenced tests would be developed and employed to assess the specific skills and knowledge. Similarly, criterion-referenced tests rather than norm-referenced tests would be used when it was necessary to certify the level of a student's educational attainments in a given area. (p. 400)

Sometimes questions arise over who should grade exceptional students when both regular and special teachers are involved. If the teachers do not work out a solution, the principal should decide on the procedure to be used. A guiding rule is that the grade should be given by the same teacher who grades the other students in the classroom for that subject or grade level and that the grading teacher should take into account the views of other teachers who work with the student on particular subjects.

PREVAILING AND PREFERRED PRACTICES

This chapter has provided an overview of the expanded uses and importance of communication among professionals in the schools and between teachers and parents. The following summary contrasts prevailing and preferred practices.

Prevailing Practices	*Preferred Practices*
1. Teachers work in solitary, "closeted" fashion, each in a boxlike room.	1. Teachers work in pairs and teams, frequently using consultants.
2. Teaching is exclusively dyadic.	2. Teachers work in both dyadic and triadic relationships.
3. Teachers tend to handle instructional and management problems alone.	3. Arrangements are made to help and support teachers in meeting instructional and management problems.
4. Teachers are untrained in professional communication and consultation.	4. Teachers, along with psychologists and other specialists, are trained in effective communication and in working in consulting relationships (as consultant or client or both).
5. Special education teachers provide direct serivces to pupils.	5. Special education teachers spend at least part of their time consulting with other teachers.

6. Advice and supervision are occasionally offered to teachers by supervisors or administrators.

7. Children presenting instructional problems are referred for study and problem definition.

8. Fellow teachers (in one's building) offer advice when asked for it.

9. Staff conferences tend to be undisciplined and full of one-sided talk, usually by administrators.

10. Teachers receive no preparation for dealing with parents and families.

11. Parents of schoolchildren have only the PTA as a group activity relating to schooling.

12. Most parent conferences about exceptional children are arranged by special education teachers and supervisors, social workers, or psychologists.

13. School staff members think of themselves as independent child advocates.

14. Teachers and other school staff members are casual about the school climate.

6. Specialized staff members offer consultation to teachers as coequals.

7. The teacher works with consultants to define children's instructional problems.

8. Teacher assistance teams are formally organized to respond to the professional needs of colleagues.

9. Staff conferences follow an agenda and are disciplined, efficient sessions directed to the solution of problems.

10. Teachers receive preparation for work with parents, including some training in parent education and counseling.

11. Formal groups of parents of exceptional children and coalitions of groups exist to advocate for their children and to train parents for their functions in educational planning.

12. Regular teachers play a central role in most parent-teacher conferences.

13. Shared staff-parent adovcacy is the expected practice.

14. Teachers and other school staff members are deliberate about creating and maintaining a positive school climate.

TOPICAL BIBLIOGRAPHY

Consultation

Bergan (1977)
Caplan (1970)
Meyers, Martin, & Hyman (1977)

Working with Parents

Kroth (1975)
Kroth & Scholl (1978)
Litwak & Meyer (1967)
Seligman (1979)
Stewart (1978)
Turnbull & Turnbull (1978)

Improving Communications

DelPolito (1977)
Giffen & Pattern (1971)
Seilor, Schuelke, & Lieb-Brilhart (1984)

Pre-referral Procedures

Chalfant, Pysh, & Moultrie (1979)

Individualized Educational Programs

Federal Register, Aug. 23, 1977, 42 (163)
Mager (1962)
Morgan (1981)
Turnbull, Strickland, & Brantley (1982)

Grading

Bender (1984)

CHAPTER 5

Advanced Cognitive Development

Students who learn rapidly and who think and perform at complex levels often are referred to as bright, high-IQ, superior, highly intelligent, brilliant, mentally advanced, high achieving, gifted, or talented. The terms *gifted* and *talented* are used here. The popular understanding of gifted and talented applies the term *gifted* more to general abilities, as shown in intellectual and academic pursuits, and *talented* more to special abilities, such as those in the arts, athletics, or leadership. We use the terms *gifted* and *talented* in these ways as a kind of shorthand.

Gifted students are not types.

These children are not special types. We consider them to be on the same continuum of development as all other children but at different points of general or special scales. The differences are mainly quantitative rather than qualitative; nevertheless, gifted and talented children may present significant challenges to educators. The following cases are examples of such challenges.

Pam was within a few months of the minimum age to enter kindergarten. She played with somewhat older children, was highly advanced in language, and was well adjusted. She almost ached to start kindergarten with her neighborhood friends. Pam's parents had her tested by a psychologist, who gave her a Stanford-Binet intelligence test that yielded an IQ of 152. That result places her within the top 1 percent in general intellectual ability. She was taken to the local school for a visit with the kindergarten teacher, who took Pam around her classroom. The teacher determined that Pam showed good background and interest as they encountered and discussed various kinds of materials and activities.

Should Pam be allowed to enter kindergarten as an exception to the chronological age rule? Is chronological age a better regulator of school entry than a more complex set of considerations that would reflect Pam's individual abilities and motivation? Pam is a real child, one we wrote about in 1962 (Reynolds, Birch, & Tuseth). She was in fact admitted early to kindergarten and proceeded successfully throughout her education. Recently she completed her PhD in archeology and took a position in one of the nation's leading museums.

Chronological age, by itself, is not the best regulator of educational progress.

A U.S. commissioner of education said, "Studies show that gifted children in our schools today are locked in by structural and administrative restrictions that inhibit their development. They are denied open access to advanced materials, a cruel kind of censorship of the mind. They are unsatisfied in their mature concern about ethical and moral questions as well as in their intellectual pursuits." (Marland, 1972, p. 19)

A 9-year-old gifted pupil, deeply interested in the comparative study of religions and their principles, did not have access to the high school library. It was miles away and was not open evenings or weekends, and there were no provisions for children or teachers to borrow from it. The youngster went to the public library in the company of a teenage sister, only to be told that the books she wanted were classified "adult" and she could not withdraw them.

In 1980, a 15-year-old self-taught computer whiz was employed by the election board of a county in a midwestern state to furnish faster, more accurate analyses of local election returns. A high school sophomore, he moved his equipment into the county courthouse and produced reports superior to any previous ones. He told officials, when asked, that his vocational-technical school wouldn't admit him to computer-related courses because he was not 16. "They don't want any "little kids" disturbing the class," he said.

Torrance (1973) told of an artistically talented black child whose graphic accomplishments, under the warm encouragement of a teacher, far outstripped the child's academic achievement. The youngster's extraordinary and botanically precise drawing of a flower was denied entry in a science contest. The reason? One of the school administrators did not believe that a pupil of limited academic attainments could produce such a picture without help.

Jonathon, a very bright, blind high school student, wished to study advanced mathematics and the Russian language. Through teamwork by teachers, parents, classmates, and volunteers, a suitable program was arranged. Volunteer braillists managed to put materials for three years of study of the Russian language into braille. Classmates became expert in gluing string to pages of Jonathon's notebooks to represent mathematical diagrams, which he could not see but could readily feel and then understand. Jonathon's experience demonstrates that there are many sound ways to provide opportunities for gifted students.

Some gifted students are also handicapped.

A major problem in education for gifted students is dispelling myths and misunderstandings.

Recent educational research has given much attention to cognitive processes (Nickerson, Perkins, & Smith, 1985). Applying the findings of that research in the schools is important for all students, but it may have special significance for students who are distinguished by their unusually advanced cognitive abilities. It would be easy, of course, to use cognitive instruction to separate gifted students from the mainstream in schools, but that would benefit neither them nor their peers. Thus it will take strong efforts by teachers, parents, school principals, and special educators to create programs that recognize students' extraordinary abilities without resorting to the excesses of special placements.

Better education should not mean only more selective education.

The 1980s so far have witnessed a rash of critiques of education in the United States, with many calling for increased rigor in academic offerings (National Commission on Excellence in Education, 1983; National Consortium for Educational Excellence, 1984; Task Force on Education for Economic Growth, 1983). Calls for excellence are never amiss except when the proposed reforms neglect equity issues and call for excesses in separateness and privilege. Movements to improve the schools always run the risk of becoming only more selective rather than genuinely more adaptive and effective. It is especially important to be mindful of this aspect of the challenge as we consider the needs of cognitively advanced students.

HISTORY AND MISCONCEPTIONS

Great intelligence and madness are not allied.

In the seventeenth century, Dryden wrote, "Great wits are sure to madness near allied, and thin partitions do their bounds divide." He was expressing the view of his day, which had its roots in early Greek misconceptions. Erroneous notions linked mental illness with precocity and creativity until the end of the nineteenth century. The attitude is summed up in this 1893 statement by Cesare Lombroso, a physician:

> The frequency of genius among lunatics and of madness among men of genius explains the fact that the destiny of Nations has often been in the hands of the insane. . . .It seems as though nature had intended to. . . preserve us from being dazzled by the brilliancy of those men of genius who might well have been compared, not to the planets which keep their appointed orbits, but to falling stars, lost and dispersed over the crust of the earth. (p. 361)

Had Lombroso looked at the published work of his contemporary, Francis Galton (1869), his confidence might have been tempered. Galton's was the first recorded effort to study objectively the characteristics of a representative group of eminent persons. Although these people were not without defects, Galton found them to display a strength and integrity of character that outweighed any personality aberrations. Moreover, Lombroso might have found some fellow physicians in truly violent disagreement with him. For example, Karl Kraus, a contemporary of Freud, said:

Nerve doctors who ruin genius for us by calling it pathological should have their skulls bashed in by the genius' collected work. . . . One should grind one's heel into the faces of all rationalistic helpers of "normal humanity" who give reassurance to people unable to appreciate works of wit and fantasy. (Quoted in Janik & Toulmin, 1973)

The need for such passionate utterances diminished as the work by Terman and his associates became better known. They began a study of 1,528 gifted children in 1921. The study continued first under the leadership of Robert and Pauline Sears and now of other scholars. Follow-up studies show that gifted and talented people enjoy, on the average, both better mental health and better physical health than most of their contemporaries. This finding was summarized in 1951 by Terman and Oden: "There is no law of compensation whereby the intellectual superiority of the gifted tends to be offset by inferiorities along non-intellectual lines" (p. 24). In 1977 another follow-up study (Goleman, 1980) reconfirmed that highly able children can expect sounder than average lifelong physical and mental health.

Longitudinal studies of gifted persons show most to be well adjusted and healthy.

Terman's sampling, carried out more than 60 years ago, did not include representative proportions of children by race, ethnicity, religion, and socioeconomic level. In the initial selection of the population, he leaned heavily on results from the intelligence tests then in existence and on children who were easily accessible in California schools. Thus caution is needed in applying the results to children from low socioeconomic backgrounds, to black, Chinese, Hispanic, and American Indian children, and to other particular groups.

Research is always conducted in limited contexts and with limited samples.

A persistent untruth about gifted and talented adults is that they were indifferent scholars as children. Perhaps some were, but the general rule holds that the potential for adult greatness shows itself in the early years. Evidence relating to outstanding painters can be seen, for example, in the Picasso Museum in Barcelona, Spain. An unusually complete record of Pablo Picasso's work as a child and teenager vividly shows extraordinary mastery of techniques plus the creative imagination that the whole world came to admire in his mature years.

Gifted adults usually showed their high ability in childhood.

The single-talent concept is another common fallacy. Actually, the majority of gifted and talented persons are well-rounded individuals; their public images are sometimes lopsided because only their major interests are presented to the world. Leonardo da Vinci's life, for example, refutes the single-talent concept; his breadth of interest and activity was recorded and widely acknowledged during his lifetime.

Most gifted persons show multiple talents.

Another artist who displayed multiple talents was Diego Rodríguez de Silva Velázquez (1599–1660). He was studying painting by the time he was 10 years old and began a formal apprenticeship at age 12. By 18 years of age, he was a known painter in Seville, and by 24, he was a widely heralded artist. He remained creative and productive until his death at age 61. A little noted fact, but one that is important here, is that Velazquez was also one of the most able and effective administrators in the Spanish court. He was the grand chamberlain of the palace of Philip IV and held major management responsibilities across all state matters and even foreign affairs.

The richness of Thomas Jefferson's gifts and talents is familiar to many Americans. Architect, writer, politician, government administrator, philosopher—this array of achievements speaks again to the breadth that can be expected from some exceptional persons.

The eminent Swiss psychologist Jean Piaget was interested in natural history before psychology. In 1907, at the age of 10, an article he wrote was published in a journal of natural history. It dealt with an unusual albino sparrow. A few years later, his writings about mollusks excited the attention of the director of the Geneva Museum of Natural History. When a vacancy occurred on the museum's staff, inquiries were initiated to determine if this very able young scientific writer might be interested in the post of curator of the mollusk collection. Imagine the museum director's surprise when it was discovered that the curatorship was being considered for a schoolboy of 14!

Fortunately for psychology, a few years later Piaget became an assistant to Theodore Simon in the Binet Laboratory in Paris. His interests shifted toward psychology, particularly learning and language development, and his subsequent work on the developmental concepts of intelligence made him a giant in the science of psychology. Varied capabilities in the same gifted and talented person are the rule, not the exception—but further study is needed on this complicated subject, to which we shall return.

INTELLIGENCE AND GIFTEDNESS

Theories and tests of intelligence have been key elements in the history of giftedness.

The history of education for gifted students has followed a course closely linked with the history of intelligence testing since the late nineteenth century. The earliest versions of intelligence tests and related theory emphasized simple sensory processes, in the belief that human discrimination, judgment, and intellectual level were based on sensory discriminations. The eyes were the "windows of the mind"; sensitivities and keenness in vision, hearing, and touch were the building blocks of keen and sensitive intelligence—or so it was believed. The educational implications of this view were devastatingly simple and wrong: They stressed sense training. It remained for Alfred Binet to show that important differences in intelligence are to be found only in more subtle and abstract functions.

The Binet test, as first developed in France and later adapted for use in America (the most prominent version is the Stanford-Binet test created by Lewis Terman, Maude Merrill, and their associates), yielded a single score that could then be transformed to a mental age and an "intelligence quotient." It was assumed that intelligence was a general ability, available for application in many life functions. Similarly, it was assumed that it could be measured by omnibus tests, or what some critics called hodge-podge procedures. Accordingly, the Binet tests included items covering vocabulary, figure copying, simple mathematics, memory for series of digits, comprehension of absurdities, and various other mental activities.

Binet's specific mission in building the test was to find the means to predict the differential achievements of children in school. He succeeded in this task better than anyone had before and about as well as anyone has since. The assumption was that if one could predict which children would lag in ordinary school programs those children could be set aside in different programs. It was an easy parallel to the conclusion that if one could predict which children would learn most rapidly in ordinary school programs, perhaps they too could be set aside, but in a different place and for a program that was accelerated and enriched.

Binet's purpose in test building was to predict school performance.

Such an orientation, using IQs for their predictive capabilities, represents the *selective* mode of education (Glaser, 1977), in contrast to the *adaptive* mode advocated in this book. The selective mode is seductive even if faulty, but that is a long story. Suffice it to say here, as a caveat, that merely to predict that a student will do well or poorly in one program yields no information on whether he or she will do better in another. Indeed, if one uses general or broadband procedures (like Binet test results) to predict performance, it is likely that the prediction will hold as well for the alternative programs and thus not be at all useful in choosing between programs for individuals. (See Chapter 2 for more discussion on this topic.)

Predicting that students will do well in a program provides no evidence in support of placing them in a different program.

Very little about the theory of intelligence was clarified by the work of Binet or Terman, but probably the most common interpretation of their work was that the tests they produced measured "abstract thinking ability." In our society, that would be indicated when a child, asked, "What is an apple?" replies "A fruit"—that is, replies by giving the taxonomic or class term rather than a function ("You can eat it") or mere description ("It is red and round") of the object. It would be indicated also by the fluent use of symbol systems (potentially in several forms as in music, mathematics, or verbal communications) and symbolic thinking. The response to this Binet-like item is an example.

Early theorizing stressed abstract thinking ability as the essence of intelligence and of giftedness.

> A father sent his boy to the lake to bring back one quart of water. He gave the boy a 5-quart jar and a 4-quart jar. How can the boy measure out exactly 1 quart of water?

Most children above age 8 or so might be expected to have no difficulty answering this question correctly on what might be called an *incipient* basis. Simply by symbolic processes, they can try various solutions and with confidence reply that by filling the 5-quart jar, then pouring the contents into the 4-quart jar to its maximum, there will be a remainder of 1 quart. A person very low in abstract thinking ability (intelligence?) might be able to pour water equally as well as others but not to answer the question on the incipient or symbolic basis. This abstract thinking theory was the basis for work by the early testers and advocates for gifted students.

British theorists, more than others, tended to view intelligence in terms of a single or unitary reasoning and learning ability. Spearman, the famous statistician, proposed the symbol g to represent this "general" ability. The story gets more complex through time, as far as theorists are concerned, but in the schools, practices were dominated by the simple g notion. Indeed, even today the g concept is probably the most commonly held in schools; that is, school records of most children still carry a single IQ as the sole representation of performance on intelligence tests.

Educators have tended to use a g-type theory of intelligence.

Among theorists, P. E. Vernon (1950) suggested that in addition to g, it is important to include at least two major group factors—one he termed verbal-educational ability ($V{:}ed$) and the other practical ability ($k{:}m$). He came to this conclusion through statistical studies of the correlations among tests of human abilities. Both $V{:}ed$ and $k{:}m$ were correlated with g, but they were not so highly correlated with each other. As in a tree (see Figure 5.1), g is the main trunk, but two major branches grow out of g and go in somewhat different directions. These represent major group factors. On the branches are many twigs, and, correspondingly, one could describe and measure many highly specific abilities. (It is noteworthy that the Vernon formulation is similar to that of the widely used Wechsler tests, which yield three IQ scores: one each for "verbal" and "performance" abilities, plus a "total" or composite IQ.)

There is no "true" approach to intelligence.

Whether one pays most attention to the trunk (g) or the main branches ($k{:}m$ and/or $V{:}ed$) or even to the minor twigs that spring from each branch would depend on one's purpose. It may be, for example, that to predict the *level* of a person's eventual vocation, a measure of g would suffice; but to predict the kind of occupation he or she might lean toward, it would perhaps be best to look to the group factors. In such a framework, there is no *true* approach to intelligence; rather there are various approaches that must be evaluated in terms of their usefulness for the different purposes.

Other theorists have proposed increasingly complex schemes. Thurstone and Thurstone (1941), for example, suggested that there are seven *primary* abilities and that if there is a meaningful concept of g, it is in secondary terms, reflected in the correlations among the seven primary abilities.

Creative abilities have been emphasized recently.

A set of ideas going beyond Binet's had a major impact on American school practices through the work of J. P. Guilford (1950, 1967). According to Guilford, a minimum of 120 abilities make up the human intellect. His "structure of intellect" was represented in a three-dimensional diagram, with the dimensions marking different operations, products, and content.

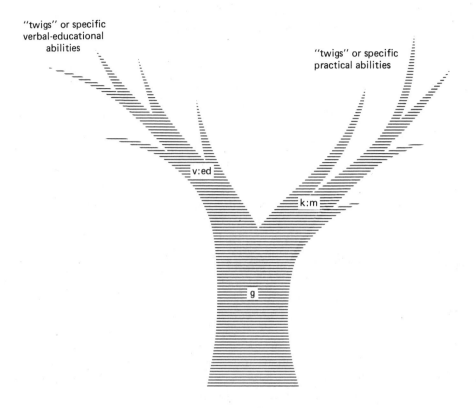

"twigs" or specific
verbal-educational
abilities

"twigs" or specific
practical abilities

v:ed

k:m

g

Figure 5.1. A hierarchical view of intelligence.

Four types of content, five kinds of operations, and six types of product in all combinations (4 × 5 × 6) yield a total of 120 intellectual functions. For present purposes, only the operations dimension is detailed.

The five types of intellectual operations Guilford identified are listed below, along with brief descriptions and examples of questions that might be asked to examine the different processes or operations.

Intellectual operations	*Description*	*Test approach*
Cognition	Learning and awareness	What is the third baseman doing?
Memory	Ability to recall what was cognized earlier	Who first handled the ball after the bunt in the game last night?

Convergent thinking	Giving the "right" or accepted answer	When is the "squeeze play" most likely to occur in a baseball game?
Divergent thinking	Creating alternative approaches	What could be done to confuse a pitcher when you have a base runner on third?
Evaluation	Weighing or evaluating alternatives	If you're one run behind with two out in the last of the ninth inning and have a man on third, how do you assess the value of the squeeze play?

Guilford and his followers (such as Torrance, 1963) argued that the widely used tests of intelligence tended to measure only cognition, memory, and convergent thinking processes, which exactly paralleled school curricula and instructional methods based on the same operations. Following Guilford's lead, strong efforts were made to give more emphasis to divergent and evaluative intellectual operations. These efforts were known widely as the "creativity movement." One now sees important results of this thinking in text materials for schools and in instructional methods but less in testing, perhaps. Clearly, Guilford's work resulted in increased sensitivity among educators to students who are creative—those who have lots of ideas, even about how they choose to be educated. There is always a risk that creativity will be lost if students are confined rigidly to listen-read-memorize-test structures and even that students will be alienated from teachers and schools that give them too little space for their intellectual activities.

The emphasis on creativity has gone to both curriculum and theories of intellect.

Highly creative students may resist rigid curricula.

Recently, several new influences have been felt in theories and practices relating to intelligence and giftedness. Gardner (1983), following a broad survey of research and theory on intelligence and a subjective "factor analysis" of findings, advanced arguments for at least seven separate intelligences. He comes close to saying that g theory is totally wrong. That puts it in the extreme, even to the point of denying what have been termed "threshold effects." According to the threshold view, it might take a certain amount (above some minimum level or threshold) of general "smartness" to get through medical school, for example, beyond which other variables may be predictive of how good a physician one becomes. In such a view, there is something to be said for both g and the more specialized intelligences, but Gardner shows little sympathy for such a view.

New ideas about separate intelligences are emerging.

Gardner's seven intelligences are (1) linguistic, (2) logical and mathematical, (3) musical, (4) spatial, (5) bodily and kinesthetic, (6) interpersonal, and (7) intrapersonal. Most of these sound familiar, and one can think of tests that have been developed to measure them. Perhaps the intrapersonal intelligence is most distinctive. However, Gardner would not be pleased to use most tests that have been devised under rubrics like his.

For one thing, he would stress that most tests of the past have been too school oriented and largely unrelated to the larger realities of life. Gardner has not produced tests, scales, or—as he prefers—means of assessing the several intelligences, but his views have stirred significant interest.

Another emerging theoretical view is that of Sternberg (1980, 1984), who also decries the inadequacy of existing intelligence tests, particularly their failure to be "consequential" in the real world beyond academics. He believes the commonly used tests overemphasize speed and tend to raise anxiety merely in the test-taking process. He says that the tests in use measure merely "last year's (or the year before's) knowledge" (1984, p. 696). A special feature of Sternberg's proposal is emphasis on what he terms "metacomponents," by which he refers to higher-order planning or strategies. For example, an "intelligent individual should know when to go fast and when to go slow" (1984, p. 696). That idea says something about advanced levels of awareness and planning in order to solve problems and learn optimally; it goes well beyond mere speed of information processing as the essence of intelligence.

Most intelligence tests have been school-centered and may be lacking in consequentiality in the larger world.

Knowing when to go slow or fast may be more important than sheer speed of information processing.

Sternberg's formulations are part of the important developments in curriculum and instruction that emphasize helping students select appropriate strategies for their own learning (Resnick, 1984). This work proceeds under rubrics such as higher-order thinking skills (HOTS) and metacognitive strategies. In this emerging framework, learning is seen as involving thinking at various levels, and stress is given to higher-order processes as a basis for better recall and generalization. The teacher may give or explain strategies to students, as part of what may be termed direct instruction, or students may be expected to develop their own metacognitive strategies (Brown, 1980; Weinstein & Underwood, 1985).

The use of cognitive instruction is advantageous for gifted students, who are most able to use cognitive strategies. Sternberg emphasizes that this is no simple matter, however, because the same situation may be mastered quite differently by different students, depending on the kinds of strategies they handle best. For example, one student might be exceptionally able to use strategies relating to social abilities. Another student may be exceptionally able to handle the verbal aspects of the same situation while being relatively less able to handle metacomponents on the social side. A third student may be able to handle the "laboratory" or practical side of the situation. Thus any given situation, according to Sternberg, might be well managed by people who have and use quite different specific abilities and strategies. The challenge for students is to become aware of and adept at using one's best abilities in an intentional, strategic manner.

Clearly, the research and theory on intelligence and intelligence testing are incomplete. They offer only limited help to practical educators. Sternberg (1984) notes that there "must be something missing [from intelligence tests]. Their ability to predict school and job performance has not changed for many years" (p. 694). New ideas on intelligence are of wide

Ideas on intelligence and giftedness are still in flux.

Substituting the predictor for the criterion may be the greatest danger in identifying gifted students.

interest, so much so that they often are publicized when only at an embryonic level of development, and that is a serious problem for the schools. We conclude by observing what Sternberg calls the "greatest danger in the use of any test," which is to substitute the test or "predictor" for the criterion. An elaboration on that point is our next topic.

EDUCATION FOR GIFTED AND TALENTED STUDENTS

Issues of Identification: The Level of the Lesson as Preferred Approach

One can proceed in two contrasting ways in identifying gifted and talented students. First, one can use tests, rating scales, or other devices. As we have noted, it is not very clear just which measures would be useful, although some general intelligence tests and special observation scales, the latter to sensitize one to the possible influences of racial, cultural, ethnic, and economic factors, may be helpful (Renzulli, 1971). Second, one can put major emphasis on the program side, that is, on the development of curricula to challenge very able learners. In this case, the gifted and talented do not emerge as special types but only as students who need and are able to profit from accelerated and enriched programs. This approach starts at the level of the lesson (see Chapter 2) rather than with test results or other factors considered to be predispositional to outstanding performance. It gives everyone a chance to qualify, and students who show the greatest profit from advanced programs are considered to be gifted or talented and are encouraged to continue enrollment in advanced programs. As a general strategy, we favor the second approach, for several reasons:

Identification should begin with program developments that challenge and assist the top learner and performer.

1. It avoids substituting the test for the criterion. It goes directly to the criterion, which is gifted performance in one or more fields. It is critical, of course, that all students be given every opportunity to develop and demonstrate high abilities in the various fields; otherwise special biasing effects obviously could appear. We feel that the obligation to offer curricular opportunities to all students is an absolute requirement no matter what one may feel about "identification," and we prefer to use this curriculum base for observing and then accommodating human differences.

2. It directs the initial attention of educators to the challenge of providing adaptive curricula and instruction rather than to the categorizing of students. To start with, the formal identification of gifted students, independent of program developments, often results in shallow programs, useless grouping practices, and confused self-concepts by selected students.

3. It avoids the potential problems of labeling students as gifted in an abstract and somewhat meaningless way and instead stresses the obvious

outstanding performances of top students. We expect that important changes in self-concept and social adjustment accrue to students when their abilities are recognized for example, when one qualifies as violinist in the highly selective citywide junior symphony orchestra or wins a position on the top debate team, rather than to be selected and placed because one is a gifted student in some abstract sense. Discussions then can be centered on programs and not on labels.

Education for the gifted should focus on programs, not on labels.

4. It recognizes that outstanding performance in a field is a function of motivation, interest, and personality variables as well as cognitive abilities.

5. It puts education for gifted and talented students in the same adaptive education framework that is created for all students. This procedure requires no sacrifice of adaptive programs for the top learners and helps to avoid the mostly wasteful and sometimes misleading practices of categorizing, labeling, and isolation. The whole process is more likely to be understood and appreciated by students in general than procedures that stress identification of the gifted in more abstract terms.

Education for gifted students is a part of adaptive education for all students.

> Is any identification procedure necessary?
> The prevailing "identification-placement" paradigm needs to be replaced by the preferred "assess-educate" model, one in which the separate "identification" step is replaced by curriculum-imbedded . . . processes for . . . gifted students. (Birch, 1984, p. 157)

Birch (1984) suggests that in addition to beginning the work of the school on the program side and in an adaptive framework, the following principles should govern identification policies and practices:

1. Work toward the capability to provide careful assessment of all children prior to school entry. Such assessments should be oriented to the planning of necessary educational adaptations for pupils at the earliest possible time. In some cases, the planning will lead to quite extraordinary arrangements to give opportunities to children who have been disadvantaged earlier for whatever reason. In other cases, it will mean accelerated and greatly enriched programs.

Early assessment and program adaptation should be a goal.

2. Link all assessment of children to the planning and conduct of education in terms of pupil needs and interests. Attention to individual differences is assured in the pace and breadth of the curriculum and in adaptive approaches to instruction. Instruction is the focus, not labeling.

3. Keep alert on a continuing basis for children who show outstanding capabilities through school achievement. If high achievement is demonstrated, any intelligence test that might or might not have predicted it is irrelevant.

4. Instruct parents, teachers, principals, librarians, and other significant adults to help spot children who show unusually high abilities at home, in school, and in the community.

5. Avoid simplistic, narrow, one-dimensional approaches to identification, even though a state or other governmental agency may seem to encourage it.

6. Provide adaptive, individualized education for all students, thus making traditional identification essentially unnecessary. Obviously, such provision means the reversal of the all-too-common pattern of teaching all children the same things, in the same ways, and in the same time periods.

The term genius *is reserved for those who have produced outstanding work for a long period.*

> [A genius is] anyone who...produces, over a long period of time, a large body of work that has a significant influence on many persons for many years; requiring these people, as well as the individual in question, to come to terms with a different set of attitudes, ideas, viewpoints, or techniques before all can have "peace of mind," that is, a sense of resolution and closure. (Albert, 1975, pp. 140–141)

EDUCATIONAL PROGRAMS

Early School Programs

Plato recommended that Greeks of outstanding ability be educated from childhood for responsible governmental positions. To detect future leaders, he suggested that promising juveniles be observed while being made to perform actions in which they were most likely to be deceived. Those who remembered and were not deceived were to be selected, and those who failed in the trial were to be rejected.

> Philip II, ruler of Macedonia, subjugated most Greek city-states, unified them without destroying personal freedoms, and became the most powerful European king of the fourth century B.C. He set the stage for his son, Alexander the Great, to change the map of the world. Less widely known is the atmosphere and instruction Philip arranged for his growing son. Through paternal encouragement, the boy was in frequent contact with gifted artists, writers, and actors, and Aristotle was summoned from Athens to tutor Alexander at the Macedonian court.

Promising children from even the poorest of homes were given encouragement and help.

The emperor Charlemagne, according to legend, urged the education of promising children among the common people at state expense.

Comenius's seventeenth-century writings frequently referred to students with extraordinary aptitude for learning. He advocated financial aid for bright students from poor homes.

The rapid rise of the Ottoman Empire in the 1500s has been credited in large part to Suleiman the Magnificent's three-step special education process. He sent teams to find the fairest, strongest, and brightest youths in the empire, regardless of social class or faith. It was made worth their while to accept tutelage under his protection in the Moslem religion, the learned disciplines of that day, and martial arts. A robe of honor was given to each boy for exceptional work in attaining strength and knowledge. Graduates were offered posts of honor and responsibility in the armed forces, the arts and sciences, and government.

The Chinese emperors sponsored instruction and a system of civil service examinations. The latter brought into government employ not only able clerks, managers, and generals but also poets, artists, and other creative persons.

The tales of other civilizations may well contain similar themes. The full story of the development of leadership in the Aztec and Inca civilizations, for instance, has yet to be told. Approaches to giftedness and talent in the nations of the African continent and Japan are now unfolding. The outstanding success of Japanese students in mathematics and science has been noted and caused some disquieting reactions in the United States. Some evidence suggests that Japanese students, on the average, may achieve as much as 2 standard deviations above the mean of American students in some subjects (Cunningham, 1984; Stevenson, Lee, & Stigler, 1986). Evidence now beginning to appear concerning similar outstanding achievements by Vietnamese immigrants to the United States, after only four or five years of studying English, adds challenge to American students and teachers.

Recent History

In 1955, Pressey put in capsule form the tenets of an educational program aimed at fostering the capabilities of gifted and talented youth. He suggested giving a precocious child "early encouragement, intensive instruction, continuing opportunity as he advances, a congruent stimulating social life, and cumulative success experiences" (Pressey, 1955, p. 14).

Early encouragement was one feature of Pressey's recommendation.

Pressey stated his view of adaptations briefly: "In proportion as [these youngsters] are very able and especially as they have special talents, special adaptations of the usual curriculums are likely to be desirable" (p. 16). With respect to acceleration, he favored admission to the first grade on the basis of readiness for school rather than chronological age, replacement of the first three grades by a "primary pool" out of which children would be promoted according to their readiness for advanced work, rapid-progress sections doing three years' work in two in junior and senior high school, and credit by examination in college—thus permitting flexible continuing progress by each student. Pressey's proposals have been confirmed as wise; early assessment and encouragement, adapted instruction and curriculum, sequential successes, and personally paced progress are still grounded solidly in the research of today (Gallagher, 1985).

Examples of special arrangements in American schools include a North Carolina residential school for students gifted in science and mathematics; special secondary day schools in New York City and Cincinnati; special classes in University City, Missouri, and those known as Major Work Classes in Cleveland; and early admission to kindergarten and first grade, as pioneered in Brookline, Massachusetts, and in Nebraska.

Most states now employ coordinators of programs for gifted students.

Recently, most states have employed coordinators in the state education department to give overall encouragement and leadership to efforts on behalf of gifted and talented children. The Association for the Gifted (TAG), a division of the Council for Exceptional Children, promoted national and regional meetings, often cooperating with other interested groups at both the national and state levels to promote planning of programs for gifted students. The Ford Foundation, the Carnegie Corporation, and other foundations have given modest but meaningful support to the preparation of program development leaders.

Sputnik caused a wave of concern for the education of gifted students in the late 1950s.

The Russian launching of *Sputnik* sparked U.S. congressional interest in improvements in American secondary school education, especially in mathematics, science, and language. The National Defense Education Act of 1957 added support for programs of education for gifted and talented children. Vigorous advocacy by parent groups has helped to propel action on behalf of such children, with the result that virtually all states now have programs for gifted students. Only small sums are available from the federal government for such programs, but increasing numbers of states offer special funding supports.

THE ROLE OF THE REGULAR CLASS TEACHER, SPECIAL TEACHER, AND PRINCIPAL

It is not new for regular teachers and principals to have daylong responsibilities for gifted and talented pupils. Among the new ideas are the following:

1. Particular attention is now called to these pupils.
2. Individualized education programs are required for them in some states, in the same pattern as for handicapped students.

Interest in education of gifted and talented students is at a high level.

3. More specialized staff, such as consultants on the gifted and school psychologists, are available from state and local school districts to offer consultation and in other ways to buttress the regular classroom teacher's work.
4. Parental involvement is increased.
5. Public interest and the interest of political leaders in programs for gifted students are at a high level.

6. Research on adaptive education and cognitive instruction provides a richer base for developing applications in school practices.

Teamwork with Specialists

In the past, regular class teachers had total responsibility for instruction of gifted pupils. Currently, the responsibility often extends to coordinating the activities of a resource teacher, specialized consultants, and volunteers. The regular class teacher's role in several states includes the joint preparation of individualized education plans with a specialist teacher and parents.

Regular teachers now have more opportunities for consultation with specialists on education for gifted students.

It may be helpful to envision the regular teacher and pupils, including those who are gifted and talented, in the center of the picture, with various services and consultants surrounding them. These services (e.g., library, guidance counseling, instructional materials center) and consultants (specialist teacher, teacher aide, volunteers) are available to the regular teacher on request. The regular teacher exercises professional generalship on behalf of the whole class while making sure that each gifted and talented pupil is accommodated by whatever form of acceleration and enrichment is most suitable.

Gifted pupils, for the most part, learn the standard curricular skills and content quickly and easily. They often move far beyond the conventional curricular offerings into advanced areas. They need teaching that does not tether them to a limited range. For gifted students, the regular class should be a forum for research, inquiry, and projects brimming with challenges. Gifted pupils learn readily and often produce imaginative ideas. They need support from principals and teachers to maintain their advanced pace of learning and confidence in their good ideas, even when those ideas differ from the norm or the vogue. It is no small talent for the teacher to be able to direct work in widely divergent areas and to guide inquiry by the most able students.

A mentor is a mature person of competence who establishes a helping relationship with a younger person.

Aware that gifted and talented pupils are not a species apart, principals and teachers see them on a continuum with all other pupils. The chief dimension of the continuum is cognitive development. Yet, realistically, gifted and talented pupils have their ups and downs on all sorts of educationally significant qualities. They are like all other pupils in more ways than they differ. This fact is well illustrated by the "talent totem poles" (Figure 5.2). Taylor (1968) depicted the many qualities that need attention when personalized education is planned for children and youth. Note in the figure that Kathy is a bit below average academically but far above average in communicating and decision making.

Gifted students are greatly variable in personality and special abilities.

A mentor is a competent older person who is able to counsel and instruct a student in areas of mutual interest. The term goes back to Mentor, the Greek protector of and adviser to Ulysses's young son. During the 20-year period

Figure 5.2. Taylor's Talent Totem Poles (*Source*: C. W. Taylor. Be talent developers as well as knowledge dispensers. *Today's Education. 57*, 67–69. Reprinted with permission.)

of the Trojan War, the faithful guardian Mentor tutored the son and helped him toward manhood. Mentor's valuable service is memorialized in today's term, which conveys the sense of continuous friendly, helpful guidance.

Acceleration

Acceleration can be accomplished in many ways.

One important way to adapt school programs for able students is acceleration. The term refers to procedures by which carefully selected students are enabled to complete a given program in less time or at a younger age than is common. Acceleration can be accomplished in many ways: early admission to kindergarten, opportunities to accomplish two grades in one year, adaptive learning systems that permit curricular advances at any stage, rapid advancement classes in secondary schools (e.g., doing two years of general math in one year; starting algebra a year early), advanced placement programs in high school, careful time-saving articulation of high school and college transitions, full-year college programs, and the like. In general, the evidence favors all forms of carefully executed acceleration, an area of needed improvement in many educational systems.

There are several reasons for considering acceleration seriously. We ask for increasing amounts of time to school our most able students, which means, in many cases, that they are able to complete formal education only in their late twenties or early thirties, well into the period of adulthood when most people are well established as independent adults. Students in special fields of medicine or advanced graduate study, for example, often find themselves in an "academic nest," even as adults. Thus when we consider early admission or other forms of acceleration for precocious children, we should be mindful that often it is not only the immediate adjustment that is our concern but those later years as well, because an early admittee may finish medical school, seminary training, or graduate school earlier than would otherwise be the case. Early career entry is a personal advantage if it can be accomplished successfully; it is also a social advantage because it adds years to the time mature contributions can be made.

Early admission to kindergarten may mean completing medical school or graduate school a year earlier than would otherwise be the case.

Another reason for concern is that we may be taking too much time for formal education during the periods of the life cycle when gifted individuals are most creative. Some of them may be better off on their own than confined to colleges or universities where their lives are managed by others. In fields of science and mathematics, especially, creative contributions of lasting significance tend to come relatively early in the cycle of adult careers (persons in their twenties and thirties), and we should make this peak period one that is fully open to creative enterprise.

We may be "mortgaging" time for schooling that would be better spent independently.

Decisions about acceleration come into focus early in elementary school. Martinson's (1972) report highlighted the difficulties teachers face if they stick to typical age-and-grade-linked curricula. In recounting the characteristics of 1,000 gifted pupils, she noted:

> In the kindergarten group, the average performance of gifted students was comparable to that of second grade students....The average for fourth and fifth grade gifted children was beyond that of seventh grade students. The average for gifted eighth grade students was equal or beyond the typical performance of twelfth grade students. (p. 81)

Most evidence on the outcomes of carefully conducted acceleration programs is positive.

There are strong reasons for providing some form of acceleration for most able students at the elementary school level and, at least equally, at the secondary level. Terman (1954) advised that the top 2 percent of students should show acceleration (by age) of at least a year and often by two years before entering college. That means that especially able students would enter college by age 17, or even 16. Beyond that point, with carefully adaptive entry into college and continuing efforts thereafter to save time, it should be possible to save at least an additional year of schooling for most gifted students. That adds up to two or three years of time saved for able students in formal education and added to their independent life in careers.

Terman favored entry to college for gifted students at least by age 17, or even at 16.

Advanced Placement

Better articulation of programs between high school and college offers opportunities for acceleration.

Some 20 years ago, my predecessors at the College Board established the Advanced Placement program (AP), which allows able high school students to study college-level courses while still in school and offers them possible advanced placement in colleges on the basis of their AP examinations.

AP provides schools with curriculum descriptions, in a variety of disciplines—American history, art, biology, chemistry, classics, English, European history, French, German, Latin, mathematics, music, physics, and Spanish. Talented and conscientious school and college teachers from each field prepare these course descriptions, descriptions that can readily be adapted to local initiatives. The course outlines and tests are revised biennially to keep current with college offerings.

For several reasons, secondary schools should seriously consider introducing the program if they have not already done so.

First, the lockstep traditional system of education is being abandoned in many schools to suit the styles and needs of individual students. AP has been in the forefront of this trend, giving able students an opportunity to stretch their minds. Every indication persuades us that more and more of our ablest students now seek this kind of intellectual challenge.

Second, the solemn progression from grades 12 to 13, long a glacial monument to the great silence between schools and colleges, is beginning to thaw as schools define multiple paths to the high school diploma and as colleges exercise flexibility in their admissions policies. Yet the abyss between school and college faculties in the curriculum area remains deep.

AP does not provide a full solution, but each year it does offer a systematic and influential meeting ground for school and college teachers, when the AP readers from both secondary schools and colleges gather to review and grade the examinations and share a full week of hard work, illuminating exchanges, and camaraderie.

Third, college credit earned by examination in myriad forms and styles is increasingly in the air. While college faculties express concern that some of these programs may result in a cheapening of academic degrees, they do not seem to view AP in this context. Perhaps this is because college faculties have always played a major role in developing the AP program.

Fourth, in the years ahead, the decline in the school-age population, already evident in the elementary grades, will move into high school and into college, where there may well be sharp declines in enrollments. This will no doubt stimulate competition among colleges for able students who have not yet received their high school diploma. Some collegiate institutions already enroll eleventh-graders. More programs of this type will come.

But secondary schools can stand their ground and preserve their eleventh- and twelfth-grade programs in this sharpening competition if they can do the job for able students in these grades as effectively as the colleges can. AP is one proven way to do this.

Many schools around the country have demonstrated that AP can be installed for a modest or even negligible incremental cost.

Beginning an AP program in a school, even for only one or two subjects, can create a dynamic concern for academic excellence that permeates the entire school and exerts a positive influence on other classes and courses as well as on members of the faculty.

Experienced AP users have found the program to be an effective instrument for serving gifted but socially disadvantaged students. I found this particularly true in my years with the Pittsburgh schools, and I suspect the same would be true in other inner-city schools where pride in the program often helps urban school leaders change negative stereotypes held by some parents and segments of the public. (Adapted from Marland, 1976, pp. 43–44)

Special Grouping

The current challenge to principals and teachers is managing pupil movement and grouping arrangements to be sure that separation from the mainstream is kept to a defensible minimum and that its true justification is instructional need, not administrative or fiscal advantages. For example, gifted and talented pupils need opportunities to socialize, plan, work, and hold discussions with like-minded peers. If that need is not satisfied in the usual course of regular class activities, then separate clubs, seminars, summer institutes, or some other special program will be needed.

It is not always necessary to segregate gifted students to encourage significant interactions among them. High-ability students tend to find and engage one another in significant interactions even if they are placed in heterogeneous groups. Third-graders who are very good in spelling tend to know who the other "good spellers" are, and they may enjoy competing in spelling within that small cohort of ability comparables.

High Jumper Extraordinaire

Alan was by far the best high jumper his high school had ever had. He no longer compared his performance with that of his classmates, nor did they seek to match him in this extraordinary ability. He did, however, follow closely the jumping performances of three other athletes in different towns in his state. These were the competitors he would meet in the state championship track tournament the next spring.

Gifted students may compare themselves and compete with other gifted students even while placed in heterogeneous classes.

Festinger (1954) advanced a theory about social comparison processes in which he suggested that people tend to make the most active comparisons of their own performance, in fields that are important to them, with

Gifted students tend to be attracted to social situations in which they are not highly discrepant in important abilities.

people who are not too greatly different from themselves in ability and that people tend to be attracted to social situations in which they are not greatly discrepant in ability. So, for example, world-class golfers such as Jack Nicklaus and Arnold Palmer probably find it less attractive to play golf with weekend duffers than with other extremely able golfers. In that exclusive company, they improve their sensitivity to the fine points of the game and their own performances. So it may be in the various aspects of schoolwork. Gifted students have an advantage when they have access to ability comparables in their special fields; that does not necessarily mean total separation from regular classmates, however. One can practice after school with the madrigal club, the basketball team, or the debate squad, or one can attend a special language camp in the summer. Some special grouping occurs quite naturally, of course, by the time students enroll for the third-year mathematics class or advanced language study in high school.

Comparisons and Competition

Cedric, the fourth-chair French horn player in the symphony orchestra, constantly complained that he was really a better player than the third- and second-ranked French horn players and was even as good as the solo player. He compared himself with his colleagues in this framework shamelessly. One day, the solo French horn player resigned, and auditions for the position were scheduled. Cedric tried for the position and won it! Soon thereafter Cedric accelerated his record collection of selections played by the solo French horn players with leading orchestras in London, Rome, Philadelphia, and Budapest. He now talked incessantly about how well he played in comparison with these long-distance colleagues.

Sometimes one's comparison or competitive cohort involves far away members.

Kulik and Kulik (1982) have provided a metanalysis of ability grouping in secondary schools. Summarizing results over 52 studies of ability grouping, these researchers found only a small effect size (.1 standard deviation) for typical students. However, for high-ability students in enriched classes, the effect size was higher (.33). This suggests that, at least for the relatively short periods of time during which ability grouping studies were conducted, high-ability pupils in homogeneous high-ability classes outperformed comparable pupils in comparison (control) classes by more than .3 standard deviation. Ability grouping was advantageous for other students as well, but by lesser amounts.

An earlier narrative review of ability grouping practices (Goldberg, Passow, Justman, & Hage, 1965) also found only small advantages for ability grouping, but it appeared that removal of bright pupils from regular classes sometimes resulted in disadvantages for the nongifted pupils. This suggests that having gifted pupils in regular classes may be enhancing in the education of other students, perhaps because the gifted students add ideas, knowledge, and broad perspectives that brighten discussions for all.

A basic problem of ability grouping research is that it usually fails to attend to what happens in ability-grouped classes. Most of the research findings may be the result not of grouping practices per se but of curricular changes that have been introduced. An interesting and challenging approach to research that attends carefully to both curriculum and grouping practices is provided by Slavin and Karweit (1985). In this research, there was indication that deliberately formed heterogeneous groups achieve as well as homogeneous groups when arrangements are made for cooperative approaches to instruction. The Slavin-Karweit research was in the field of mathematics instruction using "team-assisted individualization" (TAI), an approach to cooperative learning created by Slavin.

In general, instruction for gifted and talented pupils should be conducted in adaptive regular classes. This is to say that curricular adaptations should be made, but in the regular class. However, this should not preclude the formation of part-time special groups of gifted and talented students that provide access to ability comparables in their fields of special interest and high competence.

Listed in Figure 5.3 are a number of expressions that denote ways of organizing instruction. Some are suggested by Kaplan's (1975) lists. We have arranged them to indicate the probable degree to which they would or would not require segregation.

All these approaches may need to be used under some circumstances to organize for instruction.

Curriculum Individualization

The following are principles that we propose should have attention in arranging the curriculum for gifted students. Detailed treatment of curriculum issues is beyond the scope of this book but can be found, for ex-

Full Mainstreaming   Complete Segregation

- Special schools
- Special summer programs
- Clustered special classes in regular schools
- Limited enrollment seminars and courses
- Resource rooms and clinical centers
- Limited participation field trips and events on school time
- Cluster groups within the regular class
- Limited participation before and after school groups
- Tutoring carried on in regular class
- Independent and individualized study in the context of the regular class

Figure 5.3. Ways of Organizing for Instruction

ample, in the work of Meeker (1969), Renzulli and Smith (1978), Sellin and Birch (1980, 1981), Whitmore (1980), and Gallagher (1985).

1. Teachers and principals should be sure that all gifted and talented pupils acquire the basic skills and content of the standard curriculum and that they do so thoroughly. This means checking to see that there are no gaps in their knowledge or skills. Sometimes gifted students advance so rapidly on the basis of incidental learning (that is, without formal instruction) that assumptions are made about thoroughness of learning. Such assumptions should be checked.

Competent students should be encouraged to undertake advanced studies as soon as they are ready for them.

2. Students should be encouraged to move ahead in the standard curriculum (reading, motor development, writing, sciences, mathematics, languages, music, art, literature, etc.) as rapidly as fits each pupil's individual pace. Advanced books, materials, and instruction should be readily available in a systematic and orderly fashion, and a child's efforts at curriculum acceleration should be reinforced. The policy of holding, say, all fourth-graders to fourth-grade books, still common in too many schools, is totally inexcusable.

3. The scope of curricular offerings should be extended for students who master the regular curriculum in less than the usual time. For example, typing, foreign languages, art, and various specialized studies should be added at the times that gifted and talented students can schedule them, provided that interest is high and they promise to contribute to the students' general pattern of development.

Gifted pupils need to reach beyond the usual curriculum.

4. Teachers and counselors should encourage particularly able students to reach beyond the usual curriculum. In such cases, parents should be involved in planning. If a 10-year-old wishes to pursue content areas like astronomy, animal husbandry, ethics, epistemology, morality, Moslem culture, paper making, or population control, there must be understanding and cooperation between home and school. Such prearrangement gives parents a voice in what is going on and ensures that their values relating to the relevance and propriety of particular studies are respected. At the secondary school level, this reaching beyond may well take the form of registering for specialized advanced placement courses, working with a mentor, or special summer studies.

5. Teachers should provide opportunities for gifted students to connect whatever they are studying to what they already know and to collateral areas of study. Such opportunities might mean extending the curriculum to include exploring the history of ideas more thoroughly than is common for other students or learning how skills and knowledge relate to various professions and advanced fields of scholarship. These adaptations encourage the transfer or generalization of knowledge and the search for deeper meanings.

6. Gifted students should be encouraged and assisted to undertake independent study and to polish skills in self-directed learning. The activ-

ities should include special efforts to create awareness of their own awareness (metacognition) as an aspect of discovering their personal best
strategies for independent study, solving problems, and constructing
meaning from reading and other activities. Activities should also include
using data on their own performance as a basis for planning.

7. Gifted students should be given opportunities to explore, experiment, and create in environments that provide rich resources and guidance, along with large measures of freedom. The combination permits
students to discover that they can discover and create and to experience
the surge of motivation that usually accompanies such self-discovery.

Students need opportunities to discover that they can discover and create.

8. Students should be pressed to carry issues and discussions all the
way to culminating activities, such as decision making, policy formation,
and moral or ethical analysis, and to engage in communication activities by
making reports to or holding discussions with other people.

9. Gifted students should be encouraged and assisted to develop
leadership skills and to exercise them in the school and community. Often
the activities entail studies in social psychology, formal and informal procedures for group process (e.g., Roberts's rules of order), understanding
oneself as a social agent, and acquiring respect for all other humans, whatever their characteristics.

10. Gifted students need to build positive expectations for careers
and adult living that will optimize their talents and gifts. More than other
students, they may need special help in understanding how to accomplish
advanced and very complex learning in pursuit of high goals.

Gifted students need help in foreseeing appropriate career opportunities.

Special added attention is needed by pupils whose school performance is consistently poorer than their out-of-school attainments. Some
students show remarkable inventiveness and high leadership qualities
outside of school. This may be especially true for children whose family
and cultural backgrounds are markedly different and whose potential gifts
and talents may not be immediately evident in the dominant culture. Not
all gifted and talented children and youth find it easy to be self-starters,
especially students who are handicapped or underachieving.

Whitmore (1980) has written extensively on useful approaches to serve
handicapped and disadvantaged gifted students. Work in such areas has
come into focus much more frequently of late, probably because procedures for identifying students as gifted have been broadened substantially.
Renzulli (1973, 1978) and Renzulli and Smith (1977) have provided tools
to help teachers become more aware of the potentialities of students
whose backgrounds may be disadvantaged or atypical. A common need
among disadvantaged and handicapped gifted students is for improvements in self-concept, motivation, and goal orientation. Whitmore (1980)
reports success for programs that provide strong personal support and
guidance by teachers plus more than the usual degrees of freedom for
students.

Strong personal support by teachers is often helpful for especially able students from disadvantaged backgrounds.

The Richardson Report

A useful set of program descriptions has been provided by the so-called Richardson Report (Cox, Daniel, & Boston, 1985). With support by the Sid W. Richardson Foundation, experts on educating gifted students were able to visit many programs across the nation and to obtain information by questionnaire procedures from many more sites. With the aid of a number of adviser-scholars, a set of evaluations and recommendations was developed. The following conclusion was reached:

> From a national perspective the efforts to improve education for our most capable students look fragmented and discontinuous. There is no national consensus, not even a common pattern or generally accepted approach to meeting the special needs of this population. (p. 42)

Nevertheless, particular examples of outstanding practice were found.

Among programs observed favorably were the International Baccalaureate (IB) program, which emphasizes secondary education with a world view and advanced placement in college studies, many varieties of internship and mentoring programs, several approaches to advanced placement in college, special summer programs, and much more.[1] Perhaps the most negative conclusions related to pullout programs, practices that take gifted students out of their regular programs intermittently for specialized help.

Flexible pacing was a primary idea proposed as a result of the study.

The most important concept advanced positively as a result of the Richardson study was that of flexible pacing, the idea that students should be advanced in school on the basis of their mastery of elements in the curriculum. It seems likely that flexible pacing for the gifted will be achieved only when schools are adaptive or flexible in pacing programs for all students. Indeed, most of the recommendations of this significant study will be implemented successfully, we believe, only when total school programs become adaptive. That is the promising framework within which programs for gifted and talented students can be implemented with the promise of basic and sustained success. To achieve this framework, it will be necessary that advocates for gifted students join with their counterparts who work on behalf of handicapped students and for general improvements in the schools. It is this view that provides the theme for this entire book— that by providing adaptive school environments for all students, we also achieve the framework within which special adaptations for exceptional students, both the handicapped and the gifted, can be made.

An Appropriate Educational Program

A well-developed educational scheme for gifted and talented pupils has these six characteristics:

---

[1] For information about the IB program, write to IB North America, 680 Fifth Avenue, New York, NY 10019.

1. It is *comprehensive*, covering preschool through higher education.
2. It is *continuous*, being available for the pupil's entire school career.
3. It is *balanced*, including equal opportunity to work in all curricular and extracurricular areas.
4. It is *participatory*, involving regular and special teachers, pupils, parents, and community resources in both decision making and instruction.
5. It is *flexible*, being adaptable to changes in school and pupil conditions.
6. It is *individualized*, encouraging instruction based on close matches between pupil characteristics and what is taught and how it is taught. (Adapted from Sellin & Birch, 1980, p. 4)

PREVAILING AND PREFERRED PRACTICES

The limited administrative and program practices found in many schools are contrasted here with the preferred practices found operating successfully in some schools.

Prevailing Practices

1. Identification is sporadic, usually delayed until grade 3, 4, or later. Identification is based on group intelligence test scores, grade averages, standardized achievement test scores, teacher recommendations, or a combination of these, but most attention is paid to largely arbitrary cutoff scores.

2. Prior to classification and labeling, there is little systematic educational assessment and planning.

3. Coordination of programs for the gifted and talented is absent or haphazard.

Preferred Practices

1. Systematic assessment is made of preschool-age children to permit possible early admission to kindergarten or first grade and to check for developmental needs. Continuing efforts are made at all grade levels to identify children of high promise, with special attention to searching in minority group and disadvantaged populations. Procedures are mainly curriculum based.

2. Programs for gifted pupils are developed, and children are scheduled into advanced or accelerated programs on the basis of individualized assessments and plans.

3. A school system staff person is responsible for the overall program coordination for gifted and talented pupils.

4. Special attention to a gifted or talented pupil comes only when a regular class teacher takes an interest.

5. Parents may know that their children are in special programs, but they have little to say about the program or its content.

6. In some school systems, age or grade acceleration is arranged for a few pupils through early admission to school, double promotion, early college placement, or other means.

7. Special art, music creative writing, or other classes for elementary- or secondary-age students are occasionally offered, either during school hours or on Saturdays.

8. A few communities and states maintain special secondary schools, either for high achievers in general or designated for the sciences or the performing arts, for instance. Some are for the summer only. Other school districts offer pullout programs for selected students for one or two periods per day or per week.

4. Individualized programming is available from the preschool years through secondary and higher education. Continuous progress is monitored by teachers and coordinators of programs for gifted pupils.

5. There is full involvement of parents and the child in decision making about educational planning and evaluation of individual progress.

6. Each pupil's progress is reviewed at least annually to consider possible age or grade acceleration and program redesign.

7. There is flexible, personalized scheduling across grade levels to accommodate students' special abilities and interests and to take advantage of the many special competencies possessed by particular regular class teachers. There is open access, under reasonable supervision, to libraries and laboratories so that pupils can pursue individual projects.

8. Emphasis is kept on bringing special educational facilities, staff, and activities to gifted and talented children in the context of the regular class rather than moving the child to a special school or class. Special arrangements for grouping students of comparable abilities and interests are made to supplement regular programs.

9. Advanced placement courses are available in less than one out of six high schools.

9. Advanced placement is available in all high schools and considered by all colleges. Students are encouraged, with professional guidance, to explore the various options afforded by the advanced placement programs.

10. Regular class teachers receive little or no preservice preparation for working with gifted or talented pupils.

10. Periodic in-service minicourses are offered for regular class teachers to maintain and update understandings of and skills for individualizing programs for all pupils.

TOPICAL BIBLIOGRAPHY

General and Historical Studies

Cox, Daniel, & Boston (1985)
Gallagher (1985)
Pressey (1955)
Sellin & Birch (1980)
Terman & Oden (1947)

Intelligence and Intelligence Testing

Gardner (1983)
Sternberg (1984)

Creativity

Guilford (1967)
Meeker (1969)
Torrance (1963)

Gifted Underachievers and Disabled Persons

Renzulli (1973)
Whitmore (1980)
Whitmore & Maker (1986)

Administrative Arrangements

Cox, Daniel, & Boston (1985)
Kulik & Kulik (1982)

CHAPTER 6

Speech and Language Impairments

Speaking is so fundamental for most people that they seldom think about it. But for persons without clear, pleasant-sounding, unhesitant speech, talking can be an exercise in agony.

A TEENAGE GIRL
Even when I was a little girl I remember being ashamed of my speech. And every time I opened my mouth I shamed my mother. I can't tell you how awful I felt. If I talked, I did wrong. It was that simple. I kept thinking I must be awful bad to have to talk like that. I remember praying to God and asking him to forgive me for whatever it was I must have done. I remember trying hard to remember what it was, and not being able to find it. (Van Riper, 1978, p. 61)

Left unattended, early speech problems can leave social and emotional scars.

Problems of language and speech appear in approximately 1 out of 20 children. They occur with little regard to socioeconomic condition, family, race, rate of cognitive development, or the presence of other exceptionalities. They have potentially devastating personal, social, and academic consequences. Those facts make the prevention and correction of speech problems one of education's major challenges.

HEALTH AND SOCIAL
WELFARE CONSIDERATIONS

Professionals who concentrate on speech and language problems have developed a point of view, a terminology, and a place for themselves among the helping professions. They maintain a close alliance with dentists and physicians because some of the more complex speech problems are linked with medical and dental conditions. As will be shown, however, their closest relationship is with educators.

A small but complex group of speech problems has physiological bases.

The great majority of speech and language problems are developmental and are not tied to physiological abnormalities. This is the place, however, to describe briefly the four major kinds of medically connected speech problems that teachers may find themselves working with in collaboration with speech and language clinicians in elementary and secondary schools.[1]

Central Nervous System or Brain Damage. Injury to the brain before or after birth, from whatever cause (accident, stroke, tumor, illness), can hinder the development of language and speech. The ability to understand the speech of others may be absent or limited, too, from the same presumed cause. *Childhood* or *developmental aphasia* is sometimes used to denote such language and speech problems.

Cerebral Palsy. This faulty, slow, slurred, and difficult-to-understand speech is associated with the poor voluntary control of muscles characteristic of persons with cerebral palsy. There is no set pattern of speech disparities. It is related to the particular form and degree of the cerebral palsy, which varies from person to person.

Corrective work, begun early, produces marked improvement.

Cleft Palate or Cleft Lip. Some babies are born with a split in the roof of the mouth and/or the upper lip, leaving an opening between the mouth and the nasal cavity. Sometimes in this deformity the gap extends to the soft palate, which may be divided or missing. The difficulty in closing the nasal and oral cavities from each other during speech makes the formation of certain speech sounds, such as /v/, /t/, or /f/, particularly difficult, even following high-quality surgical repair of the cleft and remedial speech work. Dental abnormalities of teeth and gums likewise complicate articulation. Since 99 percent of cleft-palate children have middle ear disease in the early preschool years, patterns of fluctuating hearing loss are frequently found. That, too, can inhibit learning correct articulation and can slow or delay language development.

---

[1] Other serious speech and language deficiencies are connected with hearing impairments and certain physical impairments. These are taken up in other chapters.

Deformities. Occasionally children are born with other deformities of the mouth, nose, tongue, or throat, or such deformities may result from accidents or from surgery to correct other conditions. A consequence may be difficulty in producing certain speech sounds because of structural changes in the speech organs.

These four speech problems are difficult to improve or correct. Fortunately, they are also among the least frequent of all speech problems. None of them has a "typical" form, despite some common qualities. Individually designed corrective work by speech specialists often produces marked improvement, especially when started early in life.

A Personal Perspective

The following account of the first two years of Ben's life, as told by his father, highlights the human stresses that accompany physiologically based speech and language anomalies. Here are some things to think about while reading this true story:

Family effects are important to consider.

What will happen when Ben starts school?
How soon and in what ways should school personnel get involved with Ben and his family?
What parts should the principal, the teacher, and the speech and language clinician play?

The first sight of one's own child is one of life's most memorable moments. In Ben's case, that was doubly, triply true....He had a cleft lip and cleft palate. Holding him for the first time and looking through tears at those badly twisted features, I couldn't suppress the shock and despair....

An endless series of operations ahead. The possibility of mental retardation. Probable hearing loss and major dental problems. Guaranteed speech defects, and all sorts of social and self-image difficulties. Financial disaster for sure.

A full-scale tragedy.

But shock wears off, and guilt and despair finally subside once you recognize their stupidity.... Ben's sister had the right idea. Free, like all 4 year olds, from the bleeding stigmata of preconceptions, she took her first look at her...day-old brother through the hospital glass and said, "Why doesn't he have any hair?" Then added, as an offhand afterthought, "His lip touches his nose."

Young siblings are free from adult preconceptions.

Cleft lip and palate are the most common of the so-called serious birth defects. Yet the collective wisdom of the medical profession still can't explain why they occur. What is known is that all fetuses start out with bilateral clefts—a separation between the nose and mouth on either side. But by the seventh week of pregnancy, the tissue between nose and mouth comes together to form the upper lip and the normal "mustache" area between the two. By the ninth week, the roof of the mouth—the hard palate—and the soft palate behind it close up.

Except in cleft children. Their lip and nose do not separate properly on one or both sides. The palate is literally "cleft" in two parts, with a gaping hole instead of a closed inverted cup-shaped roof of the mouth. A cleft palate hinders swallowing and speech, since the muscles of the soft palate and a closed-off roof of the mouth (for suction) are essential to forming correct sounds. Lip and palate clefts do not always go together—but they most often do.

A series of fairly simple reflex tests soon established that we wouldn't have to worry about Ben's brain. Instead, we could worry about all the surgery required to fix up [his] features. . . . Even if you trust your surgeon implicitly, when your child faces a minimum of four and a maximum of perhaps eight major operations, there is only one way to deal with the prospect. That is by adapting the Alcoholics Anonymous creed of accepting the things you cannot change and taking the surgical hurdles one operation at a time. Still, no matter how well prepared you might be, there are few more upsetting sights than seeing them wheel your infant off to the operating room.

Surgery can be upsetting for parents.

He'll also have to concentrate on learning to speak properly, by means of hilarious alphabetical drills conducted by his parents and big sister. Speech progress to date has been often humorous, sometimes frustrating but generally remarkable. The vowels come out loud and clear. The consonants come out just loud—generic consonants, mostly indistinguishable one from another. Thus, for example, "Ih, ow, aey" translates—to the Ben-trained ear—as "Sit down, Daddy." But he keeps trying, and lately his *m*'s, *n*'s, *r*'s and *l*'s have been sounding the way they're supposed to.

The fourth and most recent operation is responsible for much of this progress. In it, the actual reconstruction of the palate took place and the hole—reduced by natural growth to about half an inch—was sewn shut.

Speech correction is a necessary follow-up.

The child's speaking equipment, then, is now more or less in shape. He just has to figure out how to use it and change the ways of a "lazy" tongue that has grown used to compensating in strange ways for the cleft. Often, when he rattles on excitedly about something, it is necessary to call in the outside interpreter—either his sister or his faithful young governess Megan—who understands (or pretends to) more of what he says than the old fogies. But more often, he is happy to repeat himself ad infinitum, with elaborate gestures and nonverbal cues, until a sufficient measure of his meaning is communicated—like any non-cleft 2 year old.

And then there are the teeth. They go every which way. . . . More operations will probably be needed for that. But as his second year draws to completion, it seems a relatively small thing. At 35 pounds, Ben himself is—by contrast—not at all a small thing. He's a rollicking, boisterous tornado of a little boy. A daredevil and a clown, he is impervious to the falls and bruises that reduce most kids his age to torrential tears. Perhaps, as one friend suggests, that's because he knows from his hospital stints what *real* pain is. The minor slings and arrows of daily accidents hardly faze him. . . .

Funny, but we misplaced the tragedy somewhere along the line. I think it was round about the time we stopped feeling sorry for ourselves. As for the child, he never had any tragic outlook to shed. He seemed to know better from the beginning, and his own joyous approach to life was infectious. . . . Happy birthday, Ben. (Adapted from Paris, 1981)

EDUCATIONAL CONSIDERATIONS

Most speech problems do not have a physical base. They are developmental. They respond to preventive and remedial teaching.

The improvement of speech is an important goal of elementary, secondary, and higher education. The vocational implications of effective speech today, from actor or lawyer to senator or sportscaster, are plain. The personal and social values of good speech in conversation and discussion are evident, whether in the family, among friends, or in the community. Today's culture increasingly employs such technology as dictation equipment, telephone conferences, citizen band radios, and tape-recorded messages to increase the range and variety of oral communication. A well-modulated, expressive, and easily understood voice is an unquestionable asset. It is understandable that parents and teachers show serious concern if children's speech does not develop in what they consider a normal way.

Speech is part of language arts.

Normal speech is a critical asset in today's culture.

What does being "part of the language arts" really mean? One teacher commented, "I don't feel that correcting a child's speech deviation, when I know he can produce the sounds clearly, is any different from correcting a child who says *ain't*." Another said, "Speech and grammar had slid! I'm strict about them with all children. I don't do anything different with children who show speech deviations; I'm just more conscious of their needs." (Freeman, 1977, p. 73)

Like reading and writing, speech is every teacher's business, from the primary grades through secondary school graduation. The ways in which teachers model excellent speech, give recognition for its proper use by pupils, and provide individualized instruction leading to better speech are key educational considerations.

Now another role is rapidly shaping for regular teachers, one that in the past had been reserved for the specialist only. This new trend means that

> the selection of any child for individual therapy away from the classroom would be made only after all other possible alternatives had been explored and rejected. The primary goal is to keep the child with a communication problem in the mainstream of education as much as possible. . . . This is seen as a truly cooperative effort on the part of the teacher, the speech clinician, and any other team members involved. (Hull & Hull, 1973, p. 300)

What the Hulls noted as a new trend in 1973 is now public policy in the United States. That policy includes the special education of children with speech problems in the same domain with regular class instruction. How principals, teachers, and speech and language specialists join forces to carry out that policy successfully is the main thrust of the discussion that follows.

Speech correction belongs in the mainstream.

Mainstreaming

The implementation of a new policy can be a bumpy road at first. That is especially true if there is less than adequate preparation for the new responsibilities.

This real-life story, by Linda East, of Altavista Elementary School in Virginia, tells how one determined first-grade teacher mustered the support to cope successfully with what at the outset seemed an impossible situation. In the process, it shows how similar situations might be better prepared for in the future. Significant themes introduced in the story are elaborated later in the chapter.

A Mainstreaming Success Story

I've always found it helpful as a teacher to jot down a few first impressions of children after their parents brought them by to enroll in my first grade class. My first impression of Bill seemed normal enough: brown skin, short curly black hair, large almond-shaped brown eyes filled with wonder, terribly shy but terribly excited.

His mother was a large dominating woman with eyes like Bill's that seemed to be busy looking past you as she spoke. "I'm afraid you're going to have trouble with Bill," she said. "He's never been away from home, so he may not know how to act. Didn't send him to kindergarten. I was scared the noise of so many children would upset him. Say hello to Miz East, Bill."

General development seemed grossly retarded.

A soft "low" came from Bill, who clung tightly to his mother's hand. As they left, she added an afterthought. "Oh, and Miz East, you may have to help Bill when he goes to the bathroom."

The next day was to be a sudden awakening as to just how much I would have to help Bill. Besides not being able to use the bathroom by himself, Bill couldn't eat by himself (he chewed one pea at a time); nor could he speak comprehensibly, walk properly, go up or down steps, run, or jump. When asked a question, he mumbled a stream of unrelated sounds. Bill spent most of the first three days crying in my lap as I tried to organize a new class of diverse and demanding first graders.

I quickly rushed in every specialist I could reach, the principal, and a videotape crew to film Bill in the classroom and on the playground. The tape was sent to some specialists I couldn't reach.

Formal assessment was of limited help.

Their verdicts were very discouraging, and I learned nothing new. He obviously needed special education. But mainstreaming meant Bill must remain in my room the entire school year, spending only 10 minutes at the end of each day with a learning disabilities teacher. A speech therapist worked with him twice a week for short periods of time, too.

Each day as I worked with the class, I struggled desperately to make every minute of Bill's time a learning experience. Every evening, I cursed the idea of mainstreaming and wondered what kind of thoughtless people could have instituted such an impossible program.

At lunchtime it was necessary for me to feed Bill. After a week of not eating lunch myself, I decided I would try to teach Bill to feed himself each lunchtime until one of the pupils had finished eating and could take over for me. It became apparent that I wasn't going to be Bill's only teacher—the classroom was filled with 24 eager instructors. And they put all they had into teaching Bill to walk, talk, eat, go to the bathroom by himself, run, jump, go up and down steps, and play.

As weeks went by, miracles began to happen, and each day I went home with a glowing account to give my husband. "Bill learned to say 'lunch tray' today." "Bill learned to eat a forkful of mashed potatoes today." "Bill learned to jump from a small chair today."

Informal assessment uncovered Bill's real learning ability.

Bill demonstrated one skill the first week of school which astonished me and which was to be the basis for further learning experiences. He loved the record player and learned to operate it himself after only one lesson. I realized that if Bill could work the record player by himself, he could learn to do other things as well. By the second month of school, not only could Bill turn on my cassette player, he also could set it up, record his own voice, play the tape back and listen to it. The wonder and smiles on his face delighted me. I recorded simple songs and stories for him to listen to over and over.

At Show-and-Tell time, Bill always mumbled his stories and songs. No one understood anything he said, but the whole class listened attentively to see if he would use one of the words they had taught him. Our big reward finally came at Christmastime, when Bill stood before the class and sang, "Jin'le Bells Jin'le Bells Jin'le Bells" over and over again. The class broke into spontaneous applause, and my eyes filled with tears.

By the end of the school year, Bill had learned to speak in short, comprehensible sentences. He could read ten words and recognize three numbers. He ate by himself, sang songs, walked up and down steps, and ran races.

As for mainstreaming, I learned a big lesson that year: Only a classroom full of "normal" children could have set the examples Bill needed to improve his faulty speech and coordination.

Classmate modeling and tutoring succeeded.

Epilogue: In the end, I volunteered to keep Bill in my classroom the following year. He learned to speak coherently, count to 20, recognize letters and sounds, read through three levels of Ginn, retell stories, and make up his own songs. His attention span increased to 40 minutes.

My deep thanks go to his mother, who worked closely with me, and to his speech, special education, and special reading teachers. Most of all, though, my thanks go to all of Bill's fellow classmates, who set such good examples for him. (East, 1976, p. 71)

Here are some items to notice in East's story. They reflect steps she took in working with Bill, as well as her attitude toward school resources.

1. Use of notes to record impressions of children at entry
2. Call for consultative aid from the principal and from specialists
3. Immediate check on possible help from specialist teachers and the speech clinician

Was Bill mentally retarded? How can you tell?

4. Use of peer teaching, starting with lunch and leading to other things
5. Setting of short-range objectives and rewards for their attainment
6. Objective record of Bill's accomplishments
7. Increased understanding and ability to use parent and specialist teachers as a team
8. Acknowledgment of helper roles of regular class pupils

This is a striking illustration of a teacher's high-caliber competence in the face of a difficult professional challenge. It points up how regular class pupils will react when they see that their teacher is a model of helpfulness. It shows how direct interaction can build positive character in both exceptional children and their "normal" companions. It is an example of the intelligent use of consultative services and of teamwork between regular and specialist teachers. The mainstream conditions under which East found it necessary to work were less than optimal. But her approach, the decisions she made, and the spirit with which she worked are superb evidences of preferred practices.

Teamwork paid off.

DEFINITIONS

The following definitions are broadly useful for educational purposes.

Defective (or disordered) speech interferes with communication; it lacks intelligibility. It often causes the speaker to be uncomfortable and maladjusted. Defective speech attracts attention to the speech sounds and accompanying mannerisms, and that detracts from attention to the content of what the speaker is saying.

Satisfactory speech communicates without distortion. Speech itself (apart from content) produces little or no affective reaction in the speaker. The content of what the person is saying is conveyed with little or no distraction caused by mannerisms or unusual speech sounds.

Good speech enhances the communication. It gives the speaker positive feedback, through hearing and sight, that the intended affective tone is accompanying the message. Accuracy and clarity of speech sounds, in addition to the use of appropriate face, hand, and body movements, add to the force and fullness of the message being communicated.

With good speech, content has a good chance for attention.

In short, if speech cannot be readily understood, if it is upsetting to the person speaking, or if it causes distraction or negative reactions from the audience, it is a speech problem. The definition is thus entirely functional.

LINGUISTICS

Speech and language therapists often begin their analysis of speech or language problems by assessing children according to the linguistic code (decoding and encoding) and components (phonology, semantics, syntax). Freeman (1977) proposed a simple model for organizing these ideas. Phonological decoding is indicated when a child can distinguish between sounds (as in *witch* versus *switch*); phonological encoding is the ability to produce sounds. A child with an articulation disorder (substituting *w* sounds for *r* sounds, for example) shows a problem of phonological encoding. Semantic decoding refers to meanings, as shown, for example,

Distinctions made by linguists are helpful in diagnosis.

when a child is given a vocabulary test in which the answer is given by pointing to a picture. When the child names a picture, that would be semantic encoding. Problems of semantics (meanings) often reflect basic language difficulties rather than speech problems. Syntactic decoding requires understanding of sentences or other complex structures; for example, "Put the boy in the wagon." Finally, syntactic encoding involves the use of complex sequences of linguistic elements, often assessed simply by observing the spontaneous speech of the child.

Obviously, the child may have difficulties in some of the linguistic components and not in others, for many reasons. The child may have lacked experience and simply not have many well-developed concepts, or lack of experience may show particularly in limited syntax, as in saying single words when sentences would be more adequate. Sometimes the problem is one of hearing or physical inability to produce certain sounds. Speech, language, and conceptual problems interact, but it is often useful to do an analysis from a linguistic point of view to see what pattern emerges. Teachers can expect that speech and language pathologists, called in for consultation, will be able to perform such analyses.

DIVISIONS OF SPEECH AND LANGUAGE WORK

Three concepts—speech and language development, speech improvement, and speech correction—take on a new significance in today's mainstreamed classrooms. Teachers and speech and language clinicians recognize that they have much to contribute to each of these activities and that they should share responsibilities for them, in different degrees.

Speech development, improvement, and correction have special significance.

Speech and language development is the acquisition of increasing ability to understand and produce oral language.[2] It begins at birth and should continue through life. During childhood, deliberate efforts are made to foster speech and language development by teaching new words, correct pronunciations, and forms of oral language like questions and exclamations. In the school years, it is based on sequential guidelines in curricula and textbooks.

Help communication competency increase.

Speech improvement is enhancement of the quality of existing speech. It starts informally in the preschool years when parents monitor their children's oral language and encourage increased clarity, appropriate volume, accurate expressiveness, logical organization, proper temporal sequencing, and correct sound production. Schooling continues those activities and

Sharpen communication skill and accuracy; prevent defects.

---

[2] Language can be developed independent of oral speech; see Chapter 7 on hearing impairments. Also, speech is only one of several modes or ways in which humans communicate, but it is the mode most frequently used.

uses oral reading, acting, discussion, debate, role playing, and the like as vehicles. This instruction, like that for speech development, is integral to the language arts curriculum, though it overlaps into other curricular and extracurricular sectors.

Remove or minimize existing defects or disorders.

Speech correction means the remediation of oral speech disorders that interfere with communication to a significant degree. Disordered speech in need of correction is differentiated from imperfect speech still in the normal developmental sequence. Hence, speech correction applies only to significantly deviant speech patterns habituated in the person's day-to-day talking.

No aspect of speech correction is the exclusive domain of specialists.

Teachers and speech and language clinicians can help each other in all three functions: development, improvement, and correction. Figure 6.1 represents the sharing of professional knowledge and responsibilities. There is an approximately equal division with respect to speech improvement. The regular class teacher carries the major burden for speech development. The clinician carries more of the responsibilities for speech correction. There is no sharp dividing line, no solely held territory. The pupil can always look to both for help in any of the three functions.

CORRECTION PROCEDURES

Articulation Defects

Articulation defects are the most frequent speech problems of school-age children. Most common in early elementary school, some persist into the secondary and college years. They fall into three classes:

1. Omission of certain sounds, such as "I like ou" for "I like you."
2. Substitution of one sound for another, like "acwoss" for "across."
3. Distortion of sounds, like "srimp" for "shrimp" or "schtop" for "stop."

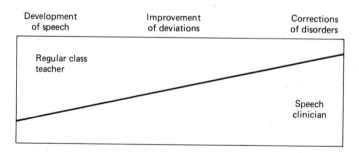

Figure 6.1. Sharing of Responsibility Between Regular Class Teacher and Speech Clinician

These three types of speech errors have been studied thoroughly, and there are proven methods of correcting them. The errors appear to be developmental in origin in the sense that a particular part of the child's step-by-step acquisition of normal speech fixated instead of moving along toward the next developmental point.

For instance, it is part of the normal speech development process for kindergartners sometimes to say "bawoon" for "balloon." But if by the end of second grade or the beginning of third grade that substitution continues, it is a sign that corrective work is probably needed.

Analysis, as follows, can illustrate this point. Johnny came to first grade with a Band-Aid on his index finger one morning in October. He held it up for the teacher to see and said, "I tut my finder on a thoup tan. Mommy wapped it up. It will det be'er thoon. Mommy thay."

The teacher knew that Johnny's cognitive development was superior because of how quickly he adapted in school and how readily he had learned daily routines. But his speech was often difficult to understand. What to do about it?

First, take note of Johnny's speech errors.

"Tut" for *"cut"*
"Finder" for *"finger"*
"Thoup" for *"soup"*
"Tan" for *"can"*
"Wapped" for *"wrapped"*
"Det" for *"get"*
"Be'er" for *"better"*
"Thoon". for *"soon"*
"Thay" for *"say"*

The next step is to look at the errors Johnny made. They are marked by asterisks in the sequences below, which show the order in which the correct use of sounds tends to develop in young children. There is one asterisk for each error.

Before starting kindergarten, children usually have good command of these sounds in oral communication:

/w/ as in *we, one, water*
/b/ as in *baby, bat, bug*
/h/ as in *hop, hair, hat*
/m/ as in *me, mad, mother*
/p/ as in *paper, pop, pole*

In kindergarten and first grade, it is natural for some pupils still to be learning to use these sounds correctly:

Four sounds give problems here.

/y/ as in *you, yes, yet*
/d/ as in *day, bed, doll*
*/ng/ as in *ring, thing, singer*
**/k/ as in *can, ink, tack*
/n/ as in *nut, knife, new*
*/t/ as in *toe, hit, batter*
*/g/ as in *big, getting, gas*
/f/ as in *fall, leaf, offer*

During second grade, a number of pupils will be gaining increased control over these sounds:

No trouble here.

/v/ as in *vase, stove, five*
/sh/ as in *shoot, shine, dish*
/th/ as in *bathe, father, this*
/l/ as in *lot, limb, bill*

By the end of the third grade, almost all children should be using these sounds properly in everyday speech:

Two sounds give difficulty here.

/th/ as in *thin, three, bath*
/z/ as in *zero, hose, his*
***/s/ as in *soap, mess, biscuit*
*/r/ as in *rain, rip, over*

Compare errors with speech development milestones.

When seen in the perspective of these lists, Johnny's imperfections are revealed to be normal, natural ones, consistent with his current development. Johnny has no difficulty with the sounds most pupils make easily by the beginning of first grade. There is some difficulty with four first-grade and two third-grade sounds.

He should not be reprimanded or teased for his manner of speech. He ought not be singled out in any way or told that his speech is incorrect or defective. Individual corrective exercises are not the most appropriate approach, either. The regular teacher's skills, augmented by consultation by a speech clinician, are best directed at helping John improve his speech in the context of speech and language development activities with the whole class. The first-grade sounds are the ones to emphasize in this speech improvement activity.

Decide on a course of action.

One of the advantages of the suggested sound groupings by grades is that they let teachers know where to begin. They are not hard-and-fast timetables. If anything, they are conservative. The sounds that are listed by grades can be linked to the sequence of the phonic elements introduced in the basic reading series; teaching one can then reinforce the other. Related illustrative material can be found in Birch, Matthews, and Burgi (1958).

Suppose now that John had been a third-grader, not a first-grader.

Corrective intervention on the first-grade sounds would be justified. A particular three-step sequence has a good record of effectiveness in remediation in such cases.

First, be sure the child hears the error. This often requires auditory training to help the child learn to notice how the correct and incorrect sounds differ. Masking the mouth with a card, one can make the sound correctly and incorrectly, in isolation and in words, to see if the child catches the differences. Tape recordings of sounds can be used, too. The speech clinician can suggest many interesting ways to conduct auditory training. Children can help each other. It is fundamentally important that the child become able to hear the correct sound made by someone else and to distinguish it from other sounds. Some sounds can be readily seen and felt, too. It helps if the child can see and feel the error and the correct sound and note the differences.

Consult a clinician about a three-step intervention.

Second, be sure the child can produce the sound correctly. Once the youngster can hear the sound, it is possible to use a tape recorder, for instance, to make comparisons between the actual sound the child produces and a correct model. Then the child can be brought, through successive approximations, to say the sound acceptably. Again, speech clinicians have identified many ways to motivate interest in achieving the correct response. Practice should continue until the pupil produces the target sound acceptably on almost every attempt.

Third, move the newly acquired correct sound into everyday speech and fix it in the pupil's spontaneous language usage. The first two steps do not result in automatic accomplishment of the third. A large amount of highly motivated and closely monitored repetition is needed to establish a new or revised speech habit.

This three-step outline of a teaching method can be fleshed out and individualized in planning sessions in which the particular child's characteristics are taken fully into account. Potential physical and environmental factors that might cause the articulation error should be investigated also. For instance, is the child's hearing in the normal range? Do the child's parents or other frequently seen adults make the same articulation error, providing a constant model? The speech clinician will know about high-interest instructional materials and procedures for use both in class and by the parents at home.

Investigate related factors.

Voice Problems

Voice problems are difficult to describe objectively. What is strange or objectionable to one person may be intriguing or distinctive to another.

Voice problems are harder to pinpoint.

Among the five types of voice problems (quality, rate, flexibility, volume, and pitch) the first in frequency is *quality*. Included under voice quality problems are voices that are so nasal, harsh, or breathy that they interfere with communication. *Rate* problems refer to dragged-out, prolonged speech or the converse, extremely quick, clipped, staccato speech—either of which is so pronounced as to diminish intelligibility. A *flexibility* disorder is exemplified by a flat, uninterrupted monotone that is difficult to attend to. *Volume* refers to too loud or too soft a voice for the situation. *Pitch* has reference to a voice that is too high or too deep.

Abrupt changes in a pupil's voice may signal a medical problem. The appropriate move is to call such a change to the parent's or school nurse's attention.

Voice problems are so idiosyncratic that the regular teacher should seek consultation with a speech clinician before attempting corrective steps. One principle to be mindful of in the meantime is to model considerate and acceptant behavior for other teachers and classmates. It is easy for a voice problem to mark a child for ridicule.

Stuttering

Stuttering refers to stoppages or pauses that noticeably interrupt the flow of speech. The stoppages are involuntary and irritating to the speaker and the listener. Stuttering is also termed *disfluency* or *nonfluency*.

Stuttering can be remedied.

Overcoming stuttering is a complex and often time-consuming process, but the rewards can be great. Shames and Florance (1980) described a five-step sequence for treatment. It can be used on a group or individual basis in school settings. Follow-up studies have shown very encouraging results.

In Phase I, the stutterer uses a delayed auditory feedback device to interfere with present speech patterns and to learn to speak in a deliberate and very controlled new way. Recognition that the stuttering can be eliminated, even though the price is constant watchfulness and somewhat mechanical delivery, offers strong motivation to continue.

Phase II is practice under the tight monitoring conditions of Phase I. The individual assesses personal speech behavior, self-administering rewards for periods of speech without disfluencies. The most reinforcing reward is to drop the tight control briefly and just speak freely for a short time.

Controlled speech must be practiced in daily activities.

The focus of Phase III is on moving controlled speech fully into daily activities. Though activities differ for each person, the underlying pattern for Phase III is similar. Contracts are written that require the individual to engage in progressively more free (nondeliberate) speech with associates, subsequently evaluate the outcomes, and report them to the speech and language clinician.

In Phase IV the clinician's role changes from close guidance and supervision to one more like that of a mentor, who is available as needed for support and understanding. Some direct instruction in effective use of the newfound freedom of speech continues. The stutterer grows in confidence, replacing more and more monitored, controlled speech with well-inflected and modulated stutter-free speech.

Phase V is evaluative, studying the effectiveness and maintenance level of the whole process. It is on the basis of such follow-up that Shames and Florance reported close to 95 percent success over a six-year period.

The time required varies greatly, from as little as two weeks to as long as two years. The youngest stutterers with whom the five-phase system has been effective were 6 years old.

With children under 8, the Shames-Florance procedure uses clinician response to replace the Phase I delayed auditory feedback device. Also, Phase IV moves into place more naturally with younger persons, sometimes proving unnecessary as a distinct step.

Whether or not stutterers are under some special form of therapy, teachers and principals have two good principles to follow to help pupils keep nonfluency in check and to be full regular class participants.

First, know that conflict or excitement tends to increase stuttering behavior. This does not mean that one should overprotect nonfluent children, keeping all stress or exuberance out of their lives. Rather, it means that one should expect and not be surprised by what happens to their speech under such conditions. Also, it means that one should help nonfluent youngsters learn to consciously control their own activity and emotional states while talking.

School climate has an effect that educators can control.

Second, treat children who stutter like the other children. Call on them. Give them opportunities to ask questions and take the time to listen. Do not fill in words for them any more than for any other child. Be a model for the stuttering pupil's classmates.

Developmental Delay

Slowed cognitive development tends to be paralleled by slow speech and language development. Speech and language stimulation is the recommended procedure in such cases. It has two components, quantitative and qualitative. The first is aimed at increasing the sheer amount of meaningful verbalization. The second focuses on raising the level of accuracy and variety of the pupil's oral expression.

Stimulate speech and language.

Speech clinicians and teachers, working at speech and language stimulation as a team with parents and aides, can prove important in the life of a pupil who shows slow cognitive development. When speech is stimulated, language growth is most likely promoted too. The effect is pronounced on some children, particularly those whose home and family lives have been relatively devoid of such stimulation.

Better speech and language mean increased learning power.

Some youngsters are kept by impairments from developing any communication ability on their own. Deaf and deaf-blind children are among that group, but there are well-worked-out ways to help them establish language systems and communication. Others, not deaf or deaf-blind, have received less attention.

Now there is a rapidly growing research and development effort to build language and communication capabilities for nonspeaking severely and profoundly impaired children, autistic and similar children, and other non-verbal or language-delayed children. These young people with severe communication handicaps make up a small but important group. Many have potential that they cannot show. Speech and language clinicians are joining with psychologists, teachers, engineers, and others to adapt old means (signing, Bliss symbols, codes) and to invent new means (communication boards, electronic devices) to break the barriers that now stand in the way of their education.

PREVAILING AND PREFERRED PRACTICES

On the left are listed practices that are usually found in speech improvement and correction programs in today's schools. On the right are preferred practices. Less common, the preferred practices are found in schools that are showing the way to others.

Prevailing Practices

1. Annually, the speech clinician screens kindergarten or first-grade pupils by taking them, one at a time, to a small, specially equipped room where speech articulation, rhythm, and voice tests are administered. Special speech-testing and instructional materials are available in the speech correction room.

2. The clinician selects certain pupils, perhaps five or six from a room, for weekly or

Preferred Practices

1. The speech clinician teams with parents, early education teachers, and kindergarten and first-grade teachers to assess children's speech and language improvement for the whole class when that is possible and for individuals as needed. The clinician notes which pupils provide excellent speech models, checks the developmental status of each pupil with regard to language and speech production, and records any serious aberrations in speech or language. This is done informally in the regular class during general speech and language instruction. Early collaborative assistance with parents is provided as necessary.

2. The regular class teacher and the speech clinician jointly plan and carry out improvement and

semiweekly correction lessons. These pupils leave their regular schedule, going to the speech clinician's room for their special instruction. There they are taught individually or in groups of three or four with similar speech problems.

3. Occasionally the clinician and the teacher have brief hallway talks about how the children designated as having speech defects are progressing. Sometimes the clinician gives suggestions for regular class help. When a child's speech is sufficiently corrected, regular visits to the speech correction room taper off to a maintenance schedule and finally stop.

4. The same pattern is followed through all the elementary, middle, and secondary schools, whether open-space or traditional in design. Some pupils continue to receive corrective attention for several consecutive years.

corrective procedures as an integral part of the language arts component of the regular curriculum. Pupils with all degrees and kinds of speech problems are helped as a matter of course, individually or in small groups, in the context of regular classwork.

3. Clinicians bring to regular classes the special equipment and materials for speech and language assessment and corrective instruction. Teachers are shown how to do speech articulation assessment and corrective instruction. Occasionally a child is moved to the speech clinician's room for intensive work, but not regularly. All pupils have been oriented to the speech correction room. It is also used by others from time to time for teacher planning sessions, parent conferences, and individual or small group tutoring.

4. This pattern continues through high school, where the child has several teachers. The closest team partner with the clinician is the language arts teacher. The other teachers are kept informed and shown how to help. In open-space schools, the clinician may team simultaneously with several teachers who are jointly responsible for larger groups of pupils. Coordination is accomplished through the team leader, but the principles illustrated here remain the same.

Total time spent by clinicians is not different in either the prevailing or the preferred practices. The preferred practices do reduce some "dead time" occasioned by back-and-forth movement of pupils and clinician from class to the speech correction room. Teacher aides can be used to good effect in either approach. The preferred practices also encourage participation by the speech clinician in the language arts curriculum. That is an advantage. Speech clinicians are among the best-informed faculty members regarding linguistics, oral expression, and the developmental aspects of human language. Their frequent presence in regular classes encourages their participation in assessing other learning problems, while making speech improvement and correction as natural to all pupils as the improvement and correction of arithmetic. A case load of names can be maintained under the preferred practices, and it can be used for administrative purposes without obtruding into the pupil's awareness.

"It points out the value of redeployment of staff energy and existing resources" (Green, 1977).

Illustration of an Effective School Program

Richardson is a rapidly growing Texas community near Dallas. It had approximately 36,000 pupils in its elementary and secondary schools in 1976. In 1968–1969, moves began to bring special education and regular education together. At the same time, decentralization started in all the school system's operations. There has been a steady march toward accomplishing both goals.

Speech and language specialists team-teach with regular teachers from kindergarten on.

Now every child who enters a Richardson kindergarten meets and talks with a speech and language clinician along with a kindergarten teacher as part of the day-to-day experience in the kindergarten class. There are 21 elementary schools in the system. Each has a full-time speech and language clinician on the faculty. They spend the first 60 days of each term with teachers in kindergarten classes working at diagnostics, individualized program planning, and speech and language development.

Before 1980, Richardson's clinicians would have waited for referrals by teachers regarding children with speech problems. At that time, case loads were 90 percent articulation errors. Today, clinicians' functions are much more extensive. Their title, speech and language therapists, tells part of that story. So does the average case load of about 70 children, of whom only about 5 percent have articulation problems. Nearly 90 percent are pupils who present language problems and with whom the therapists frequently work in small groups in the context of the regular class.

Secondary schools are served too.

The language backgrounds of the therapists in Richardson serve mainly to bolster the kindergarten and primary-grade language curriculum, though three clinicians, two full time and one part time, are assigned to service high schools too. There is cooperation, not overlap, among the therapists, regular teachers, and other special educators who work in the same settings as resource teachers. Sometimes, when it is advisable to pull one or more pupils out of a regular class for specialized instruction, the therapist may work in another location (such as a learning lab), where one-to-one instruction may be common.

Corrective speech work is intense.

For most work specific to speech—articulation, voice, stuttering, and the like—pupils are taken from the regular class to a separate therapy room in their school. Richardson's pattern in this, though, is one of intense concentration aimed at speedy results. Ordinarily, arrangements are made with the regular class teacher for a regular one-period-per-day schedule with the therapist. Progress in correction is usually so apparent that the regular teachers and other pupils quickly notice changes and take real satisfaction in giving supplemental support to the pupil. Also, the therapist makes periodic personal reports to the regular teacher.

This school district conducts prekindergarten classes, too, beginning at age 3, for children who by that time can be seen to need some form of special education. Many of them show speech and language problems in addition to other problems. In these noncategorized early childhood groups, speech and language therapists team-teach with other specialists. All work is done in the class setting.

Most special education is undifferentiated in the preschool years.

In their language instruction in regular classes, the therapists tend to work with small groups selected for basic language problems and language development needs. The therapists attend to aspects of language that underlie reading, writing, spelling, listening, and speaking, rather than attempt to teach in those curricular areas directly. The therapist and regular teacher make assessments on the basis of actual samples of the pupils' writing, speaking, and other language behavior. Sometimes clinical language tests are used, but much of the assessment is based on each pupil's day-to-day language production (or lack of it).

If a pupil's writing performance is inadequate, the assessment may reveal that the youngster is also unable to express orally what the assignment requested in written form. The speech and language therapist may trace this linguistic lack to foundational weaknesses in the pupil's conceptions about morphology or semantics. Using material from the regular class social studies texts, spelling lists, pre-primers, or whatever else is used by the regular teacher, the therapist helps the pupil develop and strengthen the ability to understand the nature of the inhibiting condition and learn to overcome it. Sometimes a third professional, perhaps a resource teacher, works with the same pupil on remedial reading, for instance, in concert with the language therapist and the regular teacher.

Communication needs are identified in the natural environment.

The consultative help of a speech and language therapist makes its way to the regular teacher through a fairly typical referral process. It usually begins with the regular teacher contacting a counselor or principal when a pupil is experiencing difficulty. From there it moves quickly through the Texas Admission-Review-Dismissal Committee process (similar to the IEP process). When special educational assistance is no longer needed, the same committee officially disengages the support linkages that had been put in place earlier by the regular and special educator team, and the speech and language therapists move to the next cases.

No intervention program can claim to be effective without ongoing evaluation. Only through such feedback can program alterations be made and teachers' responses and initiations be directed toward specific intervention strategies. When objective records on language-impaired children indicate teachers are talking less and listening more, and children are talking more and talking better, a picture is given of a truly effective classroom intervention program. (Allen, 1980, p. 10).

The process is actually much less mechanical than it might sound. Within the school, everyone is in some sense a teacher of language and speech. That helps establish and maintain a rapport among the faculty. It encourages easy informality and a shared mutual concern for all pupils, with or without speech and language problems.

Richardson's operations are not fully described in this summary. They include many other forward-looking practices. Richardson has made serious efforts to determine the value of innovative practices. Those described have had their merits tested and have won in the hard court of community acceptance.

Current Trends

Real weight is now being given to preventing speech problems and enhancing the speech and language development of all pupils. The way the clinician's time is used is becoming more related to the work to be done with regular class teachers. That teaming can be observed in other emerging trends too.

Clinicians share their know-how with others.

Like school psychologists and many other specialists, speech and language clinicians now see how important it is to "give away" many of their closely guarded skills to others. Bradley (1976) said in this connection:

> Speech pathologists have found one thing to be most critical. They must be willing to share their techniques with teachers, childcare workers, parents, and students who can assist them in the development, stabilization, and generalization of goals appropriate to the handicapped individual's present level of functioning. (p. 3)

This trend encourages principals and teachers (and often parents or aides) to help pupils in ways previously reserved for the speech clinician. Research in the early 1950s indicated that parents, working at home under the guidance of speech clinicians, produced significant, positive changes in their children's speech. Bradley (1976) commented that such findings should not surprise us, in view of the fact that "mothers, without any specific training, have been helping 80 to 90% of the population acquire and use language skills by three years of age, in every cultural and socio-economic setting" (p. 1).

Service expands through aides.

Alvord (1977) described how seven Iowa speech clinicians prepared and supervised nine communication aides to work with pupils who showed articulatory disorders that required correction. The aides produced results equivalent to those obtained by speech clinicians with similar pupils, in a comparable amount of time and with high maintenance of results. The cost-effectiveness gain was appreciable. Equally important, a marked increase in clinician time availability was noted. How best to use that time now becomes a matter of real concern, whereas before it had been only an academic question. (An earlier study reporting outcomes in the same direction was provided by Alpiner, 1968.)

Speech and language clinicians also participate more in basic elementary and secondary school programs. Ainsworth (1965) encouraged that move early. Other leaders (Hull & Hull, 1973), too, press for added integration of clinical speech work and the rest of the school's programs. The clinician's point of view can be helpful to all pupils, especially if injected during curriculum planning and program individualization design (IEP development).

Clinicians' views influence individualization.

A complementary trend is toward deeper involvement of all teachers in speech remediation for individual pupils. That involvement touches the whole range of types, severity, and ages when speech problems appear. Applied behavior analysis studies have spotlighted the significance of modeling the value of planned reinforcement schemes in changing speech patterns. The work of Bandura (1971) and others showed how observational learning helps in pupil acquisition of skills and understandings. The regular class is a favorable staging area for the application of such learning principles, in contrast to the one-to-one setting or the small homogeneous speech problem group in which speech clinicians ordinarily worked in the past. And the regular teacher is the more logical implementor of reinforcement principles, though they may well be planned, and their outcomes assessed, jointly with the speech clinician.

Applied behavioral analysis is a working tool.

A trend of great significance to principals and to nursery, kindergarten, and primary teachers is a thrust of speech clinicians toward the early childhood years. Not long ago, when clinical speech work was almost entirely corrective, it was common to hear it said that youngsters under 7 or 8 years old were too young to benefit from the assistance of the speech clinician. Now that the potentialities of speech improvement and language and speech development are better understood, that statement is heard less often. Instead, two things are happening. First, developmental and improvement speech and language procedures are being used with babies and toddlers from birth to age 3, and their parents, in home-based or center-based operations. Second, speech clinicians are pairing with early childhood teachers to foster general speech development and improvement. If these trends are attended by a sensitivity to the need for high professional standards and thoughtful evaluation, they could result in superior service to a much larger portion of the pupils who need it.

Instruction starts on Day 1.

THE ROLE OF THE REGULAR CLASS TEACHER, CLINICIAN, AND PRINCIPAL

Practices of the past took children with speech problems out of mainstream classes to special rooms for speech instruction. Many schools are showing, however, that a less restrictive alternative is to bring the speech clinician's help to the pupils who need it while they are in regular classes. Thus principals and teachers can expect speech clinicians to move step by step into the current of education's mainstream.

There are a number of guidelines that principals, teachers, and clinicians will find useful as they shape individualized programs of instruction, whether full integration has been reached or is still on its way.

Weak speech and language slow all progress.

Like the rest of the language arts, speech and language progress through a sequence to higher and more complex stages as a child matures. As in reading and the other communication skills, children learn at different rates. Some fail markedly to progress in speech and language despite serious efforts to help them. When that happens, the impact of inadequate speech and language ricochets across the rest of the school curriculum. Talking about science or social studies becomes more difficult. Asking questions in shop or health class calls attention to the defective communication. No part of schooling is unaffected.

Thus when principal, teachers, and clinicians mobilize for corrective action regarding a language or speech defect, all components of the curriculum should be thought of as resources. If music or art activities, for instance, are not enlisted in support of the remedial plan, they may not be neutral. Rather, activities and teacher expectations in art or music might inadvertently thwart the carefully designed corrective reinforcement of appropriate language or speech, for instance, during reading and arithmetic instruction. The prime principle of curriculum individualization for corrective language and speech, therefore, is to involve all elements of the school curriculum in the remedial effort in a coordinated way.

Adaptive scheduling is the key.

Regular class teachers find that four speech and language factors influence daily class activities. First, pupils are sometimes withdrawn to attend therapy sessions. That means that certain children will be away one to five times a week for 15 to 30 minutes at a time. Class plans must be adjusted if the impact of those absences is to be minimized. Second, the clinician and the regular class teacher must confer about pupils and problems. Time must be built into the schedule for that. The principal has a responsibility here, too. Third, teachers should carry on specific, individualized activities for children with speech problems to complement the activities conducted in separate sessions with the clinician. Those must be woven into the day's fabric. Fourth, the regular teacher and the clinician increasingly spend time in team teaching, both in the same class. The scenario for space allocation, pupil grouping, availability of materials and timetable calls for flexible arrangements.

The regular teacher may also be asked to sit in on or participate in therapy sessions in the clinician's room or when conferences are held with parents, the principal, or other specialist colleagues. All in all, ingenuity is needed, particularly when the regular teacher must contend with a speech and language program that removes the children from regular classes for various time periods on an irregular schedule during the week.

SUMMARY

The public schools of the nation are coming closer to fulfilling the obligation to correct or ameliorate defective language and speech among all school-age children, and services from birth to age 5 are now becoming quite common.

In many exceptional children, speech and language problems are clearly present by the third year of life. A comprehensive school-based program ought to have a staff of clinicians actively beginning corrective and preventive work by age 3. In addition, speech and language problems can arise at any later time. Therefore, a truly complete program must have the staff and facilities to bring corrective instruction to pupils in early education, elementary, middle, high, and postsecondary schools. Moreover, sufficient staff is needed to conduct thorough and intensive activity for all who need it as soon as they are identified for as long as it is required.

Older children need help, too.

The public schools, though, are not the only agencies that should take part if truly comprehensive coverage is to be assured. Health, rehabilitation, higher education, and social welfare organizations, public and private, have parts to play, for individuals not reached by the public schools.

TOPICAL BIBLIOGRAPHY

Modern School Programs for Speech and Language Impaired Pupils

Alvord (1977)
Bradley (1976)
Curran & Cratty (1985)
Dopheide & Dalenger (1975)
Freeman (1977)
Fudala (1973)
Gray & Barker (1977)
Rees (1974)
Spollen & Ballif (1971)
Van Riper (1978)
Wiig & Semel (1980)

Persons with Speech Problems

Benson (1979)
Caudill (1965)
Hart & Jones (1980)
Henry (1948)
Johnson (1930)

Speech and Language Problems among Minority Children

Anastasiow & Hanes (1976)
Jones (1976)
Simoes (1976)
Tucker (1980)

Theories and Methods in Clinical Speech and Language

Aaronson & Rieber (1975)
Birch, Matthews, & Burgi (1958)
Garcia, Billet, & Rust (1977)
Green (1977)
Hammill & Larsen (1974)
Hixon, Shriberg, & Saxman (1980)
Hull & Hull (1973)
Morehead & Morehead (1976)
Schiefelbusch & Lloyd (1972)
Shames & Florance (1980)
Van Riper (1978)

The Training of Speech and Language Clinicians

Ainsworth (1965)
Anderson (1981)
Bradley (1976)
Dopheide & Dalenger (1975)

CHAPTER 7

Hearing Impairments

Mike was the first acoustically handicapped student to be fully integrated at Robin Mickle Junior High.[1] He entered the school as a seventh-grader and graduated after three years.

In spite of a severe bilateral sensorineural hearing loss, Mike had successfully completed a program at Prescott Elementary School. For five years, he had been a full-time student in the self-contained unit for the acoustically handicapped there. Then, when he was in the fourth grade, he joined a regular class, although he still got help from teachers in the special unit.

Pupil motivation deserves to be considered in program choices.

When he had almost completed the sixth grade, Mike and his parents and teachers discussed whether he should attend Robin Mickle Junior High School or the Nebraska School for the Deaf in Omaha. (At that time, the Lincoln public school system did not have a secondary program for acoustically handicapped students.) Mike wanted to attend Mickle; it was in his neighborhood, and his sister had gone there. Mike was accepted as the first acoustically handicapped student at Robin Mickle Junior High to be fully integrated in all of his classes.

Since this was a new experience for the Robin Mickle faculty, the week before Mike started classes, an in-service program was conducted for the teachers. This venture was a cooperative effort by the resource teacher for the acoustically handicapped, the counselor, classroom teachers, Mike, and his parents.

We began the in-service program with an explanation of hearing loss and of the implications of such a loss for a student's learning. (An acoustically handicapped student will generally have difficulty with reading, language, and vocabulary development.) We displayed a hearing aid, explaining that it merely amplifies sound and does not return the individual's hearing to "normal."

Teacher preparation is basic to pupil success.

We invited Mike to attend the in-service session to meet his teachers and to

---

[1] Mike's story, told from life by Vicki Woodburn and Marge Schuster, introduces many themes that will be developed in this chapter.

give the teachers an opportunity to meet him before classes started. We gave Mike his schedule at this time and walked him through it so that he would know where each class met.

We gave the teachers suggestions on how to help Mike in class:

1. Speak naturally, without overenunciating. Speaking naturally helps the lip or speech reader.
2. Remember to face Mike while speaking or lecturing. A speech reader needs a full view of the speaker's face.
3. A student with a hearing loss will have difficulty understanding films with a lot of narration. Provide Mike in advance with notes or explanations of such films.
4. During class discussions, indicate who is going to speak so that Mike can focus his attention on that person.
5. Be aware of speech-reading distractions—mustaches, gum chewing, pens or glasses held in front of the speaker's mouth.
6. Seat Mike near the front and center of the room so that he can easily see the teacher.

Attention to communication is the key.

We emphasized an important point at the in-service session: Help Mike prepare ahead of time so that he doesn't have to catch up to the rest of the class. He can keep one step ahead of the other students by being briefed on new material before he gets to class. This approach makes the class run more smoothly for the teacher and helps make the situation more profitable and pleasant for the student.

From the opening of the school year, in order for Mike to be prepared ahead of time for each class, the teachers and the resource teacher worked together on a regular basis, informing one another of assignments, new vocabulary, and so on. Admittedly, this special effort put an extra burden on the teachers, but it contributed positively to Mike's success.

Mike was the first acoustically handicapped student in his school.

In the seventh grade, Mike registered for classes in animal science and basic studies (English and social studies), both of which required a lot of reading. To help Mike with reading assignments, the resource teacher got the assignments from his teachers before they were given in class and outlined or summarized the chapters or texts for Mike.

Special education and regular teachers worked together.

In the seventh grade, Mike also took oceanography, a course involving quite an advanced vocabulary. The oceanography teacher taped each day's lesson in advance for the entire nine weeks of the course. The resource teacher then transcribed the lessons so that Mike could read them and learn the required material.

Other classes in which Mike needed special help were construction and manufacturing—essential classes for students considering occupations that are not language oriented. These courses are detailed and relatively difficult. The teachers recognized both the difficulty of the classes and the need to give students like Mike this exposure. Consequently, they provided materials that Mike could study with the resource teacher before taking tests.

Although math was one of Mike's favorite subjects, ninth-grade algebra turned out to be very difficult for him. During the first semester, Mike became so frustrated that he asked to change his class and teacher, hoping to get a fresh start on the subject. It is school policy that a student who wants to change a class must approach the teachers involved and request the change. Mike was no exception. With the counselor, he approached the teachers and explained his desire to change. The teachers agreed to the request. This procedure helped Mike accept responsibility and become actively involved with changes that affected him.

One of Mike's assets is his athletic ability. At Robin Mickle, this ability to excel in most sports was a real asset to him in making friends.

Build on the pupil's assets.

Teachers were aware that Mike is "normal" enough to misbehave and responsible enough to correct his misbehavior. Mike has his share of ups and downs, including ninth-grade spring fever. He also taught his friends some manual communication, so that when they were too far apart to visit verbally, they could finger-spell their messages to one another.

Mike is the second child in his family. He has a sister in college and a brother in junior high. No one would be naive enough to suggest that a hearing-impaired child makes no difference in a family. Both Mike's parents and his siblings, however, appear to accept and love him unconditionally. He has the 100 percent support of his family.

Mike's family is aware of his difficulties, but they are not defensive, nor do they overreact to his problem. Quite the contrary. The family is cognizant that Mike is a "kid" with his quota of both strong and weak points. When problems arise, they approach them with openness, and teachers and parents are able to work things out together.

Family support helps greatly.

Mike's parents give this reaction to his three years at Robin Mickle Junior High:

> When Mike was ready for junior high, we were faced with making the decision as to whether he should continue in the Lincolin public school system and attend Robin Mickle or whether he should go to a school for the deaf. His three years at Robin Mickle are complete, and we can truthfully say that we feel the right decision was made in having him attend school there.
>
> Although we were a bit apprehensive at first, our minds were soon put to ease by the willingness of the administration and staff at Mickle to take on this "special" boy as part of their regular student body. During these years, the lines of communication between school and home have been kept open, and therefore most small problems have been solved before they could become large ones.
>
> We have felt free to contact the principal, the counselor, or any of the teachers at any time, and this has certainly contributed to his success at Mickle. A lot of the credit for the success is due to the very dependable, devoted resource teacher. She has worked with the staff so that before Mike ever got to a class, teachers understood his problem and knew how best to help him.
>
> Mike has had to work hard but has been rewarded greatly. We feel that Mike has truly been a part of the school in every way, which has been rewarding for him. Mike has gotten a sound junior high education.
>
> Living at home and attending Robin Mickle has allowed Mike to compete in a hearing world in all phases of his life. Although he has a severe hearing loss, he is able to participate in oral school functions. He has learned to communicate and get along with both hearing adults and peers, and his speaking vocabulary has been greatly increased by this exposure. Mike has been socially accepted by both the boys and the girls in academic and extracurricular activities.

Mike was in the mainstream at all three levels— physical, social, and instructional.

Here are Mike's own impressions of his three years at three years at Mickle:

> I really am glad I got to go to Mickle Junior High for my three years. Mickle is a good place for anybody because they have a good staff and great teachers. Teachers are willing to do the work.
>
> Another reason I was glad I joined Mickle School is athletics. I love sports like basketball, football, and especially track. If you join sports, you'll make lots of friends.
>
> I only had seven friends I knew around my neighborhood that went to Mickle. My first couple of days were kind of scary, because I hardly knew anybody and some people who knew who I was would call my name and I couldn't hear them. And they wondered what's wrong with me. Later on, I got acquainted with them and now through the three years at Mickle almost every kid in ninth grade knows I'm deaf and most of them are my friends.

Professional teamwork was an essential ingredient.

The success with Mike was the result of a team that coordinated, planned, discussed, and attempted whatever was needed to make Mike a happy, well-adjusted student.

In a way, Mike was lucky to be the first acoustically handicapped student in his school. The entire staff was able to concentrate on finding ways to help him learn in spite of his particular problem. When a school has many handicapped students with varied problems, the time for such attention is hard to find.

The faculty's experience with Mike can help other pupils in the future.

Staff members of the Lincoln schools are now planning for the integration of other handicapped students. Mike's attendance at Robin Mickle is a resource for their use.

Progress in reading for pupils who are deaf tends to be slow.

A great challenge exists to improve the education of hearing-impaired students. Some observers feel that in spite of research and heroic professional efforts, basic results in education for hearing-impaired children have improved little since the first studies of academic achievements over 70 years ago (Pintner & Paterson, 1916). The average reading level of adolescents who are deaf is only fourth or fifth grade, as judged by norms for handicapped students (Karchmer, 1985). In one study, only 10 percent of a group of deaf students 16 years old and older were above eighth-grade level in reading (Trybus & Karchmer, 1977). The average hearing-impaired adolescent achieves at about the seventh-grade level in mathematics (Karchmer, 1985). Such findings encourage no complacency.

Special and regular educators have developed practical ways to teach most hearing-impaired pupils as members of regular class groups, and that mode of education is now in a period of test. This chapter illustrates the problems in doing that and how those problems can be overcome or minimized by members of the education professions working together with other specialists and with parents.

DEFINITIONS AND PREVALENCE

Knowledge of the medical and audiological distinctions among subgroups of hearing-impaired persons is useful for teachers in their interactions with health professionals, even though such distinctions do not correspond exactly with how they will classify students for instructional purposes.

Hearing impairment is the most general term for malfunction of the auditory mechanism. It does not distinguish either the anatomical area primarily involved (central versus peripheral) or the functional nature of the impairment (sensitivity, frequency range, discrimination, sense of loudness or pitch, recognition of meaning, and the like). In a medicolegal context, *hearing impairment* implies a severity sufficient to "affect personal efficiency in the activities of daily living," specifically in respect to communication.

Hearing impairment encompasses a wide range of malfunctions.

Deafness is the traditional term for a severe or complete loss of auditory sensitivity. It implies a hearing loss sufficient to make auditory communication difficult or impossible without amplification (Davis & Silverman, 1978, p. 539).

In terms of decibels (the unit of measurement for hearing losses), persons are usually said to be deaf when they have losses greater than 90 decibels. They need to use visual channels for reception of speech (lip reading, manual communication). The term *hard of hearing* is used to refer to persons who have significant hearing impairments not severe enough to be termed *deaf*. Persons who are hard of hearing can profit from instruction and communications that involve the auditory channel.

Audiometric testing usually covers a range of frequencies from about 125 to 8,000 hertz (cycles per second), but frequencies from about 500 to 2,000 Hz are most important for the hearing of speech. Middle C on the piano is 256 hertz. Losses in this speech reception range in the better ear are critical for most common purposes.

Relatively few people are deaf; more are hard of hearing.

There is about one deaf person for each 1,000 persons in the general population, and between 15 and 30 times that number who are hard of hearing. This means that there are probably several hard-of-hearing children in every school of ordinary size in the nation—enough to warrant attention by every teacher and principal.

To communicate effectively with parents and with members of the health professions, teachers should understand the hearing sense and its operations. The external ear (Figure 7.1) collects sound waves and channels them inward through the ear canal, where they strike the eardrum.

The middle ear houses three bones called, because of their shapes, the hammer, anvil, and stirrup (malleus, incus, and stapes). They transmit, as mechanical, jointed levers, the sound waves from the eardrum to a membrane at the other end of the middle ear. The middle ear contains air, with the pressure regulated through the eustachian tube, whose other end opens into the throat.

Everyone should know how the ear works and how to protect it.

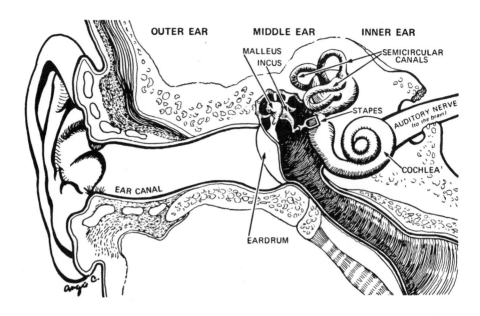

Figure 7.1. Cross Section of the Hearing Mechanism

The inner ear (the labyrinth) contains fluid. The sound waves set up waves in the liquid of the inner ear. It is here that the sound waves activate the auditory nerve. Its thousands of end fibers are attached to the roots of tiny hairs in the liquid. The hairs are stirred by the sound wave patterns in the liquid, energizing the nerve ends to form the sensation of sound. The component parts of this complex organ are illustrated in Figure 7.1. It allows one to trace the process of hearing through the reception of sound waves at the outer ear through to the excitation of the ends of the auditory nerve, which might be spoken of as the recognition of a sound signal. The perception of the sound and its integration into comprehension and memory are central nervous system functions that are only partially understood.

Anything that prevents the movement of sound waves into and through the outer ear and the middle ear obviously creates an impediment to hearing. Hearing losses that have their origin in the outer ear and middle ear are called *conductive* impairments. Children have often been warned: "Put nothing smaller than your elbow into your ear." Yet all

Ear infections can cause hearing problems.

manner of debris finds its way into the outer ear, sometimes causing scratches, infections, or punctured eardrums, which in turn can cause permanent damage.

Children are prone to conductive impairments known as otitis media (fluid in the middle ear). This may involve invasion by infection-causing agents from the throat and nasal passages via the eustachian tube. Mostly these attacks are fought off by the body's natural defenses or through help of physicians who provide antibiotics and possibly special tubes for drainage of the ear. Usually there is only minor discomfort and no lasting harm. But frequent repetitions of middle ear infections can bring about scar tissue and other changes that reduce the flexibility of the joints of the three bones whose job it is to transmit the sound waves, making it difficult or impossible for them to perform their functions.

The inner ear, too, can be reached by infections carried through the lymph. They can damage the nerve ends of the hair cells in the cochlear region. When damage occurs to the cochlea or auditory nerve, it is called a sensorineural impairment. Amplification of sound is usually less helpful in cases of *sensorineural* impairments than when losses are *conductive*. Some drugs used in controlling infections elsewhere in the body are suspected of producing degenerative changes in the inner ear structures. Also, inner ear malfunctions can be associated with prolonged exposure to high-intensity sounds, disease, and hereditary factors.

Conductive losses usually are more amenable to amplification devices.

EDUCATIONAL CLASSIFCATION

The distinction, for educational purposes, between deaf and hard-of-hearing pupils is in terms of how they can learn language. Children with little or no hearing in the first year or two of life do not learn language in the natural, informal way most children do. They are regarded as deaf. Hard-of-hearing children have significant hearing losses but do hear enough to learn language in the usual way, though imperfectly. Using this kind of grouping, one can predict that deaf pupils will usually need more special teaching than hard-of-hearing pupils.

Northcott (1973) pointed to the problem of definitions that make prophecies about personal development and social behavior and assumptions about where and how hearing-impaired pupils ought to be educated. She prefers the inclusive term *hearing impaired*.

Definitions should clarify meaning, not predict limitations.

> The general term *hearing impaired* is used deliberately because it is relatively neutral in emotional content; it does not arouse automatic prediction of the level of personal, academic, or social performance that will be achieved by any students whose hearing loss may range from mild to profound by audiological assessment and audiogram....
>
> There is ample evidence in current literature and research that the terms *deaf* and *hard of hearing* are diagnostically and psychologically unsound as a basis for judging how well a hearing impaired child will perform in the classroom. The focus today is on labeling not the child but the supplementary services and resources personnel...required to assist the child and his family. (pp. 2, 5)

In 1974, the Conference of Executives of American Schools for the

Deaf, jointly with the Convention of American Instructors of the Deaf, published an authoritative statement on definitions (Fresina, 1974). The ad hoc committee's recommendations on definitions are reflected in our use of terms. In particular, for educational consideration, we emphasize the importance of this distinction:

Educational considerations are apparent.

> *Prelingual deafness*: deafness present at birth, or occurring early in life at an age prior to the development of speech or language.
> *Postlingual deafness*: deafness occurring at an age following the development of speech and language. (p. 509).

The concepts embodied in these 1975 definitions are light-years in advance of those that appeared only a short decade before. That observation is reinforced by the ad hoc committee's indication that full integration can be feasible and appropriate for some pupils with any degree of hearing impairment, so far as "present-day implications for educational settings" are concerned (p. 510).

The following warning signs justify calling a child to the attention of parents or medical personnel because of a possible hearing problem.

All staff members and pupils should be alert to these signs.

1. On audiometric screening tests, the child shows loss of 15 decibels or greater within the speech range frequencies or extreme "spike" losses at any frequency.
2. The child appears to strain to hear, including leaning toward the speaker and cupping the ears with the hands.
3. The child asks to have comments or questions repeated and then gives correct responses.
4. The child shows speech inaccuracies, especially dropping of consonants in the middle or endings of words.
5. The child is frequently confused during discussions, even though evidently trying to participate.
6. The child has running ears, soreness, or aches and frequently rubs and scratches the outer ear canal.

A teacher's report may well prevent a hearing loss that could have a devastating effect on the child's educational development.

It has been difficult to construct a cumulative knowledge base about hearing-impaired children because of what has been called the *cohort* problem. Shifts through time in causes of hearing impairments, technological developments, methods of instruction, and environments provided all make it difficult to generalize about the development of hearing-impaired persons. Older deaf persons, for example, much more frequently than others, went through childhood without effective hearing aids and were most often educated in residential schools. Now the situation is far different, and it would be a mistake to generalize from one cohort to another.

In society, hearing-impaired persons have been exploited in a number of ways. They are underemployed, too often working at jobs below their levels of actual training. They have been the objects of crude jokes, and they have been preyed on by unscrupulous merchants.

> Hearing impairment is the leading disability in the United States. It affects more people than cancer, blindness, tuberculosis, venereal disease, multiple sclerosis, kidney disease, and heart disease combined. One out of 15 Americans is hearing impaired. . . . Even though it is the nation's most widespread impairment, the generally invisible nature of the effects of hearing loss has resulted in a dearth of public awareness and understanding. (Stewart & Chap, 1979, p. 1)

Communication is the core educational consideration with hearing-impaired pupils. At the heart of the matter is the negative impact hearing impairment can have on the normal development of language, which then is reflected secondarily in reading, writing, speaking, concept development, and many other ways. That is why educators and their helpers in psychology, linguistics, audiology, and speech pathology spend so much energy to improve the teaching of language in all of its ramifications to hearing-impaired persons. The central focus of special education for hearing-impaired pupils is the development of language and communication. While emphasizing language development, there is constant danger that other substantive aspects of education may be neglected.

Educationally, the main problems are to teach language and the means of communication.

MAINSTREAMING

Mainstreaming is achieved when children who need special education receive it on a high quality level while they enjoy the personal and social advantages of life in regular school classes with all other youngsters of their age and neighborhood. It means that quality education is going on, too, for other pupils.

Until recently, the only widely used way to bring hearing-impaired persons into the mainstream was to start them with intensive special education in preschool and elementary special separated schools or classes. Then, during the secondary, technical school, and college years, some were encouraged to attempt to attend schools with hearing students.

It is different now. Parents and teachers now start from the premise that the great majority of deaf and hard-of-hearing children can be educated from the outset in regular school and that they should be part of the school's mainstream, from the preschool years all the way through the formal education years. They do not have to begin on the outside and try to win their way into the mainstream. This was predicted by McConnell (1973) when he wrote: "The rapid increase in early detection, infant and preschool education, and day-class programs of higher quality should result in greater numbers of children able to join the regular education system" (p. 379).

Partial mainstreaming is best for some.

Not all hearing-impaired children, of course, are served best by full mainstreaming. Some profit most from partial mainstreaming, separated for short or long periods of intensified special teaching. The decision is made in the following way.

The parents and child are encouraged toward enrollment in an augmented regular nursery, kindergarten, or first grade. *Augmented* means that the school is organized, equipped, and staffed to maintain hearing-handicapped pupils as full, participating members of the group.

If, after reasonable trial, the augmented regular class cannot meet all the needs of the hearing-impaired child, consideration is given to another approach. That need not be total separation. Rather, it might be a part-time schedule in a resource room or clinical setting or full special education staffing while the child remains in the regular school with nonhandicapped pupils.

TECHNOLOGY AND SPECIAL PROCEDURES

Devices and procedures to encourage communication are under constant development.

A rich educational technology relates to teaching hearing-impaired pupils. Many will wear hearing aids, for instance, which are important elements in that technology. Understanding what a hearing aid is and does can help in teaching.

Hearing Aids

The regular class teacher can ask the special education teacher to demonstrate two or three different hearing aids and to explain how they work. All are basically similar. First, there is a device for picking up sound (a microphone). Second, there is a mechanism for making the sound louder (an amplifier). And third, there is a part that delivers the amplified sound to the hearing-impaired person (earphone or speaker). The whole thing is energized by electrical batteries, resulting in a relatively lightweight yet powerful instrument.

Many hearing-impaired children tend to have losses for high frequencies but quite normal hearing for lower tones. Such a pattern of hearing loss means that children are likely to lose certain high-frequency sounds as in *f* and *s*. A simple amplification device that increases intensities of sound at all frequencies may, in such cases, cause discomfort at lower levels while increasing intelligibility at higher frequencies. Progress is being made in "shaping" amplification at various frequencies so that a device will optimize hearing for each individual user, but practices in this domain fall quite short of desired efficiencies. Indeed, it is very difficult to achieve for children all that is feasible in using even simple hearing aids. Too often they go unused, batteries are dead, or other practical difficulties become obstacles to efficient use.

For best use of hearing aids, the regular class teacher needs agreement on certain matters with the special education teacher and the child's parents.

Agreements in advance can prevent problems.

1. Hearing-impaired pupils will be prepared, to the extent their ages permit, to take responsibility for ordinary care of their hearing aids and will know how to use them.
2. The special education teacher will be on call to help with problems with any aids.
3. The special education teacher will notify all concerned if there is to be any change in how or when a child is to use an aid.
4. The special education teacher will be kept up to date on how the child is complying with the prescribed use of the aid.

The regular teacher can also make constructive use of the natural curiosity of hearing pupils about aids by asking the special education teacher to prepare one or more lessons for the class on hearing aids. The level of complexity would need to fit the capabilities and interests of the hearing pupils. Children of nursery and kindergarten age, for example, tend to be less distracted than older children by such matters as hearing aids worn by their companions.

Instructional Aids

The design of instructional materials to help hearing-impaired pupils has concentrated, naturally enough, on the language arts. An item that came into wide use in the early phases of special media applications was the Fitzgerald Key (Fitzgerald, 1954). It uses a set of visual symbols and sentence examples to encourage accepted grammatical construction in oral and written speech. To monitor the system, such questions as "Who?" "What?" "Where?" and "How many?" are cued in visually.

AV Captions

Adding printed captions to modern instructional or entertainment films has become helpful in assisting deaf pupils in their learning. Started in 1958 through federal funding support, a substantial library of such films is now

*Improvements
appear every year.*

available for loan. Many TV broadcasts now include captions, which are made visible only by special devices.

The use of media for education and other purposes with persons who are deaf has broadened greatly in recent decades through federal supports. Governmental agencies now assist on a national scale in the development of programmed instruction, educational television, personnel training, and equipment for use not only in schools but also in the homes of hearing-impaired persons. One recent development is the adaptation for home use of teletype and telephone systems to allow communication by print rather than spoken word between hearing-impaired persons or with hearing persons.

Teletype Phone Network Helping Deaf Reach Out

*A handicap can
spark creative
contributions.*

A Pasadena dentist, who has never heard a spoken word, has made it possible for 14,000 deaf people to carry on conversations over the telephone. Dr. James C. Marsters inspired the development of a communications system that combines the telephone with the Teletype machine. Deaf persons "talk" to one another by punching teletypewriter keys. Their messages are carried from one teletypewriter to another via the telephone.

An orthodontist, Marsters, 51, is one of only three totally deaf persons in this country ever to become a dentist. Since birth he has lived in a world of complete silence. Yet, like many born without hearing, he has learned to master speech, using words he has never heard himself. He receives communications from others by reading lips.

*Adapted telephone
devices are
available.*

"A telephone for those deprived of hearing is often a matter of life and death," Marsters explains. "Imagine waking up at 2 in the morning and finding your wife having a heart attack. You are deaf. You run to a neighbor and start pounding on his door. The neighbor has no idea who's at the door. He shouts—'Who is it? Who is it?' You can't hear him, you don't answer. He doesn't open the door. He doesn't know who it is.

"What do you do? You are stuck. Multiply that by 1,000 times. It gets serious. You can't reach out when there's a need to reach out."

*Collaboration
produced fruitful
results.*

In 1963, Marsters sought out Robert Weitbrecht, a deaf astronomer and electronics engineer. "I was so frustrated trying to use the telephone," recalled the dentist. "I had heard of Bob Weitbrecht's expertise in electronics. So I flew up to San Francisco to talk with him and see if we could come up with a telephone for the deaf. We worked together for months and finally came up with the equipment we now have.

"Teletype machines were being phased out by the telephone companies, Western Union and other firms and being replaced with computers. We found a way to put the Teletype machines to work for the deaf."

The two men formed an all-deaf owned and operated company, Applied Communications Corp., headquartered in the San Francisco Bay area of Belmont. Marsters is president and Weitbrecht is vice president of research and development.

Out the their research came the Phonetype, a device that converts telephone signals into teletypewriter signals and vice versa. When the phone rings in the home or office of a deaf person who has a teletypewriter and Phonetype, lights go on and off. If a person is both blind and deaf, fans go on. The deaf-blind person uses a Braille teletypewriter.

Telephone signals are converted to teletypewriter signals.

When the phone is lifted off its cradle and placed on a recess in the Phonetype—a small black box—the teletypewriter is activated and a message from the caller begins to appear on the receiver's teletypewriter.

Research led to practical help.

The person receiving the message responds by typing a message on the teletypewriter keyboard. The conversation goes back and forth throughout the call.

In 1968, the Marsters-Weitbrecht project was given a boost when American Telephone and Telegraph Co. agreed to donate surplus Teletype machines to deaf people through the Alexander Graham Bell Association for the Deaf, Inc. (Alexander Graham Bell's wife was deaf).

That same year, Marsters, Weitbrecht and others from the National Association of the Deaf and the Alexander Graham Bell Association for the Deaf formed Teletypewriters for the Deaf, Inc. (TDI), a nonprofit organization. (*Los Angeles Times*, 1975)

While not originally designed for hearing-impaired pupils, books written with high interest appeal and low vocabulary loading have been found useful. They maintain motivation and bypass limited reading abilities. Thus their use encourages gains in concepts, understanding, and information despite the limiting impact hearing impairments can have on general language development.

Access to these and many other specialized instructional materials can be made available in any community. Local special education personnel should be familiar with nearby resources and those distributed from national centers. Regular class teachers should also ask for consultation from their colleagues to learn about materials with which they might not be familiar. Regular class teachers often find they can also make effective use of these devices with children other than those for whom they were originally intended.

Special education personnel can help locate resources.

Language and Communication

American Sign Language, or *Ameslan*, another element of special technology, uses signs to represent concepts, not words. As in English, where a word represents a concept (e.g., *time*), in Ameslan a sign represents a concept (e.g., a finger pointing at a wristwatch or the place where one would be worn). Ameslan is a form of manual communication.

The visual communication system used by most American deaf people is, in the scientific and technical sense, a language. American Sign Language (Ameslan) is not simply signed English. Actually, according to Fant (1972), its structure has more in common with Chinese. Signed English (Siglish) presents signs, interspersed with finger-spelled words, in the phrase patterns of English. Ameslan uses identical signs but orders them in unique sequences. Most deaf persons use either Ameslan or Siglish, because they have learned to read and write English and are familiar with its structure. Because English (or Siglish) has been learned as a second language (and against almost incredible odds), deaf people understand and can use it to some degree. They comprehend in a general way what is presented in Siglish, but in Ameslan the message comes through fully.

Manual alphabet refers to an alphabet with a one-to-one relationship of finger positions of one hand and the 26 English letters (see Figure 7.2). Using the manual alphabet, English words can be spelled and sequenced into sentences as a direct substitute for English speech or writing. Punctuation can be shown also.

Methods of teaching language and communication, increased interest in sign language, improvement of school achievement, and increased interest in hard-of-hearing pupils stand high on today's agenda. There are two language approaches, American Sign Language and English, and two communication forms, manual and oral (Quigley & Kretschmer, 1982).

Many deaf children acquire good oral speech and speech-reading skill under proper instruction. Conventional wisdom has it that well-functioning oral communication can be taught only if there is a start in the first years of life, no exposure to sign or finger spelling, maximum use of residual hearing, 24-hour-a-day focus on deliberate oral communication, social and educational activities primarily with hearing persons, and a positive, supportive, yet firm attitude toward the child's use of oral speech and speech reading. The sheer logistic barriers to maintaining these requirements over the years of childhood may account for the apparent reduction of interest in a solely oral approach.

A total communication approach is currently favored. Total communication, which combines oral, sign, and finger spelling, currently receives favorable attention. Suppes (1974), in a succinct review of the research, made a germane remark regarding the contention between advocates of the manual versus oral approaches to communication:

> It is hard to think of an area [of teaching] in which really careful and extended experiments would be of more use, for there is a long tradition of support of each position. Until recently, the oral position was probably the dominant one, but in the last few years there has been an increasing interest in the respect for what has been achieved by manual methods beginning with the very young child. (p. 145)

The growth in use of sign language stems from four sources. First is the conscious promotion of total communication, which combines the use of oral speech, speech reading, sign, and the manual alphabet in teaching deaf pupils.

Second is the increased proportion of deaf and hard-of-hearing pupils

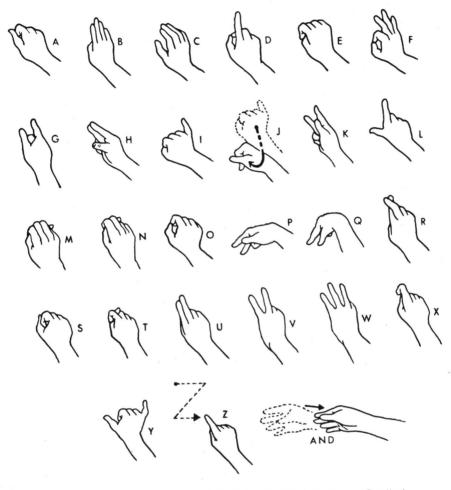

Figure 7.2. The American Manual Alphabet (As Seen by Finger Speller). (*Source:* L. J. Fant, Jr., *Say It with Hands.* Washington DC: Gallaudet College Centennial Fund Commission, 1964, p. 1. Reprinted with permission.)

who attend regular classes. Given that daily close contact, hearing pupils and their regular teachers find it interesting, useful, and not difficult to learn sign. Often it is taught as an in-service unit.

Third is the more frequent translation of television needs and features into sign by superimposing a signing person in a corner of the screen. This has markedly increased access to those programs. At the same time, it has made knowledge of sign more valuable to all hearing-impaired individuals. The increase in public visibility of special adaptations for deaf persons through TV increases public interest and understanding of deaf persons.

Fourth, sign language is increasingly employed in other phases of special education. It has opened communication channels with physically handicapped, autistic, aphasic, retarded, disturbed, and other persons whose oral expression is limited.

Mainstreaming can work with any language and communication system.

Mainstreaming is effective in oral teaching programs and in total communication programs. There is one fundamental difference between the two. The oral method requires that the pupil learn lip reading (speech reading) and oral speech as the *only* means of communication in face-to-face situations, whether with hearing persons or with deaf or hard-of-hearing persons. No gestures or movements are allowed other than those ordinarily used by hearing persons to supplement ordinary conversation.

The total communication approach also teaches the pupil to become skillful in lip reading and in oral speech. In addition, the pupil gains proficiency with communication by the manual alphabet (finger spelling) and sign language. The more detailed sign system used in total communication uses positions and movements of the hands and arms in relation to each other and the rest of the body to convey concepts, including things, places, actions, emotions, quantities, prefixes, suffixes, and other language nuances. Manual alphabet and sign are both used by the person speaking, with the manual alphabet called on to supplement the information conveyed by signs where necessary, as in proper names. Teachers and pupils who are listening observe the speaker's lip and facial movements, the signs, and the manual spelling, when it is used.

Regular class attendance is possible.

Children educated by the oral approach attend regular classes if they are skillful in oral language and lip reading and if their scholastic achievement is comparable to that of at least some of the hearing pupils. The same is true for pupils prepared by the total communication approach, for they acquire oral language and lip-reading competencies, too. In the latter case, aide-interpreters are part of the staff complement.

Some hearing children and their regular teachers deliberately learn manual communication and sign in order to communicate better with the hearing-handicapped pupils who have been prepared through total communication procedures. Both regular teachers and hearing pupils seem to acquire basic sign and finger-spelling skills rapidly.

When the same school system offers parents the choice of the method to be used with their child, it is necessary to keep pupils in the two programs separated. Otherwise, the children in the oral group tend to learn sign language and finger spelling from those in the total communication group and to use them for manual communication.

Through social and political action–oriented clubs and associations, many deaf persons have successfully helped each other in matters from employment and recreation to education, insurance, and legislative lobbying. Some writers on the sociology and social psychology of hearing impairment speak of these groups as making up the "deaf community." Many deaf persons find themselves living in two cultures: the minority deaf community and the majority general community.

The United States is also dotted with volunteer organizations, often called speech and hearing associations. They tend to be amalgams of professional persons, parents of hearing-impaired children, public-spirited lay citizens, and hearing-impaired adults. Their staffs conduct public information campaigns on prevention of hearing defects, provide free hearing tests, act as direct assistance or referral agencies for hearing-impaired persons, conduct demonstrations of education or other services they believe their communities need, and advocate for hearing-impaired persons in whatever ways are relevant and necessary.

Hearing-impaired people help each other.

These groups are strong and useful resources for teachers for direct help in planning, tutoring, interpreting, and other instruction-related matters. For broader considerations, such as helping to form and guide the policies and practices of state and local education agencies, they can have important roles. They are also potential employers of teachers in their various service projects.

Hard-of-hearing children and adults who function well with hearing aids can also use the telephone because their aids have built-in devices called telephone switches, or "T-switches." More and more American phone receivers are compatible with the telephone switches, allowing hard-of-hearing individuals access to that increasingly fundamental means of communication. It would be helpful if all telephone companies installed receivers that work with hearing-aid telephone pickups.

THE FUNCTION OF HEARING IN LEARNING LANGUAGE

Standard modern practice with newborns and infants includes efforts to determine if there is defective hearing. If infants have significant hearing losses in the speech range and do not receive special instruction, they will become victims of the most serious educational handicap an otherwise normal human can have. Through hearing, the young child learns that language exists and how to employ it to communicate.

Hearing is essential to acquiring language normally.

It is a serious matter that a congenitally deaf child, without special instruction, cannot *say* his name. It is also serious that the child does not really *know* his name. *But it is most important and most serious of all that the child does not know that there is such a thing as a name.* That most fundamental lack—absence of the most elemental concept of language—is the core of the educational problem. Language in all its ramifications is what the child must be taught. To understand that fully, one must study the typical process of learning language.

The Language-learning Process

Language comes naturally to infants and toddlers who can hear and who are not otherwise handicapped. The expression "comes naturally," stripped down to its essence, is illustrated in Figure 7.3.

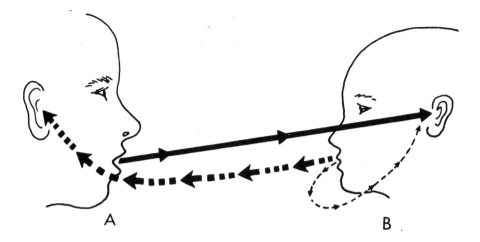

Figure 7.3. The Language-learning Process

Adult-child interaction aids language development.

Speech sounds are produced by A, the adult (see solid line). They enter the ears of B, the baby, and are perceived, that is, transmitted to the brain and recorded there. Sounds produced by B, the baby (see dotted line), are transmitted to the adult's ear, who already knows language and can compare the baby's sounds with known words or approximations of words. When the baby produces a sound that is close to a word, the adult often repeats it, delightedly, or otherwise shows pleasure selectively in favor of wordlike sounds. Thus the baby is aided in forming, producing, and repeating the sounds of the adult's language.

The baby's hearing is already involved importantly in the transaction. If the baby could not hear or heard imperfectly, there could be no perception of the adult's sounds in the first place. In the second place, there could be little or no knowledge of the meaning of the adult's reactions to sound produced by the baby.

Hearing allows self-monitoring of sounds.

Hearing plays another role in very early life, too. When the baby utters sounds, they are heard through the baby's ears almost simultaneously (see dashed line). Thus the baby's hearing provides the added capability of self-monitoring of speech sounds. Given the assumption that the baby has the remembered perception of an adult-produced sound, it is now possible for the baby to practice alone. At early stages, this is referred to as babbling.

The crucial role of adequate hearing in all of this is plain. Without hearing on the baby's part, there is a gap in the line of oral-aural communication and a similar gap in the monitoring line; the normal language-learning process is stymied.

Much more could be said about this process. Meanings get attached to spoken sounds along the way. Normal language development moves very swiftly in the earliest years. In longer term, deaf children may miss explanations for feelings, social experiences, and consequences of behavior, all of which can lead to apparent poor social comprehension. Hearing is important also for learning about music, the sounds of nature, and a multitude of other things, including safety.

Normal language development proceeds swiftly in the earliest years of life.

But the essential fact is that *adequate hearing in the speech range is a fundamental requirement for normal language development*. Its absence can cause one of the most devastating of disabilities. Fortunately, there are ways to ameliorate the impact of deafness on the child's general development and education. They will be noted later.

Hearing Loss Conditions That Influence Education

The educational influences of hearing loss stem from five factors. Technical advances have resulted in corrective procedures through which all have come increasingly under control.

1. Sounds Affected by the Hearing Defect. Many sounds such as the bass horn or the rumble of distant thunder are lower than most human voice sounds. Total loss of hearing for those low sounds interferes little with hearing for ordinary conversations. The same is true for sounds higher than those used for talking. Examples would be the tones of a piccolo or the shrill sound of a whistle. It is an inconvenience to miss those kinds of sounds or to hear them imperfectly. Loss of hearing of that kind does carry with it some educational problems. However, the most serious special educational problems arise when there is a hearing loss for the sounds ordinarily made by the human voice in conversation—the so-called speech range.

The most common losses in hearing are for high frequencies.

2. Degree of the Hearing Defect. Assume that the child's hearing loss cuts across all or most of the speech range. If so, and if the loss is complete or almost complete, nothing that is said by a teacher or by any other person will be heard. That closes off all auditory communication for the pupil—a most serious problem.

It is more difficult to focus listening than looking.

If the hearing loss is total, an ordinary hearing aid has no value. It would be like offering ordinary glasses to a totally blind person. However, if the hearing loss is not quite total, sometimes specialized hearing aids can help. But as with vision, if only a little remains, amplifying devices cannot be expected to work miracles. At best, they allow the child to hear a little more, though what is heard will usually be quite distorted. It is much more difficult to listen to something specific, shutting out the rest, than it is to look at something specific and attend to nothing else.

It takes real effort to learn to use a hearing aid well. Also, it takes practice to sustain good hearing aid use, and the aid itself needs regular care and maintenance. All of that must be made part of the child's special education.

Learning to use the aid is part of special education.

3. Onset of the Hearing Defect. A third factor of major significance is the age at which the hearing defect started. If a 15-year-old loses all hearing, it is a matter of real concern. Yet it is not as serious as losing hearing while an infant or toddler. The 15-year-old has permanent assets that the infant will to some extent be denied, despite the most expert efforts to help attain them. Here is a list of some of those assets that early profound or severe hearing impairment make it extremely difficult for a person to acquire:

1. Knowledge of one's native language
2. Clear oral speech
3. Interpreting the oral speech of others
4. Ability to read with speed and comprehension
5. Understanding of abstract concepts

Early loss of hearing inhibits all linguistic development.

Becoming deaf at age 15 would take away only the third. And with the other four, to acquire proficiency at lip reading (speech reading) would not be an insurmountable task.

But imagine beginning life with no means to make contact with others through sounds! When one recognizes that adequate hearing is the key to all five of the qualities listed, the importance of the age at which hearing is lost becomes clearer.

Two other factors rank high in significance even though they are not related directly to defective hearing. One concerns the pupil's cognitive development and the other the instruction received in early life. Proper instruction in early childhood can have positive effects on cognitive development. Thus these factors are often linked.

4. The Hearing-impaired Child's Cognitive Development. One can easily underestimate the intelligence of hearing-impaired youngsters. To people unfamiliar with the impact of hearing loss, such children are frequently thought to be mentally retarded. Therefore, it is fundamentally important to get the professional opinion of a school psychologist, an audiologist, and special educators with experience in working with hearing-impaired children. Anything short of assessment by such a team is likely to result in a false impression that can lead to serious and permanent curtailment of a child's educational opportunities. Often young hearing-impaired pupils need weeks or months of patient work by the teacher and other specialists, acting as a team, before the full extent of the child's intelligence can be brought out. Taking that time can be the most important investment ever made on the child's behalf.

Keep a positive and dynamic attitude toward potential for learning.

5. The Nature and Amount of Stimulation Provided. The fifth factor of major significance is the kind and amount of stimulation the hearing-impaired individual has received. Babies born without hearing make sounds in the first months of life, just as hearing babies do. That soon stops, however, unless it is encouraged by the adults around the baby.

Similarly, in older children, language comprehension can decline when a hearing loss develops. The speech quality of the person who is losing hearing will also diminish. However, if regular, conscious efforts are made to encourage the baby's babbling and other kinds of striving for communication and to bolster and maintain the older child's language development and speech quality, the problems associated with hearing loss can be minimized.

Stimulation prevents deterioration.

Prevailing and Preferred Practices

Preferred practices for hearing-handicapped children coalesce around two broad moves. One, a pragmatic view, says that teaching language in the earliest childhood years is of overriding importance. Second, a new position is emerging for the residential and day school as a limited regional resource, specializing in intensive work with hearing-impaired pupils with the kinds of complex educational problems and/or family and social problems that defy solution in the mainstream.

New roles for the residential and day school are emerging.

Prevailing Practices

1. Children with severe to profound hearing impairments are detected, for the most part, in the first year or two of life. Other losses tend to be identified later, usually near admission to kindergarten or first grade.

2. Otologists, audiologists, nurses, and psychologists are the contacts parents tend to have when they are learning about their children's hearing impairments and beginning to make plans to remedy them.

Preferred Practices

1. Educators press for regular and repeated screening from birth on, emphasizing very early discovery and educational intervention as necessary.

2. Teacher specialists in very early childhood (birth to 3 years) representing the local school system work directly with parents from the time the hearing loss is discovered, coordinate educational planning, and make use of otological, audiological, and psychological findings in doing so. The parent has a tie to educators from the local school system from the time the hearing loss is detected. Care is taken to match learning tasks to the child's rate and level of cognitive development.

3. Free public education for hearing-impaired pupils with severe and profound losses is provided in a few states from as early as the condition is detected and in several states beginning at age 2. Many states have not yet arranged for schooling for these children before standard admission age for all children.

3. Education for all hearing-impaired pupils is free and public, beginning in infancy or at any age hearing impairment is found.

4. Educational guidance in the preschool years emphasizes sound and intensive auditory training by audiologists or speech and hearing clinicians in one-to-one or small group clinical settings.

4. Preschool educational guidance stresses participation with hearing children and their families in all normal developmental activities while using sound amplification and receiving intensive auditory training from qualified specialists.

5. The local school system becomes aware of the existence of most of its preschool hearing-impaired children when they reach legal school entry age. Preschool educational programs, where they exist, tend to be operated by volunteer agencies.

5. The local school system deliberately seeks hearing-impaired children in the first weeks and months of life and accepts responsibility for all aspects of preschool education for them and their parents. Qualified teachers conduct the education. Volunteers help in teaching, in supplying services that supplement education, and as innovators in demonstrating new directions the school might take to make program improvements.

6. Parents immediately confront the choice of oral or total communication for their child. Acceptance of one separates the child and parents from children and adults who espouse the other. Professional persons

6. Parents receive objective information about differing forms of instruction. They have options from which they make choices for their children. School systems have qualified staff members who work effectively in all

take sides in acrimonious conflicts over the form of instruction.

7. At school admission time, parents in rural and small-town settings send their severely or profoundly hearing-impaired child to a boarding school or to a special class that usually calls for a daily bus ride to a different school from that attended by the other children of the family. In many cases, the same is true of parents and children who live in large cities and suburbs.

8. Children with mild to moderate hearing impairments usually have special education from speech therapists in their local schools. The therapists ordinarily take the child out of class to give 20 to 40 minutes of corrective and remedial language and speech instruction each week and to monitor the child's hearing aid use if one is worn. They advise teachers about favorable pupil seating and are alert to the child's other special needs. There is little or no direct contact with parents. Often the speech therapist's training and experience with hearing problems is limited or nonexistent; in some cases, however, the therapist's preparation is excellent.

9. Most hearing-impaired pupils of all degrees of hearing loss

forms of instruction.

7. Teachers and aides instruct infants and toddlers at home if parents wish. When mature enough for school, hearing-impaired pupils attend the local school or a nearby regular school. The special education they need is brought to them in the regular class context. Clinical otological, audiological, and psychological work, if needed, is done mostly outside regular school hours.

8. Educational programs are individualized. Plans are prepared in writing by a team and are coordinated by the regular class teacher. Specialist teachers work with children in the context of the regular class rather than removing them, in most instances. Parents take an active part in preparing program plans, approve them, and often work at home with their child under the supervision of the regular teacher and the therapist.

9. Special educational help outside the regular class

are separated from regular classes and other classes for part or all of each day, all year long. Relatively few severely or profoundly hearing-impaired pupils (deaf pupils) move into the mainstream for any of their formal elementary or secondary education.

is given when needed. Generally, however, mainstreaming is practiced full time or most of the time.

10. Many speech and hearing specialists and teachers of the hearing-impaired, perhaps the majority, have training or experience only in their specialties. Regular class teachers only occasionally have backgrounds that ready them for helping hearing-impaired students in their regular classes.

10. Specialists in the education of the hearing-impaired or in speech and hearing are drawn from a pool of professional educators who have training and successful experience as regular class teachers. Regular class teachers have in-service or preservice training to prepare them to instruct hearing-impaired pupils in the mainstream and for coordinating and using the help of specialists.

11. Few special classes, day schools, and residential schools have facilities for hearing-impaired pupils with other exceptionalities (giftedness, social or emotional maladjustment, mental retardation, other sensory or physical problems), from the point of view of staff preparation, physical plant, curriculum adjustments, and instructional materials.

11. Resources are available in the school system to accommodate multiple exceptional pupils, and the attitude is favorable toward doing so.

12. Liaison between regular elementary and secondary education and special classes and schools for hearing-impaired pupils is minimal.

12. Specialists in the education of hearing impaired pupils view themselves as close working colleagues of regular class teachers. They meet

There is little mingling for professional, educational, or social reasons between the staffs or the pupils of the two. frequently on professional and educational matters concerning themselves and their pupils.

REACHING HEARING-IMPAIRED PUPILS IN SPARSELY POPULATED REGIONS

A significant problem for which preferred practices are not yet clear is how best to reach hearing-impaired pupils who are isolated by geography and climate. In many parts of North America, centers give counseling and training to parents of hearing-impaired children. Yet families residing long distances from centers have little opportunity for direct contact with them. Newfoundland, Canada, where distance, geography, and severe weather conditions sharply limit travel, developed inventive ways to bring special education to preschool-age hearing-impaired children in their home communities.

There are all kinds of mainstreaming. Ken Killian, a 6-foot, 183-pound, 16-year-old sophomore, plays first-string middle guard on Baldwin High School's football team. Baldwin employs a complex, continuously maneuvering defense. They switch plans half the time at the line of scrimmage. How does a player like Killian handle such situations? The linebackers give him hand signals. They touch different parts of his body to tell him what to do. The signals are changed weekly.

The coach says, "At no time do we accept his being deaf as a handicap. A kid without desire and mental toughness has a handicap. Killian has desire and mental toughness. When he makes a mistake, he makes it in a football sense." There haven't been too many of those so far. (Adapted from Fisher, 1980)

A home-centered design was offered, combining instructional sessions and videotapes with periodic telephone talks with teachers. Beginning with children who were educationally deaf, it expanded to take in children with any degree of hearing handicap, plus those with multiple handicaps.

A home-centered design serves preschoolers in remote areas.

When an eligible child was identified, the parents received a letter describing the program and inviting family members and relatives in close daily contact with the child to attend a meeting to become fully briefed. Also, the education or health professional nearest to the family was approached. These professionals, often speech therapists or nurses, were asked to assist the family in getting to the meeting, help collect information about the child, and encourage the family to participate. Center staff main-

Equipment is supplied to parents.

tained telephone contact with both professionals and families. Financial assistance was available if the family needed help traveling to the general meeting.

Following a workshop with the families at the center, auditory-training and videotape equipment was supplied to each home. Videotaped presentations were sent as needed for home viewing and practice. There ensued weekly parent-teacher telephone contacts, an annual home visit by a teacher from the center, and attendance at another workshop at the center a year later.

The 48 videotapes available the first year had five objectives in common. They encouraged the parents to acquire these attributes of good teaching:

1. Skill in choosing materials for one-to-one teaching sessions, which would be suitable to the child's level of development and interest
2. Skill in maintaining control of a one-to-one teaching session
3. Initiative in extending the techniques taught on the tapes to day-to-day situations
4. The ability to involve other members of the family in one-to-one teaching sessions
5. Skills related to the discipline of the hearing-impaired child. (House & Neville-Smith, n.d., p. 29)

Telephone contact solves problems.

The once-a-week telephone call to parents from the center assisted in solving problems, reinforced material in the videotapes, and recorded pupil progress information. Parents used the telephone contact for trouble-shooting, as needed.

Twice a month a "More Ideas" booklet was sent to parents. These supplemented the videotapes and recommended ways to use toys, games, and ordinary home activities to strengthen language skills.

The annual home visit by a teacher from the center was both social and professional. It revived the images of the people attached to the telephone voices, and it allowed direct validation checks on the child's progress. During the home visit, the teacher renewed the relationship with the family's local contact person, the professional whose on-site monitoring served as another resource and as an advocate for the family and the center.

Technology and family involvement support mainstreaming.

From the points of view of feasibility, pupil progress, cost, and acceptability, the evaluation of the program is positive (House & Neville-Smith, n.d., pp. 83–94). It offers an excellent illustration of how to combine professional skills, modern communication and instructional technology, community support and advocacy, and family participation to bring appropriate special education to preschoolers while they continue to grow and develop in the mainstream of family and neighborhood life.

It may be that this special education design will prove to be an alternative preferable to daily aggregate instruction of hearing-impaired children at a center, even if it is otherwise feasible to bring the children together.

CURRENT TRENDS

Telephone and personal interview follow-ups were made in 1977 and in 1980 of successful mainstream programs reported earlier (Birch, 1975). Focus was on the question "What does it take to make mainstreaming effective from the point of view of teachers and those responsible for school organization and administration?" The answers were not always specific to students with hearing impairments. Indeed, they provided a general summary of the principles of adaptive education, with consideration for hearing impairment as an aspect of planning instruction. The findings of this inquiry are presented in terms of five summary principles.

Principle 1: Apply a Preteach-Teach-Postteach Strategy. When this principle operates, there is a close, cooperative instructional team relationship among regular and special teachers of the hearing-impaired in planning instruction as well as in carrying it through.

The basic principles are those of adaptive education.

Fourth- or fifth-graders are studying *Robin Hood*. The regular teacher's lesson plan calls for (among other things) discussion of a thought question: Why did Robin Hood and his men believe that they could not expect to receive justice at the hands of the Sheriff of Nottingham? The teacher of the hearing-impaired, as a matter of course, reviewed the lesson plan with the regular teacher during an earlier planning period. The pupils had a homework assignment on *Robin Hood*.

The special teacher meets the hearing-impaired boys and girls for a 20-minute period sometime before their regular class to go through the upcoming lesson. The special teacher finds that some children are not clear as to the meaning of *justice*. Other hearing-impaired children do know the meaning of *justice* but have difficulty with other expressions. The special teacher has the children discuss the terms, monitoring the exchange to ensure that the concepts are clarified. When the special teacher is satisfied that the hearing-impaired pupils are ready for instruction on about equal terms with the hearing children, the preteaching is concluded.

The special teacher offers instructional support.

The hearing-impaired pupils then attend the regular social studies or literature class studying *Robin Hood*. (The regular teacher and the other pupils have previously been oriented to working with deaf and hard-of-hearing pupils in the class.) If the special teacher has noted one or two matters that need particular attention in the lesson for certain children, they are passed on to the regular teacher by note or in a chat as the class begins.

After class, the regular teacher reports special problems encountered

The regular teacher reports problems.

with the hearing-impaired pupils. These are passed on by a short note, checks or comments on a checklist, a personal talk, or by the pupils themselves. The special teacher then takes action as necessary in the postteaching session, depending on whether it is a conceptual problem, a behavior problem, failure in communication, a lack of preparation or background, or whatever.

The postteaching time period is used flexibly. Its initial portion may be needed to top off the previous regular class lesson. Its latter portion might be employed to preteach key material for the next regular class lesson. Material related to more than one regular class lesson can be included. Other variations depend on the needs of the hearing-impaired pupils.

The preteach-teach-postteach pattern carries on until each hearing-impaired child becomes less dependent and more able to dispense with the preteaching and postteaching phases. Then the pattern changes from one of regular application of the preteaching and postteaching phases to one where the hard-of-hearing or deaf student seeks help from the special teacher only as the student feels it is needed. An important personal growth objective has been reached when a hearing-impaired student shows that degree of independence. The teachers, too, must sense when to let go.

The preteach-teach-postteach sequence is an instructional principle of adaptive education whose day-to-day details vary. Some arrangements are highly complex; others are simple. Some appear informal; others, tightly structured and regularized. Some use time before or after the school day; some do not include all of the regular school program in the hearing-impaired pupils' curriculum. Many involve parents, volunteers, buddies, or paraprofessionals in the process. But observation reveals the preteach-teach-postteach principle operating in some form in mainstreaming that works.

Principle 2: Teach Toward Hearing-World Participation. This principle makes participation in the hearing world the focus of all instruction. Every moment of the school day plus much of the child's out-of-school time is taken up with planned instruction toward that goal. It is not a pressure-cooker situation, however; the teaching is usually fun for the child.

Participation is the goal.

Also, everyone teaches: parents, aides, supervisors, regular class teachers, special educators, principals, social workers, psychologists, playground assistants—everyone who has contact with the child.

Social interaction skills must be deliberately taught.

If children are in the charge of an aide at any time before, during, or after school, there is a definite responsibility to use that time for practice of skills and abilities that are parts of the curriculum. The same is true for parents. There is a plan for each child. Every adult with the child knows what that plan is and accepts responsibility for furthering each child's education in an orderly way toward hearing-world participation.

There are times for fun, games, and unstructured romping. These are arranged so that hearing-impaired youngsters also learn important attitudes and behaviors under pleasurable conditions.

An aide in one school said that "the deaf like to play by themselves." To prove the assertion, the aide pointed across the room to a group of seven or eight nursery school- and kindergarten-age hearing-impaired children who were bouncing and swinging, climbing and whirling together on indoor play equipment. There were two hearing children in the room also. One was off alone in a corner painting at an easel. The other was at the periphery of the group of hearing-impaired children, occasionally trying to enter part of the play, not quite making it, and retiring to the edge of the group again.

Earnest efforts were being made at that school to begin integration of hearing-impaired children with others, but the principle "Teach toward hearing-world participation" was not in full operation. The effort toward mainstreaming was failing, and the people responsible did not know why. They had not conceptualized the principle fully, so the implementation needed was not clear. Not everyone understood and participated. After several days of observation, these specific gaps in implementation became apparent:

1. Aides did not understand the integration effort because it had not been explained adequately.
2. The aides had not been given specific responsibilities.
3. Written plans were not available to help teachers or aides determine what to do with pupils.
4. Neither the hearing-impaired nor the hearing pupils knew why they were together.
5. Aides were frequently with children for more than an hour with no supervision from a professional educator.
6. The aides initiated no communication with any of the children. Nor did they encourage communication the children initiated, except to stop disputes or misbehavior.

Can you turn these points around and make them positive guidelines?

The concepts central to the principle were being violated. Precious time for the children was slipping away. Some children were having fun, to be sure. All of the children, as well as the aides, were certainly learning, but the wrong things. The deaf children were learning to ignore hearing children. The hearing youngsters were learning to live beside but not with the deaf and hard-of-hearing pupils. Aides were learning that their nonguidance and noninvolvement were completely acceptable to their supervisors, for none made any efforts to get them to change.

Successful application of this principle calls for positive, planned action rather than laissez faire inaction. Effective mainstreaming requires

Planned action is needed.

that understanding and commitment be expressed 100 percent of the time in the day-to-day, hour-to-hour, moment-to-moment teaching activities of all who are in contact with hearing-impaired pupils.

Principle 3: Use a Systematic Approach. This principle says there is a design to the mainstreaming effort into which all the bits and pieces fit. It is planned; a document setting forth the plan is readily available. It is *Mainstreaming* also organized; a structure is discernible, and individuals have assigned *plans are* responsibilities. Those responsibilities are accompanied by the authority *documented.* necessary to see that the responsibilities are carried out. Further, the approach to mainstreaming flows in orderly steps.

In some places, mainstreaming activities have not gotten beyond reflecting the individual interests of principals or teachers in individual schools. In one community, for example, a substantial portion of its hearing-impaired children were mainstreamed in the elementary grades. However, there was a mainstream plan only for those grades. Children who had been mainstreamed often found themselves placed in special classes in junior and senior high schools, for no clear reason. The program design did not carry through.

Neither did policy, authority, or responsibility, for that was equally divided between elementary and secondary administrators who had differing points of view. It was a classic case of good ideas and worthy efforts losing their impact because of faulty planning.

A map and an Though it is necessary in the smallest school, this principle needs to be *itinerary help to* applied with maximum rigor in large and complex school systems. The *navigate the* principle gets excellent support when the state department of education *mainstream.* promulgates detailed program guidelines. State guidelines help local schools draft documents specific to the community.

One ever-present danger, however, is that the plan, once crystallized, becomes inflexible. The document that outlines the school's plans should be updated periodically. With that provision, the plan can serve as both a reliable anchor and a motivating guide.

Principle 4: Have Unified and Consistent Commitment and Direction. Where mainstreaming is healthy and vigorous, the groups that form the power base of schools are together in their belief in it as the preferred pattern. The school board has policies that emphasize it. New and remodeled schools make provisions for the inclusion of regular and exceptional children. Personnel policies provide for employing teachers sympathetic toward integrating pupils. The professional staff receives in-service sessions on team teaching and consultation. Collective bargaining contracts contain clauses that specify recognition of factors involved in maintaining sound special education for exceptional children in regular classes. These examples, as well as others, show unity of commitment.

Equally important is unified and consistent direction. Schools with serious problems in trying to get mainstreaming established sometimes lack power structure commitment. But more often they are without some-one clearly in charge of implementation. Nothing discourages movement more than divided and inconsistent authority. Smoothly operating and thoroughly implemented mainstream programs have one person who clearly possesses both the authority and the responsibility for the program's management. The styles and management behaviors of persons responsible for implementation may vary. But one thing is certain: They and everyone else involved recognize who has been delegated the right to guide the program and where accountability for its proper conduct rests.

Educators with decision making power must reach agreement and exert their efforts in the direction of mainstreaming.

After a detailed account of thorough academic and social integration of 63 deaf pupils in regular school classes, Reger (1977) concluded:

Deaf children do need special assistance, but there is a thin line between assistance that facilitates personal growth and assistance that stifles growth. The history...suggests that too often...well-intentioned "help" has turned into debilitating overprotection. Deaf children can be, should be, and want to be mainstreamed....With a little help from their friends, they can make it. (p. 56)

Principle 5: Bring Special Education into the Regular Class. This says a great deal about the alterations in what teachers do when progressive inclusion for pupils with hearing impairments becomes the major pattern. To operate special education within the structure of the regular class and school spells change.

More and more, both deaf and hard-of-hearing pupils are receiving education in regular schools. Practical examples abound and are on the increase (Birch, 1975; Connor, 1976; Reger, 1977). Residential and day schools are changing, partly because of decreasing enrollment and partly because remaining enrollments contain a higher proportion of children with complex conditions that go beyond hearing impairment. But even children with complicated, multiple involvements can often be accommodated in their local school system, at least at the physical and social mainstream levels. In some school districts, close to 100 percent of all hearing-impaired pupils are integrated with hearing pupils, with many being fully mainstreamed at the instructional level as well.

Local school efforts make the difference.

The gap between separation and inclusion, if it is reduced further, means potentially wrenching alterations in the professional lives of many teachers who now work in residential schools, special day schools, and self-contained special classes, to say nothing of the regular class teachers who will be called on to make changes. Fortunately, enough has been learned from teachers, pupils, and parents who have ventured into the central current to engender confidence that it can be done by others without serious hardship.

THE ROLE OF THE REGULAR CLASS TEACHER, SPECIAL TEACHER, AND PRINCIPAL

Inclusion requires new patterns of professional behavior.

The inclusion of hearing-impaired pupils means two kinds of change in work demands on educators. One is new work, such as added lesson preparation and increased chalkboard use by the regular teacher. Second, special and regular teachers and principals have to learn to become a team. That change from relative isolation means altering established patterns of daily professional behavior.

Where mainstreaming has worked out well, the extra work and the changes in work style required to get the program under way have been made rewarding. Quality in-service programs have been offered, many with credit for advanced degrees, advanced certification, and recognition toward salary increments. Teachers' aides have been furnished, many of them having specialized skills in communication. New or remodeled teaching space, modern instructional materials, added audiovisual aids, and other improvements that make teaching more satisfying have been supplied. Teachers of regular classes have had access to more help from principals and supervisors. Also, they have received direct on-site consultation and assistance with regular class pupils from the special education teachers who work with them, frequently right in their own classes.

Teamwork with Specialists

When a child receives instruction, direction, and assignments from more than one teacher, confusion and conflict can easily arise. Opportunities for misunderstanding are increased, too, when children have language and communication limitations imposed by defective hearing. Thus it proves

Role definition is essential.

important that there be clear and consistent role definition for the professional persons responsible for the various parts of mainstream schemes.

Following are examples of statements of responsibility for certain professional positions that are intended to help clarify roles and functions of mainstream team members. (These can be generalized to work with other exceptional youngsters too.)

Regular *counselors* are responsible for counseling services for all pupils, including those who are hearing impaired. They employ assistance from specialists trained to work with students who are hearing impaired, but they use the help as consultation and do not turn over counseling to those specialists. They have received some special orientation to adaptive forms of career education and counseling for hearing-impaired students, so they can help in movement beyond the common stereotypes about life-style and work for persons who are deaf or hard of hearing.

Regular *principals* have authority and responsibility for both special and regular education in the school. They have a chief voice in the selection and assignment of teachers and pupils; they use consultation from specialists in the school and on the central office staff but do not delegate decision making to them. Principals employ teacher committees and parent participation in planning and organizing individualized education for all children in the school.

All emerging professional role changes focus on coordination rather than separation.

Regular class teachers have the first voice in day-to-day decisions about educational programs for all pupils, including exceptional pupils assigned to a regular class. They can obtain assistance by specialists on the school or central office staff and have the authority to direct and supervise the work of teacher aides assigned for fixed periods of time. They may call and arrange meetings of teacher committees concerning pupils in the class, with the concurrence of the principal. Regular class teachers may deal directly with parents, with the concurrence of the principal, or may make parent contacts through the school social worker or counselor.

Teachers of hearing-impaired pupils help regular class teachers who have such pupils on their class rolls. They preteach and postteach. They accept referrals from regular class teachers for assessment and aid in planning instruction for regular class pupils who may need special education. They serve on faculty committees and make available special instructional materials to regular class teachers and hearing-impaired pupils. They provide orientation and continuing education to all teachers regarding teaching hearing-impaired pupils.

The special teacher of the hearing-impaired may teach directly parts of the curriculum that are specific to hearing-impaired students. For example, the program Providing Alternative Thinking Strategies (PATHS) consists of lessons focused specifically on social skills, emotional understanding, and self-control for hearing-impaired students (Greenberg et al., 1985). Lessons in this series lead naturally to applications in mainstream situations but may be introduced by the special teacher by special arrangements.

Increasing numbers of persons now receive preparation in vocational schools for roles in serving persons who are hearing impaired. These *paraprofessionals* are prepared to offer "total communication," for example, and to serve in mainstream classes as daily working partners with regular teachers, often extending the influence of the special teacher of the hearing-impaired who may have several classes and schools to serve and who will have only limited amounts of time in a particular class.

One reason for keeping pupil accounting and related responsibility clearly in the hands of regular education personnel is to make sure that hearing-impaired pupils maintain and increase their skills in pursuing the regular curriculum of the school and real-world resources. This should reduce the need for a special counseling center or similar services for hearing-handicapped persons. It should not make the use of such services a matter of habit for hearing-impaired persons, but rather it should strengthen their independence of those services.

Responsibility and accountability are linked.

Another reason for stressing the central role of regular teachers is to prevent superficial kinds of mainstreaming, those that may give a surface appearance of inclusion while in reality all the education of the hearing-impaired child is conducted by specialists, with regular education personnel as onlookers or bystanders. Also, specialists with pupils who are hearing handicapped need reorientation to assist them in working in new relationships with regular school personnel. Only a few have training and experience in joint professional consultation with teachers from other educational specializations and with members of other professions, yet that is a significant new skill required of them. The same is true of participating in committee decision making and team teaching. Thus there remains an important need for reeducation for persons now prepared only for special education for hearing-handicapped pupils in traditional, separate settings:

Bruce (1973) said:

> Integrated educational settings for the hearing impaired range from those that offer mere· physical proximity with hearing pupils to those in which the hearing impaired children are completely independent of supportive personnel. A child may be integrated as early as 0–3 years or as late as high school age. The effective implementation of integration is dependent on the quality of personnel, equipment, transportation, and curriulum. (p. 213)

We agree that adaptations in the school system are the primary determinants of effective mainstreaming. We see little value in approaches that ask only, "Is the child ready to adjust to the school?" It is the school that should be more flexible. We add only that the school physical plant and methods of teaching, too, need attention if instruction is to be properly individualized.

All students with special needs, as well as most other students, come to the student counseling bureau at the Area Vocational Technical Institute (AVTI). No special programs are offered at the AVTI for students with disabilities, but the counseling bureau organizes whatever special supports may be needed by individual students. Jeff, who is deaf, entered the sheet metals curriculum. A special teacher of the hearing-impaired went with Jeff to the sheet metal shops and conferred with the regular instructors about necessary adaptations in communication that Jeff would need. For the first week of his studies, Jeff received instruction from both the regular and special teachers.

Thereafter, a paraprofessional skilled in total communication made regular visits—usually quite brief—to the sheet metal shop to see that Jeff and his instructors were communicating appropriately and fully.

MOVING HEARING-IMPAIRED PUPILS FROM SEPARATED SETTINGS

When a pupil in a separate program is considered for movement into physical, social, or instructional mainstream activity, these 10 points merit consideration:

Bringing a child into the mainstream from a separate class or school calls for special care.

1. Particular attention should be paid to ability to take part in language, reading, writing, spelling, and conversation. Superior reading and understanding of the conversation of others can compensate for less satisfactory expressive skills, or the reverse.

2. As to social and emotional behavior, the issue is whether the regular class teacher, having observed and read reports about the hearing-handicapped youngster's typical behavior, feels the child can be fitted in or can learn to fit in with the regular class friendship groups and cliques. (It is good to initiate mainstream activities with the beginning of a term, so that the hearing-impaired pupil may be assimilated while social units are in the formative stages.)

3. Does the student attend and follow directions well? Familiarity with the way the regular class teacher conducts instruction allows the special teacher to help the hearing-impaired pupil sharpen necessary attending skills.

4. Some hearing-impaired pupils are able to perform well but lack self-confidence, independence, and determination to succeed in regular classes. With encouragement from teachers, they may find in the regular class the positive experience that bolsters confidence and helps them face the next of life's challenges with more assurance.

Promote self-confidence.

5. There is no reason why mainstreaming should be reserved for hearing-impaired pupils of average learning ability. Mentally retarded or gifted hearing-impaired pupils should have the opportunity to take part in mainstream-style special education programs if other appropriate criteria are met.

6. It is preferable that the hearing-impaired pupil's age be within two years of the average age of the group of hearing pupils. The child's general maturity is important, but if there is reason (e.g., if the child is unusually large or small or unusually gifted or talented), the two-year age limit should be disregarded.

7. If the regular class teacher is motivated and willing to try, that receptive attitude deserves equal weight with the teacher's understanding of the problems faced by a hearing-impaired student.

8. It is seldom necessary to reduce regular class size to accommodate hearing-handicapped pupils so long as the total class size, including the children with hearing impairments, does not exceed the typical class size for that school system and appropriate support services are provided.

Make use of equipment.

9. Proper amplifying equipment should be on hand, and the regular teacher should know how to use it.

Parental help is very important.

10. The parents should be aware of their roles and willing to play them. But the absence of such support (or even the absence of parents) need not hold an otherwise ready pupil out of the mainstream. Parent surrogates should be found to assist in the afternoon, evening, and morning.

These 10 criteria are intended to be flexible. Teachers and the pupils themselves are best able to judge who can qualify for consideration for integration. As a general rule, pupils need more opportunity to test themselves; they should not be shielded from contacts with regular classes.

Steps for Teachers and Principals

We now present some teacher-to-teacher comments and suggestions. Most come directly from professional educators experienced with mainstreaming. They found that their worries diminished when they kept to these guidelines.

Improving Communication

1. It is better, for understanding, to be near the hearing-impaired child. That applies to the child's understanding of the teacher or other pupils and the reverse.

Improved communication encourages increased learning.

2. Place the hearing-impaired child so there is face-to-face visibility of the teacher's speech movements. The child should be free to change position or seats as needed.

3. Use your natural gestures to supplement oral presentations, without exaggeration.

4. When referring to something in the room, point to it, nod in its direction, glance at it, or walk over and touch it. If discussing something in the room, manipulate it, to the extent possible, to synchronize with what is being said.

5. Take care not to talk when your face is turned to the chalkboard while you are writing, when it is turned down to see your notes, or when it is hidden by a book or papers or by your hands.

6. When showing films or slides, keep enough light on in the area so that the hearing-impaired pupils can see faces clearly when the teacher or narrator makes comments.

7. Remember, hearing children can tell how loud and how expressive their own voices are; hearing-impaired pupils cannot. You and the other pupils can find out from the special teacher how to reinforce good expression and how to help maintain appropriate voice volume with hearing-impaired pupils.

8. Talk in full sentences. If not understood, say the whole sentence again or rephrase the same thing in a new sentence. Avoid single words. It is easier to grasp content or meaning in context.

9. Use your own natural, normal teaching voice.

10. Remind hearing pupils to speak in complete sentences, to enunciate clearly, and to turn in the direction of the hearing-impaired pupils before speaking.

11. Make sure that the hearing-handicapped pupils learn any special "in" words or expressions used in the class or neighborhood. Making and maintaining a dictionary of such terms can be a class project of general value.

12. Light can be a problem in lip reading. The speaker's face should be clearly visible. Also, it is difficult to lip-read when there is a strong light behind the speaker (window, sun, lamp).

Teaching Techniques

1. Make use of captioned films. The special education teacher can help get these. Regular class pupils can profit from the combination of sound and print, too.

2. Use supplementary pictures and diagrams. As in the case of captioned films, the special teacher can help get pictures, diagrams, and other instructional materials developed especially for teaching hearing-impaired pupils. These same materials can often help the hearing pupils, too.

3. Write (or print) key words, expressions, phrases, and assignments on the chalkboard, or use an overhead projector. If an aide is available, make it a regular duty to write key words and instructions on the chalkboard.

4. Hearing-impaired students cannot take notes while they watch the faces of their teacher and fellow students. One way to help is to give all students copies of the teacher's notes. Another way is to arrange for two hearing students to make carbon copies of their notes for the hearing-impaired classmate. (Two students' notes work better than one; less will be missed.)

   Teamwork among all concerned is the key to success.

5. Share the key ideas of the lesson with the special teacher of the hearing-handicapped so that the ideas can be used in the preteach-

ing and postteaching sessions. It is helpful also to use a buddy system in which regular class students take turns reviewing their notes orally with a hearing-handicapped student in planned study sessions. That, of course, can help the hearing buddies, too.

6. Check regularly on the match between each pupil's rate and level of congitive development and the educational tasks now offered, plus those sequenced ahead for that pupil.

Class and Pupil Management

Expectations are similar for all pupils.

1. Hearing-impaired pupils welcome help in learning how to be quiet and not disturb hearing pupils by unknowingly making noises.
2. Expect hearing-impaired pupils to accept the same responsibilities for considerate behavior, homework, and dependability as is required of others.
3. Call the child's name when asking for attention. Touching or tapping the arm or shoulder should not be necessary, any more than with other pupils.
4. Everyone may profit from time to time from being reminded that hearing-impaired children have acquired an almost incredible skill. They "see" what others hear, and when they speak, they do so without hearing the sounds of their own voices.

In emergency situations (e.g., fires, auto accidents), sign language interpreters may not be on hand. Service personnel such as custodians, police, and emergency squads need to know key signs to exchange vital information. Two tools to help prepare public safety and health personnel for emergencies are 100 Medical Survival Signs, available from the Sign Language Store, 8613 Yolanda Avenue, Northbridge, CA 91328, and Silent Siren, available from the National Association for the Deaf, 814 Thayer Avenue, Silver Spring, MD 20910.

---

5. Some pupils, including hearing-impaired pupils, have learned to look attentive and to appear to be understanding when they are not. Occasionally direct a question to each of the hearing-impaired pupils to assess whether they are really tuned in to what is being taught.

Good discipline is a product of sound instructional management.

6. Your attitude is quickly caught by your pupils; they will tend to adopt your way of behaving and feeling about hearing-impaired pupils.
7. Be as consistent as you can about daily routines and requirements, particularly when a new hearing-handicapped pupil is entering your group. That will limit communication problems, especially while the process of getting acquainted takes place.

8. Give each hearing-impaired child encouragement and help in making child-to-child contacts that can lead to friendships in the regular class.

9. Detail for each hearing-impaired child what is expected in emergencies such as fire, accident, or other unusual occurrences. It is especially important that the child know what the regular class teacher expects under such circumstances.

10. Use cooperative goal-structuring techniques in which heterogeneous groups of students are formed and taught to be mutually helpful.

SUMMARY

Hearing-impaired pupils can take part in all aspects of regular education. Adaptations are needed for them, but sometimes those adaptations turn out to be beneficial for all. An example is the football huddle, used originally by deaf players so opponents would not see their manual talk while setting up the next play.

As in the case of communication in the huddle, the great bulk of curricular adjustments, special teaching methods or materials, and other accommodations relate to some aspect of the language arts. Given the staff and facilities, those accommodations can be made for hearing-impaired pupils from the very beginning of school.

PROSPECTS FOR THE FUTURE

A steady demand exists for qualified teachers of hearing-impaired youngsters. Regular class teachers who understand and can work with mainstream programs for hearing-impaired pupils can also expect to be favored for employment in forward-looking school systems. The rapid growth of interest in the very early childhood years suggests that there may be a high demand for teachers for that population.

Early childhood preparation is a growth frontier.

TOPICAL BIBLIOGRAPHY

Educational Intervention with Preschool-Age Hearing-Impaired Children

Birch (1976)
Brasel & Quigley (1977)
Brown (1973)
Kennedy et al. (1976)

Ling (1981)
Meadow (1980)
Northcott (1971)
Reger (1976)

Hearing-Impaired Students and Higher Education

Birch (1975)
Fellendorf (1973)
Jacobs (1980)
Martin (1984)
Stuckless & Enders (1971)

History of Education of Hearing-Impaired Persons

Craig (1942)
Davis & Silverman (1978)
Kirk & Lord (1974)
Lowenbraun, Appleman, & Callahan (1980)

Measurement of Sound and Hearing

Avery (1975)
Davis & Silverman (1978)
McConnell (1973)
Moores (1982)
Stillman (1976)

Modern Elementary and Secondary School Programs

Avery (1975)
Birch (1975, 1976)
Gustafson (1983)
Lowenbraun, Appleman, & Callahan (1980)
Martin (1984)
Moores (1982)
Northcott (1971)
Quigley & Paul (1984)
Reger (1976)
Ross & Nober (1981)
Yater (1976)

Persons with Hearing Impairments

Burlingame (1964)

Jacobs (1980)
Josephson (1963)

The Hearing Impaired Child's Parents

Dale (1967)
Ferris (1980)
Garrett & Stoval (1972)
Greenberg (1980)
Jacobs (1980)
Katz, Mathis, & Merrill (1974)

CHAPTER 8

Visual Impairments

Mainstream education has a long, successful history.

Imaginative principals, teachers, and parents demonstrated more than 50 years ago that by working together they could provide the specialized education needed by most students with vision impairments totally within the regular class or with only occasional removal for limited periods and purposes. The move to enroll and maintain these children in regular classes with special supports has spread widely.

Geerat J. Vermeij's (1978) first-person account tells of his integrated education as a blind child and how he now feels about it. In the process, he introduces a number of ideas that will be dealt with later in this chapter. It has been said that blind persons' views about their own condition range from seeing it as a nuisance to considering it a catastrophe. Vermeij's view tends toward the nuisance side of that continuum, as you will note.

A blind scientist speaks out on teaching the blind student.

I believe that three qualities should characterize the accommodation of the handicapped in public education: common sense, flexibility, and equal treatment. I am convinced that a change in attitude can accomplish much toward successful accommodation, and with a minimum of expense in time, money, and effort. . . . I am a totally blind scientist. I teach and conduct research. . . .

Most scientists begin their careers early, and I was no exception. My parents encouraged my first interests in natural history. So did a number of enlightened teachers at residential schools for the blind in the Netherlands, where I was born, and later in public schools in New Jersey. At the age of 10, I began to collect shells, and I rapidly became interested in other branches of biology as well. Thereafter, I pursued my scientific interests outside the classroom. My parents and brother constantly read to me. For two years, I attended Columbia University's Science Honors Program for high school students. . . .

Educators who run residential schools often maintain that blind students cannot learn essentials like braille and independent travel adequately unless they are segregated in special schools or classrooms. On the other hand, residential schools prevent blind students from being integrated into the society at large until they go to college or get jobs.

Public education, however, is a ready vehicle for social integration. Moreover, public schools can teach special skills to the blind: Training in Braille, typing, mobility, and other techniques essential to the functioning of a blind individual can supplement the standard curriculum or replace parts of it.

The regular classroom can offer needed services.

My experiences in the public schools of New Jersey prove that training and integration can coexist in the standard classroom. When I arrived in the United States in 1955, I was enrolled in third grade. Once or twice a week an excellent resource teacher from the New Jersey State Commission for the Blind came to teach me English grammer, contracted English Braille, Braille typewriting, and standard typing. Throughout my public education, the Commission provided textbooks that had been brailled by volunteers. From eighth grade on, a reader paid by the state came daily to read other books for leisure, and a Commission instructor gave me mobility training.

Already, the residential schools in the Netherlands had trained me thoroughly in Braille. One of these schools also had a small collection of stuffed animals. These specimens fascinated me and helped sustain my interest in natural history. The school frequently took me and my classmates on excursions to the woods, heaths, beaches, airports, and other places, where all of us were at liberty to experience firsthand the world around us. . . .

From the viewpoint of the blind student, it is much better to take a course in which some of the laboratory work cannot be done firsthand than to be denied the opportunity to take the course at all.

This does not mean that the criteria used in evaluating a blind student should be different from those for a sighted student. It is unfair either to relax criteria for the blind or to invent additional ones. Thus, we should not permit a student to complete a course without some understanding of techniques—nor should we demand medical information or psychological tests if these are not required of other students also. The blind and other handicapped people desire equal, not preferential or different treatment. To compete with the sighted on uneven terms severely weakens the position of the blind and impairs their chances of changing people's attitudes and of achieving integration. . . .

Equal rather than preferential treatment is desired.

I wish to emphasize that many problems which the handicapped face are those of the human population as a whole. Neither the blind nor the sighted will learn sicence or any other subject unless they are motivated, and unless teachers portray their subjects as fun, exciting, powerful, and intellectually satisfying. Those teachers who discourage the blind from taking a particular course or pursuing a field probably discourage nonhandicapped students as well. A flexible, tolerant attitude that encourages experimentation and a little risk helps lower educational barriers for blind and sighted alike.

In summary, I believe that attitudes create the greatest impediments to integrating the blind and other handicapped people in education. Common sense, flexibility, and a commitment to treat the handicapped on equal terms with others can lower and perhaps ultimately remove these barriers. (pp. 77–78)

The Vermeij story vividly illustrates both the complexity and the personal rewards of special education for a visually impaired child. The challenge is to help all such children.

DEFINITIONS, INCIDENCE, AND PREVALENCE

Blindness is a low-incidence condition.

Vision impairments occur in about 20 percent of the general population, but a large majority of the problems are corrected with prescriptive lenses. Educationally significant, noncorrectable vision impairments are found in only about 1 student in 1,000. Only about 3 out of 10 of those children are blind for educational purposes; fewer than 1 percent of the children receiving special education and related services in the United States are visually handicapped.

It is difficult to be exact about the incidence (number of new cases in any given period) and prevalence (number of existing cases at any given time) of visual impairments, for several reasons. First, there is no central registry for visually impaired persons to which one can turn for an unambiguous count. Second, many persons have multiple handicaps and may be reported in any one of several different categories when unduplicated counts are made. Third, the increasing trend toward mainstreaming means that persons with visual impairments are more widely dispersed, and it is difficult to make contacts for counting purposes. Fourth, incidence rates vary greatly over time. For example, incidence rates went down in the 1930s following improvements in immunization practices for certain diseases and the growing use of silver nitrate prophylactic treatments for infants. Rates went up in the period from the late 1940s to the mid-1950s because of retrolental fibroplasia (now referred to as retinopathy of prematurity), a difficulty associated with excessive amounts of oxygen in apparatus used for intensive infant care. Rates of incidence went down from about 1955 to 1964 when the trend reversed again for a brief period because of a rubella (German measles) epidemic. Since about 1966, incidence rates have been relatively low, but prevalence data reflect all of these variations in rates, in various patterns according to the age of persons observed. In the mid-1980s, the average person with retinopathy is about age 35, while those with rubella-caused impairments are in their early twenties. Most blindness occurs among the elderly, so the age distribution, considering the total age range, is highly skewed to the advanced side of the age continuum.

The definition of blindness most widely used in this country is not medical or educational but legal or economic. It was written into the Social Security Act of 1935, primarily for the benefit of aged persons; since then, however, it has become the basis for a broad range of categorical programs.

Blindness is . . . visual acuity for distant vision of 20/200 or less in the better eye, with best correction; or visual acuity of more than 20/200 if the widest diameter of field of vision subtends an angle no greater than 20 degrees. (National Society for the Prevention of Blindness, 1966, p. 10)

Note that this definition identifies categories or classes of persons for certain legal purposes. The legal definition of blindness includes not only persons who are totally blind, that is, unable to distinguish light from dark or without light perception, but also those who have some vision, severely impaired though it may be, in one or both eyes. By definition, then, the legal term *blindness* is not synonymous with total absence of sight. Only about 10 percent of the legally blind are totally without vision.

One can be legally blind and still have much useful vision.

To establish the eligibility of individuals to participate in federal and state aid-to-the-blind programs, most states adopted the Social Security Act definition. It is also accepted by most other agencies, official or private, that provide aid or services to blind persons. These include eligibility for income tax exemption, Talking Books from the Library of Congress, special teaching materials (braille and large print) from the American Printing House for the Blind, and state service programs.

The term *partially sighted* includes a larger group whose vision in the best eye after correction is between 20/70 and 20/200. The person with 20/70 vision sees at 20 feet what a person with normal 20/20 vision sees at 70 feet. The person with 20/200 vision sees at 20 feet what one with 20/20 vision sees at 200 feet. Anyone with 20/400 vision or worse cannot read letters of any size at 20 feet, even the big *E* on the Snellen chart. Such a person may, though, be able to function as a sighted person educationally by reading pages of normal type at the usual distance, or closer, with the aid of special lenses.

Physicians are usually concerned about classification of vision impairments according to cause (etiology), prognosis, and possible medical treatments. Thus medical classifications differ somewhat from those whose focus is legal rights, social services, education, or financial considerations.

Medical classifications differ from those of other disciplines.

Visual impairments are frequently coincident with other impairments. Fully half of blind or partially seeing children in the schools in the 1980s can be described as multiply impaired. One probable explanation is the medical advances that make it possible to keep alive newborns who have suffered adverse prenatal or perinatal influence. Diseases are another important cause. Rubella, for example, leaves in its wake large numbers of multiply impaired children, especially when the disease occurs in mothers during the first trimester of pregnancy. The last epidemic of rubella in the United States, 1964 to 1966, is estimated to have produced 30,000 children with visual and other concomitant impairments. Modern, effective immunizations, promoted by good health education and public health practices, serve to reduce that number, but further reductions, to near zero, could be achieved if available knowledge were properly applied.

20/20 to Become 4/4

One of the most common phrases connected with eyesight, "20/20 vision," may fall victim to metric conversion. This would bring the eye chart test into line with the metric system, changing the standard for perfect sight to 4/4. The American Optometric Association supports the change, stating that it will simplify the prescribing of glasses for tasks requiring good vision at great distances and will reduce the space needed in a doctor's office to perform the test from 20 feet to 4 meters, or about 13 feet. It is said that the eye chart test is the only vision test in the United States that has traditionally been nonmetric.

Parental observation in the preschool years is important.

Most children with severe visual impairments can be identified at birth or in infancy. However, not all are detected. Careful observation by parents and examinations by physicians are essential to identification of impairments of lesser degree. Teachers and principals can join in watching for such characteristics as the following (adapted from Calovini, n.d.):

Appearance

Red-rimmed eyelids
Swollen eyelids
Crust near lashes
Frequent sties
Red or watery eyes
Eyes in constant motion
Crossed eyes or walleyes
Eyes that cross when the child is tired
Eyes with pupils of different sizes

Behavior

Blinks constantly
Rubs eyes often
Tends to have eyes crossed when reading
Tries to brush away blur
Seems overly sensitive to light
Stumbles or trips over objects

Teachers can note eye problems by observing how children behave.

Holds book too close or too far away when reading
Changes distance of book from near to far frequently while reading
Shuts or covers one eye when reading
Tilts head to one side when reading

Screws up face when reading

Frowns when trying to see distant objects

Thrusts head forward in order to see an object

Holds body tense when trying to distinguish distant objects

Tries to guess words from quick recognition of a part of a word in easy
reading material

Tends to lose the place on the page

Confuses *o* and *a*; *e* and *c*; *n* and *m*; *h*, *n*, and *r*; *f* and *t*

Reads less well the longer he or she tries

Has a short attention span when doing chalkboard, bulletin board, or map
work

Has poor alignment in writing

Consistency of behaviors is a key consideration.

Any child may show these behaviors on occasion for different reasons. But when some are present day after day, whoever notices them should refer the child for an eye examination. By age 4 or 5, standard screening devices such as adapted Snellen charts or telebinocular instruments can be used to screen for vision problems. These procedures produce high rates of false positives but miss few real problems.

By the time a child's vision is checked in school, it may be too late to correct some defects. A home test parents can use is designed as a pointing game for children too young to read standard eye charts.[1] The letter *E* appears, pointing in four different directions. The child is asked to point which way the *E* is going. If there is trouble seeing the smaller rows of *E's* or if one eye performs better than the other, it is a signal to have a professional examination.

SUPPORT SERVICES

People with vision impairments, particularly those who are legally blind, have received many excellent support services. Advocacy groups working on behalf of persons who are blind have been particularly effective. A distinction in this connection, insisted on by some blind persons, is between programs *for* and *of* the blind. The prestigious American Foundation *for* the Blind welcomes help from anyone who wishes to join in efforts for improving opportunities *for* the blind; the American Council *of* the Blind, by contrast, is an important leadership agency and advocacy group consisting *of* blind persons.

Vigorous and broad-based advocacy characterizes this field.

Associations like these are effective in securing better schooling for children, services for parents, opportunities for both sheltered and competitive employment, public transportation, recreation, legal services and

---

[1] The test is free from the National Society for the Prevention of Blindness, 79 Madison Avenue, New York, NY 10016.

protection, housing, and health services. Association leaders typically give much attention to public education, to improving the general public understanding of vision impairments, and to advocating for their members before legislatures and other policymaking and administrative bodies.

Teachers of children with visual impairments will frequently have contact with organizations of parents and friends of visually handicapped children who monitor carefully the extent and quality of schooling and other services provided. The National Association for Parents of Visually Impaired is a nonprofit organization for parents who are committed to providing support to the parents and families of youngsters who have visual impairments.

Volunteer workers produce many instructional materials.

Volunteer organizations often began because of the needs of teachers who found themselves with visually impaired children but few instructional materials. Many school districts have small groups of volunteer transcribers and transcriptionists who record braille materials and other items needed in the schools. They also work for visually impaired college students or adults in professions and businesses. A number are affiliated with national agencies like the Library of Congress, the American Printing House for the Blind, the Braille Association, and National Recording for the Blind. A most gratifying experience for professional workers is to observe the highly motivated work of literally thousands of transcribers and other volunteers who devote time and energy to the production of instructional material for visually impaired children and adults.

Social workers, employed in schools or through specialized networks of state and local offices, help to identify and register children with significant vision impairments at the earliest possible age. They then direct parents to needed services, such as medical help, parent training, and preparation for schooling. Children of families who receive strong and effective services in the early years have a considerably better chance of profiting from schooling later.

EDUCATIONAL CLASSIFICATION

Classification in the schools depends on educational needs and abilities.

For educational purposes, children are considered to be blind when they must be taught to read by using braille or other means that do not involve sight. Partially sighted students, for educational purposes, have vision problems that require some special adjustments in instruction but nevertheless can be taught to read print of regular or large size. These educational classifications are functional; they are determined by the pupil's preferred mode of reading.

Deciding whether a child is educationally blind or partially sighted, in the sense of requiring a special mode of reading, is by no means simple. Researchers have not yet produced clear procedures for making this important classification decision. Some children with visual acuity measuring

20/400 may need braille, while others with the same measured acuity will be able to read clear print quite adequately.

Whether a particular child is taught to read print or braille depends on many factors in addition to visual acuity. Some of these are intellectual ability, motivation, family support, judgments of professionals on the use of low-vision aids (e.g., magnification devices), presence of secondary handicaps, preferences of the child and other significant persons, and prognosis for improvement or deterioration of vision. Only three of the decision variables listed are characteristics of the child. The others are characteristics of the total life situation.

Most of the important educational variables are external to the child.

Finally, the decision on whether a child needs accommodations for visual impairment in an instructional program must be validated by actual trials within the school situation. Even then, the child's needs will not be static, so programs will require changes with time and experience.

MAINSTREAMING

Most visually handicapped children do well in the mainstream. At the primary level, a child enrolled in a regular class may need extensive help from a resource teacher who can provide intensive instruction in orientation and mobility, typing, or braille. Later on, the student may need only occasional itinerant special teacher help to develop and maintain skills to compensate for disability. For brief occasional periods—in summer, for example—the same student may need to go to a special school for intensive instruction in daily living skills and for experience with other blind persons with whom models for learning and adjustment can be shared.

Visually handicapped children are readily educated in the instructional mainstream.

In many states, as recently as the 1950s and 1960s, blind and partially sighted students were almost automatically placed in residential schools. Since then, however, a countertrend has grown, bringing orientation and mobility training, instruction in braille reading and writing, and other special subjects into the resource rooms and regular classes of community schools. Thus the downward movement on the cascade of specialized instruction is exemplified to a high degree in programming for visually handicapped children. The prevailing practice in a great many school districts is to start visually impaired children in regular school programs from the beginning and to maintain them there by delivering the special instruction they need in that environment. That, of course, has required increasing involvement of regular teachers and principals in cooperative programming with special teachers.

Consider the following two illustrations. The first is concerned with arranging education for a partially sighted child whose vision is in a period of change; the second involves a child who has some vision but who will need braille instruction.

Judy was 8 years old and in the third grade. Her teacher asked the con-

Special and regular teachers join forces in planning.

sulting vision teacher for help because Judy's vision has diminished this year and she was beginning to drop back in her schoolwork. After their cooperative assessment and discussion, the two teachers wrote this report:

Though she tried hard, Judy had great difficulty in performing visual tasks, whether at reading distance or farther away. Glare bothered her; she was able to see better when the material was held up at an angle. She said that both the print in her regular reader and large-type print were easy to see. However, she read poorly in both and appeared to have less difficulty in seeing the large type. The general quality of Judy's schoolwork and her speaking vocabulary indicate above-average ability. The parents report that Judy will receive a new prescription for glasses soon. Also, she is to have surgery on one eye in a few months.

Medical interventions can have educational benefits.

We hope the new prescription and anticipated surgery will help solve Judy's problems in seeing. Educationally, however, she can benefit now from the use of a reading stand, a marker, dark-lined paper, and large type for at least some of her books. The dilemma of dittos can be solved by the teacher continuing to darken them or by using a transparent yellow acetate overlay to darken the purple print.

Judy's difficulty in reading may be caused by the combined effects of limited seeing and lack of experience in reading. The large type should add encouragement for her to read. Even though it is difficult, she should continue to use her eyes to read and write.

Judy's ability to see will vary from day to day. If she can see well enough and prefers to use regular type-size materials at times, she should be encouraged to do so.

Debbie, age 5, attended a day-care center seven hours a day while her parents worked. Following is part of a report prepared by the day-care teacher and a public school special vision teacher as Debbie entered kindergarten.

At the center each day, time was given to free play with toys indoors and out, walks to the parks and nearby playgrounds, small group activities, and nap time. The director set the pattern of treating Debbie normally, which carried over to the teachers and other children. She has not been pampered or given special privileges.

Debbie is very talkative, uses language well, and appears very capable of learning. She has excellent orientation and mobility skills considering that she apparently has light-perception-only vision.

The behavioral objectives worked on at the center included further language development; object identification, discrimination, and classification; self-care; math readiness; sensory listening and smell; and large muscle coordination including running, skipping, jumping, and galloping. Debbie was also taught specific skills used in kindergarten such as cutting, pasting, folding, and coloring.

The educational plan is based on individual needs and conditions.

The center teacher is concerned about Debbie's habit of rubbing her eyes (even when walking) and her frequent illnesses. She has taken a long nap each day at the center.

Recommendations and Future Plans. First, Debbie will be receiving day care in her neighborhood even after she enters kindergarten. She will be taking the same school bus as the neighborhood children. Second, a vision teacher plans to be in her school two times per week next year for direct tutoring, preparation of special materials, and interpretation of needs with the teacher, as needed.

One year later, Debbie's kindergarten teacher and the consulting vision teacher made the following report:

The behavioral objectives planned for Debbie this year for the special tutorial sessions included braille readiness, orientation and mobility, handwriting, self-care skills, and classroom maintenance needs.

Debbie completed through Book 14-E in the Lippincott reading readiness series. Portions from each book were selected, brailled, and read. She was also part of a reading group that emphasized listening skills. Many reading readiness games for the class were adapted in braille. She has been able to match, recognize, and recall all of the upper- and lowercase braille letters and has mastered beginning sounds. She has effectively blended sounds for beginning reading as a part of this series.

Steady progress resulted from detailed teacher planning.

Many of the math readiness games from the *Work Jobs* book that were in the kindergarten room were readily adapted in braille. The daily calendar program was also prepared in braille, as were experience stories.

Debbie moves freely in her classroom, to other nearby rooms, and in the physical education program. She is unafraid and has a keen awareness of herself in space. Self-care assistance has been minimal, with shoe tying receiving the greatest emphasis. She is generally responsible for her own in-class needs.

Manuscript writing of her first name was a goal recently attained through use of tactile aids. Nearly all the craft projects planned by the kindergarten teacher required no special adaptations to be meaningful.

Debbie's mother attended the meetings planned for parents and applied for Talking Book and braille book services from the regional lending library.

A concern in preschool was frequent illness and tiredness. There was little of that this year.

Recommendations and Future Plans

1. Debbie had considerable success in kindergarten. It seems likely that will continue in grade 1. She will need some aid from a vision teacher on a daily basis for direct tutoring and to prepare materials and confer with her regular class teacher.
2. A successful method to erase the eye rubbing has not been found. Debbie is aware of it and is able to talk about it, which may be a start.
3. She shows a healthy attitude about her impairment, but, as would be the case with many other blind children, she needs assistance in interpretation of social situations and awareness of her own social impact.

Plans for the following year are built on previous gains.

Judy and Debbie are fairly typical of young mainstreamed visually impaired pupils. The special equipment and procedures they and others find useful are described in more detail in the next section.

TECHNOLOGY AND SPECIAL PROCEDURES

Reading can be done by touch.

Louis Braille (1809–1852) was blinded at the age of 3 and became first a pupil and then an instructor at the Institut des Jeunes Aveugles in Paris. There he developed the system of embossed writing that bears his name. The idea came from the use of raised-dot codes, read by touch in nighttime military maneuvers. Essentially, *braille* is a code based on a cell of three embossed dots in each of two vertical rows. By varying the placement and number of dots in each row, braille provides all the letters of the alphabet and the numbers 1 through 10 (the letters *a* through *j*). Variations of placement and added cells permit the notation of all punctuation signs and the end of communication. Braille is read by passing fingertips across the braille figure from left to right, as in sight reading.

In use today, braille has two forms: full-spelling (Grade 1) braille and contracted braille; the latter consists of the first form plus 189 contractions and short-form words and is known as Grade 2 braille. Many of the contractions occur in commonly used words, which are also the words used most frequently in primer-level readers. As may be imagined, that can cause difficulties in learning to spell if one starts reading instruction with Grade 2 braille and common words. The alphabet and numbers 1 through 10 are illustrated in Figure 8.1. The raised dots that form the braille system are shown in the figure by the small black bullets.

The *Optacon* is an instrument that scans print materials electronically and raises the orthographic features. Because the print is raised, it can be read by touch. Use of the Optacon is on the increase. However, braille remains the most common medium for reading by educationally blind students.

Because braille mathematics calculations are long and slow, the *abacus* is often used instead. It speeds the processes. Sighted children also enjoy using the abacus. A special braille approach to mathematics uses what is known as the Nemeth code, and lately computers have shown promise as an instructional tool in this field.

The *braille writer*, somewhat smaller than a typewriter, produces braille print mechanically. It has a spacing bar and six keys that correspond to the six dots of the braille cell. The keys can be pressed simultaneously in any combination to produce the desired cell constellation. Commonly used by blind persons early in elementary schools, the braille writer remains a continuing aid throughout school and life.

Slate and stylus are equivalent for blind pupils to tablet and pencil for sighted persons. The equipment consists of a lapboard, special braille paper, and a slate (a template with spaces corresponding to dots and cells of braille). The student uses a hand stylus to punch the dots in each cell. A slower procedure than the braille writer, the slate and stylus work well for spelling tests, short-answer assignments, and recording study assignments made by teachers.

```
a        b        c        d        e        f        g        h        i
o •      o •      o o      o o      o •      o o      o o      o •      • o
• •      o •      • •      • o      • o      o •      o o      o o      o •
• •      • •      • •      • •      • •      • •      • •      • •      • •

j        k        l        m        n        o        p        q        r
• o      o •      o •      o o      o o      o •      o o      o o      o •
o o      • •      o •      • •      • o      • o      o •      o o      o o
• •      o •      o •      o •      o •      o •      o •      o •      o •

s        t        u        v        w        x        y        z
• o      • o      o •      o •      • o      o o      o o      o •
o •      o o      • •      o •      o o      • •      • o      • o
o •      o •      o o      o o      • o      o o      o o      o o

   1           2           3           4           5           6           7           8
• o  o •    • o  o •    • o  o o    • o  o o    • o  o •    • o  o o    • o  o o    • o  o •
• o  • •    • o  o •    • o  • •    • o  • o    • o  • o    • o  o •    • o  o o    • o  o o
o o  • •    o o  • •    o o  • •    o o  • •    o o  • •    o o  • •    o o  • •    o o  • •

   9           0
• o  • o    • o  • o
• o  o •    • o  o o
o o  • •    o o  • •
```

Figure 8.1. The Braille Alphabet and the Numbers 1–10

The *Kurzweil Reading Machine* (KRM) provides direct access to printed and typed information. Compact size, push-button control, readily understood speech, automatic tracking of text, and the ability to read at speeds faster than human speech are among its features. Blind college students read materials from the library shelves. Visually handicapped secondary and elementary school students sometimes use the KRM to keep up with reading assignments in mainstream classes. Machine maintenance costs and other practical considerations may limit the use of the KRM, but trends in this line of technology are positive.

Material is placed face down on the scanner's glass surface. A control panel activated by the user causes the machine automatically to find the first line of text and begin scanning the page. Within a few seconds an electronic voice is heard reading. Controls permit users to make choices about reading manner and speed. The machine can repeat the previous few lines or words, spell out words that may be obscure, announce punctuation and capitalization, and mark certain words or phrases for later reference.

The Talking Magazine edition makes *U.S. News & World Report* available to thousands to blind and physically handicapped people at no cost to themselves. Every Saturday, while the presses turn out the latest issue of

A variety of materials and equipment aid learning.

the magazine, professional broadcasters read nearly every word of it onto tapes, alternating their voices with each article for variety. The tapes are transcribed on master records. Thousands of the disks made from the master records are mailed, arriving at a listener's home just a few days behind the regular magazine delivery date. To hear the tapes, the blind subscriber uses a special record player, available on loan.

The National Library Services for the Blind and Physically Handicapped, a division of the Library of Congress, maintains the list of people who ask to receive the talking edition and provides the record players. It also foots the bill for the records, which are provided at cost by the magazine.[2]

Personal computers are rapidly coming into wide use by visually impaired individuals. They serve as word processors, with many advantages over ordinary typewriters—for example, in alphabetizing items electronically, checking on the spelling of common words, and storing information conveniently. For the student who has special interest in computers, it is possible to extend usage to include many important functions in communications, data management, and more.

Large print books help children with partial sight.

Large print books are used with children whose partial sight interferes with reading ordinary print but who can discriminate larger letters and words. Large print generally refers to letters 14 or more points high (see Figure 8.2). The research of Peabody and Birch (1967) and others indicated that most large print books are in 18-point type. Large print can be produced by photographically enlarging standard type, by resetting standard type in large sizes, by using a large-type typewriter, and by writing by hand in manuscript. There are several related ways to make reading easier for the visually impaired, such as low-vision aids (magnifiers that allow many students to read standard print), reading with the print close to the eyes, and devices that transfer ordinary print to larger images on TV screens. These devices are like hearing aids for the hearing-impaired. When useful, they are necessities for effective instruction and learning.

Low-vision aids and large print magnify or spread the image on the retina. The same effect can be achieved simply by getting closer to the book or object. But such enlargement on the retina reduces the amount of material that can be viewed at any given moment. The perceptual unit of a person with good vision may include several words, whereas a child using a magnifying device may be able to see only part of a word in one fixation. Enlarging the perceptual unit can thus result in limited reading speed and fatigue.

Actually, many more partially seeing pupils can learn to read ordinary print than was once believed (Barraga, 1976; Birch et al., 1966). They should be given opportunities to do so. Obviously, reading ordinary print

---

[2] Information on the Talking Magazine edition is available from Reader Service, 2300 N Street, N.W., Washington, DC 20037.

Point size		Examples
6	zyxwtvutsrqponmlkjihgfedcbsryxwv	Many maps and directories
8	zyxwtvutsrqponmlkjihgfed	Newspapers
9	zyxwtvutsrqponmlkjihgf	Magazines
10	zyxwtvutsrqponmlkji	High school texts
12	zyxwtvutsrqponml	Books for children 9–12
14	zyxwtvutsrqpon	Books for children 8–9
18	zyxwtvutsrq	Books for children 5–8 and large print texts
24	zyxwvuts	Large print books

Figure 8.2. Examples of Print Size. Print size is expressed in *points*, measured from the bottom of the lowest to the top of the highest character. One point equals 1/72 inch.

has advantages. Large books are a considerable inconvenience. With experience in reading, dependence on large print usually lessens.

Reader services come in various forms. Volunteers are frequently needed simply to read aloud to students; they may be classmates or other members of the community who have organized themselves to provide systematic reader services. In other cases, readers record materials on tape. The Library of Congress provides nationwide distribution of Talking Books, recordings of outstanding books read aloud by well-known figures. Visually impaired (and physically impaired) persons obtain the records from regional depositories. In some states, special recordings are made for occupational groups, such as blind lawyers. In at least one state, reader services are provided by radio, using the side channels of the public FM radio network. A special agency (Recording for the Blind, Inc.) provides recordings of materials for blind college students.

Services and special materials are useful and free.

Visually impaired students may select from a variety of materials and equipment shown in the checklist in Figure 8.3. Decisions regarding their selection and use should be made by the special and regular teacher after consultation with the individual student.

As rules of thumb, it can be anticipated that at high school level, non-handicapped students will read ordinary materials at a rate of about 250–300 words per minute (wpm). Braille is slower, usually about 90–120 wpm for good braille students. Most students can listen to tapes at about 150–175 wpm, but with training and special devices to compress speech (which eliminates some of the lost time between spoken words), that can sometimes be increased up to 275 wpm. Good instruction improves whatever mode of reading is used.

Special education teachers, supervisors, and coordinators are familiar

Partially Seeing Students	*Blind Students*

Paper
_____ Regular notebook paper
_____ Bold-line paper
_____ Raised-line paper
_____ Nonglare paper

_____ Braille transcription paper
_____ Graph paper
_____ Raised-line paper

Books
_____ Regular print
_____ Recorded books
　　_____ Cassette
　　_____ Reel
　　_____ Records
_____ Large print

_____ Braille books
_____ Recorded books
　　_____ Cassette
　　_____ Reel
　　_____ Records

Equipment
_____ Tape recorder
　　_____ Cassette
　　_____ Reel-to-reel
_____ Typewriter (large or regular type)
_____ Adjustable-top desk; desk-top easel or bookstand
_____ Magnification devices (low-vision aids)
_____ Lamps
_____ Closed-circuit TV system (enlarges standard point)
_____ Personal computers

_____ Tape recorder
　　_____ Cassette
　　_____ Reel-to-reel
_____ Typewriter
_____ Braillewriter (six-key machine that "types" braille)
_____ Slate and stylus (for writing braille)
_____ Abacus
_____ Braille rulers
_____ Braille erasers
_____ Talking calculator (calculator with audio output)
_____ Speech compressor

Other
_____ Large print maps
_____ Relief models
_____ Raised-line drawing kit
_____ Black felt-tip pens
_____ Large soft-lead pencils
_____ Yellow acetate (place over purple dittos to increase contrast)
_____ Writing guides (helps person write on line)

_____ Braille labeler
_____ Swail dot inverter (for making raised-dot drawings)
_____ Raised-line drawing kit
_____ Braille maps and globes
_____ Relief models
_____ Optacon (electronic device that enables blind person to read print)

_____ Raised-print and braille
clocks
_____ Writing guides (helps
person write on lines)

Figure 8.3. Materials and Equipment Checklist. (Adapted from a publication of the Ohio Resource Center for the Visually Handicapped, Columbus).

with where and how to obtain these items. Many can be borrowed as needed. Such special materials and equipment for schooling are free to the child. They must be provided, if needed, as the child's right. Moreover, use is not necessarily limited to visually impaired pupils. Frequently children with learning disabilities or other conditions that interfere with or limit writing or reading, for example, can use some of these items to good advantage.

THE VISUALLY IMPAIRED PERSON

The fairest and most accurate statement about persons with visual impairments is that they vary greatly. They are not of a kind, and no common set of expectations can be made for them. They need and deserve to be known individually. Laurie, some of whose story follows,[3] had to adapt to blindness from a life of seeing.

This is my first year in high school, and I was really kind of scared when I started. I got butterflies in my stomach and sometimes felt like I didn't want to go at all. My high school is a big place, and I was worried about being able to find my way around. I was even worried about finding the front door! Besides, everyone already knew everyone else, and I didn't know anyone. I'm glad that didn't last too long. . . .

Laurie's feelings are like those of any new student.

I don't always like to use my cane. Like, if I'm going to the store with one of my friends, it makes me feel funny to be carrying it around. It makes me feel awkward.

I guess some people think I'm stubborn because of this, but the way I figure it is, other people don't have to do it, so why should I? But then I realize that knowing how to get anywhere by myself makes learning how to use the cane worthwhile.

---

[3] Excerpted from A. J. Brightman & D. Greig, (Eds.), *Laurie* (New York: Scholastic Book Services, 1978). Reprinted by permission.

Braille is like an alphabet made up of a bunch of raised dots. So I read with my fingers instead of my eyes, even to tell what time it is. The hardest thing is learning what all the different shapes mean.

New learning presents challenges.

There are all different kinds of things for me to learn, like using a regular typewriter, writing my signature, cooking, doing laundry, making my bed, going shopping. You might not think so, but even learning how to make a grilled cheese sandwich can be a big deal for me.

I'm a pretty quiet person mostly. I guess you could say I'm kind of shy, or maybe I'm just old-fashioned. When I meet someone new—especially if that someone is a boy—my tongue gets tied up in a knot.

Before I went totally blind, I used to think that if you couldn't see, you wouldn't be able to do anything on your own. All I could think about was a little man on a street corner holding a tin cup. I never thought of a blind person being able to go to school or take a bus or do almost anything.

I guess that's the way most people think about it.

Friends can sense when help is appropriate.

My friends all understand that I don't really want to be treated differently, but I also want them to know that I do have a problem. There are some kids I know who would feel funny if I held onto their arm or asked them for help.

But once in school I was walking down the hall with one of my friends, and she just naturally took my arm...just like that, I didn't say anything, and neither did she. It's like she knew that I might have trouble or something, so she naturally reached over. That's how I like it.

Then there are some people who have trouble doing that, and that's O.K., too. I think it's something that they can learn from experience.

You want to know what makes me really uncomfortable? Every once in a while there are these people who come up to me and don't say anything. They keep real quiet and just look at me. It's as if they're going to find the answers or something all over my face. It's embarrassing when that happens, because then other people start to wonder what the person is staring at and then they begin to stare, too.

I guess people stare because they just don't understand what being blind is all about. I guess they have questions that they don't know how to ask.

Another thing that really aggravates me is when people talk about me as if I weren't there. I can't even describe how angry that makes me. Like sometimes someone will ask my mother, "And how's Laurie?"...and, I mean, I'm standing right there. I'm not invisible.

She'll usually say, "Ask her."

Future plans point to independence.

Lori's one of my best friends, and a really nice person. She doesn't put people down because they're different. She's just easygoing and nice to everybody. We hope someday we'll live together when we go to college. We'll get an apartment, you know, and have a cat. It'll be nice.

When I grow up, I want to be either a kindergarten teacher or a child psychologist, because I just love little kids. I suppose being either is going to be hard for me, but that's all right. I don't like anything that's too easy. I like something that has a challenge.

I think that I'm going to make it, and that everything's going to be all right for me. I think I'll be able to do more and more things on my own. I won't always have to have somebody else around. I'll be independent.

THE FUNCTION OF VISION IN LEARNING

Children with vision impairments who are enrolled full time in regular school programs tend not to have complicating secondary conditions. Their major problem, to put it simply, is that they do not see well. Obviously, though, reduced vision also restricts concept formation from environmental experiences, limits mobility, makes spatial orientation difficult, and alters the acquisition of personal and social behaviors that are learned by seeing and imitation.

Vision coordinates most of our sensory impressions of events and objects. True, children with little or no vision do use touch and hearing to become familiar with the sound, feel, and features of some objects and persons. But they cannot learn from feel about a bird in flight, a small insect, colors, or the moon and stars. The song of a bird alone tells nothing of its size or coloration; a person's voice tells little of appearance or behavior; running footsteps could indicate flight or sport. Coordination with visual clues is missing.

Vision facilitates coordination and integration of information.

We also use sight to relate the coordinated information received from our senses to the meaning of words, thus building concepts. Young sighted children quickly learn to distinguish between a truck and a passenger car, a fire engine and a police car or ambulance, and even the makes of their family's and a neighbor's cars. No one formally teaches those differences; sighted children develop them incidentally from the evidence of their senses and the words for the vehicles. Children without sight may learn to distinguish the sounds of the different vehicles, but they are unable to form the *same* concepts sighted children have of them.

A great deal of a child's learning derives from imitation. Blind children cannot see to imitate smiles, frowns, chewing motions, the placement of feet on stairs, the use of tableware, clapping hands, and the like. Children with very low or no vision usually must be taught such behaviors deliberately. Blind children, seldom aware of the possible range of facial expressions and their significance, do not know that they too are capable of expressing emotions facially.

Vision encourages learning by imitation.

Those who see little or nothing encounter a special set of problems in spoken communication because they lack the visual cues that help sighted persons interpret and respond to the spoken word. The movements associated with speech, including body and hand movements and facial expressions, are often as important as the speech itself. An arched eyebrow may emphasize surprise; a shrug of the shoulders may be the silent answer to a question.

Visually impaired persons can be taught techniques to minimize or overcome difficulties in speaking and responding to the spoken word. The aim is greater confidence in social conversations, family interactions, and public gatherings and in securing and refusing the help of sighted persons.

Some persons with very limited sight develop an expressionless, or "deadpan," look. Other blind people take on a fixed smile. Both are inappropriate and distracting.

Also, blind people are not always sure of the situation in which they are speaking. It is difficult for them to judge the size of a room, the number of people present, and where those people are located. Consequently, visually impaired people may speak in a voice that is either too loud or too soft for the circumstances.

Training can help social adjustment.

Lack of eye contact is one of the most common and noticeable difficulties. Untrained partially seeing or blind speakers may hold their heads down or look everywhere except directly toward the persons with whom they are conversing. Through training, they can be taught to localize the sound of the voice, to face the speaker, and to turn the direction from which the voice is coming. In this way, they achieve a good approximation of eye contact. Speech training also covers introductions, voice analysis and control, and spoken communication in public situations.

Self-stimulation replaces external stimulation.

Lack of environmental stimulation leads some young blind children to develop "blindisms," forms of self-stimulation, such as turning the head rapidly, rocking back and forth, or poking the eyes with their fingers. Young children with only light perception will often "light-play": They will look directly at a light source while moving their hands and fingers back and forth very close to their eyes. Sighted persons who do not understand the reasons for these behaviors may be troubled by them and may even misinterpret them as evidence of emotional disturbance. Blindisms can be eliminated through intensive instruction.

Mary Berkey is the chief switchboard operator at Northumberland State University. She has been blind all her life. Her job is full-time; she worked up to it over a period of three years after first being employed at the university as a department receptionist and a part-time typist.

Mary uses electronic equipment called the Talking Telephone Directory (TTD). Upon receiving a call, she types the name on a keyboard like that of a typewriter. The TTD then speaks into her headset the correct number for that name, allowing her to connect the call. From name typing to number output takes less than a second. Blind operators with this equipment handle approximately 85 calls per hour. The average for sighted operators with conventional methods is 50 to 55 calls.

Blind children display the same range and proportion of mental and emotional disturbances as other children. Partially sighted persons, perhaps because they bestride the worlds of both the seeing and the blind, "tend to be less well-adjusted than either the blind or the seeing" (Lowenfeld, 1973, p. 55). Although they have sight, seeing may require effort and strain and may be insufficient under some circumstances. They may be able to see very well at close range but not be able to read a street sign or the number of an approaching bus. If their fields of vision are very limited, they may give the impression of confusion as they try to integrate bit by bit all the information in a new environment. If they have difficulty with light, they may be blinded on entering a brightly lighted room or be unable to read the menu in a darkened restaurant.

Partially seeing children with very low vision may be misunderstood because of slow reactions or confused responses. They may have difficulty organizing their perceptions of what is around them in a noisy cafeteria, for example, a room in which the furniture has been moved about, or a sunny playground where running children and shadows blur and shift. Adults may interpret their slowness of response as a sign of mental retardation, depriving these children of appropriate help.

Misinterpretations can adversely affect individual programming.

Quality education for visually impaired pupils starts orientation and mobility training early. That involves careful orientation of children to their environment and to obstacles and cues they should be aware of in order to travel safely. Usually, it involves training in use of white cane techniques to discover elevation changes and obstacles before stumbling on them while walking. At later stages, mobility and orientation training will include topics such as using public transportation, referring to special braille maps, and maintaining orientation in large spaces. The competent use of auditory cues and modern cane techniques can build true skill and confidence about travel. When instruction is carried out in the presence of seeing children, their understanding grows as well.

PREVAILING AND PREFERRED PRACTICES

Prevailing Practices

1. Public schools accept responsibility for educating visually impaired children at kindergarten age.

2. Children with visual impairments are mainstreamed for academic instruction, but social mainstreaming is often lacking.

3. Children with visual impairments are taught mainly by one special vision teacher in cooperation with one or more regular teachers.

Preferred Practices

1. Search and outreach activities contact visually impaired children and begin their education, with family participation, as soon after birth as they can be identified.

2. Attention is given to both academic and social mainstreaming.

Social mainstreaming deserves careful attention.

3. The school principal, parents, and all teachers work together to plan and conduct the educational program.

4. Special education teachers encourage regular class teachers to send exceptional children to resource rooms for much of their instructional needs.

5. The program for students with visual impairments is mainly academic.

6. Few carefully designed support programs are available for postsecondary students with vision impairments.

7. State residential schools for the blind operate as comprehensive alternative programs.

Specialists should share their skills.

8. Programs for visually impaired students operate separately from the rest of special education, with little sharing of concepts, materials, or techniques.

9. Visually impaired persons with other impairments, except for the deaf-blind, receive little attention.

4. Special education teachers learn consultative and team-teaching skills so that they can help regular class teachers instruct exceptional children in the regular class context.

5. Emphasis is given to social skills and development as well as academics; special in-school and out-of-school arrangements are made as necessary for experience and training in social areas and daily living skills.

6. Vocational schools, colleges, and graduate schools modify admissions and develop strong support programs for students with vision impairments in mainstream programs.

7. Residential schools are much lower in enrollment and regionalized to serve specific needs, such as programming for multiply impaired students or offering short-term training on special topics for students otherwise enrolled in mainstream programs.

8. Specialists in work with visually impaired students exchange competencies and knowledge with other educators, working jointly on the educational problems of exceptional children who have multiple disabilities.

9. Physical and social inclusion of multiply impaired students in regular schools provides them with a wider range of developmental opportunities.

THE ROLE OF THE REGULAR CLASS TEACHER, SPECIAL TEACHER, AND PRINCIPAL

Principals and regular teachers may be apprehensive when they first learn that a student with visual handicaps may be enrolled with them. That concern can be reduced by visits to operating mainstream programs and by talks with successfully mainstreamed blind pupils. When specialist team members are available to assist with direct service, provide guidance, and answer questions, anxieties are reduced quite readily.

The Special Teacher of the Visually Impaired Student

Certified instructors of visually impaired students may be employed as consultants, itinerant teachers, resource teachers, or teachers in specialized settings. They may also serve in supervisory and administrative roles. Regular teachers can expect vision teachers to perform the following tasks:

The special teacher supplements and complements the work of the regular teacher.

1. Provide special materials, such as braille, large print, and recorded material, braille writers, typewriters, braille slates, and magnifiers and participate in decisions about their use.
2. Demonstrate proper use of special equipment (those listed above and others, such as the abacus, special maps, tape recorder, and records).
3. Assist in the assessment of students and in making referrals for additional studies, as needed.
4. Monitor progress and specific problems and needs as each special student proceeds through the school program.
5. Participate in team planning sessions.
6. Help to advise and counsel parents and teachers.
7. Help to organize reader and brailling services.
8. Teach students orientation, mobility, and the use of residual vision.

The special teacher offers consultation to parents.

An informative study of the functions of the teacher-consultant of children with visual handicaps was conducted by Moore and Peabody (1976). Participating were teachers from preschool through secondary school; on the average, each had about 19 students. The following functional description of an itinerant teacher teaming with regular teachers was drawn from their work (pp. 56–64).

In a typical week, the teacher spends 19¼ hours in direct instruction of children; 1½ hours consulting with regular classroom teachers; 2½ hours in procurement and construction of materials; 2 hours in consultation with parents, other professionals, volunteers or community agencies; 2½ hours in administration (i.e.,

Direct instruction and driving take up the most time.

reports, meetings) or collecting information on referrals; and 5¼ hours driving, not including home to the first school and from the last.

Typically, 11 of the teacher's 19 partially seeing (visual learner) pupils are at the elementary school level and 6 at the secondary school level. One is either a preschool visual learner or a multiply-impaired visual learner in another special program. One is a nonvisual (blind) learner, most probably at the secondary level. Only 13 children need regular service; 8 of the elementary visual learners, 4 of the secondary visual learners, and the nonvisual learner. Six children are visited infrequently during the year as requested by the regular teacher or for monitoring purposes only.

For the 8 elementary visual learners who require regular service, the teacher consults with the classroom teacher and school nurse, assesses visual functioning of the child, and interprets medical information and visual function.

Following is a set of statements selected and adapted from records of special teachers of visually impaired children. They indicate in practical terms what the functions of such a special teacher are. Judgments about effectiveness of specific functions are in parentheses.

Keeping records helps the itinerant teacher evaluate program effectiveness.

Had conference with student and teacher on completion of daily assignments. (Effective)

Had conference with mother on kinds of behaviors that would be expected of her child as he changed from an elementary class to a large junior high. (Effective)

Advised parents not to have their first-grader learn braille until absolutely necessary in spite of doctor's recommendation; two years later child is still doing well with large print. (Effective)

Tried but could not get teachers to hold the same standards for quality of work from visually impaired students as from other students. (Ineffective)

Made assessment of academic status of a student; discovered she was well below her level and arranged to place her in a special reading class. (Effective)

Reviewed picture of a rainbow with a partially seeing fifth-grader who could not see a real one and whose reading assignment required knowing about rainbows. (Effective)

Helped clarify some conceptual problems relating to mathematics lessons of a second-grader. (Effective)

Accompanied class on a field trip and described sights to the visually handicapped student in the class. (Effective)

Arranged for partially seeing student to use films and remote control projector for supplementary materials. (Effective)

Introduced playing ball to improve eye-hand coordination of a student. (Effective)

Tried to get high school student to go to Mental Hygiene Clinic where he had been previously referred. (Ineffective)

Taught personal typing to partially seeing student and noted positive attitude change. (Effective)

Had several discussions with a high school student about drugs and alcohol. (Effective)

Answered questions on birth control asked by a 16-year-old partially seeing girl about to be married. (Effective)

Arranged for student to discuss advantages of vocational rehabilitation program with another student in high school who had rejected being referred and receiving services. (Effective)

Encouraged blind student to submit her poems to a national children's magazine—published. (Effective)

Failed to convince newly blinded adolescent she needed to learn braille. (Ineffective)

Arranged for braille student to have reader service to prepare her for debate team; did some research myself for student and brailled information for her use. (Effective)

Suggested projects for a teacher to use with a nonverbal very active partially seeing boy in a "trainable retarded" class. (Effective)

Gave guidance department of a school a push to get a visually impaired/mentally retarded student into vocational technical school despite his first rejection by the school. (Effective)

Individual counseling facilitates adjustment.

A Case Study

Some pupils with more than one impairment move through regular schools with little or no difficulty if they get the right kinds of help at the right times. Georgeann, a 13-year-old blind student, also has some orthopedic problems. Her gait is slow and awkward. She needs a handrail to negotiate stairs. She has been assisted through a full year by regular teachers and a consulting vision teacher. This summary is adapted from one written by the special teacher in cooperation with Georgeann and her other teachers.

A combination of impairments can be managed.

The academic objectives for Georgeann included effective use of slate and stylus, introduction to braille shorthand, typing, review of abacus, writing her signature, writing and evaluating her own short-term educational goals, and interpretation of maps, charts, and graphs. Related objectives were learning to listen and learning to use conversational posture. Specific orientation and mobility objectives were not set.

She can use the slate and stylus for note taking, though Georgeann types most of her work. Her speed, format, and accuracy are acceptable. She overcame an initial difficulty in using quotation marks and knowing when to indent for paragraphs.

She can set up and work math problems, including problems with fractions, on the abacus. The concept of place value as it relates to fractions, percentages, and decimals is confusing to her, and she is now working on it.

She can write her name in cursive form within the signature guide, and she can use the check template. She has used the raised letters from the Optacon and identifies them easily.

A United States atlas and an African atlas have been provided for her. One hour was spent reviewing the keys to the atlas, and she now uses them independently. Her listening skills in a group have improved.

Students help establish their own goals.

Everyone in the class sets goals. At the beginning of the year, Georgeann began setting weekly goals for herself. At first, they were very broad and difficult to accomplish in a week's time. Through work in her accountability group, Georgeann's goals have become more directed. She now puts her goals on a timetable for the week and is much more successful in accomplishing them.

She received three hours of orientation and mobility evaluation and instruction per week for two months. Yet she remains a very dependent student and capable of only slow and inefficient travel in the classroom or at home. To get around in the school building, she requires sighted assistance. She walks on the level adequately but slowly. Stairs can be used if she has a handrail. Other children often carry her books.

Planning, recording progress, and projecting new plans is an essential cycle for teachers.

The full range of orientation and mobility instruction will be necessary over the next several years if she wants to be able to travel outside routes with complex intersections. A complete course requires approximately 250 hours of sequential and intensive instruction. It may be necessary to re-activate physical and occupational therapy for her, too. Consultation is needed about that.

Recommendations for next year: Direct service by the vision teacher three or more times a week, continued consultation with regular teachers, and possible occupational and physical therapy coordinated with orientation and mobility instruction.

Steps for Regular Teachers and Principals

Before a student with visual impairment enters school, a partnership should be established with regular teachers, the principal, the vision teacher, and the child's family. Together they plan any required adjustments in program, attitude, and equipment.

An early concern will be to introduce the visually impaired pupils to the spaces and places they must know. Take time at the beginning to walk with the children through the routes to be traveled. Explore and explain various parts of the classroom and school areas such as lavatories, exits, shops, gym, lunchroom, special rooms, and the principal's office. Special alerts should be given to obstructions and danger points, such as drinking fountains and staircases. Visually impaired children will need to be alerted when changes are made in routes or room arrangements. The special vision teacher assists in orientation activities and often offers direct instruction on the use of the white cane and other mobility activities. Much can be done, though, by regular teachers.

Independence is the objective. Avoid overprotection.

In travel and orientation, the aim is for independence. Once the child forms a cognitive map of the school and makes a good start on independent travel, expect consistent independent performance. Overprotection is a great disfavor.

The child should also learn to travel outside the school in an independent way, using the same means of transportation as other children. Sometimes children with visual impairments are carried to school in private taxis or special buses. Occasionally this may still be required, but generally such arrangements are not necessary and should be minimized.

Vigorous physical activities should be part of the school program, unless there are health reasons for limiting them. It is best to integrate the child into regular physical education activities with only essential adaptations. Visually impaired students need to learn the rules of common games—even those they may not engage in regularly—and the principles of fair play.

Provide a place where the child can store necessary special equipment and obtain it for use as needed. Taking care of the equipment and storing it carefully and consistently should be the child's responsibility.

Teachers, principals, and parents may be apprehensive about the attitudes of other children. Will they be unkind or overprotective? The best prediction is that other children will carry the same attitudes into their relationships with the child who has vision problems as they observe in the behavior of adults. Children tend to be realistic; they enjoy helping a classmate who genuinely needs help, but they dislike dependency. To help them understand their new classmate, give them facts about the situation, including the nature of the child's impairment and any special materials and equipment that may be used.

Adult behavior shapes children's attitudes.

In general, standards of behavior, classroom duties and privileges, and work assignments should be the same for the child with vision impairments as for all others. The principal can help all staff members in the building understand what the expectations are. Grading need not be a special concern, either. All children should receive individualized instruction according to their developmental needs; in such a context, the child with visual impairments need not be nearly so "different" as first anticipated.

Not many changes in curriculum are required specifically because of vision impairment. Certain listening skills do need to be taught, however, as do certain mental mapping skills. The vision teacher may find it desirable to teach for improvement in the use of whatever vision remains. Extra help in spelling may be required, especially for braille readers who are started on Grade 2 braille. But such curricular adaptations are relatively few. It is often necessary, though, to use special materials to *present* the curriculum (large print books or braille). It may be necessary to obtain or devise special substitutes for visual aids. Vision teachers know how to help with this. Fellow students are also quite ingenious in designing substitutes. One example is the use of string diagrams (string glued to paper) to replace visual mathematical charts. It may be necessary to use volunteers who read for the student, either directly or on audio tapes. If a student

Minimal changes in curriculum, but major changes in presenting curriculum, are needed.

uses braille, the vision teacher assigned to work with the regular teacher—and possibly a specially trained aide or volunteer—will help to prepare assignments and tests and translate the student's braille responses. Some regular teachers learn braille, reading it visually rather than by touch, but this is not a necessity.

No special extracurricular program is needed. With careful planning and a few modifications, the student with visual impairments can profit from every type of activity; field trips, student government, debate, art, music, publications, athletics, and others.

Adjustable scheduling helps the teacher provide the specialized instruction the student might need. Quite often, school systems offer special intensive training programs during the summer months on braille, orientation, and mobility to avoid excessive interruption of the regular flow of schoolwork during the academic year.

Emergency procedures should be formulated.

It is advisable to prepare one or two dependable seeing students to assist the student with visual impairments in case of special need. For example, although most students with vision problems can perform quite adequately in fire drills or other real or simulated emergencies, it is wise to have a special arrangement for assistance, a buddy system, if needed. Teachers should check their liability coverage for emergency situations and for regular school activities that have dangerous aspects, but there need be no serious problems on this account.

Plans don't always work out positively and may need to be changed.

Does it all really work? Usually progress is quite adequate. Indeed, programs in regular schools for children with vision impairments frequently become the source of feelings of great pride and satisfaction among teachers, administrators, and parents. But, of course, the story is not always one of unmixed progress. Continual appraisal is required, and when difficulties occur, changes are indicated. Perhaps, for a time, a program outside the regular class will be required. But the general rule is success in the mainstream—academic, personal and social.

SUMMARY

What Every School with Visually Impaired Pupils Should Have

This list should help principals and teachers check their preparedness for educating blind and partially seeing pupils. Of course, the number and nature of the pupils will influence the way these listed resources are deployed.

The checklist is a vehicle for self-evaluation.

Personnel
1. Teacher-consultant qualified to instruct visually impaired pupils
2. Orientation and mobility training specialist available

3. Regular administration and faculty oriented to work with visually impaired pupils
4. Pupil personnel staff (counselor, nurse, social worker, psychologist) capable of working with vision-impaired pupils and with access to specialist consultation as needed
5. Service staff of school (secretarial, custodial, food services) acquainted with special considerations for visually impaired pupils
6. Braillists and readers to assist as needed
7. Volunteers and aides trained to work with visually impaired pupils

Pupils
1. Student body oriented to visually impaired pupils
2. Seeing pupils assigned to participate in a buddy system for travel, safety, and related activities with visually impaired pupils
3. Pupil-specific materials needed for day-to-day work (magnifiers, tape recorders, batteries, typewriters)
4. Ready access to class-inclusion instructional materials such as Talking Books, brailled books, large type books, and voice response computers.

Facilities and Arrangements
1. Audible or tactile substitutes for visual signals where needed (texture footing change at stairs and doorways, audible danger signs, brailled names on doors)
2. Braille numbers and directions on telephones and switches or attached magnifiers with lights
3. Emergency local resource persons and materials (first aid, alarm) and their locations, if needed by visually impaired student, teacher, or support staff
4. Auditory alarm signals and procedure for fire and evacuation

Continuing Education
1. Annual in-service update for faculty and support staff on developments in special education
2. Special orientation for new or substitute faculty or support staff

PROSPECTS FOR THE FUTURE

It is unlikely in the foreseeable future that there will be any reduction in the need for teachers for visually impaired pupils. Rather, the need will probably increase. Education of children and youth with vision impairments presents outstanding career opportunities. The greatest demand is for vision teachers who are highly skilled in teaching braille, mobility, orientation, and related special subjects. Need also exists for professionals

The need for skilled teachers will increase.

prepared to work with multiply handicapped students, such as the retarded-blind and the deaf-blind. Several special centers[4] prepare orientation and mobility instructors. Opportunities are emerging for persons who undertake truly broad preparation in special education and who are in a position to assume support roles across a variety of the traditional categories of handicapping conditions. For example, a teacher might prepare to conduct a general resource room in a school and to develop skills to serve children who need braille or other specialized forms of instruction when that is needed. A critical need also exists for investigators who will give attention to pressing educational research and development problems.

TOPICAL BIBLIOGRAPHY

Attitudes toward the Blind

Lowenfeld (1973)
March & Friedman (1972)

People with Visual Impairments

Braddy (1933)
Chevigny (1946)
Davidson (1971)
Dickshoff (1939)
Keller (1954)

Instruction

Barraga (1976)
Buell (1966)
Foulke et al. (1962)
Franks (1983)
Hanninen (1975)
Mangold (1982)
Martin & Hoben (1977)
Napier et al. (1975)
Olson (1981)
Weisgerber (1978)

---

[4] For example, Boston College, California State University at San Francisco, and Western Michigan University.

CHAPTER 9

Physical and Health Impairments

Mary F. Ramsey taught primary grades for 5 years, then for 18 years taught physically impaired pupils who were homebound. After taking a yearlong sabbatical leave to visit school programs for physically impaired students, she taught 12 more years at a special public day school for physically impaired children, and youth. Excerpts from her remarks during an interview (Aiello, 1976b) call attention to several themes that will be developed later in the chapter.

Q: *What prompted you to become a special education teacher?*

A: When I was a child I had a sledding accident and I spent 2 years at home, with no help from the school with my school work. I spent all that time plugging along on my own, and the realization of what it meant to be handicapped always stayed with me. When I had the opportunity to work with physically handicapped[1] children I welcomed it.

A teacher "tells" it like it was and is."

---

[1] In this book we call these youngsters physically impaired. For educational purposes, physically impaired children and youth are defined as those with crippling conditions, illnesses, or other physical health problems that make some form of special education or school service necessary. Physical impairments that primarily involve hearing, vision, and speech are dealt with in other chapters.

Q: *What were some of your first experiences as a special education teacher?*

A: Back then, physically handicapped children were always taught at home. I was one of the first teachers of homebound instruction in the city and I drove all over town working with children.

Q: *Do you have any success stories to share?*

Other professions often welcome educational consultation.

A: I always felt that many of my students could be in the public school. I remember one girl in particular who had a number of operations on her face and she was quite upset by this. Even after she had very effective plastic surgery, her doctor routinely signed an excuse for her to be out of school. I tracked down the doctor—literally chased him all over the hospital—and explained to him how important the group setting of regular classes was to her social adjustment. The doctor said he hadn't thought of that, so together we got her back into school.

Q: *What were some of your most difficult moments?*

A: Back in the 1930s medical technology wasn't what it is today and some of my children died. It was terribly difficult for me when a child died . . . .

Q: *Over the years you've seen successful and unsuccessful teachers. What do you feel accounts for success?*

A: When teachers were successful they showed genuine caring and empathy for all children. These teachers were exceptionally creative and they always made the child aware of what he could do.

Q: *Mainstreaming, or the placement of exceptional children in the least re-strictive alternative of the regular class, is an important issue for special educators today. Does the mainstreaming issue relate to your past experiences?*

Knowledge reduces fear.

A: Children who posed behavior problems tended to frighten the regular class teacher, and the basic problem with mainstreaming back then and today is that teachers are afraid when it comes to handicapped children. They don't know what to expect.

Q: *What was the attitude of public school people when you tried to place your physically handicapped students in the regular class?*

A: I found then, in the 1940s right up through the 1970s, that often public school people have difficulty accepting handicapped children. But I found that when I myself worked with the regular class teacher and helped develop the necessary skills, I could pave the way for a more positive reception for my students.

Q: *What is your opinion of the mainstream movement?*

Regular school socialization is preparation for life's mainstream.

A: The school experience should prepare all children to live well in the mainstream of society. It is our responsibility as teachers to make that happen, and placement in regular settings is one of the best ways I know. (pp. 4–5)

HEALTH AND SOCIAL WELFARE CONSIDERATIONS

Not so long ago, physically handicapped persons were ridiculed and derogated and were, at best, the objects of a doubtful charity. The legal foundations for real equality of opportunity are now in place, however. They are interlocked with increased medical and psychosocial knowledge and with changes in the health and social welfare professions.

The major concern of the health professions is increasing life expectancy. It is accomplished in two ways: (1) by preventing accidents, anomalies, and diseases and (2) by limiting the effects of accidents, anomalies, and diseases that do occur. Despite strong efforts, however, success is only partial. Each advance in the health sciences is bought at some price, such as increased viability of impaired infants. The net result is that every wave of newcomers to kindergarten contains crippled and otherwise health-impaired children who need teaching, facilities, and services of special kinds.

First-class citizenship builds self-esteem and feelings of self-worth.

Health Professions Terminology

The following medical terms identify those children with special needs who are most often found in educational programs for pupils with physical and other health-impairing conditions. It is important to point out three things immediately: (1) The names of medical conditions give few clues to individual special educational needs, (2) only a minority of children with these conditions have any special education needs at all, and (3) there is no educational justification for grouping these children in school by their medical diagnoses.

Understanding common disorders strengthens communication.

> *Allergies.* Adverse sensitivities or low tolerances to specific substances that are not problems to people in general. Reactions may take many forms; the most common are watering eyes, sneezing, nasal discharge, itching, or rash.
>
> *Arthritis.* Inflammation of a joint, making motion difficult, painful, and limited.
>
> *Asthma.* Repeated occurrence of wheezing coughs, difficult breathing, and feelings of constriction because of bronchial contractions.
>
> *Autism.*[2] Severe communication and other developmental problems

---

[2] Autism was placed in the category of physical and other health impairments in January 1981, when a revision of the regulations governing Public Law 94–142 removed this condition from the category of seriously emotionally disturbed. For purposes of instructional planning, however, children who manifest autistic behavior are generally considered severely handicapped. Their needs and characteristics are described more fully in Chapter 10.

generally characterized by disturbances in interpersonal and object relationships and in language, often evidenced by stereotypic behavior and/or self-stimulation.

Cerebral Palsy. Several forms of paralysis due to brain damage. The most common forms are *ataxia*, shown by marked inability to coordinate bodily movements; *athetosis*, appearing as slow, repeated movements of the limbs; and *spasticity*, characterized by abrupt contractions of muscles or muscle groups, producing interference with and distortion of movement. All forms involve involuntary movements, and they appear in various combinations in different body locations depending on the nature and sites of the brain damage.

Congenital Anomaly. Any body organ or part existing in an abnormal form from the time of birth. This condition can affect the whole body, as in dwarfism (unusually small size) or albinism (absence of pigmentation), can be limited to one part (absence of an arm or a leg), can be expressed as clefts (cleft lip or palate), or can affect internal parts like the spine or spinal cord (spina bifida) or the heart.

Diabetes. Disorder of metabolism of carbohydrates that is indicated by excessive amounts of glucose in the blood and urine.

Epilepsy. Disorder of the brain sometimes resulting in convulsive movements and periods of unconsciousness lasting several minutes and sometimes in brief lapses of consciousness (up to 10 seconds) or feelings of unreality, dizziness, or semiconsciousness.

Hemophilia. A condition in which the normal blood clotting procedure is defective, with consequent difficulty in stopping bleeding when it occurs for any reason on the surface or within the body.

Leukemia. A form of cancer affecting the balance of cells in the blood and, therefore, the normal functioning of the blood.

When I first found out I had diabetes I was scared and almost started to cry. I did not know what to expect or what my life was going to be like. But after my doctor, nurse, and dietitian taught me the things I would have to do each day—taking insulin, urine testing, and eating right—I decided that diabetes wasn't that bad.

Basketball was my major concern. I don't feel that diabetes affects how I play, but, when I was first released from the hospital, I was worried. My diabetes was diagnosed in May 1979, when I was a high school junior, and I had been looking forward to playing during my senior year. At first, my fears seemed to be coming true. Nothing I tried to do on the court happened the way I wanted it to. I guess I was hesitant. But, after about six games and a lot of help from my dad, I finally got my act together. My dad gave me the incentive to make the best of my condition. He said, "Chuck, there are two things you can do: feel sorry for yourself because you have diabetes, or exercise hard, gain all of your weight back, and go out on the basketball court, giving it all you have." I chose to give all I had to my games. It was the right decision. (Ray, 1980, p. 34)

Muscular Dystrophy. A group of chronic inherited disorders characterized by progressive weakening and wasting of voluntary skeletal muscles.

Poliomyelitis. A viral infection that can result in the paralysis of body parts or systems, depending on the parts of the central nervous system attacked.

Rheumatic Fever. A disease characterized by fever, inflammation, and pain around the joints and inflammation of the muscle and valves of the heart.

Spina Bifida. An anomaly characterized by a defect in the bone that encases the spinal cord.

Traumatic Injuries. Impairments that result from accidents. They encompass a great variety of conditions, including amputations, paralyses, and limitations of body function.

Common Greek and Latin Combining Forms Used to Describe Persons with Disabilities

Forms and Meanings	*Examples of Use*
Greek	
a-, an- (*not, without*)	anoxia
di- or dis- (*twice, double, both*)	diplegia
dis- (*reversal, opposite*)	disorder
dys- (*ill, bad, hard, impaired*)	dysfunction, dysgenic, dysphoria
endo- (*from within*)	endogeneous
exo- (*from without*)	exogeneous
-ia (*disease, disorder*)	phenylketonuria, anoxemia
-iatry, -iatric (*healing*)	psychiatry, psychiatric
iatric- (*diagnostician*)	iatrogenic illness
idio- (*self*)	idiopathic, idiosyncratic
-itis (*inflammatory disease*)	encephalitis, encephalomyelitis
-oma (*tumor*)	sarcoma, encephaloma
-trophy (*nutrition*)	dystrophy, atrophy
Latin	
bi- (*two, twice, doubly*)	bilateral
-osis (*condition, process*)	psychosis

Friedman and MacQueen (1971) attempted to identify from among the 45,000 children in six Iowa counties those whose physical impairments had educational and psychological relevance. They found that approximately 4 children out of 1,000 had such conditions.

VOLUNTEER AGENCIES

Teachers and principals can get information and help from two kinds of organized volunteer groups. One is comprised of interested citizens whose objective is to assure that proper health, education, and social services are readily available. The second is made up of handicapped persons themselves.

Citizen groups act as advocates to assure appropriate services.

Citizen groups include such organizations as the Muscular Dystrophy Association of America, National Easter Seal Society for Crippled Children and Adults, National Epilepsy League, National Foundation—March of Dimes, and United Cerebral Palsy Associations. These groups distribute suggestions for teachers and other professionals who work directly with handicapped children. They offer counsel to parents and distribute curriculum materials for use in regular grades to help all pupils understand impairments and feel at ease with their exceptional classmates.

Volunteer groups of physically handicapped persons do similar things, but they also have thrusts of their own. During one month, for example, a local chapter of Open Doors for the Handicapped conducted the following activities:

1. Held a meeting of its subcommittee on barrier-free design.
2. Sent a delegation to the annual state meeting of the Governor's Committee on Employment of the Handicapped.
3. Announced its intent to host the first of four regional meetings to identify major problem areas in providing opportunities for the handicapped.
4. Took part in and invited local employers to join in a seminar on affirmative action, with particular emphasis on the regulation that "every Government contractor must prepare and maintain an affirmative action program for the employment and advancement of qualified handicapped workers."
5. Had 30 of its members attend a meeting with a representative of the Regional Office for Civil Rights, Department of Health and Human Services, to learn in detail the implementation procedures for federal regulations concerning access to public facilities.

Self-help groups of handicapped persons are growing in influence.

6. Gave members information on a new mode of transportation, a pedestrian vehicle that allows a handicapped person in a wheelchair to load and unload himself unaided. A ramp is part of the machine. It travels over hard-surfaced roads, on sidewalks, up and down inclines, and through gravel, sand, mud, and snow.
7. Published editorial comments on the problems associated with

being a handicapped member of a minority group. (For an example of publishing activities by handicapped persons, see the magazine *Mainstream*, "the magazine of the able-disabled," available from P.O. Box 2781, Esondido, CA 92025.)

8. Published a note speculating that the wavy signature of Rhode Island governor Steven Hopkins on the Declaration of Independence may have been because of cerebral palsy. On placing the deciding signature on the document he is reported to have said, "My hand may be shaky, but my heart is firm."

Citizen and self-help groups have three other activities in common. They advocate vigorously for all impaired children and adults. They encourage continuing education with respect to impairments for health, education, and welfare professionals. Finally, they press both government and private foundations to sponsor research aimed at preventing or ameliorating impairments.

EDUCATIONAL CONSIDERATIONS

There is no justification today for assembling children with crippling and health impairments into one group for schooling. Educationally, no more heterogeneous array of pupils could be found. And the special help they need is usually more portable than the children.

Conglomerate classes of physically disabled pupils do not make educational sense.

Mullins (1971), one of the first to call attention to the great within-group differences, spoke of "untenable groupings." She said:

> Many teachers have reported an I.Q. range of over one hundred points in their classes. It is not unusual to find a gifted child with muscular dystrophy sitting next to a cerebral palsied child with unmeasured intelligence or vice versa. In the same class there may be children with communication problems such as blindness or deafness who may also be physically handicapped. There will often be one so-called "brain-damaged wall-climber." The age range of such a class may extend from pre-puberty through adolescence. (p. 15)

She pointed out that "the best teachers cannot supply the kind of group cohesiveness and peer motivation essential to social learning in such a heterogeneous class" (p. 15) and called the teacher's task of individualized modification of methods, curriculum, and materials "gargantuan."

Noneducational considerations initially brought physically disabled youngsters together in special classes. First, many needed to be transported if they were to attend school at all. It was more convenient and economical to transport them all to one central place. Second, many required frequent and intensive occupational, physical, and speech therapy, as well as medical consultation and nursing and dietary supervision. It proved

Noneducational considerations should not dictate educational placements.

It was easier to have one building with elevators and ramps than to make all school buildings fully accessible.

more feasible to group those therapies and related health services in one place and to bring the pupils to them. Third, many of these pupils could not manage stairs, and many used mobility aids such as crutches, walkers, and wheelchairs. To design and construct one school building to accommodate those factors seemed far less difficult than to make all existing and future school buildings barrier free. So transportation, health-related care, and architectural accessibility were the factors responsible for the original tendency to cluster crippled and other health-impaired pupils in their own special schools or classes.

Even with special transportation and facilities, it was not feasible to move some children, such as those in traction or in iron lungs. Also, there were always some children who could be accommodated in their local schools with modest adaptations. By the late 1940s, it had become customary to speak of a need for a spectrum of six types of school settings essential for adequate educational opportunity for physically- and health-impaired pupils.

Early versions of the cascade or continuum of educational arrangements stressed places.

1. *Regular class* attendance for pupils who can do the work of the regular school if minor adjustments in such things as seating, scheduling, and instructional materials can be made.
2. *Special day classes in regular schools* for pupils who can attend a regular school but who need a specialist to teach them all or most of the day.
3. *Special day schools* for pupils who need a school building and equipment totally adjusted to their needs.
4. *Homebound instruction* for pupils who must remain at home (either in bed or with extremely limited activity) for periods of time long enough to interfere seriously with their education.
5. *Hospital instruction* for pupils well enough to receive instruction who must be hospitalized for medical treatment on a 24-hour-a-day basis for a long enough period of time to constitute a major interruption in education.
6. *Residential schools* for pupils who are undergoing long-term convalescence or rehabilitation that necessitates living in a specialized setting adapted for that purpose.

Under Public Law 94–142, "orthopedically impaired" means having a severe orthopedic impairment that adversely affects a child's educational performance. Included are impairments caused by congenital anomaly (e.g., clubfoot, absence of some member) or from other causes (e.g., cerebral palsy, amputations, fractures or burns).

"Other health impaired" means of limited strength, vitality, or alertness due to chronic or acute health problems such as a heart condition, tuberculosis, rheumatic fever, nephritis, asthma, sickle cell anemia, hemophilia, epilepsy, lead poisoning, leukemia, or diabetes that adversely affects a child's educational performance.

All of these arrangements have been changing in one significant way, however, since the 1940s. They have moved into closer contact with regular education.

There have been wide fluctuations in the nature of the physically- and health-impaired population. When special schools for physically handicapped pupils began, for example, they catered to pupils with "lowered vitality." Improved nutrition, the almost complete eradication of childhood tuberculosis, and surgical procedures that effectively repair heart anomalies in the first few months of life are the kinds of influences that have brought marked changes in the proportions of such pupils. At one time, the most common of the crippling conditions was poliomyelitis, but vaccines have sharply reduced the incidence of this disease. Cerebral palsy, which often leaves children with very complex physical and educational problems, is now the most prevalent crippling condition seen in special education programs.

General group characteristics changed significantly.

Today's education for children who are physically impaired and who have health problems is projected against four main considerations. First, it is an "artificial" grouping of children, educationally speaking. No common threads of special instructional needs provide a rationale for bringing them together. Second, a spectrum of school settings is needed for these pupils, ranging from extraschool situations like the home or the hospital through various levels of integration within the orbit of the schools.

Flexibility is a key requirement.

Third, there is a strong trend toward moving physically challenged and health-impaired pupils into their local schools for all their education and bringing special services to them before or after school so as to not rob them of academic instructional time with their teachers. Fourth, the pupil population characteristics have changed markedly, largely in relation to changes in health care. That now keeps more and more children with complex physical, mental, and emotional or social conditions in their own family homes, neighborhoods, and schools.

This amalgam of background educational considerations, joined with legal, medical, and social welfare factors, poses a formidable set of educational challenges. The remainder of this chapter shows how principals, teachers, and the specialists who work with them are responding to those challenges.

Mainstreaming: A Case Example

Lisa Blumberg was born with cerebral palsy. She tells how it affected her education and makes recommendations for teaching exceptional students.

The Case for Integrated Schooling

The impaired child and the regular school deserve the chance to test each other's limits.

Although I have an obvious and, in some respects, limiting physical disability as a result of having been born with cerebral palsy, I have always attended schools with nondisabled students. I feel that I benefited academically, emotionally, and socially from having gone to regular schools rather than to special ones.

Imagination plus common sense solves problems.

Often the roadblocks that seem to stand in the way of a disabled child attending a regular school are not real or can, with a little ingenuity, be circumvented. A child who does not write legibly can do his written work on a typewriter. A child who walks very slowly should be able to arrange to leave each class two minutes early so he can get to the next one on time.

I cannot truthfully say that I have always been "just part of the gang." In my high school years especially, I think my disability did put some distance between my classmates and me, although this was no doubt partly due to my growing awareness of myself and my disability. However, although many of my relationships have been more superficial than I would have liked, for the most part I have gotten along well with people in school.

Real-world experiences teach independence.

Today, stairs are absolutely no problem for me. As long as there is a railing, I can go up and down flight after flight without thinking twice about it. This is because I have always been in places where I have had constant practice with them.

Your first goal should be to promote the acceptance of handicapped children as individuals, more like than unlike other children, and to encourage their participation in regular group activities.

Explain the nature of certain limitations to all students and encourage them to probe these handicaps with perceptive questions. Whenever possible, have students try to imagine themselves in a handicapped child's place. Would they like to feel isolated? Inferior? As you are trying to improve attitudes, present children with facts. Talk openly about the causes of some of these handicaps. Point out the aids available. . . . Disabled children do have abilities. Emphasize what they can do. (Pieper, 1974, p. 128)

Beware of stereotyping.

It may be thought that those who work with people with disabilities are far less prejudiced against such people than most people, but from my experience, this is manifestly not so. Thus parents should be aware that a disabled child in a regular school may in fact be less a victim of categorization than a disabled child in a special school.

Full membership in the neighborhood is basic.

As a child, most of my friends' talk revolved around school happenings. If I had gone to a special school, I would have been barred from most of these conversations. Sending a disabled child to a special school creates a further distinction between him and the neighborhood children. (Adapted from Blumberg, 1973, pp. 15–17)

TECHNOLOGY, SPECIAL PROCEDURES, AND PREFERRED PRACTICES

The status of special education for children with crippling and health disabilities does not lend itself to a simple listing of technologies and special procedures due to the heterogeneity of the population and their great variety of service needs. However, a number of principles can be used in planning education for children who have physical or health limitations.

The first principle is that *all children should begin school in regular classes unless there are insurmountable transportation problems*. If transportation to a special school is feasible, it must also be feasible to a regular school. If the regular school presents architectural barriers, they should be removed. If attendant and aide services are needed by the pupil and are available in a special school or class, they should also be made available to the regular school to support the child's attendance there. In short, special education staff, facilities, and support services that make attendance feasible in a special school or class should be redeployed to make the same available in the regular class setting.

Second, *keep schooling a continuous and full-time process adjusted in intensity to the child's vitality, mobility, and general pace of behavior*. If a child needs to be admitted to a hospital, education should follow the child. The criterion should be whether the child is able to receive instruction, not how long the hospital stay will be. The time allocated for teaching (how much time the child can tolerate instruction) should be a joint decision of the physician and the specialist teacher. The content of teaching should be the teacher's decision. Also, when the child is not hospitalized and when there is not an emergency, any speech, occupational, or physical therapies, medical examinations, and conferences involving the child should be scheduled before or after school or on weekends. The slowed physical pace of some pupils may cause their school programs to move at a slower than typical rate. Their schooling should not be further decelerated by non-school matters that can be arranged outside of regular school time.

Adjust the program to meet changing needs.

Third, *pupils should attain self-regulation with regard to exertion and scheduling of activities*. Many children, while still quite young, are required by their physical condition to husband strength and to budget energy output. Other children, having the normal amount of energy, simply cannot move themselves with the speed and coordination that intact bodies and brimming energy banks allow for other pupils. It is preferred practice to give these youngsters opportunities to test themselves. The same reasonable monitoring any child needs—no more and no less—should apply for those with crippling and health impairments. All children should be guided to discover their own limits and the effects of their disabilities, if any, on their daily lives.

Avoid overprotection.

Fourth, *organize educational programs in terms of pupils' educational needs;*

Grouping should be in accord with educational needs.

match both short- and long-range instructional designs to the pupils' own characteristics and present educational achievements. The diagnoses of most physically challenged and health-impaired children tells little if anything about their educational abilities and requirements.

It is a violation of this principle to group children together *for education* simply because they all need *physical therapy*. Decisions about each child's educational program should be made as though crippling or health impairment is not a factor. Then, adjust the program and the local school setting to take into account any impairment the child has. Often that proves a less formidable task than first assumed.

Look for simple solutions first.

Jack Cappa, a teacher and father of a son with spina bifida, said a cooperative school board and understanding parents and teachers have effected changes for handicapped children. One grade was moved from the second to the first floor, another grade was moved to a different building, and the library and music room have been moved downstairs. "These things have made our son a normal student. He's accepted," Cappa said. (Rosensweet, 1976, p. 9)

Fifth, *make technology the servant of pupils and teachers.* Making this principle operational requires two actions. One is to assure that every technical aid of established value is available for use in regular schools by children who need them. For instance, if a teacher concludes that a mechanical page turner or some adapted paper and paper holders are needed to make it feasible for a pupil to work in the regular class, those materials should be supplied by the school district. The specialist teacher should have up-to-date knowledge about relevant educational technology. That teacher should also have quick access to needed items and should help the pupil and the regular class teacher become skilled in their use.

The second action needed to operationalize this principle goes further. Teachers must form cooperative relationships with engineers, psychologists, and other scientists who work at the interface of machines and people. Here is an illustration.

Extraordinary measures may be needed to provide full opportunities to some students.

A student named Upjohn at the University of the Pacific School of Pharmacy of Stockton, California, developed a device that made written communication possible for a girl who was unable to write for 12 years. [This device] allows 29-year-old Cass Moreland to activate a special typewriter by using the frontalis muscles in her forehead.

Ms. Moreland, because of congenital cerebral palsy, is unable to speak, and uses a wheelchair. Previously, her only form of written communication was a special typewriter that she could activate with her shoulder muscles—until surgery in the early 1960's made this impossible. Despite these handicaps she completed high school and attended enough classes to be a sophomore at the local community college. However, her inability to write prevented her from going much further through college.

The small box that Upjohn constructed amplifies the electrical activity from muscles responsible for the movement of the girl's eyebrows—via electrodes placed on her forehead with a band and wired to the box. This allows her to activate a switch and control panel and thus use the specially designed typewriter.

For Ms. Moreland, the device is a slow process of written communication, but it does allow her to convey her thoughts in written form. "Cass has been able to adjust to the new device with a minimum of training time and now has a slow but viable method of communication," explained Upjohn. "This will allow her to complete her college education." (U.S. Department of Health, Education and Welfare, 1976, pp. 11–12)

Certainly this is a highly complex writing assistance device. It may have limited generalizability. But it is right for Cass Moreland. Like every other person, she has the right to as full an education as her cognitive reach will allow.

Technology, ingenious teachers, and helpful classmates bring even homebound pupils into close contact with regular school activities. Home-school telephone hookups became generally available in the early 1950s. The child at home is able to participate in class and teacher dialogues, listen and respond, and ask for attention by flashing a light on the in-class sender-receiver. Teachers adapt by talking about what they put on the chalkboard or the visuals they use. Classmates carry the portable telephone apparatus from room to room and plug it in. Other classmates carry books and assignments to the child's home and back, thus maintaining a thread of direct social contact.

Sixth, *provide a continuum of expert educational assessment, instruction, and counseling.* This principle emphasizes the everyday working partnership that principals and teachers should have with specialists. Because of the differences among pupils, expertise in assessment, instruction, and counseling are not always found in the same consultant. Designing quality schooling for a kindergarten child with slow cognitive development and muscular dystrophy is widely different from counseling and helping plan education for an eleventh-grade honor student and athletic star whose recent injury resulted in permanent paralysis from the waist down. The solution here is simply to become well acquainted with the psychologists, physicians, rehabilitation counselors, and other specialists of the community and the region and to use them selectively.

The teacher should "quarterback" the consultation.

THE ROLE OF THE REGULAR CLASS TEACHER, SPECIAL TEACHER, AND PRINCIPAL

Teamwork with Specialists

The regular class teacher takes the lead in arranging instructional activities, with the specialist teacher a participating partner. Activities include

Teamwork facilitates mainstreaming.

assessment of educational needs; obtaining specialized instructional materials; designing the psychoeducational match that guides both what is taught and how it is taught; personalized instruction in tutoring, small group, or total class settings; developing instructional plans and schedules; helping select and train peer tutors and helpers; and guiding the work of employed aides and volunteers.

The special teacher and the principal ordinarily have chief responsibility for attending to service activities, although the regular teacher should take part in making plans and decisions. Some of the service activities may best be delegated to aides and helpers, with teachers monitoring. Service activities include arranging pupil transportation; scheduling therapies; assisting in proper use and maintenance of braces, crutches, and wheelchairs; obtaining and maintaining special instruction-related equipment such as personal microcomputers; and having special-purpose ramps, handrails, and the like made and installed. These last might be temporarily necessary, for instance, if the class is putting on a play and the stage needs adapting so that a physically impaired pupil can take part in the production as an actor or stagehand.

At least half of excellence is attention to details.

The special teacher assists regular teachers in prereferral program adjustments that may prevent referral to special education; receiving pupil referrals from regular class teachers or others when that is necessary; working with parents; processing referrals; contacting community social and medical agencies; acting as a liaison with other schools regarding transfers, promotions, and other matters; participating in staff meetings; and interfacing the pupil with vocational rehabilitation services. The special teacher—regular teacher relationship here is mainly one of maintaining an effective two-way flow of information between themselves and significant others. School social workers and psychologists often plan important roles in coordination, too.

Information is shared.

The two-teacher team periodically updates in-class records of pupil plans and progress. Critical to this process are discussion and agreement on what should become part of the record. The same approach applies to the report card (or other form of regular achievement report to parents) and to teachers' entries in the school and central office cumulative folders. Usually the regular class teacher has final responsibility for these items. The special teacher or school nurse records data concerning medicines, prescribed physical activity routines and limitations, and other medical information.

Parent Relations

It is advisable for the regular teacher and the special teacher to confer with parents. That helps ensure accurate communication and strengthens parents' resolve to follow through at home with school-related procedures. Joint discussions with parents also help to open out-of-school social activi-

Parents should be partners.

ties and recreation to physically challenged and health impaired pupils, especially in cases where parents tend to be overprotective.

Curriculum Individualization

Physically and medically impaired pupils seldom need instruction outside the regular curriculum. Mullins (1971) highlighted that point vividly with an illustration of twin brothers, one with spina bifida, who have attended three grades together in their local school. The major portions of their curricula needed no substantive changes.

Some things, though, do call for adaptation or particular emphasis. Here are some examples.

1. *Habits of planning*. Retracing one's route unnecessarily is too time and energy consuming for youngsters whose supply of those commodities is less than average.

2. *Choosing the essentials*. Most pupils can carry along an additional book just in case it is found to be required later. This is not so for pupils who need one or both hands to help with movement and who may already be carrying a heavy brace.

3. *Mobility training*. All children have to learn how to travel with increasing independence. Special added instruction is required when only certain routes, buses, buildings, and streets are sufficiently barrier free to use and when weather changes pose extraordinary hazards. *Adapt and adjust the regular curriculum.*

4. *Health habits*. Personal health takes on special meaning when functionally limiting impairments already exist. For example, toileting care for a child with spina bifida needs to be handled efficiently and sensitively, always with emphasis on self-management to the maximum. From the point of view of safety, pupils with diabetes need instruction in the prevention of coma. Epileptic pupils who are liable to seizures or brief blank periods must have instruction in the management of those incidents.

5. *Physical education and recreation*. Physical educators have long recognized the need for individual adaptations. They help pupils with physical and health impairments to acquire and maintain superior levels of general fitness through individualized programs termed *adaptive* physical education. Special attention spotlights body alignment, posture, and the adjustments needed to facilitate participation in recreational sports such as bowling, fishing, and golf.

6. *Handwriting*. Some pupils with hand or coordination difficulties will attain competence in writing if templates and line guides are employed and if simpler and larger letters are substituted for those conventionally used. Others may have to bypass handwriting altogether, except for learning a signature, and do all their writing on typewriters or microcomputers. *The curriculum is more than academics.*

7. *Socialization and personal development*. This part of the curriculum refers to what students learn in school about cooperation, respect for in-

dividual rights (both personal and property), consideration for others, their own strengths and weaknesses, and the generally accepted values of the child and adult worlds in which they live. These and related matters make up what some educators call the affective curriculum. The presence of physically disabled and health-impaired pupils among other pupils encourages social and personal considerations that can contribute to positive mental health for all.

8. *Other curricular areas.* Vocal music may be extremely difficult for pupils with slowed speech and distorted articulation due to cerebral palsy. Studio arts may require adaptations in technique and media for pupils without the use of hands and arms. Playing wind instruments may be too dangerous for pupils with weak arterial walls or asthma. Chemistry experiments may have to be adapted for youngsters still learning to manipulate objects by means of prostheses. Wood or metal shop machinery may require added safety devices and special signs and fixtures. Calculators may have to be supplied in mathematics classes. Relevant adjustments may also need to be made in other curricular components, all highly individualized.

These examples show that adaptations must be personalized, whether in arithmetic and the language arts, in the social and natural sciences, in the health and physical development areas, or in the creative and performing arts. As a general rule, curricular adaptations ought to allow these pupils equivalent access to content and skills with other pupils of like levels and rates of cognitive development.

Instructional Materials

Special adaptations make materials usable.

Concern here is with arranging for the child to be able to use instructional materials with ease. Children in wheelchairs may have difficulty using the ordinary chalkboard, reaching the globe, or manipulating a large dictionary. Some need stands for textbooks, plus mechanical page turners. As part of a physical therapy routine, some pupils may need to stand for a large part of the day.

The challenge is to achieve a comfortable and efficient interface between the pupil and the material the pupil has to use. This calls for contrivances that bring those materials under the pupil's control.

School Physical Plant

Some elementary and secondary schools, designed for typical pupils, effectively bar exceptional children. The same is true of some colleges, but progress is being made under federal regulations that require accessibility to the disabled as a condition for receiving federal funds of various kinds. Teachers and parents with physically limiting conditions are also excluded by architectural barriers whenever they exist.

New construction, fully accessible to exceptional persons, is appearing. Remodeling is achieving the same result in many older facilities. Guides for architects and school planners are now available to assist them in planning and creating barrier-free environments.[3]

ILLUSTRATIONS OF EFFECTIVE SCHOOL PROGRAMS

A particularly illuminating investigation of inclusion of physically handicapped students in regular school environments was reported from England by Anderson (1973). This study involved 99 moderately and severely disabled children who were educated in "ordinary" primary schools. The first words of the first chapter of Anderson's book are "No handicapped child should be sent to a special school who can be satisfactorily educated in an ordinary school." The study followed children with cerebral palsy, spina bifida, thalidomide-caused deformities, hemophilia, and a variety of other disorders into the ordinary schools not just to test how well they were doing but also to seek guidance on how better program planning might proceed. The book-length report includes much detail on school, family, and community aspects of programming for the physically handicapped pupils in regular schools.

Research leads to practical programming guides.

General findings of the study can perhaps be summarized through a series of brief quotations from Anderson's concluding comments.

> There can be little doubt that the majority of the parents...preferred ordinary school placement....The amount and quality of social integration between handicapped and nonhandicapped children both inside and outside of school was very encouraging....Findings suggest that most children without neurological disorders are able to cope, emotionally, with the environment of an ordinary primary school....It is not the physical handicap *per se* but the existence of learning disorders which is important....Given special provisions of the kind I have described, it is possible to offer even severely handicapped children a satisfactory education in an ordinary school. Given imagination, backed up by expertise and by financial resources, it is possible to provide for children with additional specific learning difficulties without segregating them. (pp. 289, 290, 293, 297, 303)

Preschool and Elementary Level: An Example

The Urbain Plavan School is in Fountain Valley, California. It was designed for regular school pupils as well as those with cerebral palsy, polio, birth defects, accident-caused limb losses, and other physical and health-

---

[3] Legal guidelines come from the U.S. Architectural and Transportation Barriers Compliance Board, Washington, DC 20201.

impairing conditions. It opened in 1973, having been planned and built specifically to integrate orthopedically handicapped and typical children.

Because moving requires considerable effort for many handicapped children, the school was designed for maximum circulation efficiency. It is an irregular oval-shaped building. Four distinct elements surround and feed into a fifth element—an 8,100-square-foot central learning center. The four elements are an administrative section, classrooms, a special services section, and a music platform and storage facility. The focus of the complex is inward. Eleven circulation paths lead to, through, and out of the learning center.

Space and design allow full participation.

Although there are special service facilities to accommodate handicapped students, no real boundaries exist. Orthopedically handicapped and health-impaired children participate in all regular activities.

A total of 96 handicapped pupils and 330 typical children, preschool through eighth grade, attend the school. Most are drawn from a "walk-in" area surrounding the site. Some of the orthopedically handicapped children are transported from four cooperating school districts. The staff includes 10 regular teachers, 8 teachers, and 8 teacher's aides for orthopedically handicapped children, 2 learning center coordinators and 2 aides, a teacher of educable mentally retarded children, and a speech and language therapist.

Special equipment in the school includes electric parallel bars, balance beam, rocking beam, rocking boat, walking rails, bicycle exerciser, foot placement ladder, triplex pulleys, punching bag, shoulder wheel, finger ladder, wrist roll, and standing tilt table. There is also a training bedroom for daily-living skill adaptation, a training bathroom, training kitchen, and hydrotherapy room.

Parents receive clinic services.

The special services section of the school functions as a full-time psychoeducational planning, programming, and evaluation clinic. Parents can bring children here for examinations, consultation, and therapy. A separate reception and waiting room with an outdoor play area serves these parents and children. (Adapted from Russo, 1975, pp. 18–21)

COORDINATION OF SERVICES

Education for physically challenged and health-impaired pupils has to be seen as one important part of a complex of developmental support systems aimed at maximum normalization. Others deal with health services, home and family living, religion, social services, vocationally oriented training, and recreation. To be sure, these are interactive systems. Education overlaps to some extent with each of them, and each with the other. They should also support each other. Comprehensive programming is necessary. Teachers must see that it happens, but not at the price of shortchanging education.

TOPICAL BIBLIOGRAPHY

Orientation of Regular Classes to Pupils with Physical and Health Impairments

Allen, 1980
Anderson, E., 1973
Billings, 1963
Blackman, 1983
Brolin, 1978
Buchanan & Mullins, 1968
Dibner & Dibner, 1973

McNett & Merchant, 1981
Pell, 1973
Pieper, 1974
Rapier et al., 1972
Richardson, 1971
Swan, 1980
Wendland, 1972

People with Physical and Health Impairments

Agrault, 1963
Batshaw & Perret, 1981
Berg, 1966
Blanchard, 1980
Douglas, 1950
Gallico, 1941

Jones, 1977
Lukens & Panter, 1969
McNett & Merchant, 1981
Schary, 1958
Zimmer, 1980

School Adaptations for Pupils with Physical and Health Impairments

Abeson & Blacklow, 1976
Aiello, 1976a
Anderson, R., 1973
Anderson, W., 1978
Birch & Johnstone, 1975
Calovini, 1969
Campbell, 1980
Connor, Williamson, & Siepp, 1978

Goldenson, 1978
Green, 1974
Gromek & Scandary, 1977
Hawkins-Shepard, 1978
Marr, 1969
Molloy, 1975
Mullins, 1971, 1979
Umbreit & Cardullias, 1980
Weishahn & Mitchell, 1971

CHAPTER 10

Severe and Profound Handicaps

Practices are changing.

Until recently, America had a history of segregating severely and profoundly impaired individuals in separate and isolated, distant places. Practice in the Western world for many years was to construct and staff specialized schools and other centers to house, educate, and care for these very exceptional persons apart from society's main current. It is understandable, then, that some principals, teachers, and parents may be unfamiliar with the technical and philosophical changes that now make it preferred practice for severely and profoundly impaired children to live in their home communities and to attend regular schools.

This shift in technology and in societal attitudes and the resultant modern expectations for educational programming are the focus of this chapter. An exploration of definitions and related considerations sets the stage for a fuller understanding of the needs of severely and profoundly impaired persons. First, however, the story of Adele describes the problems and experiences of one family, as well as possibilities for progress.

Adele's problems affected the family dramatically.

Adele was a great worry to her parents from the moment of birth. Her delivery was difficult and much delayed. Fears were magnified during the first months of life because of great difficulties in feeding and health problems of many kinds. Adele's mother was unable to give needed attention to her two older children, and family tensions mounted.

Within the first year, it was clear that Adele was impaired by cerebral palsy. She was severely uncoordinated in motor behavior on both sides of the body. The parents were concerned that she might also be retarded in mental ability.

Because the family lived in a small, rural town that had only part-time medical service provided by a family-practice physician, Adele and her parents were referred to a clinic in a large city 150 miles away. For the first five years of her life, Adele was transported for medical treatment back and forth to the clinic frequently. The family was alerted to educational and related services available to preschoolers in the city environment, but Adele's mother preferred to keep her at home, in spite of the constant and extraordinary care required in feeding and caring for her.

At age 5, Adele showed few signs of talking. Her physical limitations prevented all but the simplest kinds of functions. She could swallow food with difficulty but was unable to sit up or crawl. She still needed help in toileting.

Adele's parents attended occasional meetings of the county Cerebral Palsy Association and found it helpful to share experiences with other parents. But gradually the father and mother came to hold different opinions about Adele's future. The father was persuaded that Adele was profoundly and irreversibly retarded in intellectual abilities as well as in motor functions; the mother felt strongly that Adele was not retarded in any irreversible way and that she would someday begin to develop and eventually overcome her problems, so that she could live in a semi-independent way. When Adele was refused admission to the local school, which had no special education program for profoundly handicapped children, her mother became all the more determined to help Adele at home. Tensions mounted, and finally the parents separated.

In the past, schools could refuse admission to disabled pupils.

Adele and her mother moved to the city, where Adele was enrolled in a special school for severely and profoundly impaired children. Progress in schooling was slow. At age 10, however, Adele showed beginning ability to respond to a symbol board (a board containing small pictures that Adele could point to in communications with her teachers). From there progress continued slowly. The mother was able to take a job and work while Adele was in school in order to help provide the financial support they needed.

By age 22, Adele had progressed sufficiently to be placed in a group home in her community. There she still requires much supportive help, but she has learned to speak in elementary fashion and to handle most of her own bodily needs. She lives with other handicapped persons and goes each day, by special bus, to a sheltered workshop where she is learning to perform simple task sequences and to care more fully for herself in daily life. Adele's mother, still separated from her husband and the other two children, visits Adele frequently while continuing on the job she started some 15 years ago.

Group-home living was eventually achieved.

If Adele were born today, it is likely that she and her family would receive many more supports early in life. It is much more likely that she would be accepted in the local schools, even in a rural area. More technical aids would be available to provide Adele with communication skills at the earliest possible age. Because her parents would be likely to receive more help as well, it is possible that the family would be better able to maintain itself and grow with Adele.

DEFINITIONS

The main characteristic that identifies children as severely and profoundly impaired is their apparent gross intellectual retardation and the very severe

Apparent severe retardation is the main defining characteristic of severe and profound impairment.

and early derailment of cognitive development and, often, to a great degree, of affective development. Physicians and clinical psychologists might call these youngsters mentally retarded, autistic, or schizophrenic. Many of these children's conditions are further complicated by sensory deficits, particularly in vision and hearing. Neurological and/or orthopedic conditions such as cerebral palsy, spina bifida, and hydrocephalus are also frequently seen.

In short, these children present an extremely complex picture. They offer little apparent prospect of acquiring what is conventionally called an academic education; their prospects for becoming socially and vocationally independent seem sharply limited, too. As we shall see, though, these appearances may be deceiving.

Terms like *mild, moderate, severe,* and *profound* seem to enter the literature on handicapping conditions inconsistently, despite or because of their vagueness. An important inconsistency arises in the use of these modifiers (like *mild* or *severe*) because, although they may be recognized medical terms, educators often use them differently from health professionals. For example, a condition such as blindness is certainly a severe or profound *impairment*, and blindness may appear to many to be a very severe *handicap*, yet from the educator's view blindness is a far less complex educational problem than such conditions as severe deafness or mental retardation. Moreover, students who show mild and moderate degrees of impairments or handicaps have much more often been part of the professional and personal lives of teachers and school principals than students with more severe or profound impairments or handicaps. This statement is true for at least two reasons: (1) There are many more persons with mild and moderate degrees of impairments and handicaps, and (2) they usually can be integrated into regular school and community life more easily. But even people with severe and profound handicaps are now being integrated into the regular schools, and it is important to be aware of them in order to accept the challenge of serving them effectively.

Regular teachers should expect to encounter many mildly and moderately handicapped children but also some severely handicapped students.

Stevens (1962) suggested a distinction among the terms *impairment, disability,* and *handicap* that serves our purposes here. By *impairment* he referred to defective tissue (e.g., a diseased or disordered muscle), *disability* is used for the loss of organ function (e.g., a knee that will not bend), and *handicap* refers to the personal or social burden imposed on an individual because of an impairment or disability and the ways the person is received or treated in the community. A person who is disabled by the paralysis of both legs may become so adept at managing a wheelchair and other technical aids and be so well accepted and integrated into the community that the term *handicap* would hardly be applicable. Although the three terms are used in this chapter according to Stevens's distinctions, be aware that the terms are used variously and even interchangeably in current literature. It is not the impairment or the disability, but the functional handicap (difficulty in acquiring a normal education, for example) that educators are considering when they use the terms *severe* and *profound*.

Some impairments do not cause disabilities.

An Approach to Definition

The severely handicapped individual is one whose ability to provide for his or her own basic life-sustaining and safety needs is so limited, relative to the proficiency expected on the basis of chronological age, that it could pose a serious threat to his or her survival.

"Basic life-sustaining and safety needs" are defined as those requirements necessary for maintaining and furnishing nourishment to one's body and for avoiding, defending against, or escaping physical harm. Requisite skills include self-care (feeding, toileting, dressing, grooming), communication, and physical mobility. . . . To ensure one's safety further requires that one maintain contact with reality and refrain from self-mutilation. (Baker, 1979, pp. 60–61)

The important point noted here is that *there is no direct or necessary connection between a disability and a handicap.* Technical aids, unusually high motivation, compensatory skills, and supportive social environments can all mitigate the effects of a disability and lessen the likelihood or degree of associated handicaps. Thus when we speak of persons as severely or profoundly impaired, we are saying something about a very complex and constantly changing set of circumstances. When we speak of children who are severely and profoundly impaired, we are saying something about their need to be understood and served in the schools, but we have only limited ability to make predictions about their future status as adults.

Some disabilities do not result in handicaps.

We do not know enough to predict the life course for disabled children.

What are the ways in which one can be handicapped? Prehm and McDonald (1979) and subsequent investigators have suggested five possible general areas of handicapping condition, and they have used this framework to define handicapped children. The five areas are motor, self-help, cognitive, personal and social, and vocational skills.

The central defining characteristic of a severe or profound handicap is extreme inadequacy in *cognitive functioning*, which then encompasses all other kinds of handicaps. The person shows little, if any, language, is unresponsive to ordinary social stimuli, fails to develop self-help skills, and lacks vocational skills. The person may be vegetative (extremely nonresponsive) or hyperactive but in either case shows little evidence of rationality or judgment. It should be noted that the definition is in *functional* terms, which is meant to imply that the behavior need not always remain so extreme.

Some children who show severe or profound impairments in early life are demonstrated, through very intensive diagnosis and instruction, to have specific problems that can be treated with favorable results, and such children may progress in ways that make them less handicapped. For example, children who are both deaf and blind are likely also to be severely limited in cognitive functioning unless and until specialized methods of teaching are applied. Similarly, some children who exhibit irrational, even

Educators are increasingly successful in reducing severe and profound handicaps.

bizarre behavior may gradually respond to intensive treatment and come to be understood principally in terms of personality problems. Over time, such children may show improvements in functional intelligence and no longer be classified as profoundly impaired or handicapped, at least educationally.

In recent decades, special educators have led an assault on the classification of children as severely or profoundly handicapped. Many children formerly considered hopelessly uneducable have been taught by informed and caring teachers and raised from levels of profound impassivity or destructiveness to a level of purposive behavior in at least simple social settings. In the process of this work, teams of psychologists and special and regular teachers have demonstrated repeatedly that these children are really very different from one another and are heterogeneous in educational potential. In common, in the beginning, they have a profound functional handicap in cognition and other problems, but with good efforts the problem may differentiate. It becomes possible then to distinguish a variety of educationally handicapping conditions, some of them treatable with positive outcomes.

Professionals do not have skills and insights necessary to overcome all disabilities.

In this context, it becomes clear that severe and profound handicaps are a function not only of the characteristics of the individual but of the person's life situation as well. If that life situation includes people who have the necessary technical skill to diagnose and teach in special ways, the likelihood of remaining severely handicapped is reduced. There are conditions that no one currently understands or can reverse through education, but it is almost always impossible to be precise about the extent to which human problems might eventually be remediable. The struggle for educational solutions goes on.

Guidelines for degree of handicap change as educational technology advances.

Actually, there are no hard and fast rules for characterizing levels of handicap. Viewpoints change when new or adapted educational technology makes it more feasible to meet the educational needs of an exceptional child. For example, a new procedure for eliminating stuttering (Shames & Florance, 1980) promises to move that condition from the severe level toward the mild level. Several decades ago, the invention of individual electronic hearing aids allowed a major educational shift for some hard-of-hearing persons, just as the development of the braille reading and writing system opened a whole new world to people who are blind. In this chapter, central attention is given to the extreme condition characterized by very limited cognitive functioning, usually accompanied by other handicaps as well. But attention is also given to some of the less extreme handicapping conditions that tend to emerge as children who show the most extreme handicaps are given needed attention and help.

What all severely handicapped persons have in common, unless they are aided effectively, is a significant limitation in the range of purposes and goals that can be set for their lives, the skills that they are able to develop in pursuit of such purposes and goals, and the joys and rewards of life in which they can share—in short, they are limited in human freedom. The challenge to educators and others is to serve fully and well all current severely handicapped persons and also to help advance the frontiers of knowledge and skill so that more can be done for such persons in the future. The boundaries of knowledge, skill, and service can be extended, and that can be the basis for expanding the freedom of persons who are otherwise confined to limited purposes, ignorance, and neglect.

Because a number of special concepts and terms are used in this chapter and in other discussions of severely and profoundly handicapped persons, a brief set of additional definitions is offered here.

Deinstitutionalization refers to the declining use of residential institutions for handicapped persons. Admission rates have been reduced, especially for children, and residents are returned to the community whenever possible. Related aspects include adherence to the due process and other legal rights of handicapped persons, the development of habilitation and transition programs for institution residents, and the rapid development of appropriate community resources to serve persons who would otherwise be in institutions. Unfortunately, no aspect of deinstitutionalization proceeds perfectly (Bruininks & Bruininks, 1981).

Institutionalization rates for children have dropped sharply.

Normalization is a principle developed by Nirje (1969) and advocated in the United States and Canada, notably by Wolfensberger (1972). It argues for the "normal" treatment of handicapped persons in normal or everyday environments to the maximum possible extent (Flynn & Nitsch, 1980).

Bengt Nirje, in the 1960s, introduced the principle of normalization to the system serving persons who are mentally retarded. In a simple but eloquent way, he explains what the application of the principle means.

NORMALIZATION*

Bengt Nirje

Normalization means...A normal rhythm of the day.
You get out of the bed in the morning, even if you are
Profoundly retarded and physically handicapped;
You get dressed,
And leave the house for school or work,
You don't stay home;
In the morning you anticipate events,
In the evening you think back on what you have accomplished;
The day is not a monotonous 24 hours with every minute endless.

---

* In *Information Exchange*, monthly newsletter of the Development Disabilities Program of the Metropolitan Council, St. Paul, Minn., January 1986, p. 1.

You eat at normal times of the day and in a normal fashion;
Not just with a spoon, unless you are an infant;
Not in bed, but at a table;
Not early in the afternoon for the convenience of the staff.

Normalization means...A normal rhythm of the week.
You live in one place,
Go to work in another,
And participate in leisure activities in yet another.
You anticipate leisure activities on weekends,
And look forward to getting back to school
Or work on Monday,

Normalization means...A normal rhythm of the year.
A vacation to break routines of the year.
Seasonal changes bring with them a variety
Of types of food, work, cultural events, sports,
Leisure activities,
Just think...We thrive on these seasonal changes.

Normalization means...Normal developmental experiences
Of the life cycle;
In childhood, children, but not adults, go to summer camps.
In adolescence one is interested in grooming, hairstyles,
Music, boy friends and girl friends.
In adulthood, life is filled with work and responsibilities.
In old age, one has memories to look back on, and can
Enjoy the wisdom of experience.

Normalization means...Having a range of choices,
Wishes, and desires respected and considered.
Adults have the freedom to decide
Where they would like to live,
What kind of job they would like to have, and can best perform.
Whether they would prefer to go bowling with a group,
Instead of staying home to watch television.

Normalization means...Living in a world made of two sexes.
Children and adults both develop relationships with
Members of the opposite sex.
Teenagers become interested in having
Boy friends and girl friends.
Adults may fall in love, and decide to marry.

Normalization means...The right to normal economic standards.

All of us have basic financial privileges, and responsibilities,
Are able to take advantage of
Compensatory economic security means,
Such as child allowances, old age pensions, and
Minimum wage regulations.
We should have money to decide how to spend;
On personal luxuries, or necessities.

Normalization means...Living in normal housing
In a normal neighborhood.
Not in a large facility with 20, 50 or 100 other people
Because you are retarded,
And not isolated from the rest of the community.
Normal locations and normal size homes will give residents
Better opportunities for successful integration
With their communities.

The term *developmental disabilities* gained widespread use with congressional passage of the Developmental Disabilities Act in 1970. Under this act, many local and state programs for severely handicapped persons began. Early efforts built upon work with persons classed as mentally retarded, but through the years other exceptional conditions were added. Public Law 95-602 provided the following definition:

Knowledge of common terms is professionally useful.

Severe, chronic disability which...(a) is attributable to a mental or physical impairment; (b) is manifested before the person attains age 22; (c) is likely to continue indefinitely; (d) results in substantial functional limitations in three or more of the following areas of major life activity: self-care, receptive and expressive language, learning, mobility, self-direction, capacity for independent living and economic sufficiency; and (e) reflects the person's need for a combination and sequence of special, interdisciplinary, or generic care, treatment, or other services which are of lifelong or extended duration and are individually planned and coordinated.

The concept of developmental disabilities has broadened over the years.

Developmental programming is adaptive education for persons who are handicapped; it is systematic, sequential instruction based on the assumption that all persons can learn to some degree, whatever the nature and extent of their impairment. Furthermore, it is assumed that people learn best in environments that offer them the opportunity to learn through orderly, structured steps that take into account what they already know. Many varieties of task sequences for diagnosis and teaching have been developed.

"Infantizing" is overprotecting and creating dependency in disabled persons. Expectations for development are low.

"Adultizing" is the opposite of infantizing. It means giving the disabled person every opportunity and encouragement to become as self-sufficient as possible in mobility, self-help, social relationships, and work.

There is some decline in support of sheltered workshops, with supported work models gaining in favor.

The *sheltered workshop* is a specialized training and work setting for persons who are judged to lack readiness for competitive community employment. In the sheltered workshop, individuals receive training in general and specific work skills plus on-the-job work experience. The workshop often engages in industrial tasks (such as sorting or assembling items) on contracts with local businesses and industries; on this basis, it is able to offer the workers hourly pay. Training in daily living, social skills, financial management, grooming, and similar topics is usually part of the total program. Assistance in gaining less sheltered employment is offered when individuals show readiness. The use of sheltered workshops grew rapidly for at least a quarter of a century, beginning in the 1950s. In recent years, there has been a tendency to seek a broader range of employment opportunities for disabled persons in "normalized" settings.

Supported work is a term to describe training and other supportive activities provided to disabled persons who are employed in carefully selected competitive employment situations. The supported work model may be used in connection with schools or rehabilitation agencies. It deals with transition into competitive employment (Rusch, 1986).

Community living arrangements (CLA) are small group homes or foster home situations created specifically to house and supervise persons who are not yet capable of fully independent living. Often CLAs are used to serve individuals who have been discharged from institutions and are seeking gradual integration into community life. Group homes are usually managed by persons (often married couples) who have a broad interest in education and social services of all kinds. Residents of group homes or foster homes are frequently enrolled in sheltered workshops or other community agencies for training and employment. Sometimes distinctions are made between ICFMRs (intermediate care facilities for mentally retarded persons) and SILs (semi-independent living arrangements).

Under federal law, each state is required to designate one or more agencies to operate a *vocational rehabilitation* (VR) program for handicapped persons. The services that must be provided include diagnostic and evaluation services; counseling and guidance; medical services; training; income maintenance; transportation; family services; interpreting services for the deaf; reader services for the blind; telecommunications, sensory, and other technical aids and devices; job placement services; and postemployment support to maintain suitable employment. A vocational rehabilitation counselor is assigned to each client and acts to purchase and arrange necessary programs. Concerns are often expressed that VR services exclude many severely handicapped persons in favor of clients whose employability is easier to establish.

HEALTH CONSIDERATIONS

The survival rate among premature infants has gone up quite steadily, and many infants who suffer difficult births or who show congenital anomalies are kept alive. The rate of disabilities found in such cases is higher than for infants in general. Thus we have the ironic condition that the improvement in health services has increased the numbers and proportions of persons with impairments, disabilities, and handicaps.

Better health services means more disabled persons.

Canadian Hospital Teams Aid in "Mainstreaming" Each team includes a physiotherapist, occupational therapist and speech-language pathologist who travel together daily to specific quadrants of the city of Calgary. They provide therapy to the children on-site in the community programs and also help ease the process of integration through supportive consultation to teachers and parents. Vans to transport the teams and their equipment are donated by the Calgary Shrine Club. Three or four children are grouped in some preschool facilities to maximize efficient use of resources.

Through gradual phases of growth, beginning with the transfer of five children, the project has, in five years, integrated 128 children from the specialized segregated hospital programs. An additional 186 children, referred to the project by hospital clinics and departments, have been maintained in their neighborhood facilities.

Initially, mild and moderately handicapped children were placed in community daycare centres, nursery schools, kindergartens and schools. More recently, severely physically handicapped children have been accepted in the project. The age range extended from two to sixteen years. Forty-three percent are in the preschool programs, while the majority of school-aged children under treatment are in the first or second grade. (Cripps & Innes, 1980)

Many children with severe and profound handicaps are readily discovered in infancy or early childhood by physicians, nurses, or other health professionals. Pathognomonic physical signs or marked delays in language and motor development sometimes give clear indication of problems. Sometimes parents who suspect delays in their children's development or become anxious about their limited functions will seek medical or psychological advice. Certainly it is helpful if these children, in their very early years, are subjects of joint planning by parents and health professionals. It is well to bring early childhood educators with special education training into such planning, too. Pediatricians, hospital nurses, and other health professionals may tend to focus mainly on the physical impairments they encounter among young children and not be so aware of how educational procedures can stimulate flagging development.

Educators can provide a helpful perspective even in the period of infancy.

Increasingly, physicians are able to treat disabilities in early years, thereby often preventing conditions that would otherwise be likely to develop into handicaps. For example, it is now common to use surgical procedures to provide a shunt for the excessive fluid that sometimes develops in a baby's head and, if left untreated, can cause severe mental retardation. Metabolic and genetic studies reveal other disorders, such as phenylketonuria, which, if untreated, leads to mental retardation; when treated by a special diet, it may have only limited effects on cognitive development.

Much work remains to be done to achieve good medical services for all children. Screening tests at infancy are not yet performed routinely on all children; only a small proportion of young children are screened for health problems, and, unfortunately, follow-up diagnostic studies are sometimes performed poorly.

The incidence of severe handicapping conditions tends to increase with age and accelerates in later life. Someone has suggested that the population of the whole world can be divided into the handicapped and the temporarily nonhandicapped, thus reminding us that limitations in function tend to be the eventual fate of all persons. Because of increased longevity, the numbers and percentages of people with severe handicapping conditions are increasing steadily. One result is a large increase in the demands on rehabilitation and health services.

EDUCATIONAL CONSIDERATIONS

Severely and profoundly impaired children are leaving the isolation of institutions to enter regular schools.

Severely and profoundly handicapped children are entering their local schools much more frequently than in the past. They are coming from homes where in the past they might have been isolated and from institutions where they have been sequestered. They bring with them many challenges for school administrators as well as for regular and special teachers.

Residential Settings

America has grown grievously and increasingly disappointed in most residential institutions that were supposed to rehabilitate disabled individuals. They are being used much less frequently. Rates of referral for residential care of children were relatively stable in the 1950s, 1960s, and early 1970s (Lakin, Krantz et al., 1982). Since then, substantial changes have occurred. For example, between 1968 and 1978, the average age of first admission increased approximately five years (Lakin, Hill et al., 1982). That means that most severely and profoundly handicapped children remained in their own homes or other community settings. In the same period and in succeeding years, much deinstitutionalization has occurred, meaning that much of the population in institutions has been returned to the community.

"People Are Better Off," Pennhurst Study Proclaims

Conclusions drawn from a five-year longitudinal study of people who have left the Pennhurst State School and Hospital in Pennsylvania revealed the following:

1. By every scientific design and test available, people who have gone to community living arrangements (CLAs) are better off.
2. They have made more progress than similar people still at Pennhurst and more than they themselves made during their prior time at Pennhurst.
3. These people have become better able to do things for themselves, rather than having things done for them.
4. The people who seem to make the greatest gain in adaptive behavior tend to be those who start out the lowest. That is, the people with the most severe impairments turn out to benefit the most from community placement.

These and many other observations are included in *The Pennhurst Longitudinal Study: Combined Report of Five Years of Research and Analysis*. The study was conducted as a collaborative effort by the Temple University Developmental Disabilities Center in Philadelphia and the Human Research Institute in Boston. It was supported by the U.S. Department of Health and Human Services.

Important efforts are under way to change the functions of residential institutions and to bring them up to new standards of excellence. Their former all-purpose, long-term containment functions are now being reduced, even to the point of abolishment in many places. They are now being expected to serve highly intense, short-term needs. Family members and local school representatives are also more closely involved in the work of residential institutions.

The functions of institutions are changing, and community services have improved.

Almost all of the special education and rehabilitation that residential institutions were formerly supposed to do can now be accomplished in the local community.

Special Day Schools

But isn't there an intermediate step or arrangement, something between the residential institution and mainstreaming? Wouldn't a special day school, one apart from the regular school that enrolls only handicapped students, be the ideal? The day school would seem to offer children the advantages of life at home with their families and still give them the full and expert attention they need from full-time teams of professionals. For youngsters found to be severely and profoundly impaired, is it truly important or desirable that they attend regular schools? These are some of the questions to be answered in the context of rapidly changing arrangements for the care and education of severely handicapped children.

Most advantages of the special day school can be achieved in regular schools.

Special, centralized day schools for exceptional children are nearer to what is needed, we believe, than separate residential settings. Separate residential schools, or schools within institutions, tend to be farther away from the child's home, both in actual distance and in life-style, than special day schools to which children are transported daily. Thus the latter does allow each child much more family and neighborhood life. Also, the faculty of the special day school can more readily have access to specialists and can share in the use of instructional materials, technical equipment, and other resources that are available through the school system and other community support systems. Nevertheless, the trend—which we believe has both philosophical and research support—is toward more inclusive arrangements, in regular school settings. That is part of what is meant by the principle of the least restrictive environment.

The Regular School Setting

The positive and favorable qualities found in special day schools can be made part of the regular school. Indeed, some elements of a sound and complete education are difficult or impossible to supply when a severely handicapped child attends a separate, special day school. These elements can readily be provided by regular schools, as demonstrated in many places.

For example, interaction between children with severe impairments and other children is very important; it can be part of daily life when both are in the same school. Such interaction is mutually beneficial; each has something to give to and gain from the other. It needs to be added quickly, however, that it would be too easy to assume that simply putting severely and profoundly impaired students in "normal" or "natural" environments automatically ensures favorable results. Specific teaching for specific results is required (Voeltz, 1984).

The provision of training in the natural environment is clearly not a simple proposition....If a simple train-and-hope approach is adopted in the natural environment, however, it may result in a substantial decrease in the probability of skill generalization beyond the training situation. Those problems can apparently be avoided through careful planning and the adoption of one or more strategies specifically designed to facilitate generalization. (White, Leber, & Phifer, 1984, p. 26)

A large part of the teacher's work with severely and profoundly impaired children consists of stimulating them to attend to sounds, sights, and other contacts with the environment. Another significant portion of the teacher's work with these children is to construct, step by step, some meaningful system of communication with them. That may take years. It may be established through pointing to pictures, eye-blinks, Morse code or special language boards, or a means that the teacher and the child invent together, over long months of trying to establish contacts. The "real world" of the regular school can be engineered to promote the motivation and the means for communication.

The main point of the teacher's efforts to stimulate attending behavior and create communication bridges is to bring out and put to constructive use whatever cognitive powers the impaired child has. That is consistent with the basic meaning of *education*, from the Latin root meaning "to lead out."

The rewarding part of the teacher's work is to see positive changes, however small they may be. From time to time, though, the changes are great. Sometimes a teacher finds the key to unlock a robust intellect that had been imprisoned for years, locked behind a facade of *apparent* absence of cognitive powers.

When severely and profoundly impaired children are taught in the same building with regular classes, the general atmosphere is that of the real world. It does not have to be fabricated or simulated. Even in regular schools, impaired children may often be kept much to themselves because of their unusual program needs. But they do see other children and are seen by them. Moreover, children from regular classes hold doors open for them, say "Hi" when they pass in the hall, and in countless other ways are a part of their daily lives. It is common, also, for individual children from regular classes to volunteer to help in the impaired pupils' teaching and recreation activities. In a very similar way, the interactions between special and regular teachers grow, and so do parent interactions in the school and community. They build and maintain a subtle though solid base for promoting progressive inclusion. These important elements of normalization are much less likely to develop in separate schools.

All children profit from experience in the real world.

A Family Lesson on Genetics

At a general meeting of parents at the Franklin Elementary School, the parent of a nonhandicapped 7-year-old told about asking her son to describe for the family the new class in the school. A class for handicapped students had been moved from the regional center to Franklin. "Yes," said the boy, "I've been down to the new class, and you can tell they're all from the same family." The mother told, to the delight of other parents, how that observation had led to a family discussion about genetics and Down syndrome.

When children with severe impairments are served in regular schools, there are understandable debates and tension concerning the curriculum that should be provided for them. Some educators argue:

> Once again, we are in danger of embarking on a program for a handi-capped population, while lacking the knowledge base to support our efforts and we are unfortunately committing ourselves to doing before we know what needs to be done....Let us not sacrifice the child to the con-cept by forcing, for our own edification, normal educational experiences and expectations on them. (Burton & Hirschoren, 1979, p. 599)

Achievement expectations must be flexible and individualized.

Others argue strongly "that attempts at setting limits regarding severely and profoundly handicapped learners encourage the risk of developing yet another self fulfilling prophency in the field of special education" (Sontag, Certo, & Button, 1979, p. 605). This debate is reminiscent of the compar-able debate in the 1950s that centered on so-called trainable retarded children. Probably there is no clear answer to issues of curricular expec-tations for broad groups of children. Solutions must be found case by case in the context of developmental programming. Tensions will probably always exist between those who wish to be conservatively realistic about children, especially in creating parental expectations, and those more hopeful professionals who find it hard to be sure about limits but see new frontiers being reached quite regularly.

SOCIAL CONSIDERATIONS

As more and more severely and profoundly handicapped individuals remain in the community rather than being placed in separate, closed insti-tutional environments, the challenges to all community institutions mount rapidly. Attention must be given to recreation, housing, employment, pro-tection, travel, independent living, family burdens, financial needs and management, crisis management, children's attitudes, and much more (Voeltz, 1982).

Community facilities have proliferated.

A concomitant of the deinstitutionalization movement has been the rapid development of community residential facilities for severely handi-capped persons, mostly in the form of group living arrangements. It has been estimated that in the period 1973 to 1977, the number of such com-munity facilities doubled in the United States (Bruininks, Hauber, &

Kudla, 1979). Even keeping records of the housing and care of individuals has become a massive problem because of the increase in the number of widely dispersed small group homes. At the same time, the challenge to local social agencies to provide quality social services for group-home residents has accelerated.

In the mid-1980s, a new and powerful force for deinstitutionalization was created in the form of Medicaid waivers. In effect, this program permitted the transfer of massive amounts of federal money from institutions to local community services (Jones, 1985). States and localities were permitted to apply for waivers of procedures that formerly had directed funds only to residential settings and to plan programs—such as parental training and respite care—that would make it feasible for disabled persons to live with their own families or in community settings of some other kind.

Various other federally sponsored social programs that call for operations outside of schools have been launched. For example, the U.S. Social Security Administration provides Supplementary Security Income (SSI) to handicapped children under certain conditions. Food assistance and outpatient and inpatient psychiatric services may be provided, and early education programs are expected to grow rapidly. All these programs require the attention of community social agencies; often they must coordinate their concerns with those of the schools and health agencies.

Early education programs may be expected to grow rapidly following new federal legislation.

The movement toward community-based care for persons who are severely or profoundly handicapped remains somewhat controversial. Introducing the report of a symposium on outcomes of such care, Birenbaum (1986) summarized in these words: "The individuals with mental retardation who are reported on here seem to be in the community but not of it" (p. 145). Large numbers of retarded persons (more than 100,000 in the mid-1980s) are placed in nursing homes. The amount of participation in community programs by retarded nursing home residents is apparently less than desired. Younger and more mobile male residents appear most likely to participate in such outside programs (Benz, Halpern, & Close, 1986). There are no magic solutions to problems of severely handicapped persons in community programs. Successful programs will require much work and development by many people.

Who Gets the Training

A small group of severely handicapped young adults took their places on the waiting benches of the training school for beauticians. They would take their turns along with others to get their hair washed, cut, and treated in other ways. The teacher who accompanied them went immediately to the staff of the school to give them brief lessons on their "special" customers—who might not know whether their hair was oily or dry or be unable to read directions on the bottles of shampoo. The beauticians understood the situation

> quickly, and everything went "beautifully." Note who received the training and how everyone learned!

SPECIAL PROBLEM AREAS

The term *severely and profoundly impaired* obviously covers a very hetero-geneous group of persons, many having more than one identifiable impairment. We can identify a number of dyads, for example, deaf-retarded and blind-retarded. The additional presence of speech or behavior problems can turn each dyad into a triad. The following discussion centers on several of the common dyads and on cerebral palsy, an impairment that often includes more than two disabilities. Two conditions that are often difficult to distinguish until instruction has been attempted for some time—autism and severe mental retardation—are also discussed. A longer section is devoted to mental retardation in order to attend to the major shift from institutional to community-based programming.

Sensory Dyads

Deaf-retarded and blind-retarded children are not beyond being taught in today's schools.

Being deaf or hard of hearing poses a recognizable educational difficulty under the best of conditions. When hearing impairment is compounded with severe intellectual limitations, the result taxes the skills of all special and regular educators.

The needs of hearing-impaired–retarded pupils, however, are not beyond the capabilites of today's educators. The first step is to assess the pupil's educational needs and to devise plans to meet them. The assessment inevitably specifies critical needs in the areas of language and communication, as well as important needs in social and emotional de-velopment and self-help skills. In almost all cases, deliberate cognitive stimulation appears to be a need, because a combination of handicaps tends sharply to reduce a child's interaction with the ordinary environment and thus opportunities for intellectual development. Similarly, blind-retarded children will also need special stimulation, though of different kinds. Inability to see often means difficulty in mobility as well.

Special projects offer promising practices.

Approaches to meeting the needs of severely disabled school-age children with hearing impairments are offered by the Multiply Handi-capped Education Project at the Speech Pathology and Audiology (SPA) Program of the Pennsylvania State University. Principal project goals include the identification of children in the service area who are hearing impaired and have one or more other severe handicaps and the provision of adequate intellectual and psychosocial evaluations for all children in the demonstration classroom and a limited number of other environments.

Important aspects of the project include development of a service delivery model for a rural population of multiply handicapped hearing-impaired children; the Child-based Information System, in which a bank of strategies and a detailed record of goals and accomplishments aid teachers in planning and conducting a multiply handicapped child's educational program; involvement of parents, with an extension of classroom educational programs into the home and an effort to help parents better understand and cope with their handicapped child (Program Development Assistance System, 1980).

Cerebral Palsy. Cerebral palsy comprises a variety of syndromes, most of which include multiple disabilities (see Chapter 9 for definition). Common difficulties are paralysis, mental retardation, epilepsy, vision and hearing impairments, and speech problems. One wonders, in view of the variety of disabilities, how decisions are ever made about classification. Why is a child who has both vision problems and cerebral palsy not classified as blind? This question leads to the concept of *primary* handicap. The term *cerebral palsy* is used only for cases of multiple disability in which the neuromotor disability is judged to be the *primary* or *outstanding* factor in designing the pupil's mix of special and regular education. When limitations in cognitive functioning are also prominent, the person may be considered to be profoundly or severely handicapped as defined by educators and not classed primarily as CP.

Classification decisions are complex.

The Children's Rehabilitation Center of the University of Virginia provides a program to train service providers of southwestern Virginia who work with cerebral palsied children. The project has a demonstration classroom for pupils who are physically handicapped, located in a rural elementary school. Neurodevelopmental therapy techniques are given prominence. Target developmental areas are ambulation, feeding and speech, nonverbal communication systems, and improving functional use of the limbs.

The program procedures emphasize parent training and instruction in the main. Weekly meetings are held to integrate physically handicapped preschoolers and nonhandicapped children in parent-led sessions. These sessions serve to expand on the model classroom and adapted model sites for multihandicapped pupils (Program Development Assistance System, 1980).

Autism.[1] Autistic and autistic-like children relate very poorly to other people, lack communication skills, often exhibit stereotyped behavior, and usually prefer an unchanging environment. Autistic children are

---

[1] See Chapter 9 for definition. Autism is included in the category of "other health impairments" for purposes of Public Law 94–142. In the context of instructional planning, however, it is most usefully described as a severe and profound impairment.

Programming for autistics children stresses communication skills.

frequently very difficult to diagnose; they are often considered mentally retarded in early life. School programs for them emphasize intensive inter-personal interactions to encourage trusting relationships and the general development of responsive behavior; other commonly emphasized curriculum targets are language, self-care, and preacademic skill development. With increasing frequency, the children who first appear to be intellectually retarded and then emerge as autistic make progress and are introduced into mainstream school environments, but in strongly supported programs. Principles of applied behavior analysis are commonly used in programs for these children. Parents usually participate intensively.

Project Educate, initiated by the Indiana University Developmental Training Center, is an example of one such program. The primary aim of Project Educate has been to develop a model school program for autistic and severely emotionally handicapped children and their parents that can be successfully implemented by the public schools in Indiana. Children throughout the state are screened for the program. In case conferences, parents and schools agree to train with the project staff to facilitate the child's placement back in the local educational agency and home. An inter-disciplinary staff works with the clients in the elementary school–based classrooms, in communities, and in the home programs to ensure genera-lization of learning and work toward gaining as much independence in functioning as possible (Program Development Assistance System, 1980).

Staff support helps to solidify gains.

Who Needs Friends Like This?

Left to his own resources, even in a grocery store, the profoundly retarded person dies within a matter of days of starvation, if he does not meet with accidental death before that. . . . It is 'heroic optimism' to think that with proper habilitation, the level of functioning of every retarded person may be improved. . . . The court's belief that virtually all the retarded people in institutions could be "normalized" in "less restrictive settings" is . . . divorced from reality. . . . The personal life of the retarded person [in a community living situation] is reduced to more and more frustration and isolation.

An Argument in Response

All individuals could be trained to "survive" in grocery stores and a variety of other community environments if they had regular access and reason to use those environments. (*Newsletter of the Association for the Severely Handicapped*, 1981, 7(1), pp. 1, 2)[2]

---

[2] These statements were part of a brief filed in the *Haldeman* v. *Pennhurst* case as quote in the *Newsletter*.

TECHNOLOGY, SPECIAL PROCEDURES, AND PREFERRED PRACTICES

Today, prosthetic devices can help disabled persons with almost every aspect of their lives. A prosthetic device, in a very broad sense, is used to modify the functioning of the disabled person or to modify the environment in such a way that it eradicates or reduces the effects of a disability. *Everybody uses prosthetic devices.* Smith and Neisworth (1975) specified five general categories of such devices: locomotion, life support, grooming and hygiene, communication, and household assistance. A few examples of prosthetic devices follow.

For severely handicapped persons who have communication problems, simple electronic communication boards can be constructed to signal common needs (e.g., to use the bathroom, mobility help) or to give simple responses (e.g., "yes," "no," "I don't know"). The user may be required to make only one simple motion to activate one of a number of widely spaced push buttons.

More complex communication boards exist or can be created. Some devices call for a teacher or other nonhandicapped person to scan a sequence of possible responses; at the proper moment, the handicapped person gives a signal, however slight, such as an eye-blink or touching a switch. From the signal, the teacher can determine the response intended by the handicapped person. The Bliss Symbol Scanner (Prentke Romich Co., Shreve, Ohio) is a widely used scanning board that presents a variety of images and symbols that disabled children use to communicate with their teachers, classmates, and aides.

Everybody Uses Assistance Devices

Babies need strollers; hikers need backpacks. Special adapted devices are everywhere you look—glass elevators to revolving tower restaurants, for example—how specially adapted can you get? (Corcoran, 1980, p. 1)

Wheelchairs of many varieties are used widely; some have mirrors, allowing users to signal by eye movements to the drivers of the wheelchair the directions in which they wish to travel. Eye movement signals can also be used with countless other prosthetic devices relating to communication and mobility.

The rapid invention of prosthetic devices by technicians and the co-invention of devices by handicapped persons and engineers has been one of the most encouraging developments in programming for disabled persons. Computer-assisted devices are being developed widely and rapidly. It is hard to imagine the limits of technical aids at a time when talent of high order is available to analyze and solve problems of coping at the interface of a handicapped person and the environment.

Methods of behavior analysis have become prominent.

The systematic application of the methods of behavior analysis to the teaching of severely handicapped persons has been probably the major breakthrough in education in recent decades. Through behavioral methods, individuals considered to be hopelessly handicapped have been taught complex chains of behavior that add richness to their lives and to those of their families and associates. Again, it is difficult to set the limits of this technology, which is a contributing factor to the greater optimism often expressed about the developmental potentialities of severely handicapped children.

The problem of generalization, that is, of carrying or transferring what is learned in school to daily life situations, is often critical in the lives of students who are severely handicapped. For this reason, it is important to relate the curriculum of the school to the realities of the home and community and even to specific futures anticipated for individuals. For example, for an adolescent who may be anticipated to live semi-indepen-

At times, training is designed to support specific transitions and future situations.

dently in an apartment, training would be offered in how to clean and maintain an apartment, prepare simple meals on an electric stove, use the public transportation system to and from the sheltered workshop and the Y or a similar place (where an evening social club is operated), and handle problems or emergencies. For most individuals, such specificity in a future-referenced curriculum could not be justified, but for some individuals it may be the only option, considering the problems of generalization. Always, of course, it is essential to involve the individual as well as the parents in such planning.

No other aspect of special education has changed quite so rapidly in recent decades as that of services to severely disabled children. Elements listed here as preferred are rapidly becoming prevailing practices.

Prevailing Practices

1. Screening and preventive programs for severely disabled children are available only to the minority population.

2. Professionals usually recommend that severely and profoundly impaired children be institutionalized.

Preferred Practices

1. Screening programs (e.g., for metabolic disorders) and preventive programs (e.g., early care for at-risk children) are provided uniformly to the entire population of children.

2. Parents are encouraged to provide care for their severely and profoundly impaired children at home and to seek supports for their home-based program.

3. Severely and profoundly impaired children attend centralized or regional special schools.

3. Severely and profoundly impaired children, in small clusters, attend regular schools and interact with nonhandicapped children in as many ways as are feasible, including helping relationships.

4. Programming in institutional settings is oriented to long-term care.

4. Programming in institutional settings is oriented maximally to helping residents return to their families and communities to the fullest possible measure of independent living.

5. Public policy and funding arrangements for community facilities to serve severely disabled persons are inconsistent and inadequate.

5. Careful study and policy development lead to long-term, stable development of community-based services for severely handicapped persons.

6. It is assumed that severely impaired children cannot learn academic skills, and the school curriculum is oriented to other matters, such as self-care and leisure skills.

6. Curriculum planning for severely handicapped children is an individual matter and does not preclude academic training; preparation for employment or other form of economic usefulness is common.

7. It is assumed that severely handicapped persons will live, as adults, in sheltered environments.

7. Severely and profoundly impaired students are prepared as fully as possible for independent, adult living arrangements.

THE ROLE OF THE REGULAR CLASS TEACHER

Regular class teachers ordinarily do not find services to severely handicapped children to be overly burdensome. There are not many such children, and those who attend regular schools (an increasing number, to be sure) are usually well supported by special education teachers and other specialists. Following is a brief list of some of the challenges that regular teachers may face, however, along with guidelines for meeting them.

Specialists provide extensive support.

1. Regular teachers may be expected to support the enrollment of severely handicapped children in the least restrictive environment, which means regular schools.
2. Regular teachers should expect to be informed, at least at a basic level, of the nature of the disabilities and handicaps of the children and should expect to help *all* children to become aware of such conditions and to develop positive attitudes toward the disabled children.
3. If severely handicapped children are enrolled directly in regular classrooms, teachers should expect to consult with special education staff members and parents concerning the nature of the programs that should be provided and to participate fully in the evaluation of the children's progress and their impact on the regular class as a whole.
4. The regular classroom teacher who participates directly in programs for severely handicapped children should expect to receive the training, assistance, and additional equipment and supplies needed to conduct quality program for all children in the classroom.

CHARACTERISTICS OF A COMPREHENSIVE PROGRAM

Briefly, the following list summarizes the characteristics of a full and adequate community program for severely and profoundly impaired children.

1. Parents of severely and profoundly impaired children are contacted by school authorities as soon as a handicapping condition is discovered. The school's interest in the child is expressed, contacts are continued, and the child is enrolled in appropriate school programs as soon as feasible. Parent education is offered from the moment of discovery.

All community services are effectively coordinated.

2. School authorities develop clear patterns of communication and coordination with all health, rehabilitation, and social service agencies in the community for the purpose of coordinating services to the children and their families.
3. The children are enrolled in regular schools, at least for an initial period of schooling, and a place is held in a regular school for each severely handicapped child, even when the child is enrolled in a special center or school for a period of time.
4. All children and all parents in the community are informed about disabled children, and many are engaged in helping to conduct the school programs; nonhandicapped children may serve as peer tutors, for example, and parents often act as aides or assistants.

5. Preparation programs for teachers of severely disabled children are significant parts of college and university programs serving the area schools. Specialized teachers from such programs are employed, as are all necessary additional staff, such as speech and language therapists, psychologists, social workers, and school nurses.

6. All teachers are given training to help them develop awareness and skills so that they can take an important part in programming for severely disabled children in the regular schools.

7. Comprehensive diagnostic services are provided by the schools, including educational, psychological, social, and medical services (arranged outside the school).

8. Intensive programs of parent education and counseling are available through the schools and related agencies.

TOPICAL BIBLIOGRAPHY

Characteristics

American Psychiatric Association (1979)
Baker (1979)
Gardner (1977)
Quay & Werry (1972)
Wolf & Anderson (1969)

Instruction

Balow & Reid (1980)
Brown, Nietupski, & Hamre-Nietupski (1976)
Burton & Hirschoren (1979)
Haring & Brown (1977)
MacMillan (1973)
Sontag, Certo, & Button (1979)
Stainback & Stainback (1980)

Care and Rehabilitation

Bruininks, Hauber, & Kudla (1977)
Flynn & Nitsch (1980)
Halpern, Close, & Nelson (1986)
Lakin & Bruininks (1984)
Lakin, Hill, Hauber, & Bruininks (1982)
O'Connor, G. (1983)
Rothman & Rothman (1984)
Rusch (1986)
Wolfensberger (1972)

Autism—What It Means for Educators

Bettelheim (1967)
Bower (1974)
Lovatt (1962)
Lowry, Quinn, & Stewart (1981)
Shopler & Olley (1981)

Family Supports

Bilotti & Kettrick (1984)
Bradley (1984)
Cina & Caro (1984)
Earhart & Sporakauski (1984)
Featherstone (1980)

CHAPTER 11

Facing the Future

The programs described early in this chapter are now present for everyone to see. They include the growing pains of early childhood education, new programs to deal with child abuse, and new approaches to funding systems. The emerging issues considered later in the chapter, however, especially the future of education for exceptional students, are frankly speculative. Our views of the years ahead are written from a perspective with which some other educators may not agree.

We see important shifts in our society in attitudes toward atypical individuals, in the legal framework for special education programs, and in performance expectations for teachers, principals, and other educators. Change is going on in communities and schools at a very rapid pace. Old certainties, and even some that are relatively new, are being challenged. It seems clear to us that in the United States, the arrangements made to serve exceptional students in the future will be quite different from those of the past. In these final pages, we offer a glimpse of the future as we anticipate it, however tentatively. Obviously this is an invitation to others to join in thinking of the future and to make their commitments.

Attitudes toward atypical persons are changing.

As a people, we have long been concerned with the physical welfare of children and youth. That concern now extends to psychosocial development, career development, and opportunities for better lives. Programs are being developed for young people who have, until now, been on the fringes of society: high-risk preschool children, drug-handicapped learners, school-age parents, and neglected and abused children. A fundamental element in all of these programs is mainstreaming, the attempt to accommodate exceptional children while they remain in their own homes and regular schools and to conduct the research, development, and training necessary to make that more feasible for more children.

EARLY CHILDHOOD EDUCATION

Historical Background

An important change in rationale for early education has occurred.

Except for a growing kindergarten movement, teachers heard little about early childhood education until the 1960s. Between 1960 and 1970, public awareness of the importance of early education was heightened as a result of Head Start and similar pre-kindergarten programs, which focused on 3-, 4-, and 5-year-old children, especially those who were members of economically poor families, physically handicapped, or both (Zigler & Valentine, 1979). Understanding of the value of early education grew in this period, but ideas fell far short of universal application.

Only a few years ago, children who needed help in eating or toileting were excluded from school.

Early childhood instruction for exceptional children increased during the 1950s and 1960s, and it had a pragmatic base. It just seemed to "make sense" to start earlier to educate chidlren who were economically disadvantaged or handicapped. For children with emotional problems, nursery school was usually prescribed, mainly to relieve a troubled home situation or to provided a therapeutic setting for long stretches of time. It was assumed that with a good start, the future would be better.

The pragmatic approach was inconsistent, however. In some cases (e.g., deafness, cleft palate, blindness), free education and related service started at birth or by age 2. Yet some other exceptional children (e.g., cerebral palsied, autistic) were denied early education on the grounds that they were not mature enough to profit from the experience; they required dressing, toileting, and other physical care that was generally not supplied in preschools.

Preschool enrollment is steadily increasing.

In 1965, fewer than 30 percent of all children in the appropriate age range attended preschool. By 1978, 50 percent of young children were in preschool programs. With the increased birth rate during the 1980s and with more mothers getting paying jobs, preschool enrollment is expected to continue increasing.

Public Law 94–142, passed in 1975, provided incentive grants to school districts that planned programs for 3- to 5-year-old handicapped children. Public Law 99–457 (1986) extended the incentive program downward to the period of infancy, from birth to age 3, and required a free, appropriate education for handicapped preschoolers age 3–5 by the 1990–1991 school year. Age 3 has been considered a reasonable breakpoint in the continuum, with programs for handicapped children up to age 3 being mainly home or hospital based and with emphasis on the child's relationships with parents and a less formal curriculum, while programs for 3- to 5-year-olds tend to be center based, more focused on the child, and more structured in curriculum. Provisions for preschoolers vary greatly among states and localities.

The recent surge of interest in infancy and the early childhood years holds promise for improving the lives of exceptional children. The purpose of this earliest form of intervention is threefold: to help babies and their families live fuller, happier lives together from the outset; to prevent or minimize the development of problems that are rooted in the first years of life; and to increase the chances for satisfactory future schooling and wholesome life patterns.

Project Home Base

One of several nationally validated early education projects was developed at Yakima, Washington.[1] Project Home Base was originally conducted under Title III of the Elementary and Secondary Education Act of 1965. After it showed success, the project was submitted for national review, approved, and given funds for dissemination to other communities under the auspices of the National Diffusion Network of the U.S. Department of Education. The following description is adapted from an abstract submitted by Carol Jackson, Project Director.

Project Home Base is founded on the belief that parents are a child's first and best continuous teachers. It is aimed at supporting and enhancing the parents' teaching and parenting behavior and thereby influencing development of the child's growth and learning potential. The central feature of the project is a weekly home visit by a paraprofessional parent-educator. The parents are given a task selected to meet the developmental needs of the child and are provided with information about child growth and development, health care, and related matters. The parents then work with their child on the selected task during the week. As a result of these contacts, it is hoped that the parents will be better able to identify and meet their child's developmental needs, thus positively affecting growth and learning potential. The child will be better prepared to learn and will become a more efficient and effective learner.

Parents are a child's first teachers.

Evaluation results show that the principal project objectives have been met consistently. Home Base children entering Head Start performed better on a preschool inventory than non–Home Base children, and they completed 92.5 percent of the tasks taught them by parents. Home Base parents increased their use of desirable teaching behaviors, as measured by a locally constructed directed observation instrument. Desirable teaching behaviors for parents were described as follows:

1. Explain what is going to happen before you start. *If children have an idea of what is expected before they start, they learn to think about what they will be doing.*

Specific teaching skills can be strengthened.

---

[1] This project was reviewed by the Joint Dissemination and Review Panel (JDRP) of the U.S. Department of Education. An annual publication, *Education Programs That Work*, published for several years by the Far West Laboratory for Educational Research and Development, San Francisco, provided abstracts of projects approved through the JDRP process and included in the diffusion program of the National Diffusion Network, also sponsored by the U.S. Department of Education.

2. Give time to look at the materials before starting work. *If children become familiar with the materials first, they learn to become organized and better prepared to do the task.*

3. Ask questions that require more than one right answer. *If children see more than one point of view, they learn to be open to ideas.*

4. Ask questions that require more than one or two words to answer. *If children learn to give more than a yes or no answer, they learn to think their answers through.*

5. Get children to talk about their answers. *If children talk about their answers, they learn to think more deeply about things.*

6. Get children to ask questions. *If you encourage children to ask questions, they learn to look for answers.*

7. Give time to think about a problem. *If children are given time to think, they learn to think for themselves.*

8. Get children to back up answers with facts and evidence. *If children can explain how they got an answer, they have learned to find the correct answer without guessing.*

9. Praise children when they do well or when they take small steps in the right direction. *If children hear from you how well they are doing, they learn to feel good about themselves.*

10. Let children know when their answers are wrong, but do it in a loving way. *If children see the difference between right and wrong, they learn to keep working until they find the correct answer.* (Yakima Public Schools, 1977)

Who Is for Children?

By 1990, there will be an estimated 24.3 million preschool children in the United States, an increase from 1979 of 36 percent. At least 10.5 million of these children will have mothers in the labor force—a 63 percent increase since 1979.

At least half a million children in this country live in out-of-home care and may well grow up there. (Edelman, 1981)

Head Start Mainstreaming

Mainstreaming in Head Start reaped benefits for all children.

The Head Start program has become an important source of information about the mainstreaming of handicapped children. In 1972, amendments to the Head Start law stipulated that at least 10 percent of the children enrolled should be handicapped. The intent was to give handicapped and nonhandicapped children a chance to live and learn together (Zigler & Valentine, 1979).

Klein (1977) summarized the Head Start experience in mainstreaming as follows:

> Observations of early childhood programs indicate that even the most severely impaired children can benefit from integrated preschool programs. Head Start staff members who have worked with handicapped children as part of their regular program believe firmly that mainstreaming is beneficial to both handicapped and normal children. Parents of both nonhandicapped and handicapped children have expressed very positive attitudes toward Head Start in general, and particularly toward efforts on behalf of the handicapped. Most parents of disabled children in Head Start report that the program has had a significant impact on their children. These observations reinforce the belief that handicapped children should not be isolated. Mainstreaming is difficult, but its impact can reach far beyond the child and the immediate situation.
>
> Handicapped individuals have become increasingly vocal in the past few years. They are cognizant of their rights to education, employment, information, and all the other things associated with a full and useful life. Whether these rights are attained and how they are used are dependent on the motivation, goals, and abilities of the individuals concerned—all factors that are influenced by early experiences. The formative years may determine whether individuals are boxed in by the things they cannot do or whether they focus on the things they can do. Reaching out requires a kind of realism that is nurtured in the world of the nonhandicapped where the individual has the opportunity to know and observe many people without disabilities.
>
> If handicapped persons have the right to share the world of the normal, we as educators have a responsibility. We are obligated to try to help children develop the outlook and skills which may enable them to function effectively in spite of a handicap. What better place to start than in a preschool group? (p. 9)

Special Group Programs

Early education programs are commonly conducted by health or welfare agencies as well as by schools. Many offer comprehensive services; others are limited to certain categories of children (e.g., blind or deaf) or families (e.g., low-income). Such programs sometimes serve families on a broad citywide, county, or regional basis.

Outlook for Early Education

Most evidence points to the advantages of early education, especially for high-risk and handicapped children, but some doubts about programs still exist. Some early evidence indicated that early gains shown by preschoolers tended to dissipate over time and that progress in early years was not a good predictor of later success. A recent study (McKey et al., 1985) tends to

The outlook is favorable, especially for handicapped and at-risk children.

revive doubts about long-term outcomes of Head Start programs. There is little argument about positive short-term outcomes, which is to say that when children are enrolled in intensive programs, they do tend to show progress. In any case, the continuity assumption—that a good start gives continuing advantage—has continued to remain somewhat in doubt.

Executive Summary of a 1985 Report of Evaluating Head Start

Children enrolled in Head Start enjoy significant immediate gains in cognitive test scores, socioemotional test scores and health status. In the long run, cognitive and socioemotional test scores of former Head Start students do not remain superior to those of disadvantaged children who did not attend Head Start. However, a small subset of studies finds that former Head Starters are more likely to be promoted to the next grade and less likely to be assigned to special education classes. (McKey et al., 1985, p. 1)[2]

Some research shows a 50 percent reduction in needs for special education.

Other recent evidence is quite positive, at least for professionally conducted high-quality programs, and policymakers, and the general public seems convinced that early education really works. The series of reports for the Consortium for Longitudinal Studies (Lazar & Darlington, 1982) and reports of the Perry Preschool Project (Schweinhart & Weikart, 1980) have been particularly persuasive. They show that children who participated in preschool programs are more likely to stay up with classmates in school achievement and less often placed in special education programs. Most communities that started preschool programs for handicapped children are continuing to provide them (Swan, 1980). But early education programs were still the exception in the 1970s, not the rule. No more than one-fourth of the children who could profit from them were enrolled in such programs.

The outlook for the future of early education is more promising. A 1987 report of a survey conducted by the National Association of State Directors of Special Education shows that 40 states and territories expected to participate in 1987 in programs for infants and toddlers authorized under Public Law 99–457 (Viadero, 1987). Public and legislative interest in early education is growing. Many opportunities are appearing for persons prepared as early childhood teachers or administrators.

Often it is difficult to classify young children according to the usual categorical methods used by special educators. Therefore, it may be necessary to adopt noncategorical approaches in the emerging programs. Indeed, the programs may well need to deal with at-risk and handicapped children in quite open ways with regard to classification.

---

[2] For criticism of the McKey report, see Schweinhart & Weikart (1986).

There are a few dark clouds on the horizon in the field—or at least some difficult questions to be answered. One leading researcher, David Elkind (1986), has suggested that the field of early education was made the "ground on which to fight social battles that had little to do with what was good pedagogy for children" (p. 632). He makes an impassioned plea for professional educators to oppose extremely formal approaches to education for young children, which he believes put excessive demands on the children. Programs can be informal, in which case they become mainly a variety of social support for families and present little or no difficulty, in Elkind's view.

Some difficult issues have arisen concerning the long-term effects of various forms of early education. For example, it has been argued that adolescents who experience early education programs that are highly directive more often show patterns of delinquent behavior than adolescents who were in less directive programs (Berruetta-Clement et al., 1984). Another disquieting finding, reported by researchers at Utah State University on their meta-analyses of early education interventions, is that degree of parental involvement in programs seems unrelated to outcomes for the children (Castro, White, & Taylor, 1983). No doubt these issues and unexpected findings will receive further analysis and discussion.

There are some unexpected findings and issues in the field of early education.

A specific issue awaiting resolution concerns the sponsorship of early education programs. Should they be offered by the schools or by other agencies, such as health or welfare agencies? In our view that issue should be resolved early in favor of asking the schools to take the lead, but in a flexible fashion that would permit and encourage cooperation with agencies of other kinds, including industrial and other private corporations as well as public agencies.

EXTENDED EDUCATIONAL PROGRAMS

Extended forms of education besides early education are emerging as well. One of these is the extended school year, usually involving the addition of summer programs for handicapped students. Such programs often arise from a concern that handicapped students require more than 180 days of education per year and particularly that a long vacation period may cause a significant regression in what has already been learned plus a need for re-teaching time in the next school year.

The Extended School Year

On February 19, 1985, the U.S. Supreme Court declined to review the federal appeals court decision requiring the state of Georgia to provide more than 180 days of schooling per year to mentally retarded children who need the extended school year.

Attention has focused on transition programs, moving from school to work.

Another extension is in the form of transition programs, designed to assist students in making the transition from school to work and community adjustment. The Office of Special Education and Rehabilitation Services (OSERS) has proposed a transition model with several components (Will, 1984a):

1. Transition without special services. Students find their own way.
2. Time-limited service, using vocational rehabilitation, vocational education, and other specific job-training programs.
3. Transition with ongoing services, such as in mental health.
4. Transition with supported employment; special subsidies are offered to employers of handicapped persons coming out of school in transition.

"Turning 22" Law

Massachusetts has enacted school-to-work legislation (Chapter 688) that authorizes services for severely disabled persons beyond ordinary school age. It calls for individual transition plans (ITPs) for every person eligible who will need continuing services and supports.

Career education concepts and skills are infused in the regular school curriculum.

The focus on transition programs has heightened concern for career and vocational education. A common approach in career education is to work for infusion of curricular components that relate to real-world needs and skills as a part of every general curriculum segment (Brolin, 1982). For example, in teaching mathematics, careful attention would be given to applications in the practical aspects of consumerism and other daily living skills; also, time would be given, however briefly, to exploration of vocations and professions that use a knowledge and skill base in mathematics. It is intended that through carefully developed attention to career-based curriculum elements, all students will be enabled to move more efficiently and confidently through the transition period from school to work.

MINORITIES WITHIN MINORITIES

Migrant Education

Migrant children face difficult discontinuities in their educational experiences.

Exceptional students, already in the minority in schools, can be minorities in other respects as well. For example, about a million children in the United States are members of migrant families. Most fathers and frequently mothers as well in such families are agricultural workers who travel with their families from place to place in seasonal patterns to help plant and harvest various crops, or they may travel to help in the seasonal fish industry. About 60 percent of such migrant children enroll in schools in the three states of Texas, Florida, and California. Many of these families are Hispanic and require special language instruction in addition to other adaptations in school programs.

Besides farm and fishery workers, many others move frequently, moving children from school to school. Included are affluent families that move to and from special winter residences each school year and families of military personnel. Some children move about among foster homes or to and from the juvenile detention center, and some economically distressed families move frequently because they never quite make it financially and are pushed out and about. About 15 percent of the total U.S. population is estimated to change residences each year. Whatever the cause, mobility tends to "interrupt learning, health care, training, teacher-student rapport, and personal relationships" (Barresi, 1982, p. 473).

Migrant Education

Gloria Medina, 16, traveled northward from crop to crop following the California lettuce harvest. Most of the family of 10 rode in the trailer towed by the family pickup truck. Gloria and her seven brothers and sisters get what education they can as they move from one school district to another, usually enrolling in four or five different schools each year.

High mobility often leads to school dropouts.

The parents work hard to support the family. Gloria is expected to work and help in family support. She has never been fully involved in extracurricular activities at school. In academics, she is placed with younger students and, like her siblings, falls two or three years below the average of her classmates. It's very likely that Gloria will drop out of school within a year.

It might be expected that migrant children would show a higher than average incidence of impairments and handicaps in school situations—and they probably do. Nevertheless, only about 1 percent of migrant children receive special education, compared with about 10 percent of children in general (Will, 1984b). When migrant children are identified as handicapped and IEPs are prepared, the information is only rarely transferred between schools, even though such information is often found to be useful when transferred (Pyecha & Ward, 1982).

The rates of enrollment in special education by migrant children is relatively low.

A national system has been developed to help transfer information about migrant children, including those with handicaps. It is called the Migrant Student Record Transfer System (MSRTS). In 1982, some 500,000 children were recorded in the system, but that was estimated to be only about half the potential enrollees. Special federal funding is available to schools to help defray costs of special programs for migrant children. Special characteristics are required to qualify for both migrant education and special education, and even though valiant efforts are made by many educators, it appears to be difficult to cross boundaries of these two "categorical" programs and the bureaucracies that manage them. A major problem is generating data on the nature and extent of educational problems in this minority among minorities.

Bilingual Education

Another area of high challenge, again a minority within a minority problem and with yet another form of special federal financial support, is bilingual education. Some children with limited proficiency in the English language require instruction through the medium of two languages, affirming in the process the value of cultural diversity.

The number of children whose primary language is not English is growing.

It was estimated in 1976 that as many as 5 million students of school age, about 10 percent of the school-age population of the nation at that time, were bilingual (Baca & Cervantes, 1984). If one assumes that about 10 percent of this total might be expected to be "handicapped," the total estimated number of children in this minority within a minority would be about 500,000. All of these numbers are expected to increase.

Hispanics comprise the largest subgroup, making up about 60 percent of the total. All states now have substantial numbers of refugees from Southeast Asia and other immigrants. At a recent meeting of school psychologists, it was reported that certain tests given to schoolchildren required to be in the child's first or primary language involved over 29 different languages in Chicago and 33 in New York City. San Jose County, California, was reported several years ago to have 25,000 bilingual pupils, about 10,000 of them Hispanic and the remainder representing many other languages and cultures, mainly Asian.

"Bilingual special education programs provide special instruction using the student's primary language while providing opportunities for the student to acquire and reinforce English language skills" (Payan, 1984, p. 94). Leaders in the field insist that adequate programs require personnel from both fields, bilingual education and special education, while emphasizing that the administrative arrangements for programs might vary widely, so long as the needs of individual students are well understood and served.

Classification of bilingual children as mentally retarded has caused court challenges.

The field of bilingual education has been subject to much controversy. For example, it has been viewed as a separatist movement, posing threats to national unity. A particular problem has been the tendency to label bilingual children mentally retarded or emotionally disturbed at a high rate; this has led to court battles about classification problems, which have in turn caused major reconstruction of school programs of screening, diagnosis, classification, and placement (*Diana v. State Board of Education,* 1970; *Law v. Nichols,* 1974).

The commingling of bilingual and special education programs and funds presents many difficulties, most of them yet to be solved. In many respects, the programmatic problems are experienced worldwide, for the rate of human migration is high. Even movements within one nation from rural areas into the large cities, as in the United States, where large numbers of children from southern rural areas have moved to large cities of the northeast, or in Brazil, where large numbers of poor northern rural families have moved to Rio de Janeiro and São Paulo, the problems of educational accommodation are difficult. But when the moves involve major language differences, as in the case of rural Turkish families moving to Germany or Vietnamese moving to the United States, the difficulties are all the greater.

CHILD NEGLECT AND ABUSE

The Challenge

The Kempe (1973) report, showing that more than 60,000 children were seriously abused in the United States in 1972, alerted many professionals and the general public to the apparently growing problem of child abuse. A report by Nagi (1975) suggested that the problem may even be 10 times larger. Yet the phenomenon is far from recent. Abandoning unwanted children was once common in many cultures (Hurt, 1975), but interest in child advocacy has grown to the point where society recognizes that children have rights of their own and that they should be removed from homes in which they are maltreated.

Child abuse is not new, but public interest in the problem is rising.

Reluctance to report suspected cases of child abuse still exists, however. Wolfson (1980) cited the following reasons why child abuse is unreported by professionals:

1. Ignorance or misunderstanding of the reporting law; for example, the tendency to apply one's own more restricted definitions of abuse or neglect and report only abuse or neglect that is severe

2. Ignorance or misunderstanding of child protection procedures; for example, fear that the child will be automatically removed from the home and the parents criminally prosecuted

3. Belief that child protection services are not of the same quality as the services that oneself could render or belief that the child protection services may even be harmful

4. Failure to comprehend or accept that severe maiming or even death may result from one's failure to report

5. Fear of losing clients or at least incurring their anger and, especially in rural areas, fear of jeopardizing one's personal or social relationship with the parents

6. Inadequate diagnostic capabilities so that child abuse and neglect simply occur without detection

7. Frustration with the results of previous reports of suspected mal-

Child maltreatment is undoubtedly much underreported.

treatment: mishandled in an embarrassing way, no action taken, and so on (p. 3)

Theories and Models

A variety of viewpoints have been advanced to help explain child neglect and abuse. Some theorists believe that the explanation, and presumably the treatment, should focus on the psychiatric problems of the parents (Parke & Collmer, 1975). Unfortunately, there is little evidence to suggest that parents who abuse their children share consistently similar traits. However, it is widely held that many abusing parents were themselves the objects of early mistreatment (Greens, Gaines, & Sandgrund, 1974).

Other theorists take a sociological perspective. They focus on the extent to which an adequate "social support system" exists for parents (Bronfenbrenner, 1974) and believe it is possible to construct predictive or risk indexes concerning the likelihood of child abuse or neglect, thus enabling the community to launch preventive programs.

Inexperienced parents who have little outside help may be especially likely to mistreat their children.

Still other theorists suggest that child characteristics (for example, the irritating quality of an infant's crying) may interact in complex ways with stressful conditions weighing on parents to precipitate abusive behaviors. Many theorists connect child abuse to the widespread acceptance of violence in our society, in entertainment, on television, and in discipline. The use of corporal punishment in schools suggests to some that personal aggression is still a socially acceptable mode of behavior control (Zigler, 1976).

Taking a broad ecological view, Belsky (1980) suggested that parents with little experience in child care are likely to maltreat children who are handicapped, temperamentally difficult, or premature, especially if there is no exosystem (close community of friends and relatives) to help them. Such factors as unplanned births, scarce resources, and parental history of abuse or neglect add to the likelihood of maltreatment.

What Is Not Valued Is Not Well Treated

What is not valued is not well treated.

Despite the fact that advances are being made in the fight for children's rights, it is doubtful that maltreatment can be eliminated so long as parents rear their offspring in a society in which violence is rampant, corporal punishment is condoned as a child-rearing technique, and parenthood itself is construed in terms of ownership. It is likely, moreover, that recent cultural developments, such as the denigration of the role of child care, stimulated in part by the women's movement, and the narcissistic "me first" approach to life that seems to be rapidly enveloping contemporary American society, work against efforts to prevent maltreatment by devaluing the responsibilities of parenthood. . . . That [what] is not valued is not well treated should come as no surprise. (Belsky, 1980, p. 329)

Legal Systems of Reporting

All 50 states have systems to expedite the reporting of suspected abuse and neglect of minors. The Pennsylvania procedure is illustrative. Pennsylvania state law requires the reporting of suspected cases, not only by school personnel but also by physicians, nurses, dentists, hospital employees, day-care center workers, and other persons whose employment brings them in close contact with children. The mandated procedure is to file a written statement with the local county welfare agency. When reports are made in good faith, those reporting are protected from legal reprisals. If the reports prove to be unfounded, those reporting are notified, and all pertaining records are destroyed.

Teachers must report observed cases of child abuse.

Pennsylvania's Child Protective Services Law became effective in November 1975. It provides an initial report channel, the Child Line, a toll-free 24-hour telephone service with a multilingual staff. Reports can be made by any citizen, and they may be anonymous. The calls may not substitute, though, for the written statements required of persons in certain roles. Calls on the Child Line are noted, and data are fed to appropriate county welfare agencies. Investigations are subsequently made and suitable actions taken.

Signs of Child Abuse and Neglect

Evidences of abuse and neglect may be signaled by the child's appearance or behavior, by parental behavior, or by some combination of these factors. Pennsylvania's public information material highlights the following warning signs:

Child's Appearance

1. Does the child often bear bruises, welts, or burns?
2. Does the child complain of beatings or other maltreatment?
3. Is the child usually unclean or wearing clothing that is consistently torn and unwashed? Is the child often dressed inadequately for the weather?
4. Is the child underfed? Does the child complain of hunger, going to bed hungry, or missing meals because of punishment?
5. Does the child linger at neighbors' homes at mealtime?

Child's Behavior

Observe the child's behavior.

1. Does the child cry constantly?
2. Is the child extremely fearful?
3. Does the child miss school frequently?
4. Is the child left unattended or allowed to wander about alone?
5. Does the child run around the neighborhood at odd hours? Is the child frequently locked out of his own home or not allowed in?

6. Is the child emotionally disturbed due to family breakdown or serious illness? Do the parents neglect or refuse to secure medical care and treatment?
7. Is the child forced to take over adult responsibilities at too early an age?
8. Is the child exposed to degenerate conditions in or out of the home?
9. Is the child overworked or exploited?

Parental Behavior

Adults exhibit warning signs too.

1. Do the parents leave small children unsupervised or at home alone?
2. Does the parents' excessive use of alcohol or drugs interfere with the care of the child?
3. Are the parents disinterested when approached about problems concerning the child?
4. Does the parent administer unusual punishment such as excessive shaking of the child, locking the child in a room or closet, or using objects such as belts or cords to strike the child? (Adapted from Pennsylvania Office of Children and Youth, 1976)

Hunger. A particularly worrisome aspect of child neglect is hunger. Hunger increases nervousness, irritability, and inattentiveness in pupils. Those qualities appear as disinterest and lack of concentration, and they can contribute to failure to learn. Long-term malnutrition is accompanied by lethargy resulting from a general low energy level. Children whose nutritional needs are simply neglected or those from families with little money and little health care can be profoundly and adversely affected.

It has been estimated that about one-fourth of all American school-children go to school without having eaten breakfast. Even if they get sufficient nutrients later in the day to sustain them, a skipped breakfast can result in hunger pangs and depleted energy by midmorning.

An early part of the assessment of any school learning problem should be a probe into general nutritional level as well as regularity of food intake. The school nurse can be helpful if asked to check the child's appearance and eating habits. It is often necessary to verify the situation by actual family contacts. Children, especially older ones, may be unwilling to reveal home conditions of which they think school personnel may not approve.

It is a safe guess that poor general nutrition and improper eating habits are the culprits in a significant number of school learning problems and that they aggravate other problems. Since improper nutrition and food intake habits are amenable to correction, they should be checked out early in the assessment process and changed if necessary.

Educational Adaptations

As might be expected, abused and neglected children present a great variety of educational and background characteristics. They may come from the well-to-do homes or from abject poverty. Their parents may be young or old, well or poorly educated academically, and of any race or religion. The children themselves may have records of doing well or poorly in school. Sometimes the school setting is a haven or refuge. At other times, it adds to the child's problems when failure and rejection by other pupils and staff occur.

Poor nutrition contributes to learning problems.

Teachers have four functions to perform with regard to this problem: (1) to identify and report instances of child neglect and abuse, (2) to see that neglected and abused children do not lose out on education as a result of their other misfortunes, (3) to teach each new generation the child-rearing principles and practices that will act as preventive measures for the future, and (4) to support comprehensive school policies that in turn support community efforts in the prevention and treatment of child abuse and neglect (McCaffrey & Tewey, 1979). Teachers, school psychologists, counselors, and others who have frequent contact with children can form an early warning network. Such an alarm system can pick up signs, report them, and often avert tragedy.

Solutions require broad community cooperation.

Teachers should display warmth and acceptance toward abused and neglected pupils; at the time, the teacher may be the only adult in whom the child can consistently place confidence. All teachers should be encouraged to start an informal educational assessment with any child who displays any signs of abuse and neglect. The assessment should be made whether or not the suspected case is reported to local or state authorities. It is advisable to ask a special teacher, school social worker, or school psychologist to join in the initial informal assessment.

Informal assessment is a first step.

The educational procedure of choice, then, is the familiar one of establishing the best possible match between the child's needs, as determined by the assessment, and the instructional program. Concomitantly, the involvement of parents in developing and agreeing to an individualized education program may open the door to a better understanding of the home situation. Instructional programs that alert children to aberrant forms of treatment and of the kinds of help available also are of assistance.

Serving the children of battered women is a related and potentially growing problem for the schools. A *New York Post* article (1978), noted reports of "more than 4,000 women beaten by husbands in the past fifteen months" in New York City alone. More and more battered women placed in protective shelters take their children with them. Fear of reprisal is often given as a reason for not divulging new home and school addresses. Home contacts are difficult because of frequent moves. Extremely sensitive treatment by teachers, counselors, and other school staff is a necessity (Zuckerman, 1979).

Centers for battered women bring new children and new challenges to some schools.

Teaching Better Parenting

Teachers have a huge stake in the effectiveness of the nation's parents now and in the future. When teachers and parents together help youngsters

Parent education is a must.

establish self-control and thoughtful consideration of others, the results are favorable for the future of those children both as parents and as well-educated people. So one place for teachers to concentrate is on those pupils now in school. Sequential instruction at all grade levels in attitudes and behaviors conducive to mature and mentally healthy development is probably the best assurance that neglect and abuse of children will diminish and disappear.

Another area for concentrated effort is with the parents of children now in school. Continuing parent education and counseling have important places in the mission statements of public and private schools. Parents, especially parents of exceptional children, are almost always interested in becoming more helpful and skillful with their children. Increasing numbers of valuable learning opportunities are available to all parents. Many volunteer groups, such as the National Collaboration for Youth, an affinity group of the National Assembly of National Voluntary Health and Social Welfare Organizations, Inc., gladly offers help.[3]

Organizations offer help.

Resources to help the chronic child abuser are growing, too. The National Committee for the Prevention of Child Abuse issues educational materials on child abuse, prevention of child abuse, and parenting. There are hundreds of local chapters of Child Abuse Anonymous in the United States. When fathers and mothers recognize in themselves the conditions that trigger episodes of child abuse, preventive support is only a telephone call away. In a model similar to that of Alcoholics Anonymous, this organization's members aid each other by distraction, positive modeling, peer counseling, and professional help when needed. Teachers may locate nearby chapters by telephoning the local public welfare office or social services clearinghouse or by asking the school social worker.

The most promising preventive measures through improved parenting are imbedded in very early childhood intervention systems, as illustrated earlier in this chapter. Early intervention models typically establish and maintain relatively frequent and regular contacts with the parents of young children in a framework of friendly interest and support. This is the key to prevention of most child neglect and abuse and to its prompt detection if it does occur.

Better parenting, then, can be approached in four ways: (1) sequential instruction of parents-to-be while they are in school, (2) in-service education for parents of school-age youngsters, (3) referral of parents, when appropriate, to agencies designed to help them, and (4) guidance of parents in the earliest weeks, months, and years of their children's lives, as part of the new move toward very early childhood education. Each approach has the potential for effective provision of needed educational

---

[3] The National Collaboration for Youth is headquartered at 346 Connecticut Avenue, N.W., Suite 424A, Washington, DC 20036.

opportunities under conditions of close cooperation between school and home.

DRUG-HANDICAPPED LEARNERS

In a survey that polled a sample of United States youth about their key problems (Gallup, 1977), drug use and abuse was ranked highest. More than one-fourth of American young people (27 percent) called it a major problem. An estimated 3.3 million teenagers between the ages of 14 and 17 are "experiencing problems with the use of alcohol," according to the administrator of the Alcohol, Drug Abuse and Mental Health Administration, U.S. Department of Health and Human Services (Macdonald, 1985, p. 47). In 1984, fully 39 percent of high school seniors reported taking five drinks or more "in a row" at least once in the prior 10 weeks (p. 47).

Youth cite drug abuse as a major problem.

The majority of children from families affected by chemical dependency will do what these children have done for generations—keep their fear, pain and emotional isolation to themselves. They will not even share it with their non-alcoholic parent or other siblings. Often, they do not know that alcoholism/chemical dependency is the name of what is happening in their homes because they have not been given accurate, age-appropriate information about this disease. They don't know that there are millions of children just like them and that they have a right to talk about what is happening to them and to ask for help. (Wenger, 1985, p. 94)

Children whose parents are drug or alcohol addicts often do not know how to get help.

The effects of parental alcoholism and drug abuse are significant in the lives of children. According to Wenger (1985), "One of every five or six students in every classroom in America lives in a home with an alcoholic (or other drug-addicted) parent" (p. 93). The children of chemical-abusing parents exhibit more anxiety, more aggression, lower self-esteem, and more psychosomatic symptoms than other children. Drug abuse in the family is sometimes described as an "iceberg problem," meaning that what is exposed to public view is often but a small part of the problem.

Five million Americans now use cocaine on a regular basis.
There are more than 28 million children of alcoholic parents in the United States
Of infants born to heroin addicts, by age 6 months to 1 year, 85 percent no longer live in their own homes, 30 to 40 percent have been abused, and 10 to 15 percent have been killed.
29 percent of all women smoke, and only 10 to 15 percent of them stop

> smoking during pregnancy. A woman who smokes has at least twice the ordinary risk of having a low-birthweight baby.
>
> In 1983, the New York City Health Department estimated the birth rate for mothers on drugs at 7.9 per 100 live births.
>
> In 1982, some 1.2 percent of the babies born in San Francisco had drug- or alcohol-related symptoms. (U.S. Congress, 1986)

Drugs increase accidents.

The continued use of drugs, alcohol, and narcotics may produce irreversible nervous, muscular, digestive, and circulatory system damage. Even occasional use can result in disturbed mental processes and the loss of behavioral controls. In connection with motorbike or automobile operation and in sports such as swimming, boating, skiing, skating, snowmobiling, and surfing, even a small amount of alcohol, tranquilizers, amphetamines, barbiturates, hallucinogens, or narcotics sharply increases the risk of serious injury or death. The danger is not only to the user but also to innocent bystanders (Armor, Polich, & Stambul, 1976).

What Teachers Can Do

Reluctance to acknowledge the problem has kept both parents and their children ignorant about drugs, alcohol, and narcotics. Children who are emotionally unprepared to handle a confrontation with users may be easy converts to the idea that it is the "thing to do." The fact that the escape provided is fleeting, deluding, and ultimately deflationary eludes them until too late. It is only recently that schools have been enlisted in the correction of the situation. The strategies listed here are familiar, but their application to this problem is relatively new.

Familiar strategies can be applied.

1. Make school an exciting and fulfilling place for each pupil, thus reducing the likelihood that "kicks" will be sought through drugs, alcohol, and narcotics.
2. Provide students with more authentic information. Since experimentation with drugs often begins before adolescence, educational activities should begin in elementary schools. Teachers can obtain resources through mental health agencies.
3. Seek family counseling services on behalf of children who are seriously disturbed by use of alcohol or drugs by their parents or other family members.
4. Think of educational offerings as multidisciplinary. Use regional and community resources such as lawyers, narcotics agents, pharmacists, physicians, agencies such as Alcoholics Anonymous, and rehabilitated drug addicts.
5. Bring the educational effort to a strong focus at the middle school level and maintain its vigor throughout the secondary school years.

Arrange for educational services to follow and maintain the participation of potential dropouts.

6. Establish an emergency center in the school system where students
   may be taken if they are discovered to be experiencing a drug
   episode. The center staff should also provide emergency help on a
   self-referral basis for students who consider themselves in danger
   from drugs.

7. Orient staff, students, and parents to possible indications of drug
   abuse. Use these indicators with sensitivity, but do use them to
   help in indentifying and referring drug, alcohol, or narcotics
   abusers:

Regular wearing of sunglasses, even indoors, to hide dilated pupils

Long-sleeved clothing worn at all times to cover needle scars on the
   arms

Marked changes in appearance over a short time

Sharp drop in quality of schoolwork and in dependability regarding
   completion of assignments

Temper tantrums that originate suddenly with apparently little
   provocation

Drowsiness or sleeping in class

Teachers need to be alert to signs of drug abuse.

Exceptional children are not exempt from the ignorance, curiosity, and
social pressure that contribute to drug, alcohol, and narcotics use. All
teachers should therefore be familiar with the problem in order to talk
about it knowledgeably with pupils, both in class and individually. Open
and honest communication will help pupils feel that they can talk without
fear that their confidences may be violated, that they are not inviting
punishment when they reveal problems, and that they will be listened to,
understood, and helped.

Scare tactics have no place in the direct interaction of teachers,
parents, and pupils regarding drug, alcohol, and narcotics abuse. Instead,
in-service and adult education should help both teachers and parents
understand the situation more fully and react sensibly when faced with
such problems in young people.

Rehabilitation

The rehabilitation of youthful alcoholics and students addicted to drugs is a
task extending far beyond the responsibility of the schools. Certainly,
though, teacher organizations and school boards can help other agencies
by adopting policies and developing practices that address that problem
intelligently and constructively, such as vigorously driving pushers away
from the school environs and educating teachers and parents to do a better
preventive job. Most important, however, are the models that teachers,

Teacher and pupil models send effective messages.

parents, and other pupils represent. If pupils in trouble are helped by the people around them in school to learn to live as well-adjusted citizens— people who are "turned on" by their own lives without need for the highs, jolts, and dependencies engendered by alcohol, drugs, and narcotics—the schools will be making their best contribution.

SCHOOL-AGE PARENTS

Annually, in the United States, more than half a million births to teenage mothers are recorded. Seven out of 10 mothers under 15 years of age receive no prenatal care in the first three months of pregnancy.

The rate of teenage pregnancy is higher in the United States than in any other part of the industrialized world. That may be because there has been such controversy about giving unmarried teenagers information about birth control, with the result that many who are sexually active lack thorough knowledge about contraceptive procedures. The school is perhaps the most efficient place in which to organize preventive services, and a few schools have done so, usually in cooperation with parents and community agencies. Teenagers are more willing to go to the health service in the school seeking information on contraception and for follow-up services if it is the same center to which they go for physical education activity checkups and for eye and ear exams. The presence of such clinics in the schools is deeply controversial, however, and is likely to remain so.

Usually, the prospective parents have known each other for some time.

Girls who become pregnant during school age come from all socio-economic classes and attend both public and private schools. All races, all religions, and all parts of the country are represented. The pregnancy is not typically the consequence of a casual or fleeting relationship. Ordinarily, the mother and father have known each other at least a year, and they had strong feelings for each other for some time before sexual relations began (Howard, 1975).

The parents are usually close to the same age, come from the same socioeconomic background, and achieve at about the same level in school; neither is typically more worldly-wise than the other. Pressure to initiate the sexual relationship may have come from either partner. When it does take place, it is most often in the context of two individuals who are embarking, for the first time, on an interpersonal relationship they both consider serious.

Most teenage unmarried mothers now keep their children.

A generation ago, most teenage mothers gave up their infants for adoption without ever seeing them. In the 1980s, about 80 percent of school-age mothers keep and raise their own children.

Early Patterns of Schooling

The traditional pattern of educating school-age parents had three characteristics. First, mothers-to-be were excused from school as soon as the condition was known, and home instruction was provided. Second, if the mother returned to school after the baby was born, it was usually to a standard program in a different school. Finally, nothing was done to change the father's school status.

That pattern prevailed until approximately 1960. Whether or not the parents were married did not affect how the public schools educated them, though marriage did make a difference in their social acceptance. Beginning about 1960, a number of school districts took more constructive steps, especially for school-age expectant mothers. The most common decision was to establish a special center with the following features:

1. Pregnant girls who wished to continue to attend school were supplied with transportation to the center.
2. The center was located apart from regular school buildings or in a separated section of a regular school.
3. The curriculum was extended by prenatal and marriage counseling as well as intensive child-care instruction.
4. The typical curriculum was restricted to core academic subjects because the centers were not ordinarily equipped for laboratory sciences, business practice, physical education, art, and music.

Today, pregnant teenagers tend to stay in school.

Students who elected to attend the centers did so until giving birth. Afterward, they were allowed to return to regular schools if they wished and if circumstances permitted. Often, they returned to a regular school different from the one attended previously or to an evening high school, if one was available. Alterations in educational programs for school-age fathers remained uncommon.

Weaknesses in Traditional Approaches

In 1973, a school law expert began a series of articles that were influential in revealing the inequities of prevailing educational practices and in turning education for school-age parents in a new direction. Nolte (1973) reported that the restrictive school board policies guiding the education of pregnant girls dated from an era when pregnant women were expected not to appear in public, much less attend public schools. These policies, ostensibly intended to protect the health of the mother and discourage marriage and pregnancy among students, did not work and did not stand up under court challenges.

Restrictive policies did not work.

School officials are not competent to judge whether school attendance constitutes a health hazard to pregnant girls. Moreover, competent medical personnel do not believe that it does. Also, as far as the courts are concerned, to deny education to a pregnant girl either as a punishment or as an example is unjustifiable. Such action infringes on the right to due process and the right to equal protection under the law. Attempts to prove immorality, disruptive behavior, or danger to the welfare of other students

The courts support rights to education.

simply on the basis of presence in school are very difficult to substantiate, especially as a basis for a general policy of exclusion. Furthermore, when schools have tried to limit the participation of pregnant students in extra-curricular activities, the courts have lifted the restrictions.

Some actions of school boards or school administrators seem arbitrary, capricious, and unreasonable, even without the intervention and inter-pretation of the courts. In one instance, a high school principal would not permit a 17-year-old unmarried mother to be a candidate for homecoming queen. In another community, two high school graduates challenged the board of education's decision to keep their pictures out of a high school yearbook because they had become pregnant in their senior year (*Sharing*, 1974).

Nolte (1973) concluded that it is legally irrefutable that schools should be just as open to students who are pregnant as to all other students. In addition, there are sound reasons for adding to the usual curriculum and for individualizing instruction to satisfy the special educational needs occasioned by pregnancy.

A Modern Approach to Education

Today's preferred educational practice is to afford each school-age parent or parent-to-be two options: to attend a special center or to continue at the regular school with needed supports.

Garmezy (1975) described how one district moved to ensure that pregnant girls and young mothers might continue their education in their regular school. Purposes of the program were stated as follows:

Regular classes and schools are preferred.

1. To enable student mothers to remain in the regular schools
2. To provide them with practical information and supervised experi-ence in child care and parenting
3. To provide their children with individualized care in a safe and stimulating environment (p. 4)

For 10 years, Minneapolis operated a separated program for pregnant girls and young mothers. Increasingly, it was found that these pupils wanted to continue their schooling where they were already enrolled. In 1971, that was made possible in a pilot secondary school in order to deter-mine what would need to be done to make it feasible elsewhere.

Extrapolating from Garmezy's (1975) report, certain characteristics exemplified preferred practice in maintaining pregnant girls and young mothers in their regular school programs and in personalizing education to suit their needs. The focus here is on secondary schools. Although the age range of pregnant girls takes in some 11- and 12-year-olds, the numbers in the school-age group do not loom large until ages 13 and 14. Where younger girls are involved, they too should have opportunities to continue in regular schools. The preferred practices cited are as follows:

1. Home economics facilities should be equipped and staffed for day care, including food service, for infants and toddlers during the school day. A staff-to-child ratio of 1 to 4 is suitable, although service should be provided even if only one child needs day care. (The service may be extended to married teachers and other staff members, if desired, as a fringe benefit or for a fee.) Basic equipment extends from diapers and cribs to toys and indoor play areas. The day-care service should be free to pupil-parents and available until the mother's graduation.

    Preferred practices benefit mothers and their infants.

2. Pupils should have prenatal counseling and postnatal instruction in parenting skills. If permission is obtained from the parents of children in day care at the school, other pupils, boys as well as girls, may participate in their care as part of the home economics curriculum.

3. The city or county public health service should furnish medical supervision as needed. A public health nurse should be assigned to work at the school, with the amount of time dependent on the number of babies involved.

4. The fact of pregnancy or motherhood should not be allowed to overshadow the pupil's continuing need for individualized education matched to cognitive level, interests, and present achievement, like all other pupils.

5. Transportation should be supplied, if needed, to and from school.

6. Recognition should be given to the needs and rights of both fathers and mothers, whether married or unmarried.

7. Mothers should have appropriate opportunities to feed and play with their children during the school day.

8. The entire professional and support staff of the school needs orientation to the program long enough before it is started to allow questions to be raised and answered and to allow everyone to make progress in working out their moral and ethical feelings about it.

Agencies dealing with school-age parenthood are turning more attention to fathers also. There is evidence to justify the belief that many very young fathers wish to take the actual father role with their babies (Howard, 1975). Of the others, most will want a future marriage in which they will have true father roles. So the long-range goals of young fathers are not essentially different from those of young mothers:

Fathers' needs and goals deserve attention.

1. To complete schooling and acquire the competencies to maintain independence in competitive society

2. To learn to be a worthy parent

3. To acquire maturity in personal and social behavior

4. To be a contributing and stabilizing force in family life

It is a fact of life that teenage parents are and probably will continue to be part of every community. In earlier days, the unmarried parents and their child were objects of scorn, punishment, or both. These attitudes are not yet uncommon. However, many people realize that traditional responses to the problems of school-age parents and their offspring have been inadequate, and thus a new look is being taken at young families.

Services are individualized.

The new approach offers services on an individualized basis, including the additional measures of support that are needed by both parents. They included information, practical help, counseling, job guidance, loans, and personalized education. The consequences can only better individual and family life for young parents and give their children a better start.

EMERGING PROBLEMS

The problems and issues discussed in this section, although recognized for some time, have taken on new urgency in the social, political, and economic context of the late 1900s.

Changing Demographics

In 1975, the year Public Law 94–142 was enacted, there were approximately 51 million children of school age in the United States. In the first decade under that law, the school-age population dropped to about 44 million, making it a period of declining need for teachers and lesser demands for school funds than would otherwise have been the case. In many states, the rapid development of special education and related services during that decade came with relatively little competition for funds with regular education. In Minnesota, for example, the number of special education teachers increased by 95 percent from 1974 through 1983; in the same period, the number of regular secondary and elementary teachers decreased by 25 percent and 9.5 percent, respectively (*Newsletter*, 1984).

From 1975 to 1985, the school-age population in the nation declined, but then the trend reversed.

In 1985, a small increase in the national school-age population was observed, and that is predicted to become a trend, moving the child count back to a total of about 50 million school-age children by the year 2000 (U.S. Bureau of the Census, 1982). This will create needs for general expansion of education in all forms and a much more competitive climate for the further development of specialized school programs.

The proportion of children with special needs is rising.

But general data on population trends tell only part of the story. There are many indicators showing that the numbers of children with special needs will increase much more rapidly than in the past. Approximately 6 percent of the newborn, most of them showing low birthweight, are now placed in hospital intensive neonatal care units. Such children are now kept alive at sharply increasing rates, but a high percentage of them show significant lifelong impairments (12 percent according to one estimate, in comparison with 2 percent for the general population; Zill, 1985). Other causes of the increasing rates of impairment among children include increasing rates of children living in poverty and higher than average birth rates among underprivileged families. All these considerations suggest that the final years of the twentieth century may be especially challenging and difficult as attempts are made to serve the needs of all children (Reynolds & Lakin, 1987).

Categories and Labels

Many voices are telling special educators these days to drop the degrading, nonfunctional categorical systems of the past. (See Chapter 2 for detailed discussion.) A more sophisticated conceptualization of the classification is needed. Suppose, for example, we offered the following kind of rationalization for a new approach.

> There are children whose general cognitive development is unusually slow, some who do not respond well to ordinary forms of instruction, and others whose behavior is disturbing in school situations. In times past, we have used various categories and labels for such children, like *mentally retarded*, *learning disabled*, or *emotionally disturbed*; and we have even been caught up in systems that segregated special groups of such children.
>
> But now we are discovering more promising approaches to developmental problems. In the process, we see the necessity of much more detailed and broader classification systems, encompassing not only the child but his or her life situation as well.
>
> So, while we recognize that terms such as *mentally retarded*, *emotionally disturbed*, and *learning disabled* have been and continue to be affectively loaded rallying points for social action, legislation, parent groups, and even professional associations and literature, we urge everyone to understand that these terms need no longer be the starting points for special education programs. There is no special merit in sending children off to isolated classes and centers for instruction by separate categories. Instead, the study of children and of their life situations is now proceeding to finer points, all of them oriented to improving instruction. And, as we take this new approach, we can spread attention to other children as well, many of whom do not fall within the traditional categories and yet they may be well served by some of the approaches created by special educators.

By using the rationale suggested and implementing it at many levels, perhaps we can extricate ourselves and the children we serve from the confinements and hurts of an outdated categorical system, at the same time maintaining the basic commitments made to the children.

Related Services

Under United States law, the schools are required to provide instruction and *related services* to handicapped children. A difficult problem has

The definition of related services poses difficulties.

emerged concerning the definition of related services, which are described as "transportation, and such developmental, corrective, and other support services...as may be required to benefit from special education" (Public Law 94–142, Sec. 602.17). Within this definition, the term *other supportive services* has presented the most difficulty.

While many of the related services, such as those provided by audiologists and psychologists, are easily recognized as important and appropriate, what about recreation, protracted psychotherapeutic services, parent counseling, and medical services? In one midwestern community, an issue arose over "equestrian therapy" and supervision (giving horseback riding lessons) for treatment purposes. Some observers have been especially concerned about the rapid development of physical and occupational therapy programs in the schools. These are sometimes initiated on the basis of only perfunctory approvals, nominally supervised by physicians, and appear to have only tenuous connections to instructional programs. At a time of budgetary revisions, there are fears that all sorts of functions may be forced on the schools and their limited budgets.

Budgetary restraints affect attitudes toward related services.

A review of judicial interpretations of the "related services" concept clarified certain points:

> The concept is extremely broad and...has been expanded, rather than limited, by most judicial interpretations. This result is not entirely attributable to the passage of Public Law 94–142. Given an expanded school clientele, judicial concepts of education, and educational opportunity, related services are merely those services inevitably associated with assisting children in reaching basic objectives such as walking, talking, socializing, or otherwise becoming prepared for life. (*FOCUS*, 1981, p. 18)

Obviously, this is a problem area that has implications for school curriculum and budgets. It will receive continuing attention in the future.

The Large Cities

Problems in implementing new policies that address the education of exceptional students have been especially severe in many of the nation's large cities. Factors contributing to these problems include the following:

Large urban settings have special problems.

1. Resources are unusually scarce. Large numbers of children and families in major cities live in a culture of poverty; similarly, many large city governmental bodies have experienced extraordinary budgetary problems.
2. The number of exceptional children identified from minority groups is high, and minority children tend to be concentrated in large cities. Despite broad efforts to be nondiscriminatory in assessment and program decisions, assessment personnel tend to rec-

ommend minority children for special education programs at a much higher rate than other children. Special education classification systems are resisted and resented in many big cities.

3. Major revisions of educational bureaucracies have been required and have proved to be difficult, especially in large cities, where specialty groups tend to be well organized and deeply protective of members.

4. Educational directives that flow from governmental monitoring and court decisions have profound effects, causing more than the usual difficulties in large cities.

5. Teenagers in inner-city environments tend to show poor achievement in basic academic skills, along with increasingly high unemployment.

6. Teacher's associations and unions are especially strong; that can be a great strength, but it sometimes also complicates the processes of leadership, priority setting, and change. For example, there is a strong tendency to protect tenure for teachers even if it means shifting essentially untrained personnel into special positions. At the same time, constructive assertiveness on the part of teacher organizations has proved a positive force in assuring that teachers are less often arbitrarily given assignments for which they are not prepared.

7. The great complexity of urban environments results in many breakdowns and loss of trust in institutions and systems.

Loss of trust in institutions is a by-product.

8. School matters have enormous impact on governmental budgets and thus tend to bring the schools into the political arena in complicated, unpredictable ways. Some of our largest cities still have their school budgets determined by city councils rather than by independent school boards.

It is quite clear that if the new educational policies cannot be carried out effectively in the large cities, they will lack credibility and effectiveness everywhere (Levine, 1978). Improving special education programs and services to high-risk students belongs high on the agenda of leaders in the large cities of the nation.

Rural Areas

Rural areas experience many of the same problems as the large cities, particularly the problems associated with poverty. The problems of bureaucratic restructuring, complexity of systems, and loss of morale are not as immediate, but they do exist; the struggles for improvement are carried on at regional or state levels.

Special education services have always been maldistributed, but never so obviously as in recent years under "right to education" directives.

Recruitment of specialists is a major difficulty.

Special problems exist in poor rural areas, particularly in the area of recruitment and retention of special educators. Specialized training programs are usually developed in large universities in urban settings; their graduates tend not to accept teaching positions in rural areas.

Solutions to the problems in rural areas probably will require several kinds of efforts, among them the following:

1. Employment of more generic specialists at local levels, backed up by regional consultants
2. More delivery of specialized continuing education to rural educators by college staffs and regional staff development specialists
3. Training of local personnel in effective staff recruitment and retention strategies.
4. Provision of special incentives to attract qualified professionals to rural and remote areas

> The largest problem confronting new rural teachers in the plains and mountains of the northern Rocky Mountain region is the reality of rural living. Romantic and idealized notions of rural life create disillusions that often send the unprepared hurrying back to the city lights. Ironically, these same shock elements when viewed positively are the very features that are viewed by others as essential to the chosen rural lifestyle. . . . One must live ruralness after the novelty is gone to truly appreciate the reality. That is the acid test separating those who can successfully cope from the short-term romantics. (Zetler, 1980, p. 1)

5. Building stronger support systems for beginning teachers in rural and remote areas
6. Increased use of modern technology (such as miniaturized electronic devices, new forms of radio and television transmission, and remote-access computer terminals) to deliver training to both teachers and pupils
7. Increased recruitment of outstanding educators from rural areas for specialized training and return to their home communities
8. Increased use of special services cooperatives (Widvey, Edeburn, & Ristow, 1985)

Training of indigenous teachers is desirable.

Some training funds may have to be reserved for use by local schools in rural areas as they recruit, select, and support the training of indigenous teacher candidates—those who are firmly committed to return, with their specialized skills, to the sponsoring communities.

Rural educators are not simply waiting for others to come up with solutions to their problems; they have formed networking groups to share information and resources.[4]

Private Schools

One convenient method that allows local schools to comply with education rights directives is to send difficult children to private residential or day schools. That approach is beset with difficulties. It is probably illegal unless handled with great care to comply with the "least restrictive environment" imperative. If the movement in the direction of using residential private schools is great, costs can be enormous, as they are already in several states. Furthermore, political forces can develop to remove more and more of special education from public control. Powerful, well-meaning advocates for private schools can use their resources and the due process mechanisms to build a new private school system in the nation and, in the process, deprive local public schools of the energies and resources necessary to develop broad and effective programs for exceptional children.

Due process rights can be misused to secure placements in private schools.

Sometimes a special version of the medical model emerges in this context in which psychiatrists or other noneducational specialists virtually control referrals and admissions to private schools. The whole system can be turned to the advantage of relatively affluent families—whoever can secure private diagnoses and maneuver through the necessary steps of referral and placement. In some places, expensive private schools are used mainly by white handicapped children and thus tend to create or preserve racial segregation.

Exceptional children need all the help they can get, and some of it, appropriately, comes from the private sector. Some private schools are excellent, and the education of exceptional children has been aided by many other forms of private contributions. We need to make visible the examples of healthy interaction between public and private programs for exceptional children and, equally, to expose and oppose unhealthy operations and trends.

Staff Preparation

Public Law 94–142 was thrust upon largely unprepared educators. In the 30-year period from the end of World War II to 1975, the numbers of exceptional children referred out of mainstream classes to special classes and centers increased about sevenfold. Similar pullout or set-aside programs

Teachers were not trained to accommodate a broad range of differences.

---

[4] Information is available from the National Rural Development Institute and the American Council on Rural Special Education (ACRES), both at Western Washington University, Bellingham, WA 98225.

were developed in other special areas, such as bilingual education and education for the disadvantaged. The schools accommodated special needs by removing the children from regular classes rather than by becoming more adaptive to individual differences within the regular classes. Correspondingly, teacher preparation never seriously faced up to the challenge of individual differences (Howsam et al., 1976; Smith, 1980). Some discernible progress became evident in the late 1970s, but basic difficulties in teacher preparation and performance remain.

Even before P.L. 94–142 came fully into effect, the comptroller general of the United States made the following observations in a report to Congress:

> More and more handicapped students througout the country are now being integrated into regular classrooms, and educators view specialized training of regular classroom teachers as essential to effective education of the handicapped. The Department of Health, Education and Welfare should now move to insure that regular classroom teachers receive more training in the special skills required for teaching the handicapped. (Comptroller General, 1976).

Beginning in the mid-1970s, the U.S. Office of Education offered financial support in the form of "deans' grants" to help colleges revise their preparation programs in the direction of broadening the roles of regular teachers to serve handicapped children. A similar set of grants to colleges and state departments of education assisted in the in-service reeducation of regular teachers for the same purpose. Further, the federally supported Teacher Corps mandated the installation of components relating to exceptional children in each of the approximately 100 teacher preparation projects it supported across the nation in the late 1970s. (The Teacher Corps program was folded into one of the block grant programs of the federal government in 1981.) These efforts were helpful, but they clearly fell far short of what was needed.

Awareness of the need for changes in teacher education is growing.

Changes in special education programs are occurring so rapidly in the late 1980s that training for new functions and roles will be an imperative for some time to come. Much of what is needed may be *retraining* for in-service teachers (both regular and special), principals, school psychologists, and other personnel. The organization and management of in-service education programs designed to help implement the policies expressed in P.L. 94–142 have received the specific attention of teacher educators and staff development specialists (Corrigan & Howey, 1980).

Increasingly, in-service education is organized on a total school or district basis, thus linking it to specific programmatic changes occurring in the schools. Rather than serving random collections of teachers who want to "take a course," it is more often provided systematically for specific groups of personnel who are engaged in institutional change processes.

It is also increasingly common for schools to organize their own in-service education programs or negotiate with institutions of higher education for carefully tailored courses to meet local needs. Teacher centers and other organized projects, representing permanent forms of collaboration between schools and institutions of higher education, can help negotiate in parity the emerging in-service or continuing education programs.[5]

Professional associations have been increasing their involvement in retraining and in-service training for teachers. For example, the Council for Exceptional Children, through its Teacher Education Division (TED) and a national RETOOL center, has started a special project for the training of college teacher educators and special education teachers. The council conducts training on a broad range of topics, such as effective instruction. Through TED, the teacher educators are being taught to use microcomputers and special education teachers are being instructed in the effective use of paraprofessional personnel.

In the mid-1980s, two major reports treating issues of teacher education have captured wide public attention. The earlier wave of interest in improvements in elementary and secondary schools caused by the 1983 report entitled *A Nation at Risk* has now been extended to include teacher preparation. One of the recent reports was produced by a coalition of representatives of about two dozen of the nation's leading research universities, the Holmes Group (1986). The second report was produced by a special group, including representatives of the American Federation of Teachers, the National Education Association, Chief State School Officers, teacher educators, and general public interests, under the sponsorship of the Carnegie Foundation Task Force on Teaching as a Profession (1986). Both reports suggest the further professionalization of teaching, which is anticipated to involve the extension of teacher preparation into a post-baccalaureate period and considerable differentiation among levels of professional status, responsibility, and salaries for educators. A large challenge exists for fields of specialized teaching such as special education, to support these general efforts for the upgrading and professionalization of teaching and then to refashion the ways by which some teachers can be routed into advanced and/or specialized preparation for work in special education and other special fields. The period of the late 1980s and 1990s promises to be busy, productive, and difficult in the field of teacher preparation.

---

[5] Although in-service and continuing education are sometimes distinguished usefully, no distinction between the two is intended here. When treated separately, however, the term *in-service education* designates strictly local adaptations and training problems (e.g., preparing teachers for a reading series just adopted), whereas *continuing education* refers to more general studies (e.g., a course on the latest theories or principles of language development), usually conducted by college or university staff.

> Disabled people are moving into education in increasing numbers. They serve as teachers, college professors, administrators—and in a host of other educational roles. They share educators' common problems in building careers, but their contributions to education are unique.
>
> Teachers with disabilities make a difference in the classroom. They are sometimes students' only contact with a disability....
>
> The American Association of Colleges for Teacher Education in cooperation with the National Education Association has begun to document disabled educators' experiences in teacher training and employment. The program is part of Project HEATH (Higher Education and the Handicapped). (McNett & Merchant, 1981, p. 34)

Effective training and use of paraprofessionals is a major challenge.

Paraprofessionals have become an important and integral part of many special education teams. In some schools, the number of paraprofessionals exceeds the number of teachers. Volunteers also add to the staff rolls. In a speech given at a National School Volunteers Conference in 1978, then U.S. commissioner of education N. E. Boyer estimated that there were 6 million unpaid volunteers working in the schools; their work was valued at more than $1 billion per year. The effective preparation of such personnel and their use in classrooms, resource rooms, home teaching programs, and special classes has become a major challenge. Paraprofessionals and volunteers who work with exceptional students also enhance the performance of teachers (Greer, 1978; Kaplan, n.d.).

Relatively little has been done so far in organizing the preparation for paraprofessionals and volunteers or in evaluation of programs in which they are employed. Experimentation has been undertaken in several two-year community college preparation programs (Kaplan, n.d.), but major questions and issues remain, such as whether they should produce "all-purpose" special education aides or specialists in fields such as sign language or speech technology. In the meantime, the number of persons employed as paraprofessionals has grown spectacularly and is likely to continue to grow.

It has been estimated that about one-half of the nation's 2.2 million public school teachers will retire or leave the profession between 1987 and 1993. That would mean that 1.1 million new teachers would be required in that same period if present staffing patterns in the schools are maintained. It is estimated that 23 percent of all college graduates would need to enter teaching in each of the six years (1987–1993) to meet that need, whereas only about 6 percent of college students enrolled in the mid-1980s indicated an intention to become teachers. Obviously, simple replacement of the present teaching force by traditional means will not work, and it seems likely that increasing numbers of former teachers, new types of teaching personnel, and paraprofessionals will be employed as one part of a complex solution to the staffing problem.

Evaluation

Special education may well be approaching a crisis in evaluation. When Dunn (1968) said he doubted that much of specialized education for retarded children could be justified, he triggered a wave of concern and some evaluation in special education. Since then, several large-scale metanalyses of special education evaluative studies have turned up largely negative results (Arter & Jenkins, 1979; Carlberg & Kavale, 1980; Kavale, 1981). Evaluations of both psycholinguistic approaches to the teaching of children with learning disabilities and special versus regular school placements for exceptional children showed near zero effects of special education as compared with regular school services.

Greater effectiveness of specialized education has not been validated.

Although many detailed quibbles could be offered in criticism of these reports of metanalyses, they nevertheless stand largely unchallenged by contrary evidence; they document a major failure by special educators to validate their work.

Change Processes

College teachers know very well that changes cannot be brought about simply by explaining the contents of books like this one to experienced teachers or trainees. Regular teachers who take courses on mainstreaming insist that their school systems revise special education programs and provide the supports that teachers require. Training must be imbedded in a larger set of change-oriented activities if mainstreaming is to be accomplished.

When mainstreaming becomes the new policy or strategy in a school system, the following basic changes must be made, we believe, roughly in the order listed:

Efforts toward significant change and development require training.

1. Top school leaders (school superintendents and other central staff members, heads of professional associations, and members of boards of education) must be aware of new possibilities and make commitments to the specifics of a new orientation.
2. Principals and teachers must be given opportunities to study the new proposals and to participate in planning specific steps to be followed in accomplishing the planned changes.
3. Needs assessments and plans should be developed in each school as well as in whole districts. Parents, parent groups, and other organized community interests should be closely involved. Changes in services for exceptional children often draw high general community interest.
4. Training activities should be mounted in each school building, oriented at first to the specific problems and needs identified in the building. Teachers should be helped with their problems, recog-

nizing that they have many children needing special help in their regular classrooms.

5. Special education programs will need to be reorganized to begin to offer more support, indirect services, and team cooperation to regular teachers. The retraining of special education teachers, school psychologists, and other support staff should be an integral part of the change process.

If these steps are taken carefully, there is a good chance that the energies of regular and special education will be joined more effectively and that quality mainstream programming will ensue. Indeed, dozens of schools have undertaken serious efforts at mainstreaming in recent years, with encouraging results.

Several models or systems for planning change procedures are available to educators who wish to develop mainstreaming models with all possible awareness and care. The Research and Development Center and Teacher Education at the University of Texas, for example, developed a Concerns-based Adoption Model (CBAM) that can be adapted to local needs. This model focuses on the personal concerns of individuals when changes affect their life patterns. Hall, Wallace, and Dosseth (1973) and others who have advanced the CBAM model suggest that all changes involve a highly reliable series of developmental stages or "concerns." At the earliest stages, concerns tend to focus on personal matters, such as how much time is needed for training, changes in working regularities, and partners. Only later, according to the CBAM model, do concerns rise to the level of substantive details of the new operations. By assessing patterns of concerns felt by staff facing the change effort, programs can be tailored for maximum effects. Until concerns at the early stages are satisfied, it seems likely that efforts for solution at higher levels will be fruitless.

Useful models focus on the change process as it affects individuals and organizations.

Other approaches to change give attention to fundamentals of organizational processes and developments (Bennis, Benne, & Chin, 1969; Havelock, 1973; Miles, 1964). Some of the broad systems for instructional management include mechanisms for managing change processes as part of implementation. The Adaptive Learning Environments Model (ALEM), for example, includes detailed training and monitoring procedures that can be used to manage the difficult processes of change involved in moving toward individualization for all students (Wang, 1980a).

ISSUES AND THE FUTURE

Here we share our views about emerging issues and possible strategies that may help to mold education for exceptional children in the future. This entire book has been directed to the need for change. Despite the many difficulties and candid treatment of problems, we have intended to express our optimism for the future of education in general and the education of exceptional students in particular. Especially in these final pages, that is the spirit we want to convey. Before outlining our view of the future for the education of exceptional students, however, a few general observations are in order.

Shifting Priorities for Education

Schools in the United States in the early 1980s experienced a paradigmatic downshift in the priority given to education in the allocation of resources. A similar trend was noted in other parts of the world. During the 1960s, when the gross national product (GNP) was advancing healthily in most of the world, allocations of resources to education were advancing at about twice the rate of GNP increases (Husen, 1981). In the early 1980s, GNP increases flattened out, and allocations to education dropped below the GNP rate in most parts of the world. In the United States, less national attention and fewer resources were given to public purposes, and more to the private sector and to military expansions. In the United States and throughout the Western world, educators have faced the serious problem of meeting rising needs with fewer dollars.

The rate of increase in dollar allocations has dropped sharply.

Since about 1983 and the publication of the report *A Nation at Risk*, some parts of the United States have made remarkable moves to increase supports for education, but the situation is very uneven across the nation. Changes in economic circumstances, such as the rapid drop in the price of oil, have had effects on public functioning including the schools. In oil-producing states, it has been very difficult to support school improvements. It remains to be seen whether there will be strong supports for the general improvement of education; the situation in the late 1980s is mixed and highly uncertain.

Disjointed Incrementalism

The expanding federal role in education since 1965 has largely taken the form of narrow categorical programs addressed to the needs of "marginal" students—those classified as handicapped, migrant, disadvantaged, or bilingual, for example. Each program has been created with its separate bureaucracy, timeline, and evaluation-monitoring system. The apparent assumption is that none of these programs affects any of the others. However, as noted earlier, a student who is poor or from a minority family is still many times more likely to be classified as retarded than is a child from other sectors of society. The interactions of these many programs are important.

Can we move on from the categorical stage to a more interactive stage?

In almost all of the narrowly framed categorical programs there has been a turn to regular classroom teachers and the mainstream for help. The resulting pull-out programs, in which children spend some time with specialists and some with regular teachers, have a number of disquieting effects:

1. Discontinuities in school programs for almost all teachers and children when pupils travel in odd patterns throughout the school day from regular classes to Title I classrooms, speech therapy, learning disability resource rooms, and so on.
2. A narrowing of leadership and control of total programs at the local school level as increasing numbers of special programs come under the "ownership" of Title I supervisors, the bilingual community, the special education director, or others.
3. Increasing use of school staff time and resources just to make eligibility or entitlement decisions. In many places, for example, school psychologists have been withdrawn from practicing the broader application of their profession and required to concentrated on simple psychometric gatekeeping, a change resulting in severe losses in morale and program development potentialities.
4. The buildup of political constituencies that tend to protect narrow but hard-won territories (e.g., "learning disabilities") and to oppose broader systems approaches to school improvements.
5. Sometimes allowing the provision of services in a special program to justify continuation of a nonadaptive curriculum in the regular classroom. The result is a totally inappropriate program.

Special programs are sometimes misused to support continuation of nonadaptive regular school programs.

One possible solution to the disjointedness problem is to go to block grants rather than categorical supports and to allow states and local districts to reorganize their programs in more coordinated forms. For example, a school principal might be permitted to bring together all of the specialized staff of the building to serve children who have special needs. There is great concern among advocacy groups, however, that the rights of certain categories of children might be lost in the process of implementing block grants. We agree and would oppose that strategy for reform.

It seems likely that a limited set of waivers of rules and regulations might be negotiated with federal and state authorities to permit a limited number of districts to try fully coordinated programming. Then longer-range changes could be made, based on outcomes in experimental situations. Several representatives of advocacy groups have published a statement, titled "Rights Without Labels," that specifically outlines how experimental trials of coordinated programs might be undertaken while still maintaining accountability to children.[6]

---

[6] For a copy of "Rights Without Labels," write to the National Coalition of Advocates for Students, 76 Summer Street, Suite 350, Boston, MA 02110.

A Search for Better Answers

New approaches are needed.

We believe that the time is ripe for special educators to undertake a systematic search for better answers to the problems we have described here. We have in mind broad-scale developmental projects that realign the structure of school programs for special pupils. Special education administrators at the state and federal levels might offer opportunities to local school districts to present broad plans for new ways of addressing the problems of marginal students. As part of the plan, applicants might specify how they intend to work with pupils, evaluate the outcomes of instruction, and meet national, state, and local governmental requirements. Instead of launching a new set of definitions and requirements or totally devolving present federal responsibilities to state and local levels, leaders in high offices would recognize that no one really knows the answers to the difficult problems we face and, while protecting basic rights of children and their families, would support a strong experimental effort to find valid new approaches.

Plans must address individualized programming for all children.

In operationalizing this strategy for the future, we believe, first, that the present general structure of federal laws and regulations for exceptional students should be held in place, at least for a time. It would be an unconscionable disservice to exceptional children and their families to change policies entirely and require a total restructuring of programs without evidence for validity. Second, we believe that the U.S. Department of Education should work out ways of providing funds that will permit crossovers among the various categories to support selected, carefully evaluated development and demonstration programs. Third, we believe that this strategy would work only if programs included mainstream programs as well as the broad set of special programs. In other words, plans should address the problems of individualizing school programs for *all* children and should certainly include provisions for exceptional students while placed in regular classes. Fourth, as long as certain basic accountability standards are met, it would be necessary to waive some particulars of rules and regulations at the federal, state, and local levels so that responsible experimentation and evaluation could take place. If such moves are undertaken, there is a chance for the gradual restructuring of policies and programs by processes that depend mainly on data rather than on raw political forces.

Some of the essential requirements that proposed innovative programs should meet follow:

Instructional effectiveness is paramount.

1. *Program evaluation.* Proposals for educational innovation must, above all, hold promise to enable children to learn efficiently and well, particularly in the basic skill subjects. Parents of marginal children have been misled by too many panaceas; now they want evidence that proposed

programs will work, and that requires careful programmatic evaluations. Consider the following real-life incident:

SCENE: A meeting of the city advisory committee on special education programs.

EDUCATOR (*addresses the group*):   Suppose we established in every school building a system whereby *all children* were observed very carefully. When a particular child was noted to be not responding or learning well, resources would be drawn in to study that child very carefully and to arrange alternative and possibly more intensive forms of instruction, at least for a while. Parents would be involved all the way. Notice that we're not labeling any child, but careful note would be made of the progress of every child and help given when it is needed.

(*The educator then turns to Mrs. Anthony, an active leader in the local association for children with learning disabilities and the mother of a child classified as learning disabled*): Mrs. Anthony, please note that we wouldn't be classifying children as learning disabled anymore. Would that be acceptable? Remember that we would be working intensively with any child who fell behind.

MRS. ANTHONY: Yes, that's what we'd like best of all.

EDUCATOR (*addresses two black women, Mrs. Jones and Mrs. Smith, who are members of the advisory committee and mothers of children in the local schools*):   It might be found in operating the new system that more black children showed poor progress in early schooling than other children. Thus more black children might be studied intensively and given extra help. Remember, we're not going to label the children as EMR or LD or in any other way, but we're going to be very straightforward about their educational needs and arrangements for extra help. Would that be OK?

MRS. SMITH (*after some delay and quiet discussion with Mrs. Jones*):   Yes. That would be OK, except that we would want a very strong evaluation of the program to be sure that it's really working.

Rights to education must continue to be protected.

2. *Continued guarantee of basic educational rights for all children.* The hard-won victories for handicapped children in the decade of the 1970s should not be lost. It seems likely that any proposal for change will suffer impossible political difficulties unless, at a minimum, it involves a full commitment to the following principles:

a. Every child, no matter how special his or her needs may be, shall be provided a free public education.

b. The education provided to each child shall be appropriate to individual readiness and needs.

c. Teachers and other school professionals will cooperate fully with parents in making written plans for the education of individual children whose needs are unusual or whose progress in school is of concern.

d. Parents (including surrogates when appropriate and students themselves as they mature) will be afforded *due process* in connection with all major decisions about education, including the right to appeal against educational authorities any decision that they consider to be in violation of the child's best interest.

e. School programs should be conducted in accordance with the principle of the least restrictive alternative as it has been interpreted in recent years.

3. *Adaptive instruction for all students*: All students are entitled to and should be provided individualized education programs, not just those who are exceptional. Within such a context, school personnel must have the capacity to spend more time on both diagnostics and instruction with certain students, a situation in which special education teachers can be employed effectively. Adaptive instruction refers mainly to the differentiation of curriculum to meet individual needs at the level of the lesson, not at the level of presumed predispositional states, except when evidence to justify complex diagnostic procedures is very strong. Each student's mathematics lesson, for example, should be arranged at an appropriate level, taking into account the scope and sequence of the curriculum and the individual's current level of mastery in mathematics.

Adaptive instruction responds to individual needs at the level of the lesson.

4. *Management assistance and support for regular teachers.* Management demands on regular teachers should be eased. Through training, teachers can acquire the skills needed for new forms of consultation and assistance; pupils can be taught self-management procedures; modern information systems and technology can be made available; and procedural requirements for the use of special resources can be reduced. Special educators and aides who now work mainly in special centers can be moved into regular class settings for much of their work and can help with some of the management of regular classes and schools.

Regular teachers must receive stronger supports.

5. *Support for early education and preventive instruction.* Evidence indicates the advantages of earlier schooling for many children and their families, especially children who are disadvantaged by physical or intellectual handicaps or the lack of intellectual stimulation. Early education will require changes in funding systems to reward the positive *outcomes* of school operations (e.g., fewer disabled learners) rather than to offer rewards only for increases in the rosters of school casualties.

Early education is one avenue to cost effectiveness.

6. *Cost effectiveness.* Any solution must be cost effective. Programs should either show no increases in costs over programs now in effect or provide clear justification for increases. There should also be readiness to make structural changes in programs when they are cost efficient and do not detract from program outcomes.

7. *Full use of technologies.* Among the most promising aspects of special education development in the future is that of applying appropriate technologies. Throughout this book, many examples of the use of technology to provide prostheses for disabled individuals have been discussed (electronic hearing aids, motorized wheelchairs, electrically powered page turners, symbol boards, etc.).

Perhaps most important of all of the technologies available to assist in special education is the computer. Applications of computer technology can be made in class management, assisting teachers in keeping track of the myriads of data about individual students. Applications for this management purpose are at only beginning stages.

Computers can also be used directly in instruction of children, and that may be their most promising application. Students who show limited progress in early phases of instruction in basic subjects, such as reading, show cumulative disadvantages, but computers can be used to help solve problems. It has been estimated that by the middle elementary grades, the least motivated children may be reading only one-tenth as many words as children in a highly skilled group (Stanovich, 1986). This refers only to reading in school; presumably the differences in volume of out-of-school reading would be equally large or probably even greater. Nagy and Anderson (1984) describe these differences as "staggering." Merton (1968) and Walberg and Tsai (1983) have described this situation in which early progress leads to more experience and accelerated progress in terms of "Matthew effects." This follows the Gospel according to Matthew 25:29: "For unto every one that hath shall be given, and he shall have abundance: but from him that hath not shall be taken away even that which he hath."

A solution to this problem for the slow learner, at least in part, may be to provide opportunities for poor beginning readers to use reading materials in which they can "touch" unknown words and have them "spoken"—all through a computerized system. McConkie and Zola (1985) have produced such a system (see also Olson, Foltz, & Wise, 1986). This approach assumes that poor readers have particular difficulty in recognizing new words and that this results in slow, discouraging reading experiences. By having difficult words "spoken" to them immediately, the volume of their reading experiences can be expanded easily. Early studies using such computer-assisted approaches to reading instruction have been positive, and applications in other areas, to extend the experiences of handicapped students, are virtually unlimited.

8. *Differential educational staffing patterns.* Productive educators must be afforded greater influence and must receive greater rewards. This possibility requires systems-oriented efforts to establish more serviceable links between researchers and teachers, better monitoring systems to improve relations between supervisors and direct service personnel, more recognition and use of highly professionalized teachers as instructional leaders and mentors, and increased use of paraprofessional personnel.

Attention to staffing patterns can benefit both teachers and children.

Figure 11.1 suggests a direction that we believe role revisions need to take regarding mildly and moderately handicapped children. At the first-

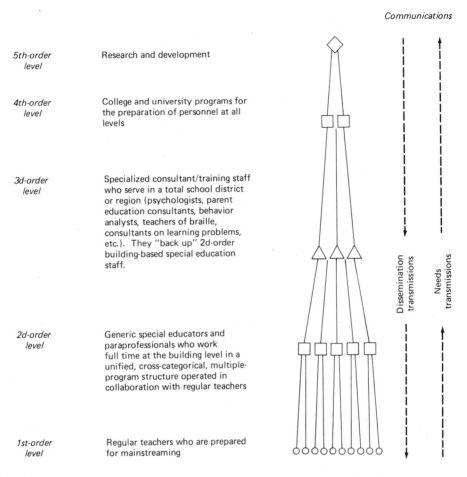

Figure 11.1. A Special Education Structure for the Future. (Adapted from Birch & Reynolds, 1982)

order level ("street level") are the regular school staff members who engage children and their parents directly in regular classes.

The second-order level consists of special educators and paraprofessionals at the building level. Envisioned here is a totally coordinated second-order system that encompasses all the special education conducted in a particular school building plus programs for disadvantaged, bilingual, migrant, low-English-proficiency, or other children with special needs. Regular teachers would turn to this source of help within their school to deal with *all* children who reside in a school's attendance area and who have special needs. Together, teachers and other staff members would operate a carefully developed system for the individualization of instruction of all pupils. Included in the system would be the capacity for

The proposed model addresses the educational needs of all exceptional children.

intensive work with children who have special needs, but these children would not be given traditional labels. A school with 25 to 30 regular teachers would have a second-order staff of 3 to 5 special education teachers and 4 to 6 paraprofessionals.

As more and more of the direct instruction of exceptional students is managed by regular teachers and generic special educators (levels 1 and 2), the demand for consultation and training help from specialists is increased. This provision is represented by the third-order level in Figure 11.1. A local school might be able to serve some children with complex educational needs very effectively through a combination of the regular teacher and the resources of a special educator, working together. These two teachers may need additional help, however, in such functions as managing the system for individualizing instruction, carrying out special assessments, selecting and supplying special materials, and consulting with parents. Thus they would call on consultants from the school district general offices. First-order and second-order staff members can enlarge their areas of expertise through consultation with computer experts, educational audiologists, psychological experts on behavior management, experts on learning problems, parent educators, or other specialists. In rural areas, the specialists at the third-order level might be employed on a regional basis or by cooperative arrangements among several school districts.

The fourth-order level consists of college and university professionals who prepare personnel for all levels. At the fifth level are research and development (R&D) personnel who are often but not always employed in universities. They lead efforts to build the knowledge base that undergirds special education practices.

Desirable communication links across all levels are indicated on the right of Figure 11.1. Strong two-way communication is needed (a) *outward* from the first-order level to keep everyone informed about the needs and realities of the teaching and learning situation (the *needs transmissions*) and (b) *inward* from R&D personnel to all other levels to keep staff members informed of important developments in the knowledge base related to instruction (the *dissemination transmissions*).

In a sense, this conception turns the structure for special education and other programs for marginal pupils on its head. In the past, narrow categorical specialists were employed at the street level in the schools. Now we think it is appropriate to move toward the greater involvement of regular teachers and a broadly prepared group of generic special educators at the school-based levels and to back them up with specialists. It has become unrealistic and defeating, we think, to propose that all schools can employ highly specialized categorical specialists at the street level. (Note that the specializations at the third-order and higher levels are not necessarily categorical in the traditional special education sense.)

Narrow specialization is no longer an effective approach.

The strucuture proposed in Figure 11.1 for the future of education for marginal students requires radical changes in the training, deployment, and certification of school personnel. It acknowledges the move toward the unification of regular education and all forms of special education, as well as the assumption of leadership by broadly prepared regular-line administrative officers in the school system. It calls for the deployment of a back-up cadre of specialists who can support building-level programs through consultation and training. Such specialists also should be able to make contributions to preparation programs conducted by colleges and universities and research programs conducted in special centers.

CONCLUSION

The federal government's involvement in public education in the United States since the mid-1960s has resulted in enormous gains in education for exceptional students, but it has also taken us down a very rocky and deeply rutted road comprised of narrowly framed programs to meet the needs of various categories of students. The needs have been very great and the moral commitments beyond reproach, but the professional quality of the response has been equivocal, the procedural load heavy, and coordination very much neglected. Possibly too much of the attention of educators has turned to procedural rather than substantive norms.

The disjointedness of these developments has been a burden, based largely on doubtful assumptions and procedures, that subtracts from needed services to children. Many teachers and principals are rightfully complaining and asking for help.

The time may be at hand for a basic restructuring of the schools, especially the reworking of relations among categorical programs and regular education, and for a major upgrading of the teaching profession. A key to the necessary changes could be to use some of the various special or categorical funds for a period of time as developmental capital to rework the system and increase its capacity to address individual differences. If we draw on the best ideas now available, divest ourselves of some of the errors of the past, and commit ourselves and our resources to the task ahead, we can enter an important and exciting period of development and improvement in education in which exceptional students are given a more integrated place in the schools and a better education.

The time for basic restructuring has arrived.

THE CHALLENGE OF THE FUTURE

Romeo was a severely retarded 19-year-old when taken under public guardianship and assigned to a state residential institution. His mother was no longer able to care for him. In the institution, his behavior was troublesome, even dangerous to himself and others. The staff at the institution placed him in physical restraining devices. When his mother became aware of this, she sued to secure removal of the restraints. Romeo's "liberty needs," the mother argued, called for training rather than for physical restraints. The case (*Youngberg v. Romeo*) reached the Supreme Court and was decided in 1982. The court case involved only the claim for "liberty needs," and this was decided in favor of Romeo: He was ordered to be released from physical restraints so that he could move about with some freedom, and the institutional staff was directed to give Romeo the training necessary to make him safe in his own person and as a member of the institution.

What is more interesting for our purposes, however, was the fact that the court went beyond the immediate claims of the case and commented on the larger range of possible public obligations to Romeo. Should the institution be responsible for maintaining preexisting skills (the language abilities he had when institutionalized, for example)? Some jurists thought that the provision of food, shelter, medical care, and safe living conditions was enough—hardly more than could be said of animals in a zoo. What about training and education that would give Romeo some options in his life, even if it was to be spent in an institution? Apparently the case for education and for the cultural imperatives is yet to be made positively and persuasively, because the Supreme Court came down on the conservative side, attending only to Romeo's "liberty needs" and the obvious biological imperatives. We find the *Youngberg v. Romeo* decision deeply disturbing for its failure to take with equal seriousness needs for education, "liberty," and survival. Apparently there is much work yet to be done to win a high place for education and the cultural imperatives.

We live in an environment that is increasingly synthetic. It is not made perfectly for anyone and probably never will be, but it can be improved. The point is often made that a good way to test how well we've created our own environment is to look to the life situation of those who are least powerful—the young and the elderly, the poor and the disabled. We think that such a test will show that there has been progress in recent years, even if somewhat uneven, but that there are miles and miles to go.

In the past several decades, the rights of children to receive education and, furthermore, education that is appropriate to their needs have been well established. We need argue no longer about those basic matters. Attention must now be directed to the problems of providing quality education to all.

TOPICAL BIBLIOGRAPHY

Emerging Programs

Allen (1980)
Gallagher (1980)
Jordan, Hayden, Karnes, & Wood (1977)
Karnes, Teska, & Hodgins (1970)

McCaffery & Tewey (1979)
Warfield (ed.) (1974)
Wright (1980)
Zigler & Valentine (1979)

Emerging Issues and Problems

Bernstein, Kirst, Hartman, & Marshall (1976)
Hobbs (1975)
Howard (1975)
Klerman & Jekel (1973)
Kline (1977)
MacMillan, Jones, & Aloia (1974)
Milofsky (1974)
Sarason & Doris (1979)
Thomas (1977)

The Future

Deno (1978)
Menolascino (1979)
Reynolds (1978)
Stainback & Stainback (1980)
Weatherley (1979)
Wolfensberger (1973)

References and Suggested Readings

Aaronson, D. R., & Rieber, R. W. (1975). *Developmental psycholinguistics and communication disorders*. New York: New York Academy of Sciences.

Abeson, A. (1976). Legal forces and pressures. In R. L. Jones (Ed.), *Mainstreaming and the minority child*. Reston, VA: Council for Exceptional Children.

Abeson, A., & Blacklow, J. (1976). *Environmental design: New relevance for special education*. Reston, VA: Council for Exceptional Children.

Agrault, E. W. (1963). *Take one step*. Garden City, NY: Doubleday.

Aiello, B. (Ed.). (1976a). *Places and spaces: Facilities planning for exceptional children*. Reston, VA: Council for Exceptional Children.

Aiello, B. (1976b). A very special special teacher. *Teaching Exceptional Children, 9,* 4–5.

Ainsworth, S. (1965). The speech clinician in public schools: "Participant" or "separatist"? *American Speech and Hearing Association, 7,* 495–503.

Albert, R. S. (1975, February). Toward a behavioral definition of genius. *American Psychologist,* 140–151.

Algozzine, B., & Maheady, L. (1986). In search of excellence: Instruction that works in special education classrooms. *Exceptional Children, 52*(6), entire issue.

Allen, K. E. (1980). The language impaired child in the preschool: The role of the teacher. *Directive Teacher, 2*(3), 6, 8–10.

Alley, G., & Deshler, D. (1979). *Teaching the learning disabled adolescent: Strategies and methods*. Denver: Love Publishing.

Alpiner, J. G. (1968). *The utilization of supportive personnel in speech correction in the public schools*. Denver: Colorado State Department of Education (Title VI, ESEA, BEH, U.S. Office of Education).

Alvord, D. J. (1977). Innovation in speech therapy: A cost effective program. *Exceptional Children, 43,* 520–525.

American Foundation for the Blind (AFB). (1954). *The Pine Brook report: National work session on the education of the blind with the sighted.* New York: Author.

American Psychiatric Association (APA). (1968). *Diagnostic and statistical manual* (2d ed.). Washington, DC: Author.

American Psychiatric Association. (1980). *Diagnostic and statistical manual* (3d ed.). Washington, DC: Author.

Anastasiow, N. J., & Hanes, M. L. (1976). *Language patterns of poverty children.* Springfield, IL: Charles C. Thomas.

Anderson, E. M. (1973). *The disabled school child: A study of integration in the primary schools.* London: Methuen.

Anderson, J. (Ed.). (1982). *Curricula for high-risk and handicapped infants.* Chapel Hill, NC: Technical Assistance System, Frank Porter Graham Child Development Center.

Anderson, J. L. (1981). Training of supervisors in speech-language pathology and audiology. *ASHA, 23*(7), 8–14.

Anderson, R. Mainstreaming is the name for a new idea. *School Management, 17*(7), 28–30.

Anderson, W., Chitwood, S., & Hayden, D. (1982). *Negotiating the special education maze.* Englewood Cliffs, NJ: Prentice-Hall.

Armor, D. J., Polich, J. M., & Stambul, H. B. (1976). *Alcoholism and treatment.* Santa Monica, CA: Rand Corp.

Arter, J. A., & Jenkins, J. R. (1979). Differential diagnosis-prescriptive teaching: A critical appraisal. *Review of Educational Research, 49*(4), 517–555.

Avery, C. B. (1975). The education of children with impaired hearing. In W. M. Cruickshank & G. O. Johnson (Eds.), *Education of exceptional children and youth* (3d ed.). Englewood Cliffs, NJ: Prentice-Hall.

Baca, L. M., & Cervantes, H. T. (Eds.). (1984). *The bilingual special education interface.* St. Louis MO: Times Mirror/Mosby College Publishing.

Baker, D. B. (1979). Severely handicapped: Toward an inclusive definition. *Journal of the Association for the Severely Handicapped, 4*(1), 52–65.

Ballard, J., Ramirez, B., & Weintraub, F. (1982). *Special education in America: Its legal and governmental foundations.* Reston, VA: Council for Exceptional Children.

Balow, B., & Reid, G. (1980). *Autism sourcebook for parents and professionals.* Minneapolis: University of Minnesota, Special Education Programs.

Bandura, A. (Ed.). (1971). *Psychological modeling.* Chicago: Atherton.

Barraga, N. (1976). *Visual handicaps and learning: A developmental approach.* Belmont, CA: Wadsworth.

Barresi, J. G. (1982). Educating handicapped migrants: Issues and options. *Exceptional Children, 48*(6), 473–488.

Batshaw, M. L., & Perret, Y. M. (1981). *Children with handicaps: A medical primer.* Baltimore: Paul Brookes.

Becker, H. S. (1963). *Outsiders: Studies in the sociology of deviance.* Glencoe, IL: Free Press.

Belsky, J. (1980). Child maltreatment: An ecological integration. *American Psychologist, 35*(4), 320–335.

Bender, W. N. (1984). Daily grading in mainstream classes. *Directive Teacher, 6*(2), 3–6.

Benham, H. (Ed.). (1973). *Feeling free.* Englewood Cliffs, NJ: Scholastic.

Bennis, W. G., Benne, K. D., & Chin, R. (1969). *The planning of change* (2d ed.) New York: Holt, Rinehart and Winston.

Benson, D. F. (1979). *Aphasia, Alexia and Agraphia.* New York: Churchill Livingstone.

Benz, M., Halpern, A., & Close, D. (1986). Access to day programs and leisure activities by nursing home residents with mental retardation. *Mental Retardation, 24*(3), 147–152.

Berbow, C. (1980). *Review of instructionally effective schooling literature* (Urban Directory Series, No. 70). New York: Columbia University, Teachers College.

Berg, N. A. (1966). *Wednesday's child: A tale of love and courage.* Philadelphia: Muhlenberg Press.

Bergan, J. R. (1977). *Behavioral consultation.* Columbus: Merrill.

Bernstein, C. D., Hartman, W. T., Kirst, M. W., & Marshall, R. S. (1976). *Financing educational services for the handicapped.* Reston, VA: Council for Exceptional Children.

Berruetta-Clement, J., Schweinhart, L. J., Barnett, W. S., Epstein, A. S., & Weikart, D. P. (1984). *Changed lives: The effects of the Perry pre-school program on youths through age 19.* Ypsilanti, MI: High/Scope Press.

Bettelheim, B. (1967). *The empty fortress.* New York: Free Press.

Betts, E. A. (1946). *Foundations of reading instruction.* New York: American Book.

Billings, H. K. (1963). An exploratory study of the attitudes of noncrippled children in three elementary schools. *Journal of Experimental Education, 31,* 381–387.

Bilotti, E., & Kettrick, R. (1984). Innovative approaches to financing home care. In Association for the Care of Children's Health, *Home care for children with serious handicapping conditions: A report on a conference held May 27, 1984, Houston, Texas.* Washington, DC: Association for the Care of Children's Health.

Birch, J. W. (1955). *Retrieving the retarded reader.* Indianapolis: Bobbs-Merrill.

Birch, J. W. (1975). *Hearing impaired children in the mainstream.* Reston VA: Council for Exceptional Children.

Birch, J. W. (1976). Mainstream education for hearing-impaired pupils: Issues and interviews. *American Annals of the Deaf,* 69–71.

Birch, J. W. (1984). In *any* identification procedure necessary? *Gifted Child Quarterly, 28*(4), 157–161.

Birch, J. W., & Johnstone, B. K. (1975). *Designing schools and schooling for the handicapped.* Springfield, IL: Charles C Thomas.

Birch, J. W., Matthews, J., & Burgi, E. (1958). *Improving children's speech.* Indianapolis: Bobbs-Merrill.

Birch, J. W., & Reynolds, M. C. (1982). Special education as a profession: Where we came from and where we're going. *Exceptional Education Quarterly, 2*(4), 1–10.

Birenbaum, A. (1986). Symposium overview: Community programs for people with mental retardation. *Mental Retardation, 24*(3), 145–146.

Blackman, J. A. (Ed.). (1983). *Medical aspects of developmental disabilities in children birth to three.* Iowa City, IA: Department of Pediatrics, University of Iowa Hospital School.

Blanchard, E. (1980). People with facial disfigurements. *Disabled USA, 4*(1), 1–3.

Block, E. (1984). *Effective schooling: A summary of research.* Washington, DC: Educational Research Service.

Blumberg, L. (1973). The case for integrated schooling. *Exceptional Parents, 3*(4),

15–17.

Bodgan, R. (1983, Summer). A closer look at mainstreaming. *Educational Forum*, 425–434.

Bookbinder, S. R. (1978). *What every child needs to know about disabilities*. Providence: Rhode Island Easter Seal Society.

Borg, W. R. (n.d.). *Classroom management* (Protocol materials). Tampa: University of South Florida. National Resource and Dissemination Center.

Bower, E. M. (1973). *Teachers talk about their feelings*. Rockville, MD: National Institute of Mental Health.

Bower, E. M. (1974). *Early identification of emotionally handicapped children in school*. Springfield, IL: Charles C Thomas.

Bower, E. M. (1980). *The handicapped in literature*. Denver: Love.

Boyer, N. E. (1978). *Address at National School Volunteers Conference*. Arlington, VA.

Braddy, N. (1933). *Anne Sullivan Macy—The story behind Helen Keller*. New York: Doubleday.

Bradley, D. P. (1976, June). Expanded speech pathology services, *Prise Reporter, 7*, 1–3.

Bradley, V. (1984). Enhancing the families' role in the care of persons with developmental disabilities. In National Association of Developmental Disabilities Councils, *The community: Living and working there*. Washington, DC: National Association of Developmental Disabilities Councils.

Brasel, K., & Quigley, S. (1977). The influence of certain language and communication environments in early childhood on the development of language in deaf individuals. *Journal of Speech and Hearing Research, 20*, 95–107.

Brightman, A. J., & Greig, D. (Eds.). (1978). *Laurie*. New York: Scholastic Book Services.

Bringuier, J. C. (1980). *Conversations with Jean Piaget*. Chicago: University of Chicago Press.

Brokes, A. (1975). A process model of consultation. In C. Parker (Ed.), *Psychological consultation: Helping teachers meet special needs* (pp. 185–203). Reston, VA: Council for Exceptional Children.

Brolin, D. E. (1982). *Vocational preparation of persons with handicaps*. Columbus: Merrill.

Brolin, D. E. (1978a). *Mainstreaming handicapped students in vocational education: Resource guide and administrators guide*. Columbia, MO: University of Missouri, College of Education.

Brolin, D. E. (1978b). *Life centered career education: A competency based approach*. Reston, VA: Council for Exceptional Children.

Bronfenbrenner, U. (1974). Developmental research, public policy, and the ecology of childhood. *Child Development, 45*, 1–5.

Brown, A. L. (1980). Metacognitive development and reading. In R. J. Spiro, B. L. Bruce, & W. F. Brewer (Eds.), *Theoretical issues in reading comprehension*. Hillsdale, NJ: Erlbaum.

Brown, L., Nietupski, J., & Hamre-Nietupski, S. (1976). *Criterion of ultimate functioning*. In M. A. Thomas (Ed.), *Hey, don't forget about me* (pp. 2–15). Reston, VA: Council for Exceptional Children.

Brown, R. (1973). *A first language: The early stages*. Cambridge, MA: Harvard University Press.

Brown v. Board of Education of Topeka. (1954). 347 U.S. 483, 493.

Bruce, W. (1973). The parents' role from an educator's point of view. In W. H. Northcott (Ed.), *The hearing impaired child in the regular classroom*. Washington, DC: A. G. Bell Association for the Deaf.

Bruininks, R. H. & Bruininks, V. L. (1981). Deinstitutionalization: Implications for special education. In P. Bates (Ed.), *Mainstreaming: Our current knowledge base* (pp. 113–139). Minneapolis: University of Minnesota, College of Education, National Support Systems Project.

Bruininks, R. H., Hauber, F. A., & Kudla, M. J. (1979). *National survey of community residential facilities: A profile of facilities and residents in 1977*. Minneapolis: University of Minnesota, Department of Psychoeducational Studies.

Buchanan, R., & Mullins, J. B. (1968, September). Integration of a spina bifida child in a kindergarten for normal children. *Young Children*, 339–344.

Buell, C. E. (1966). *Physical education for children*. Springfield, IL: Charles C Thomas.

Burlingame, R. (1964). *Out of silence into sound: The life of Alexander Graham Bell*. New York: Macmillan.

Burton, T. A., & Hirschoren, A. (1979). The education of severely and profoundly retarded children: Are we sacrificing the child to the concept? *Exceptional Children, 45*(8), 598–603.

Calovini, G. (Ed.). (n.d.). *Mainstreaming the visually impaired child*. Springfield IL: Instructional Materials Center, Office of the Superintendent of Public Instruction.

Calovini, G. (1969). *The principal looks at classes for the physically handicapped*. Reston, VA: Council for Exceptional Children.

Campbell, J. (1980). Summer marine science program has disabled students hitting the beaches. *Disabled USA, 4*(1), 15–17.

Caplan, G. (1970). *The theory and practice of mental health consultation*. New York: Basic Books.

Carlberg, C., & Kavale, K. (1980). The efficacy of special versus regular class placement for exceptional children: A meta-analysis. *Journal of Special Education, 14,* 295–309.

Carnegie Foundation. (1986). *A nation prepared: Teachers for the 21st century*. Hyattsville, MD: Carnegie Forum on Education and the Economy.

Carpenter, F. (1974). *The Skinner primer: Beyond freedom and dignity*. Riverside, NJ: Free Press.

Castro, G., White, K., & Taylor, C. (1983). *Final report 1982–83 work scope*. Logan: Early Intervention Research Institute, Utah State University.

Caudill, R. (1965). *A certain small shepherd*. New York: Holt, Rinehart and Winston.

Chalfant, J. C., Pysh, M. V., & Moultrie, R. (1979). Teacher assistance teams: A model for within-building problem solving. *Learning Disabilities Quarterly, 2,* 85–96.

Chevigny, H. (1946). *My eyes have a cold nose*. New Haven, CT: Yale University Press.

Cina, S., & Caro, F. G. (1984). *Supporting families who care for severely disabled children at home: A public policy perspective*. New York, NY: Community Service Society of New York.

Cohen, S. (1977). *Accepting individual differences*. Allen, TX: Developmental Learning Materials.

Comptroller General of the United States. (1976, September 28). *Report to the Congress. Training educators for the handicapped: A need to redirect programs*. Washington, DC: GPO.

Connor, F. P., Williamson, G. G., & Siepp, J. M. (1978). *Program guide for infants and toddlers with neuromotor and other developmental disabilities.* New York: Teachers College Press.

Connor, L. E. (1976). Mainstreaming a special school. *Teaching Exceptional Children, 8,* 76–80.

Corcoran, P. (1980). Address at Tufts University. *Science and Technology for the Handicapped, 1*(3), 1.

Corrigan, D. C., & Howey, K. R. (1980). *Concepts to guide the education of experienced teachers.* Reston, VA: Council for Exceptional Children.

Cox, J. L. (1984). An exploration of issues regarding evaluation activities related to the effectiveness of special education programs, a policy-oriented study of special education service delivery systems: Executive summary for Vol. III. Research Triangle Park, NC: Research Triangle Institute.

Cox, J. L., Daniel, N., & Boston, B. O. (1985). *Educating able learners.* Austin: University of Texas Press.

Craig, S. B. (1942). Fifty years of training teachers of the deaf. *School and Society, 56*(1449), 301–303.

Cripps, R., & Innes, R. L. (1980, June). *Mobile team project 1974–1979: Children's Hospital outreach therapy teams support mainstreaming of cerebral palsied and developmentally delayed children into local preschool and school facilities.* Paper presented at the convention of Rehabilitation International, Vancouver, British Columbia.

Cromwell, R. (1976). Ethics, umbrage, and the ABCDs. In M. C. Reynolds (Ed.), *Mainstreaming: Origins and implications.* Reston, VA: Council for Exceptional Children.

Cronbach, L. J. (1967). How can instruction be adapted to individual differences? In R. M. Gagne (Ed.), *Learning and individual differences.* Columbus: Merrill.

Cronbach, L. J., & Gleser, G. C. (1965). *Psychological tests and personal decisions* (2d ed.) Urbana: University of Illinois Press.

Cronbach, L. J., & Snow, R. E. (1977). *Aptitude and instructional methods.* New York: Irvington.

Cruickshank, W. M. (1972). Some issues facing the field of learning disability. *Journal of Learning Disabilities, 5,* 380–383.

Cunningham, S. (1984, September). Cross-cultural study of achievement calls for changes in home. *APA Monitor,* 10–11.

Curran, J., & Cratty, B. (1985). *Speech and language problems in children.* Denver: Love.

Dale, D. M. C. (1967). *Deaf children at home and at school.* Springfield, IL: Charles C Thomas.

Davidson, M. (1971). *Louis Braille, the boy who invented books for the blind.* New York: Hastings House.

Davis, J. (Ed.). (1977). *Our forgotten children: Hard of hearing pupils in the schools.* Minneapolis, MN: University of Minnesota, Audio Visual Library Service.

Davis, H., & Silverman, R. (Eds.). (1978). *Hearing and deafness.* New York: Holt, Rinehart and Winston.

DelPolito, C. M. (1977). *Intrapersonal communication.* Menlo Park, CA: Cummings.

Deno, E. (Ed.). (1973). *Instructional alternatives for exceptional children.* Reston, VA: Council for Exceptional Children.

Deno, S. L., & Mirkin, P. K. (1977). *Data-based program modification: A manual.* Reston, VA: Council for Exceptional Children.

Design for Change. (1983). *Caught in the web: Misplaced children in Chicago's classes for the mentally retarded*. Chicago: Author.

Deutsch, M. (1979). Education and distributive justice: Some reflections on grading systems. *American Psychologist, 34*(5), 391–401.

Diana v. State Board of Education. (1970, Jan. 7). Civil Action No. C-70 37REP. (N.D. Cal.)

Dibner, S., & Dibner, A. (1973). *Integration or segregation for the physically handicapped child?* Springfield, IL: Charles C Thomas.

Dickshoff, J. (1939). *Milton on himself*. New York: Oxford University Press.

Dopheide, W. R., & Dalenger, J. (1975). Improving remedial speech and language services through clinician-teacher in-service interaction. *Language, Speech and Hearing Services in Schools, 6*, 196–205.

Douglas, W. (1950). *Of men and mountains*. New York: Harper & Row.

Dunlap, J. M. (1955). Gifted children in an enriched program. *Exceptional Children, 21*, 135–137.

Dunn, L. M. (1968). Special education for the mildly retarded: Is much of it justifiable? *Exceptional Children, 35*, 5–22.

Earhart, E., & Sporakowski, M. (1984). *Family Relations, 33*(1), entire issue.

East, L. (1976, November-December). A mainstreaming success story. *Today's Education, 71*.

Ebel, R. L. (1983). The practical validation of tests of ability. *Educational Measurement, 2*(2), 7–10.

Edelman, M. W. (1981). Who is for children? *American Psychologist, 36*(2), 109–116.

Ekstein, A., Shulman, L., & Sprafka, S. (1978). *Medical problem solving: An analysis of clinical reasoning*. Cambridge, MA: Harvard University Press.

Elkind, D. (1986). Formal education and early childhood education: An essential difference. *Phi Delta Kappan, 67*(9), 631–636.

Emmer, E. T., Sanford, J. P., Evertson, L. M., Clements, B. S., & Martin, J. (1981). *The classroom improvement study: An experiment in elementary school classrooms*. Austin: University of Texas, Research and Development Center in Teacher Education.

Evans, S. (1980). The consultant role of the resource teacher. *Exceptional Children, 46*(5), 402–403.

Evertson, L. M., Emmer, E. T., Clements, B. S., Sanford, J. P., Worsham, M. E., & Williams, E. L. (n.d.). *Organizing and managing the elementary school classroom*. Austin: University of Texas, Research and Development Center for Teacher Education.

Exceptional Children, (1985, November). Entire issue.

Eysenck, H. J., Wakefield, J. A., Jr., & Friedman, A. F. (1983). Diagnosis and clinical assessment: The DSM-III. In M. R. Rosenszweig & L. W. Porter (Eds.), *Annual review of psychology, 4*, 167–193.

Fant, L. J., Jr (1972). *Ameslan, an introduction to American Sign Language*. Silver Spring, MD: National Association of the Deaf.

Featherstone, H. (1980). *A difference in the family*. New York: Penguin.

Federal Register. (1977 August 23). *42*(163).

Federal Register. (1981 January 19).

Fellendorf, G. W. (1973). Hearing impaired graduates of regular schools. *Volta Review, 75*(2), 232–255.

Ferris, C. (1980). *A hug just isn't enough*. Washington, DC: Gallaudet College Press.

Festinger, L. (1954). A theory of social comparison processes. *Human Relations, 7,* 117–140.

Fiscus, E., & Mandell, C. (1983). *Developing individualized education programs.* St. Paul: West Publishing.

Fish, J. (1985). *Educational opportunities for all?* London: Inner London Education Authority.

Fisher, R. L. (1980. April). First string mainstreaming. *Western Pennsylvanian,* 56–58.

Fitzgerald, E. (1954). *Straight language for the deaf: System of instruction for deaf children* (2d ed.). Washington, DC: Volta Bureau.

Flynn, R. J., & Nitsch, K. E. (Eds.). (1980). *Normalization, social integration, and community services.* Baltimore: University Park Press.

FOCUS on special education legal practices. (1981). 1(2).

Foster, G. G., Ysseldyke, J. E., Casey, A., & Thurlow, M. (1984). Congruence between reason for referral and placement outcome. *Journal of Psychoeducational Assessment, 2,* 209–218.

Foulke, E., et al. (1962). The comprehension of rapid speech by the blind. *Exceptional Children, 29,* 134–141.

Fox, W. L., Egner, A. N., Paolucci, P. E., Perelman, P. F., & McKenzie, H. S. (1975). An introduction to a regular classroom approach to special education. In E. Deno (Ed.), *Instructional alternatives for exceptional students.* Reston, VA: Council for Exceptional Children.

Freeman, G. G. (1977). *Speech and language services and the classroom teacher.* Reston VA: Council for Exceptional Children.

Friedman, R. J., & MacQueen, J. C. (1971). Psychoeducational considerations of physical handicapping conditions in children. *Exceptional Children, 37,* 538–539.

Frisina, R. (1974). *Report of the committee to redefine deaf and hard of hearing for educational purposes.* Washington, DC: GPO.

Fudala, J. B. (1973). Applied awareness: Speech improvement in an elementary classroom. *Teaching Exceptional children, 5,* 190–194.

Gallagher, J. (Ed.). (1980). *Ecology of exceptional children.* Reston, VA: Council for Exceptional Children.

Gallagher, J. J. (1985). *Teaching the gifted child* (3d ed.). Boston: Allyn & Bacon.

Gallico, P. (1941). *The snow goose.* New York: Knopf.

Gallup, G. (1977, May 23). *Gallup youth survey.* Princeton, NJ: Gallup Polls.

Galton, F. (1869). *Hereditary genius.* New York: Macmillan.

Garcia, E. E., Billet, O. J., & Rust, F. P. (1977). The experimental analysis of language training generalization across classroom and home. *Behavior Modification, 1*(4), 531–550.

Gardner, H. (1983). *Frames of mind.* New York: Basic Books.

Gardner, W. I. (1977). *Learning and behavior characteristics of exceptional children and youth.* Boston: Allyn & Bacon.

Gargiulo, R. (1985). *Working with parents of exceptional children.* Boston: Houghton Mifflin.

Garmezy, E. (1975, Winter). The mother and infant care education project, Minneapolis public schools. *Sharing,* 4–5.

Garrett, C., & Stoval, E. M. (1972). A parent's views on integration. *Volta Review, 74*(6), 338–344.

Giffen, K., & Pattern, B. R. (Eds.) (1971). *Basic readings in interpersonal communica-*

tion. New York: Harper & Row.

Gilhool, T. (1976). Changing public policies: Roots and forces. *Minnesota Education,* 2(2), 8–14.

Gilhool, T. K., & Stutman, E. A. (1978). Integration of severely handicapped students. In *Developing criteria for the evaluation of the least restrictive environment provision* (p. 215). Washington, DC: Department of Health, Education and Welfare, Office of Education, Bureau of Education for the Handicapped.

Glaser, R. (1975). *The school of the future: Adaptive environments for learning.* Pittsburgh, PA: University of Pittsburgh, Learning Research and Development Center.

Glaser, R. (1977). *Adaptive education: Individual diversity and learning.* New York: Holt, Rinehart and Winston.

Glass, G. V. (1977). Integrating findings: The meta-analysis of research. *Review of Research in Education,* 5, 1351–1379.

Glass, G. V. (1983, January). Effectiveness of special education. *Policy Studies Review,* 2(Special No. 1), 65–78.

Glass, G. V., McGaw, B., & Smith, M. L. (1981). *Meta-analysis in social research.* Beverly Hills: Sage.

Goldberg, M., Passow, A., Justman, J., & Hage, G. (1965). *The effects of ability grouping.* New York: Columbia University.

Goldenson, R. M. (Ed.). (1978). *Disability and rehabilitation handbook.* New York: McGraw-Hill.

Goldstein, H., Moss, J., & Jordan, L. (1964). *The efficacy of special class training on the development of mentally retarded children.* (Cooperative Research Project No. 619, July 1, 1959, to November 30, 1964.) Champaign: Institute for Research on Exceptional Children. University of Illinois.

Goldstein, A. P., Sprafkin, R. P., Gershaw, N. J., & Klein, P. (1980). *Skill-streaming the adolescent.* Champaign, IL: Research Press.

Goleman, D. (1980, February), 1,528 little geniuses and how they grow. *Psychology Today,* 28–53.

Goodlad, J. I. (1985). Foreword. In J. Oakes, *Keeping track: How schools structure inequality* (pp. ix–xii). New Haven, CT: Yale University Press.

Gorham, K. A. (1975). A lost generation of parents. *Exceptional Children,* 41, 521–525.

Goss v. Lopez. (1975). 419 U.S. 565.

Graden, J. L., Casey, A., & Bonstrom, O. (1985). Implementing a prereferral intervention system: Part II. The data. *Exceptional Children,* 51, 487–496.

Gray, B. B., & Barker, K. (1977). Use of aides in an articulation therapy program. *Exceptional Children,* 43(8), 534–538.

Green, A., Gaines, R., & Sandgrund, A. (1974). Child abuse: Pathological syndrome of family interaction. *American Journal of Psychiatry,* 131, 882–886.

Green, P. (Ed.). (1974). *One out of ten: School planning for the handicapped.* New York: Educational Facilities Laboratories.

Green, R. A. (1977). *Implementation of a speech improvement program at the kindergarten level.* Unpublished doctoral dissertation, Nova University, Fort Lauderdale, FL.

Greenberg, M. T. (1980). Hearing families with deaf children: Stress and functioning as related to communication method. *American Annals of the Deaf,* 125, 1063–1071.

Greenberg, M. T., Kusche, C. A., Gustafson, R., & Calderon, R. (1985). The

PATHS project: A model for the prevention of psychosocial difficulties in deaf children. In G. B. Anderson and D. Watson (Eds.), *The habilitation and rehabilitation of deaf adolescents*. Washington, DC: Gallaudet College Press.

Greer, J. V. (1978). Utilizing paraprofessionals and volunteers in special education. *Focus on Exceptional Children, 10*(6), 1–15.

Gromek, I., & Scandary, J. (1977). Considerations in the educational placement of the physically or otherwise health impaired child. *DOPHHH Journal, 3*(1), 8–11.

Grossman, H. J. (Ed.). (1973). *Manual on terminology and classification in mental retardation*. Washington, DC: American Association on Mental Deficiency.

Grossman, H.J. (Ed.). (1977). *Manual on terminology and classification in mental retardation* (rev. ed.). Washington, DC: American Association on Mental Deficiency.

Grossman, H. J. (Ed.). (1983). *Classification in mental retardation*. Washington, DC: American Association on Mental Deficiency.

Grotsky, J., Sabatino, D., & Ohrtman, W. (Eds.). (1976). *The concept of mainstreaming: A resource guide for regular classroom teachers*. King of Prussia: Eastern Pennsylvania Regional Resources Center for Special Education.

Guilford, J. P. (1950). Creativity. *American Psychologist, 5*, 444–454.

Guilford, J. P. (1967). *The nature of human intelligence*. New York: McGraw-Hill.

Guskin, S. L., Bartel, N. R., & MacMillan, D. L. (1975). Perspective of the labeled child. In N. Hobbs (Ed.), *Issues in the classification of children* (Vol. 2). San Francisco: Jossey-Bass.

Gustafson, G. (1983). *Teaching and learning signing exact English*. Los Alamitos, CA: Modern Signs Press.

Haitema, J. S. (1947). Administrative research necessary for special education. *Journal of Educational Research, 40*, 627–637.

Hall, G. E., Wallace, R. C., Jr., & Dosseth, W. F. (1973). *A structural model for developing a case study of PTE adoption: A developmental conceptualization of the adoptive process within educational institutions*. Austin: Research and Development Center for Teacher Education, The University of Texas.

Hallahan, D. P., & Kauffman, J. M. (1986). *Exceptional children* (3d ed.). Englewood Cliffs, NJ: Prentice-Hall.

Halpern, A., Close, D., & Nelson, D. (1986). *On my son*. Baltimore: Brookes.

Hammill, D. D., & Larsen, S. C. (1974). The effectiveness of psycholinguistic training. *Exceptional Children, 41*, 5–14.

Hanninen, K. A. (1975). *Teaching the visually handicapped*. Columbus: Merrill.

Haring, N. G. (1975). Application of behavior modification techniques to the learning situation. In W. M. Cruickshank & D. P. Hallahan (Eds.), *Psychoeducational practices* (Vol. 1). Syracuse, NY: Syracuse University Press.

Haring, N. G., & Brown, L. J. (Eds.). (1977). *Teaching the severely handicapped* (Vol. 2). New York: Grune & Stratton.

Haring, N. G., & Krug, D. A. (1975). Placement in regular programs: Procedures and results. *Exceptional Children, 41*, 413–417.

Haring, N. G., & Phillips, E. L. (1972). *Analysis of modification of classroom behavior*. Englewood Cliffs, NJ: Prentice-Hall.

Haring, N. G., & Schiefelbusch, R. L. (1976). *Teaching special children*. New York: McGraw-Hill.

Hart, J., & Jones, B. (1980). *Where's Hannah?* New York: Penguin Books.

Havel, S., & Anastasiow, N. (1985). *The at-risk infant*. Baltimore: Brookes.

Havelock, R. G. (1973). *The change agent's guide to innovation in education.* Englewood Cliffs, NJ: Educational Technology Publications.

Hawkins-Shepard, C. (Ed.). (1978). *Making it work: Practical ideas for integrating exceptional children into regular classes.* Reston, VA: Council for Exceptional Children.

Heinz, R. W. (1971). Special education: History. *The encyclopedia of education* (Vol. 8). New York: Macmillan & Free Press.

Heller, K. A., Holtzman, W. H., & Messick, S. (Eds.). (1982). *Placing children in special education: A strategy for equity.* Washington, DC: National Academy Press.

Henry, N. (1948). *King of the wind.* Chicago: Rand McNally.

Hersh, S. P. (1976). Epilog. In H. Yahraes & S. Prestwich, *Detection and prevention of learning disorders.* Washington, DC: Department of Health, Education and Welfare. (U.S. Government Printing Office Publications No. [ADM]77-337; Stock No. 017-224-00524-0.)

Higbee, D. R. (1981). More over, David Premack! *Directive Teacher, 3*(2), 4, 19.

Hill, A. L. (1978). Savants: Mentally retarded individuals with special skills. In N. Ellis (Ed.), *International reviews of research in mental retardation* (Vol. 9). Orlando, FL: Academic Press.

Hillinger, C. (1975, December 7). Teletype communication puts the deaf in touch. *Los Angeles Times.*

Hirsch, S. P. (1976). Executive high school internships: A boon for the gifted and talented. *Teaching Exceptional Children, 9,* 22–23.

Hively, W., & Reynolds, M. C. (1975). *Domain-referenced testing.* Reston, VA: Council for Exceptional Children.

Hixon, T. J., Shriberg, __., & Saxman, J. H. (Eds.). *Introduction to communication disorders.* Englewood Cliffs, NJ: Prentice-Hall.

Hobbs, N. (1975). *The futures of children.* San Francisco: Jossey-Bass.

Hobbs, N. (1980). An ecologically oriented service-based system for the classification of handicapped children. In E. Salzinger, J. Antrobus, & J. Glick (Eds.), *The ecosystem of the "risk" child.* Orlando, FL: Academic Press.

Hocutt, A. M., Cox, J. L., & Pelosi, J. (1984). *An exploration of issues regarding the identification of LD, MR and ED students.* (Phase I report of a policy-oriented study of special education service delivery systems.) Research Triangle Park, NC: Research Triangle Institute.

Hodges, D. J. (n.d.). *Sounds of a "quiet revolution."* New York: Hunter College, Department of Educational Foundations.

Holmes Group. (1986). *Tomorrow's teachers: A report of the Holmes Group.* East Lansing: The Holmes Group, Inc., Michigan State University.

Homme, L. (1970). *How to use contingency contracting in the classroom.* Champaign, IL: Research.

House, A. M., & Neville-Smith, C. (n.d.). *Home centered videotaped counseling programmes for parents with hearing impaired children (0–5 years of age) in rural Newfoundland and Labrador* (Vol. 1). St. Johns: Newfoundland School for the Deaf.

Howard, M. (1975, Spring). Improving services for young fathers. *Sharing,* 10–22.

Howsam, R. B., Corrigan, D. C., Denemark, G. W., & Nash, R. J. (1976). *Educating a profession.* Washington, DC: American Association of Colleges for Teacher Education.

Hull, F. M., & Hull, M. E. (1973). Children with oral communication disabilities. In L. M. Dunn (Ed.), *Exceptional children in the schools.* New York: Holt, Rinehart and Winston.

Hunt, D. E. (1975). Person-environment interaction: A challenge found wanting before it was tried. *Review of Educational Research, 45*(2), 209–230.

Hunt, J. M. (1961). *Intelligence and experience.* New York: Ronald.

Hurt, M. (1975). *Child abuse and neglect: A report on the status of research* (Office of Human Development/Office of Child Development, Publication No. 74–20). Washington, DC: GPO.

Husen. (1981). *University of Sweden.* Unpublished address, University of Minnesota.

Idol-Maestas, L. (1983). *Special educator's consultation handbook.* Rockville, MD: Aspen Systems.

Jacobs, L. M. (1980). *A deaf adult speaks out* (rev. ed.). Washington, DC: Gallaudet College Press.

Janik, A., & Toulman, S. (1973). *Wittgenstein's Vienna.* New York: Simon & Schuster.

Johnson, D. W., & Johnson, R. T. (1975). *Learning together and alone.* Englewood Cliffs, NJ: Prentice-Hall.

Johnson, R. A., & Grismer, R. M. (1972). The Harrison School Center: A public school–university cooperative resource program. In E. Deno (Ed.), *Instructional alternatives for exceptional children.* Reston, VA: Council for Exceptional Children, pp. 93–103.

Johnson, W. (1930). *Because I stutter.* New York: Appleton.

Jones, M. L. (1985). *Home care for the chronically ill or disabled child: A manual and sourcebook for parents and professionals.* New York: Harper & Row.

Jones, P. R. (1981). *A practical guide to special education law: Understandig and implementing P.L. 94–142.* New York: Holt, Rinehart and Winston.

Jones, R. (1977, June). The acorn people: What I learned at a summer camp. *Psychology Today,* 70–81.

Jones, R. (Ed.). (1983). *Reflections on growing up disabled.* Reston, VA: Council for Exceptional Children.

Jordan, J. B., Hayden, A. H., Karnes, M. B., & Wood, M. (Eds.). (1978). *Early childhood education for exceptional children: A handbook of ideas and exemplary practices.* Reston, VA: Council for Exceptional Children.

Josephson, N. (1963). *Edison, a biography.* New York: McGraw-Hill.

Kaplan, G. R. (n.d.). *The vital link: Paraprofessionals and the education of handicapped children.* New York: City University of New York, Center for Advanced Studies in Education, New Careers Training Laboratory.

Kaplan, S. N. (1975). *Providing programs for the gifted and talented: A handbook.* Reston, VA: Council for Exceptional Children.

Kappelman, M., & Ackerman, P. (1977). *Between parent and school.* New York: Dial Press.

Karchmer, M. (1985). Demographics and deaf adolescence. In G. B. Anderson & D. Watson (Eds.), *The habilitation and rehabilitation of deaf adolescents.* Washington, DC: Gallaudet College Press.

Karnes, M. B., Teska, J. A., & Hodgins, A. S. (1970). The effects of four programs of classroom intervention in the intellectual and language development of 4-year-old disadvantaged children. *American Journal of Orthopsychiatry, 40,* 58–76.

Katz, L., Mathis, S. L., & Merrill, E. C., Jr. (1974). *The deaf child in the public schools: A handbook for parents of deaf children.* Danville, IL: Interstate Printers and Publishers.

Kaufman, M., Agard, J. A., & Semmel, M. (1985). *Mainstreaming learners and their environment.* Cambridge, MA: Brookline Books.

Kavale, K. (1981). Functions of the Illinois Test of Psycholinguistic Abilities (ITPA): Are they trainable? *Exceptional Children, 47*(7), 496–510.

Keller, H. (1954). *The story of my life.* New York: Doubleday.

Kempe, C. H. (1973). A practical approach to the protection of the abused child and rehabilitation of the abusing parent. *Pediatrics, 51,* 804–812.

Kennedy, P., et al. (1976). Longitudinal sociometric and cross-sectional data on mainstreaming hearing impaired children: Implications for school programming. *Volta Review, 78,* 71–81.

Keogh, B. K., Major, S. M., Omori, H., Gandara, P., & Reid, H. P. (1980). Proposed markers in learning disabilities research. *Journal of Abnormal Child Psychology, 8*(1), 21–31.

Kirk, S. A. (1941, November). The president's page. *Journal of Exceptional Children, 8,* 35.

Kirk, S. A., & Gallagher, J. J. (1986). *Educating exceptional children* (5th ed.). Boston: Houghton Mifflin.

Klein, J. W. (1977). Head Start services to handicapped: Mainstreaming the preschooler. *Head Start Newsletter, 9*(6), 1–9.

Klerman, L. V., & Jekel, J. F. (1973). *School-age mothers: Problems, programs and policy.* Hamden, CT: Sinnet Books.

Kline, D. F. (1977). *Child abuse and neglect: A primer for school personnel.* Reston, VA: Council for Exceptional Children.

Kounin, J. S. (1970). *Discipline and group management in classrooms.* New York: Holt, Rinehart and Winston.

Kroth, R. L. (1975). *Communicating with parents of exceptional children.* Denver: Love.

Kroth, R. L., & Scholl, G. (1978). *Getting schools involved with parents.* Reston, VA: Council for Exceptional Children.

Kulik, C., & Kulik, J. A. (1982). Effects of ability grouping on secondary school students: A meta-analysis of evaluation findings. *American Educational Research Journal, 19*(3), 415–428.

Lakin, K. C., & Bruininks, R. H. (1984). Challenges to advocates of social integration of developmentally disabled persons. In K. C. Lakin & R. H. Bruininks (Eds.), *Strategies for achieving community integration of developmentally disabled citizens.* Baltimore: Brookes.

Lakin, K. C., Hill, B. K., Hauber, F. A., & Bruininks, R. H. (1982). Changes in age at first admission to residential care for mentally retarded people. *Mental Retardation, 20*(5), 216–219.

Lakin, K. C., Krantz, G. C., Bruininks, R. H., Clumpner, J. L., & Hill, B. K. (1982). One hundred years of data on populations of public residential facilities for mentally retarded people. *American Journal of Mental Deficiency, 87*(1), 1–8.

Larry P. v. Riles. (1972). Civil Action N.C.-71-2270, 343 F. Supp. 1306. (N.D. Cal.)

Lauer, R. M. (1979). *New York State Psychologist,* p. 5.

Law v. Nichols. (1984). 414 U.S. 563, 391. Ed 2dl, 94 S Ct. 786.

Lazar, I., & Darlington, R. (1982). Lasting effects of early education. *Monographs of the Society for Research in Child Development, 47* (2–3, Serial No. 195).

Leinhardt, G., Bickel, W., & Palloy, A. (1982). Unlabeled but still entitled: Toward more effective remediation. *Teachers College Record, 84*(2), 391–422.

Levin, H. M. (1978). Some economic considerations in educating handicapped children. In M. Reynolds (Ed.), *Futures of education for exceptional students: Emerging structures.* Reston, VA: Council for Exceptional Children.

Levine, D. V. (1978). The social context of urban education. In E. A. Erickson & T. L. Reller (Eds.), *The principal in metropolitan schools* (pp. 106–129) Berkeley, CA: McCutchan Publishing Corp.

Lindsley, O. R. (1972). From Skinner to precision teaching: The child knows best. In J. B. Jordan & L. S. Robbins (Eds.), *Let's try doing something else kind of thing: Behavior principles and the exceptional child* (pp. 2–11). Reston, VA: Council for Exceptional Children.

Ling, D. (1981). Teaching hearing impaired children to use spoken language. *Prise Reporter, 12,* 1–2.

Litwak, E., & Meyer, H. J. (1967). The school and the family. In P. F. Lazarfeld & E. Katz (Eds.), *The uses of sociology*. New York: Basic Books.

Lombroso, C. (1893). *The man of genius*. London: Walter Scott.

Lora v. Board of Education. New York City. (1979). 75 Civ. 917. (J.B.V.) U.S. District Court, Eastern District of New York.

Loring, J., & Burn, G. (Eds.). (1975). *Intergration of handicapped children in society*. London: Routledge & Kegan Paul (in association with The Spastics Society).

Lortie, D. (1978). Some reflections on renegotiating. In M. C. Reynolds (Ed.), *Futures of education for exceptional students. Emerging structures*. Reston, VA: Council for Exceptional Children.

Los Angeles Times. (1975, December 7). Teletype phone network helping deaf reach out.

Lovatt, M. (1962). Autistic children in a day nursery. *Exceptional Children, 29,* 103–108.

Lovitt, T. C. (1978). *What research and experience say to the teacher of exceptional children: Managing inappropriate behaviors in the classroom*. Reston, VA: Council for Exceptional Children.

Lowenbraun, S., & Affleck, J. (1976). *Teaching mildly handicapped children in regular classes*. Columbus: Merrill.

Lowenbraun, S., Appleman, K., & Callahan, J. (1980). *Teaching the hearing-impaired*. Columbus: Merrill.

Lowenfeld, B. (1973). History of the education of visually handicapped children. In B. Lowenfeld (Ed.), *The visually handicapped child in school*. New York: John Day.

Lowry, C. K., Quinn, K., & Stewart, M. A. (1981). *Serving autistic children within a large rural area*. Iowa City: University of Iowa Press.

Lukens, K., & Panter, C. (1969). *Thursday's child has far to go*. Englewood Cliffs, NJ: Prentice-Hall.

Lundstrom, K. (1974). *Case studies in special education: Cuba, Japan, Kenya, and Sweden*. Paris: UNESCO Press.

Lynn, L. E. (1983, January). The emerging system for educating handicapped children. *Policy Studies Review, 2*(Special No. 1), 21–58.

Macdonald, D. I. (1985, March 18). *Prepared statement before the Select Committee on Children, Youth and Families, U. S. House of Representatives*. Washington, DC: GPO.

MacMillan, D. (1973). *Behavior modification in education*. New York: Macmillan.

MacMillan, D. L., Jones, R. L., & Aloia, G. F. (1974). The mentally retarded label: A theoretical analysis and review of research. *American Journal of Mental Deficiency, 79*(3), 241–261.

MacMillan, D. L., & Meyers, C. E. (1979). Educational labeling of handicapped learners (pp. 151–194). *Review of research in education*. Washington, DC: American Educational Research Association.

Madden, N., & Slavin, R. E. (1983). Mainstreaming students with mild handicaps: Academic and social outcomes. *Review of Educational Research, 53*, 519–569.

Madsen, J. M. (1980). *Please don't tease me.* Valley Forge, PA: Judson Press.

Mager, R. F. (1962). *Preparing instructional objectives.* Palo Alto, CA: Fearon.

Magnetti, S. S. (1982). Some potential incentives of special education funding practices. In K. A. Heller, W. H. Holtzman, & S. Messick (Eds.), *Placing children in special education: A strategy for equity.* Washington, DC: National Academy Press.

Maker, C. J. (1979). Developing multiple talents in exceptional children. *Teaching Exceptional Children, 11*(3), 120–124.

Mallis, J. A. (1956, November). Seminar for superior students. *Clearing House,* 175–178.

Mangold, S. S. (Ed.). (1982). *A teacher's guide to the special educational needs of blind and visually handicapped children.* New York: American Foundation for the Blind.

Marland, S. P., Jr. (1972). *Education of the gifted and talented.* Washington, DC: U.S. Office of Education.

Marland, S. P. (1976, January-February). Advanced placement. *Today's Education,* 43–44.

Marr, H. (1969, September). Education of the physically handicapped: An urban approach. *Newsletter,* Division on Physically Handicapped, Homebound and Hospitalized. Reston, VA: Council for Exceptional Children.

Marsh, V., & Friedman, R. (1972). Changing public attitudes toward blindness. *Exceptional Children, 38,* 426–428.

Martin, D. S. (Ed.). (1984). *International symposium on cognition, education and deafness* (Vol. 2). Washington, DC: Gallaudet College Press.

Martin, G. J., & Hoben, M. (1977). *Supporting visually impaired students in the mainstream: The state of the art.* Reston, VA: Council for Exceptional Children.

Martinson, R. (1972). *An analysis of problems and priorities: Advocate survey and statistical sources. Education of the gifted and talented.* (Report to the Congress of the United States by the U.S. Commissioner of Education and background papers submitted to the U.S. Office of Education). Washington, DC: GPO.

McCaffrey, M., & Tewey, S. (1979). *We can help.* Reston, VA: Council for Exceptional Children.

McConkie, G. W., & Zola, D. (1985). *Computer aided reading: An environment for developmental research.* Paper presented at the meeting of the Society for Research in Child Development, Toronto.

McConnell, F. (1973). Children with hearing disabilities. In L. M. Dunn (Ed.), *Exceptional children in the schools.* New York: Holt, Rinehart and Winston.

McCubbin, H., Cauble, A., & Patterson, J. (1982). *Family stress, coping and social support.* Springfield, IL: Thomas.

McDowell, R., Adamson, G., & Wood, F. (Eds.). (1982). *Teaching emotionally disturbed children.* Boston: Little, Brown.

McKey, R. H., Condelli, L., Hanson, H., Barrett, B., McConkey, L., & Plantz, M. (1985). *The impact of Head Start on children, families and communities.* Washington, DC: CSR, Inc.

McNett, I., & Merchant, D. (1981 February-March). Disabled educators: Assets—not handicaps—to good teaching. *Today's Education,* 34–37.

Meadow, K. (1980). *Deafness and child development.* Berkeley, CA: University of California Press.

Meehl, P. (1972). Specific genetic etiology, psychodynamics and therapeutic nihilism. *International Journal of Mental Health, 1,* 10–27.

Meehl, P. E., & Goldberg, R. R. (1983). Taxometric methods. In P. C. Kendall & J. N. Butcher (Eds.), *Handbook of research methods in clinical psychology.* New York: Wiley.

Meeker, M. M. (1969). *The structure of intellect: Its interpretation and uses.* Columbus: Merrill.

Mehrens, W. A., & Ebel, R. L. (1979). Some comments on criterion-referenced and norm-referenced achievement tests. *Measurement in Education, 10*(1), 1–7.

Menolascino, F. J. (1979). Handicapped children and youth: Current-future international perspectives and challenges. *Exceptional Children, 46*(3), 168–173.

Merton, R. (1968). The Matthew effect in science. *Science,* 56–63.

Metropolitan Educational Cooperative Service Unit. (1983). *School improvement: Research-based components and processes for effective schools.* Minneapolis-St. Paul, MN: Author.

Meyers, J., Martin, R., & Hyman, I. (Eds.). (1977). *School consultation: Readings about preventive techniques for pupil personnel workers.* Springfield, IL: Charles C Thomas.

Miles, M. B. (1964). *Innovation in education.* New York: Bureau of Publications, Teachers College, Columbia University.

Milofsky, R. D. (1974). Why special education isn't special. *Harvard Education Review, 44*(4), 437–458.

Molloy, L. (1975). The handicapped child in the everyday classroom. *Phi Delta Kappan, 56*(5), 337–340.

Moore, M. W., & Peabody, R. L. (1976). *A functional description of the itinerant teacher of visually handicapped children in the Commonwealth of Pennsylvania.* Pittsburgh: School of Education, University of Pittsburgh.

Moores, D. (1982). *Educating the deaf: Psychology, principles and practice* (2d ed.). Boston: Houghton Mifflin.

Morehead, D. M., & Morehad, A. E. (Eds.). (1976). *Normal and deficient child language.* Baltimore: University Park Press.

Morgan, D. P. (1981). *A primer on individualized education programs for exceptional children: Preferred strategies and practices.* Reston, VA: Council for Exceptional Children.

Morgan, D. P. (1981). *A primer on individualized education programs for exceptional children: Preferred strategies and practices* (2d ed.). Reston, VA: Council for Exceptional Children.

Morse, W. (Ed.). (1979). *Humanistic teaching for exceptional students.* Syracuse: Syracuse University Press.

Morton, M. (1975, November). Your community—goldmine. *Talents and Gifts,* 25–26.

Mullins, J., & Wolfe, S. (1975). *Special people behind the 8-ball.* Johnstown, PA: Mafex Associates.

Mullins, J. B. (1971). Integrated classrooms. *Journal of Rehabilitation, 37*(2), 14–16.

Mullins, J. B. (1979). Making language work to eliminate handicapism. *Education Unlimited,* 20–24.

Nagi, S. (1975). Child abuse and neglect programs: A national review. *Children Today, 4,* 12–17.

Nagy, W. E., & Anderson, R. C. (1984). How many words are there in printed school English? *Reading Research Quarterly, 19,* 304–330.

Napier, G., Kappan, D. L. Tuttle, D. W., Schrotberger, W. L., & Dennison, A. L. (1975). *Handbook for teachers of the visually handicapped*. Louisville, KY: American Printing House for the Blind.

National Coalition of Advocates for Students (NCAS). (1985). *Barriers to excellence*. Boston: Author.

National Commission on Excellence in Education. (1983). *A nation at risk: The imperatives for educational reform*. Washington, DC: U.S. Department of Education.

National Consortium for Educational Excellence. (1984). *An agenda of educational renewal: A report to the Secretary of Education, U.S. Dept. of Education*. Nashville: Vanderbilt University (Peabody College).

National Society for the Prevention of Blindness. (1966). *Fact book: Estimated statistics on blindness and vision problems*. New York: Author.

National Society for the Study of Education (NSSE). (1949). *The education of exceptional children* (49th Yearbook, Part II: *The Society*). Chicago: University of Chicago Press.

Newman, R. G. (1959). The assessment of programs in the treatment of hyper-aggressive children with learning disturbances within a school setting. *American Journal of Orthopsychiatry, 29*, 633–643.

Newsletter. (1984, February 9). Minneapolis: Education Student Affairs Office, College of Education, University of Minnesota.

New York Post. (1978, December 6).

New York Times (1980, July 2). U.S. court tells New York to aid more with learning disabilities.

Nickerson, R. S., Perkins, D. N., & Smith, E. E. (1985), *The teaching of thinking*. Hillsdale, NJ: Erlbaum.

Nirje, B. (1969). The normalization principle and its management implications. In R. Kugel & W. Wolfensberger (Eds.), *Changing patterns in residential services for the mentally retarded*. Washington, DC: U.S. GPO.

Nolte, M. C. (1973, March). Why your school board should review and (probably) remake its policy toward pregnant school girls. *American School Board Journal*, 23–27.

Northcott, W. H. (1971). The integration of young deaf children into ordinary educational programs. *Exceptional Children, 38*, 29–32.

Northcott, W. H. (Ed.). (1973). *The hearing impaired child in a regular classroom: Preschool, elementary, and secondary years*. Washington, DC: A. G. Bell Association for the Deaf.

Northeast Ohio Special Education Regional Resource Center. (1980). *The Serrculator, 9*(7–8).

Oakes, J. (1985). *Keeping track: How schools structure inequality*. New Haven, CT: Yale University Press.

O'Connor, G. (1983). Social support of mentally retarded persons. *Mental Retardation, 21*, 187–196.

Olson, M. R. (1981). *Guidelines and games for teaching efficient braille reading*. New York: American Foundation for the Blind.

Olson, R., Foltz, G., & Wise, B. (1986). Reading instruction and remediation with the aid of computer speech. *Behavior Research Methods, Instruments, and Computers, 18*, 93–99.

Palincsar, A. S. (1986). Metacognitive strategy instruction. *Exceptional Children, 53*(2). 118–124.

Parents in Action on Special Education (PASE) v. Joseph P. Hannon. (1980). U.S. District Court for the Northern District of Illinois, Eastern Division, No. 74C3586.

Paris, B. (1981, August 10). Cleft palate: The long, long journey. *Pittsburgh Post Gazette*, 17.

Parke, R. D., & Collmer, C. W. (1975). Child abuse: An interdisciplinary analysis. In E. M. Hetherington (Ed.), *Review of child development research* (pp. 509–590) (Vol. 5). Chicago: University of Chicago Press.

Payan, R. (1984). Development of the bilingual special education interface. In L. M. Baca & H. T. Cervantes (Eds.), *The bilingual special education interface.* St. Louis: Times Mirror/Mosby College Publishing.

Peabody, R. L., & Birch, J. W. (1967). Educational implications of partial vision: New findings from a national study. *Sight-Saving Review, 37*, 92–96.

Pegnato, C. W., & Birch, J. W. (1959). Locating gifted children in junior high school: A comparison of methods. *Exceptional Children, 25*, 300–304.

Pell, D. M. (1973). Teacher acceptance and preception of behavior transferred from special to regular classes. *Dissertation Abstracts International, 33*(8), 4209–A.

Pennsylvania Association for Retarded Children (PARC) v. Pennsylvania. (1971). 334 F. Supp. 1257 (E. D. Pa.).

Pennsylvania Office of Children and Youth. (1976). *Won't you speak for them?* Harrisburg: Department of Public Welfare, Commonwealth of Pennsylvania.

Perry, J. (1982). The ECS interstate migrant education project. *Exceptional Children, 48*(6), 496–500.

Peterson, J., Peterson, D., Heistad, D., & Reynolds, M. C. (1985). Montevideo individualized prescriptive instructional management system. *Exceptional Children, 52*(3), 239–243.

Pieper, E. (1974). Preparing children for a handicapped classmate. *Instructor, 84*(1). 128–129.

Pierson, D. E. (1974). The Brookline Early Education Project: Model for a new education priority. *Childhood Education, 50*(3), 132–134.

Pintner, R., & Paterson, D. (1916). A measurement of the language ability of deaf children. *Psychological Review, 23*, 413–436.

Prehm, H. J., & McDonald, J. E. (1979). The yet to be served: A perspective. *Exceptional Children, 45*, 502–509.

Premack, D. (1959). Toward empirical behavioral laws: I. Positive reinforcement. *Psychological Review, 66*, 219–233.

President's Committee on Mental Retardation. (1969). *The six-hour retarded child.* Washington, DC: GPO.

Pressey, S. L. (1959). Concerning the nature and nurture of genius. In J. L. French (Ed.), *Educating the gifted.* New York: Holt, Rinehart and Winston.

Program Development Assistance System. (1980). *Overview, directory and product guide 1979–80, handicapped children's model programs.* Seattle: University of Washington.

Public Law 94–103. (1975).

Public Law 94–142. (1977, August 23). *Federal Register.*

Pyecha, J. N., & Ward, L. A. (1982). A study of the implementation of Public Law 94–142 for handicapped migrant children. *Exceptional Children, 48*(6), 490–495.

Quay, H. C. (1972). Patterns of aggression, withdrawal and immaturity. In H. C. Quay & J. S. Werry (Eds.), *Psychopathological disorders in children.* New York: Wiley.

Quay, H. C. (1972). Patterns of aggression, withdrawal and immaturity. In H. C. Quay & J. S. Werry (Eds.), *Psychopathological disorders in children*. New York: Wiley.

Quigley, S., & Kretschmer, R. (1982). *The education of deaf children: Issues, theory and practice*. Baltimore: University Park Press.

Quigley, S., & Paul, P. (1984). *Language and deafness*. San Diego, CA: College-Hill.

Rapier, J. et al. (1972). Changes in children's attitudes toward the physically handicapped. *Exceptional Children, 38*, 219–223.

Ray, C. L., III. (1980). Bouncing back. *Diabetes Forecast, 33*(4), 34–35.

Redden, M. R., Fortunato-Schwandt, W., & Brown, J. W. (1976). *Barrier-free meetings: A guide for professional associations* (Publication No. 76–7). Washington, DC: American Association for the Advancement of Science.

Rees, N. S. (1974). *I don't understand what you mean by comprehension*. Paper presented at the annual meeting of the American Speech and Hearing Association, Las Vegas, Navada.

Reger, R. (1977). Commentary. *Audiology and Hearing Education*, 54–56.

Renzulli, J. (1971). Teacher identification of superior students. *Exceptional Children, 38*(3), 211–214.

Renzulli, J.S. (1973). Talent potential in minority group students. *Exceptional Children, 39*, 437–444.

Renzulli, J. S. (1978). What makes giftedness? Phi Delta Kappan, *59*(3), 180–184, 261.

Renzulli, J. S., & Smith, L. H. (1977). Two approaches to identification of gifted students. *Exceptional Children, 43*, 512–518.

Renzulli, J. S., & Smith, L. H. (1978). *Individual educational program strength-a-lyzer*. Mansfield Center, CT: Creative Learning Press.

Resnick, L. B. (1984). Cognitive science as educational research: Why we need it now. In *National Academy of Education. Improving education: Perspectives on educational research*. Pittsburgh: Learning Research and Development Center, University of Pittsburgh.

Reynolds, M. C. (1962). A framework for considering some issues in special education. *Exceptional Children, 28*, 367–370.

Reynolds, M. C. (1971). Policy statements: Call for response. Basic commitments and responsibilities to exceptional children. *Exceptional Children, 38*, 421–433.

Reynolds, M. C. (1973). *Delphi survey*. Reston, VA: Council for Exceptional Children.

Reynolds, M. C. (Ed.). (1978). *Futures of education for exceptional students*. Reston, VA: Council for Exceptional Children.

Reynolds, M. C. (1980a). *A common body of practice for teachers: The challenge of Public Law 94–142 to teacher education*. Washington, DC: American Association of Colleges for Teacher Education.

Reynolds, M. C. (Ed.). (1980b). *Social environment of the schools*. Reston, VA: Council for Exceptional Children.

Reynolds, M. C. (1984). Classification of students with handicaps. In E. W. Gordon (Ed.), *Review of research in education* (Vol. II, pp. 63–92). Washington, DC: American Educational Research Association.

Reynolds, M. C., & Balow, B. (1972). Categories and variables in special education. *Exceptional Children, 38*, 357–366.

Reynolds, M. C., & Birch, J. W. (1977). *Teaching exceptional children in all America's schools*. Reston, VA: Council for Exceptional Children.

Reynolds, M. C., & Birch, J. W. (1982). *Teaching exceptional children in all America's schools* (2d ed.). Reston, VA: Council for Exceptional Children.

Reynolds, M. C., Birch, J. W., & Tuseth, A. (1962). Review of research on early admission. In M. C. Reynolds (Ed.), *Early school admission for mentally advanced children*. Reston, VA: Council for Exceptional Children.

Reynolds, M. C., & Lakin, K. C. (1987). In M. C. Wang, M. C. Reynolds, & H. J. Walberg (Eds.), *Handbook of special education research and practice*. Oxford, England: Pergamon.

Reynolds, M. C., & Wang, M. C. (1983). Restructuring "special" school programs. *Policy Studies Review, 2*(Special No. 1), 189–212.

Richardson, S. A. (1971). Children's values and friendships: A study of physical disability. *Journal of Health and Social Behavior, 12*(3), 253–258.

Rimland, B. (1978). Savant capabilities of autistic children and their cognitive implications. In G. Serban (Ed.), *Cognitive defects in the development of mental illness*. New York: Brunner/Mazel.

Robbins, L. L. (1966). A historical review of classification of behavior disorders and one current perspective. In L. D. Eron (Ed.), *The classification of behavior disorders*. Chicago: Aldine.

Roberts, K. (1985, Summer), Clarification of negative reinforcement. *Directive Teacher*, 17.

Rogers, L., & Farrow, F. (1983). *Effective state strategies to promote interagency collaboration*. Washington, DC: Center for the Study of Social Policy.

Rosensweet, A. (1976, September 17). "Give us compassion and help," handicapped urge. *Pittsburgh Post Gazette*, 9.

Ross, M., & Nober, L. W. (Eds.). (1981). *Special Education in Transition (No. 2), Educating Hard of Hearing Children*. Reston, VA: Council for Exceptional Children.

Rothman, D. J., & Rothman, S. M. (1984). *The Willowbrook wars*. New York: Harper & Row.

Rusch, F. R. (Ed.). (1986). *Competitive employment issues and strategies*. Baltimore: Brookes.

Russo, J. R. (Ed.). (1975). Mainstreaming handicapped students: Are your facilities suitable? *Education Digest, 40*, 18–21.

Sage, D. D., & Fensom, H. C., Jr. (1985). *A study of mixed category special education programs in the Commonwealth of Pennsylvania*. (A final report to the Bureau of Special Education, Pennsylvania Department of Education.) Syracuse, NY: Syracuse University.

Sansone, J. (1984). Scheduling as a variable in the mainstreaming of mildly handicapped elementary students. Pittsburgh: University of Pittsburgh, unpublished doctoral dissertation. (See also J. Sansone & N. Zigmond, 1986, Evaluating mainstreaming through an analysis of students' schedules. *Exceptional Children, 52*(5), 452–458.)

Sapon-Shevin, M. (1982). Mentally retarded characters in children's literature. *Children's Literature in Education, 13*(1), 19–31.

Sapon-Shevin, M. (1983, January). Teaching children about differences: Resources for teaching. *Young Children*, 24–32.

Sarason, S. B., & Doris, J. (1979). *Educational handicap, public policy and social history*. New York: Macmillan.

Sattler, J. L., & Graham, L. P. (1984). Special education content included in regular teacher education programs. *Teacher Education and Special Education, 6*(2), 124–136.

Schaefer, E. S. (1972). Parents as educators. In W. W. Hartup (Ed.), *The young child: Reviews of research* (Vol. 2). Washington, DC: National Association for the Education of Young Children.

Schary, D. (1958). *Sunrise at Campobello.* New York: Random House.

Schiefelbusch, R. L., & Lloyd, L. (1972). *Language perspective: Acquisition, retardation, and intervention.* Baltimore: University Park Press.

Schulz, J., & Turnbill, A. (1974). *Mainstreaming handicapped students* (rev. ed.). Newton, MA: Allyn & Bacon.

Schweinhart, L. J., & Weikart, D. P. (1980). *Young children grow up: The effects of the Perry Preschool Program on youth through age 19.* Ypsilanti, MI: High Scope Press.

Schweinhart, L. J., & Weikart, D. P. (1986, Winter). What do we know so far? Do Head Start programs work? *High Scope Resource, 1,* 20–21.

Scriven, M. (1983, January). Comments on Gene Glass. *Policy Studies Review, 2*(Special No. 1), 79–84.

Seiler, W. J., Schuelke, L. D., & Lieb-Brilhart, B. (1984). *Communication in the contemporary classroom.* New York: Holt, Rinehart and Winston.

Seligman, M. (1979). *Strategies for helping parents of exceptional children.* New York: Macmillan/Free Press.

Sellin, D. F., & Birch, J. W. (1980). *Educating gifted and talented learners.* Rockville, MD: Aspen Systems Corp.

Sellin, D. F., & Birch, J. W. (1981). *Psychoeducational understandings of giftedness and talent.* Rockville, MD: Aspen Systems Corp.

Semiawan, C. (1980). *Applying integration when resources are limited.* Paper presented at the World Congress, Rehabilitation International.

Shames, G. H., & Florance, C. L. (1980). *Stutter-free speech: A goal for therapy.* Columbus: Merrill.

Sharing. (1974, Winter). News notes, p. 28.

Sharma, S. L. (1970). A historical background of the development of nosology in psychiatry and psychology. *American Psychologist, 25*(3), 348–353.

Sharp, B. L. (Ed.). (1982). *Challenge and change in teacher education.* Washington, DC: American Association of Colleges for Teacher Education.

Shaver, J. P., & Curtis, C. K. (1981). *Handicapism and equal opportunity: Teaching about the disabled in social studies.* Reston, VA: Council for Exceptional Children.

Shopler, E., & Olley, J. G. (1980). Public school programming for autistic children. *Exceptional Children, 46*(6), 461–463.

Simoes, A., Jr. (Ed.). (1976). *The bilingual child: Research and analysis of existing educational themes.* Orlando, FL: Academic.

Skinner, B. F. (1971). *Beyond freedom and dignity.* New York: Knopf.

Slavin, R. E., & Karweit, N. L. (1985). Effects of whole class, ability grouped and individualized instruction on mathematics achievement. *American Educational Research Journal, 23*(3), 351–367.

Slavin, R. E., Madden, N., & Leavey, M. (1984). Effects of cooperative learning and individual instruction of mainstream students. *Exceptional Children, 50*(5), 434–443.

Smith, B. O. (1980). Pedagogical education: How about reform. *Phi Delta Kappan, 62,* 87–93.

Smith, G., & Smith, D. (1985). A mainstreaming program that really works. *Journal of Learning Disabilities, 18*(6), 369–372.

Smith, J. (1976). *David's story: Programs for the handicapped* (No. 0-76-22000). Washington, DC: Office of Special Education and Rehabilitation.

Smith, R. M., & Neisworth, J. T. (1975). *The exceptional child: A functional approach.* New York: McGraw-Hill.

Sontag, E., Certo, N., & Button, J. E. (1979). On a distinction between the education of the severely and profoundly handicapped and a doctrine of limitation. *Exceptional Children, 45*(8), 604–617.

Spollen, J., & Ballif, B. L. (1971). Effectiveness of individualized instruction for kindergarten children with developmental lag. *Exceptional Children, 38*(3), 205–209.

Sprinthall, N. A. (1982). *Counseling skills for classroom teachers.* Minneapolis: University of Minnesota, National Support Systems Project.

Stainback, S., & Stainback, W. (1980). *Educating children with severe maladaptive behaviors.* New York: Grune & Stratton.

Stainback, S., & Stainback, W. (1985). The merger of special and regular education: Can it be done? *Exceptional Children, 51*(6), 517–521.

Stanovich, K. E. (1986). Matthew effects in reading: Some consequences of individual differences in the acquisition of literacy. *Reading Research Quarterly, 21*(4), 360–407.

Stephens, T., Blackhurst, A., & Magliocca, L. (1982). *Teaching mainstreamed students.* New York: Wiley.

Stephens, T. M. (1979). An interview with Dr. Sidney L. Pressey. *The Directive Teacher, 2*(2), 1, 23.

Sternberg, R. (1980). Sketch of a componential subtheory of human intelligence. *Behavioral and Brain Sciences, 3,* 573–584.

Sternberg, L., Ritchey, H., Pegnatore, L., Wills, L., & Hill, C. (1986). *A curriculum for profoundly handicapped students: The Broward County model program.* Rockville, MD: Aspen.

Sternberg, R. J. (1984). Testing intelligence without IQ tests. *Phi Delta Kappan, 65*(10), 694–698.

Stevens, G. D. (1962). *Taxonomy in special education for children with body disorders.* Pittsburgh: Department of Special Education and Rehabilitation. University of Pittsburgh.

Stevenson, H. W., Lee, S. Y., & Stigler, J. W. (1986). Mathematics achievement of Chinese, Japanese, and American children. *Science, 231,* 693–699.

Stewart, J. (1978). *Counseling parents of exceptional children.* Columbus: Merrill.

Stewart, L. G., & Chap, E. (1979). *An introduction to hearing impairment for workers with the developmentally disabled.* Tuscon: University of Arizona.

Stillman, R. D. (1976). *Assessment of deaf-blind children: The Callier Azusa Scale.* Reston, VA: Council for Exceptional Children.

Strother, D. B. (1985). Adapting instruction to individual needs: An eclectic approach. *Phi Delta Kappan, 67*(4), 308–311.

Stuckless, E. R., & Enders, M. (1971). A study of selected support services for post-secondary deaf students in regular classes. Rochester, NY: National Technical Institute for the Deaf.

Suppes, P. A. (1974). A survey of cognition in handicapped children. *Review of Educational Research, 44*(2), 145–146.

Swan, W. M. (1980). The handicapped children's early education program. *Excep-*

tional Children, 47(1), 12–16.

Task Force on Education for Economic Growth. (1983). *Action for excellence: A comprehensive plan to improve our nation's schools.* Washington, DC: Education Commission of the States.

Taylor, C. W. (1968). Be talent developers as well as knowledge dispensers. *Today's Education, 57,* 67–69.

Taylor, R. L. (1980). Use of the AAMD classification system: A review of recent research. *American Journal of Mental Deficiency, 85*(2), 116–119.

Terman, L. (1984). The discovery and encouragement of exceptional talent. *American Psychology, 8*(6), 221–230.

Terman, L., & Oden, M. (1951). The Stanford studies of the gifted. In P. Witty (Ed.), *The gifted child.* Boston: Heath.

Thomas, M. A. (Ed.). (1977). *Children alone: What can be done about abuse and neglect.* Reston, VA: Council for Exceptional Children.

Thorndike, R. L. (1975). Mr. Binet's test 70 years later. *Educational Researcher, 4*(5), 3–8.

Thurstone, L. L., & Thurstone, T. G. (1941). Factorial studies of intelligence. *Psychometric Monoraph, 2.*

Tobias, S. (1976). Achievement treatment interactions. *Review of Educational Research, 46*(1), 61–74.

Torrance, E. P. (1963). *Education and the creative potential.* Minneapolis: University of Minnesota Press.

Torrance, E. P. (1973). *They shall create: Gifted minority children.* (Cassette). Reston, VA: Council for Exceptional Children.

Trybus, R., & Karchmer, M. (1977). School achievement scores of hearing impaired children: National data on achievement status and growth patterns. *American Annals of the Deaf, 122,* 62–69.

Tucker, J. A. (1980). Ethnic proportions in classes for the learning disabled. *Journal of Special Education, 14*(1), 93–105.

Tucker, J. A. (1985). Curriculum-based assessment. *Exceptional Children, 52*(3), entire issue.

Turnbull, A. P., Strickland, B. B., & Brantley, J. C. (1982). *Developing and implementing individualized educational programs* (2d ed.). Columbus: Merrill.

Turnbull, A., & Turnbull, H. (1978). *Parents speak out: Views from the other side of the two-way mirror.* Columbus: Merrill.

Umbriet, J., & Cardullias, P. S. (Eds.). (1980). *Educating the severely physically handicapped* (Vol. II). Reston, VA: Division for Physically Handicapped, Council for Exceptional Children.

U.S. Bureau of the Census. (1982). *Statistical abstract of the United States, 1982–1983.* Washington, DC: GPO.

U.S. Congress. House of Representatives. Committee on Education and Labor. Subcommittee on Select Education. (1983). *Report from the Commission on the Financing of a Free and Appropriate Education for Special Needs Children.* Washington, DC: GPO.

U.S. Congress. House of Representatives. Select Committee on Children, Youth and Families. (1986, May 21). Hearing summary.

U.S. Department of Education. (1985). *Seventh Annual Report to Congress on Implementation of P.L. 94–142.* Washington, DC: GPO.

U.S. Department of Health, Education and Welfare. (1976). UOP pharmacy student makes writing possible for cerebral palsy victim. *Programs for the handicapped.* Washington, DC: Author.

U.S. Office of Education. (1977). Implementation of Part B of the Education of the Handicapped Act. *Federal Register, 42,* 42474–42518.

U.S. Office of Education. (1978). *Developing criteria for the evaluation of the least restrictive environment.* Washington, DC: U.S. Office of Education, Bureau of Education for the Handicapped.

Van Riper, C. (1978). *Speech correction: Principles and methods* (6th ed.). Englewood Cliffs, NJ: Prentice-Hall.

Vaughan, M., & Shearer, A. (1986). *Mainstreaming in Massachusetts.* London: Centre for Studies on Integration in Education.

Vermeij, G. J. (1978). A blind teacher speaks out on teaching the blind student. *Today's Education, 67*(4), 77–78.

Vernon, P. E. (1950). *The structure of human abilities.* New York: Wiley.

Viadero, D. (1987, April 1). Most states adopt programs for handicapped preschoolers. *Education Week,* 1, 57.

Voeltz, L. M. (1980). Children's attitudes toward handicapped peers. *American Journal of Mental Deficiency, 84*(5), 455–464.

Voeltz, L. M. (1982). Effects of structured interactions with severely handicapped peers on children's attitudes. *American Journal of Mental Deficiency, 86,* 380–390.

Voeltz, L. M. (1984). Programs and curriculum innovations to prepare children for integration. In N. Certo, N. Haring, & R. York (Eds.), *Public school integration of severely handicapped students: Rational issues and progressive alternatives* (pp. 155–183). Baltimore: Paul H. Brookes.

Walberg, H. J., & Tsai, S. (1983). Matthew effects in education. *American Educational Research Journal, 20,* 359–373.

Wallin, J. E. W. (1955). *Education of mentally handicapped children.* New York: Harper and Row.

Wang, M. C. (1980a). Adaptive instruction: Building on diversity. *Theory into Practice, 19*(2), 122–127.

Wang, M. C. (1980b). *Mainstreaming exceptional children: Some instructional design and implementation considerations.* Pittsburgh: Learning Research and Development Center, University of Pittsburgh.

Wang, M. C. (1981). *A report on the implementation and effects of the adaptive learning environments model in the Brentwood School District for the 1980–81 school year.* Pittsburgh: Learning Research and Development Center, University of Pittsburgh.

Wang, M. C., Anderson, K. A., & Bram, P. J. (1985). *Toward an empirical data base on mainstreaming: A research synthesis of program implementation and effects.* Pittsburgh: Learning Research and Development Center, University of Pittsburgh.

Wang, M. C., & Birch, J. W. (1984, 1985). Reports on the implementation and effects of the adaptive learning environments model in general and special education settings. *Exceptional Children, 50,* 391–398, and *51,* 33–40.

Wang, M. C., & Birch, J. (1986). Reports on the implementation and effects of the adaptive learning environments model in general and special education settings. *Exceptional Children, 50,* 391–398, and *51,* 33–40.

Wang, M. C., & Reynolds, M. C. (1985). Avoiding the "catch 22" in special education reform. *Exceptional Children, 51*(6), 497–502.

Wang, M. C., Reynolds, M. C., & Walberg, H. J. (1986). Rethinking special education. *Educational Leadership, 44*(1), 26–31.

Wang, M. C., Reynolds, M. C., & Walberg, H. J. (1987). *Handbook of special education research and practice.* Oxford. England: Pergamon.

Wang, M. C., & Walberg, H. J. (Eds.). (1985). *Adapting instruction to individual differences.* Berkeley, CA: McCutchan.

Warfield, G. J. (Ed.). *Mainstreaming currents: Reprints from Exceptional Children 1968– 1974.* Reston, VA: Council for Exceptional Children.

Warnock, H. M. (1978). *Report of the committee of enquiry into the education of handicapped children and young people.* London: Her Majesty's Stationery Office.

Weatherley, R. A. (1979). *Reforming special education.* Cambridge, MA: MIT Press.

Wehman, P., & Hill, J. (1980). *Instructional programming for severely handicapped youth.* Richmond, VA: School of Education, Virginia Commonwealth University.

Weinstein, C. E., & Underwood, U. C. (1985). Learning strategies: The how of learning. In J. Segal, S. Chipman, & R. Glaser (Eds.), *Thinking and learning skills: Relating instruction to basic research.* Hillsdale, NJ: Erlbaum.

Weintraub, F. J., Abeson, A., Ballard, J., & LaVor, M. L. (Eds.). (1976). *Public policy and the education of exceptional children.* Reston, VA: Council for Exceptional Children.

Weisgerber, R. (1978). *Vocational education: Teaching the handicapped in regular classes.* Reston, VA: Council for Exceptional Children.

Weishahn, M. W., & Mitchell, R. (1971). Educational placement practices with visually disabled and orthopedically disabled children: A comparison, *Rehabilitation Literature, 32*(9), 363–366.

Wendland, L. (1972, April). Personal communication.

Wenger, S. (1985, May 2). *Prepared statement before the select committee on children, youth and families, House of Representatives.* Washington, DC: GPO.

White, O. R., Leber, B. D., & Phifer, C. E. (1984). Training in the natural environment and skill generalization: It doesn't always come naturally. In N. G. Haring & K. A. Liberty (Eds.), *Research in education of the severely handicapped.* Seattle: University of Washington, Washington Research Organization.

Whitmore, J. (1980). *Giftedness, conflict, and underachievement.* Boston: Allyn & Bacon.

Whitmore, J. R., & Maker, C. J. (1986). *Intellectual giftedness in disabled persons.* Gaithersburg, MD: Aspen.

Widvey, L., Edeburn, C., & Ristow, R. (1985). A systematic process for developing special services cooperatives in rural school districts. *Rural Special Education Quarterly, 6*(2), 13–15.

Wiig, E. H., & Semel, E. M. (1980). *Language assessment and intervention for the learning disabled.* Columbus: Merrill.

Will, M. C. (1984a, June). Bridges from school to working life. *Interchange,* 2–6.

Will, M. C. (1984b). *Proceedings of the national policy workshop on special education needs of migrant handicapped students.* Address to the Interstate Migrant Education Council, Denver.

Will, M.C. (1984c). Let us pause and reflect—but not too long. *Exceptional Children, 51*(1), 11–16.

Mill, M. C. (1986). *Educating students with learning problems: A shared responsibility.* Washington, DC: U.S. Department of Education.

Wolf, J. M., & Anderson, R. M. (1969). *The multiply handicapped child.* Springfield, IL: Thomas.

Wolfensberger, W. (1972). *The principle of normalization in human services.* Toronto: National Institute on Mental Retardation.

Wolfensberger, W. (1973). The future of residential services for the mentally retarded. *Journal of Clinical Child Psychology, 2*(1), 19–20.

Wolfensberger, W. (1983). Social role valorization: A proposed new term for the principle of normalization. *Mental Retardation, 21*(6), 234–239.

Wolfson, D. J. (1980, Summer). Confidentiality and the mandatory reporting of child abuse. *Minnesota Psychological Association Newsletter,* 1–8.

Wood, F. H. (1979). Defining disturbing, disordered, and disturbed behavior. In F. H. Wood & K. C. Lakin (Eds.), *Disturbing, disordered, or disturbed?* Minneapolis: University of Minnesota, Department of Psychoeducational Studies.

Wood, F. H. (1980). Introduction. In F. H. Wood (Ed.), *Teachers for secondary school students with serious emotional disturbance: Content for training programs* (pp. 1–2). Minneapolis: Department of Psychoeducational Studies, University of Minnesota.

Wood, F. H. (1981). *Perspectives for a new decade: Education's responsibility for seriously disturbed and behaviorally disordered children and youth.* Reston, VA: Council for Exceptional Children.

Wood, F. H., & Lakin, K. C. (Eds.). (1979). *Disturbing, disordered, or disturbing?* Minneapolis: University of Minnesota, Department of Psychoeducational Studies.

Wood, M. M. (Ed.). (1975). *Developmental therapy.* Baltimore: University Park Press.

Woodburn, V., & Schuster, M. (1978, April-May). Mike was our first deaf student. *Today's Education,* 77–78.

Wright, A. R. (1980). *Local implementation of PL 94–142: Second year report of a longitudinal study.* Menlo Park, CA: SRI International.

Yakima Public Schools. (1977). *Project Home Base.* Yakima, WA: Author.

Yater, V. V. (1976). *Mainstreaming of children with a hearing loss: Practical guidelines and implications.* Springfield, IL: Thomas.

Yi Shui. (1981, June 8). *South China Morning Post.*

Youngberg v. Romeo. (1982). 102 S Ct, 2452.

Ysseldyke, J. E., & Algozzine, B. (1984). *Introduction to special education.* Boston: Houghton Mifflin.

Ysseldyke, J. E., Alpozzine, B., & Epps, S. (1983). A logical and empirical analysis of current practice in classifying students as handicapped. *Exceptional Children, 50,* 160, 166.

Ysseldyke, J. E., Algozzine, B., Shinn, M., & McGue, M. (1982). Similarities and differences between low achievers and students classified as handicapped. *Journal of Special Education, 16,* 73–85.

Zetler, A. (1980, December). Population sparsity and geographic isolation as it relates to staff recruitment and retention. *NRP Newsletter,* National Rural Project, Murray State University, KY, 2–3.

Zigler, E. (1976, February). Controlling child abuse: An effort doomed to failure. In W. A. Collins (Ed.) *Newsletter of the Division of Developmental Psychology,* American Psychological Association, 17–30.

Zigler, E., & Valentine, J. (1979). *Project Head Start: A legacy of the war on poverty.* New York: Free Press.

Zigmond, N., Vallecorsa, A., & Silverman, R. (1983). *Assessment for instructional planning in special education.* Englewood Cliffs, NJ: Prentice-Hall.

Zill, N. (1985, June 25). *How is the number of children with severe handicaps likely to change over time?* Testimony prepared for the Subcommittee on Select Education of the Committee on Education and Labor, U.S. House of Representatives.

Zimmer, G. (1980). Multiple sclerosis. *Disabled USA, 4*(1), 18–20

Zubin, J. (1967). Classification of the behavior disorders. In P. R. Farnsworth, O. McNemar, & Q. McNemar (Eds.), *Annual review of psychology* (pp. 373–406). Palo Alto, CA: Annual Reviews, Inc.

Zuckerman, J. (1979, Spring). Battered wives and their children. *New York Supervisor,* 14.

Index